Windows' Hidden Tools for Secure Sharing, Communi... and Collaboration

The XP Files

McGraw-Hill Osborne

New York Chicago San Francisco Lisbon
London Madrid Mexico City Milan New Delhi
San Juan Seoul Singapore Sydney Toronto

Guy Hart-Davis

McGraw-Hill/Osborne
2600 Tenth Street
Berkeley, California 94710
U.S.A.

To arrange bulk purchase discounts for sales promotions, premiums, or fund-raisers, please contact **McGraw-Hill**/Osborne at the above address. For information on translations or book distributors outside the U.S.A., please see the International Contact Information page immediately following the index of this book.

The XP Files:
Windows' Hidden Tools for Secure Sharing, Communication, and Collaboration

1234567890 CUS CUS 0198765432

ISBN 0-07-222401-0

Publisher:	Brandon A. Nordin
Vice President & Associate Publisher:	Scott Rogers
Editorial Director:	Roger Stewart
Project Editor:	Julie M. Smith
Acquisitions Coordinator:	Tana Diminyatz
Technical Editor:	Felicia Buckingham
Copy Editor:	Bart Reed
Proofreader:	Linda Medoff
Indexer:	Jack Lewis
Computer Designers:	Tara A. Davis, Lauren McCarthy, and John Patrus
Illustrators:	Michael Mueller and Lyssa Wald
Series Design:	Mickey Galicia
Cover Design:	Jeff Weeks

This book was composed with Corel VENTURA ™ Publisher.

Dedication

To the memory of my grandmother,
Diana Barstow

Contents

Acknowledgments xiii
Introduction xiii

CHAPTER 1 **Meet Windows' Hidden Internet Communication Tools** **1**
XP: Built to Take Advantage of the Internet—and of You 2
Windows Messenger 3
NetMeeting 4
.NET Passport 5
Hotmail and Outlook Express 5
HyperTerminal 6
Phone Dialer 6
Which Program Should You Use for Which Task? 6
Summary 7

CHAPTER 2 **Get the Best Internet Connection and Secure It** **9**
Choose an Internet Connection Type 10
Dial-Up Connections via POTS 11
ISDN Connections 12
Wireless Connections 13
Satellite Connections 14
DSL Connections 15
Cable Modem Connections 16
Optical-Fiber Connections 17
Choose an ISP 17
Cost 17
Connection Speed 18
Limited or Unlimited Plan 18
E-mail Accounts and Newsgroups 18
Web-Based Access to E-mail 18
Multilink 19
Backup Connectivity for Failure and Travel 19

Set Up and Configure Your Internet Connection 19
    Connect Your Communications Device 19
    Create the Internet Connection 24
    Configure Your Internet Connection 26
    Set Up a Multilink Modem or ISDN Connection 33
Share Your Internet Connection with Internet Connection Sharing 36
    Advantages and Disadvantages of ICS 36
    What ICS Is and How It Works 37
    Alternatives to ICS 39
Secure Your Internet Connection with ICF 39
    Enable ICF 41
    What ICF Does and Doesn't Block 41
    Poke Holes in Your Firewall 42
    Allow Incoming Services via ICS and ICF 42
    Allow ICMP Requests 44
    Use ICF's Security Logging Feature 45
    Open Ports Manually on ICF 46
Troubleshoot Your Internet Connection, ICS, and ICF 47
    Troubleshoot Your Internet Connection 47
    Troubleshoot ICS 49
    Troubleshoot ICF 52
Summary 53

CHAPTER 3   **Establish Your Digital Identity—and Protect Your Privacy** **55**
Establish Identity in the Physical World 56
Establish Identity Online 58
Privacy and Anonymity Online 60
    The Erosion of Privacy in the Modern World 61
    The Differences Between Privacy and Anonymity 61
    The Illusion of Anonymity Online 63
    Who's Watching You Online? 63
Understand .NET and Neutralize Its Threat 69
    What Is .NET? 69
    What Is .NET Good For? 70
    .NET Detriments 73
    Protect Yourself from .NET 74
Understand .NET Passport 75
Get a .NET Passport and Add It to XP 76
    Edit Your .NET Passport's Profile 77
    Should You Use Passport Wallet? 77
    How Secure Is Passport Wallet? 78
    Passport Wallet: What Is It Good For? 81
What Happens When You Use .NET Passport 81

Use Digital Certificates to Prove Your Identity and Protect Yourself .. 82
    Get a Digital Certificate 84
    Manage Your Digital Certificates 88
Summary 99

CHAPTER 4   **Create, Manage, and Use Free E-mail Accounts**
          and Outlook Express **101**
    A Brief History of Hotmail 102
    Get a Hotmail Account 104
    Access Hotmail via the Web 106
    Configure Hotmail to Suit Your Needs 106
        Update Your Personal Profile, Password, and Secret Question 106
        Choose Whether to Be Listed in the Hotmail Member Directory 107
        Choose Free Newsletters and Special Offers 107
        Filter and Delete Junk Mail 107
        Filter Mail to Specific Folders 109
        Receive Alerts 112
        Get Your POP Mail via Hotmail 112
        Apply a Signature to Your Messages 113
        Choose Mail Display Settings 114
        Choose Reply-Related Settings 115
        Turn Off Sent Message Confirmation 116
        Choose to Have Hotmail Expire a Session After a Given Time 116
        Access Hotmail via Outlook Express 117
    Start Outlook Express 117
    Set Up Your E-mail Account 117
    Configure Outlook Express for E-mail 119
        Make Outlook Express the Default Mail Handler 119
        Prevent Outlook Express from Signing You into Messenger 119
        Set Up the Outlook Express Window for Easy Reading 120
        Request and Return Read Receipts 124
        Send and Check for Messages 125
        Choose Fonts, Stationery, and Business Cards 127
        Choose an E-mail Format: HTML or Plain Text 128
        Include the Original Message in the Reply 129
        Add Correspondents to Your Address Book Automatically 129
        Turn AutoComplete On and Off for E-mail Addresses 129
        Get Notification of New Messages 129
        Apply Signatures to Your Messages 130
        Choose Virus-Protection Options 132
        Choose Options for Sending Secure Mail 133
        Choose Spelling Options 137

Make Outlook Express Ask Before Changing the
Dial-Up Connection 137
Make Outlook Express Hang Up the Internet Connection
After Sending and Receiving Messages 138
Empty the Deleted Items Folder Automatically 138
Remove Deleted Messages from IMAP Folders 139
Compact Old Messages to Save Space 139
Change the Location of Your Message Store 140
Add an E-mail Account to Outlook Express 140
Configure an E-mail Account 140
Send and Receive E-mail 147
Create a Message 147
Read E-mail 155
Work Offline with Outlook Express 159
Create Rules to Protect Your POP3 Mailbox from Spam 159
Examples of Creating a Mail Rule 161
Arrange Your Mail Rules into Order 166
Apply Your Mail Rules 166
Modify a Mail Rule 168
Derive a New Mail Rule from an Existing Rule 168
Maintain a Blocked Senders List 168
Perform a Local File Clean Up 169
Other Free E-mail Services 171
Yahoo! Mail 171
Hushmail 172
Netscape Mail 173
Bigfoot 174
Summary 174

CHAPTER 5   **Chat with Anyone in Public or Private** **175**
Should You Use Messenger or NetMeeting for Chat? 176
Messenger 176
How Messenger Works: The Lay Version 177
Understand the Privacy Implications of Messenger 178
Configure Messenger 179
Troubleshoot Messenger Configuration and Connection Issues 187
Create and Manage Your Contact List 189
Connect with Messenger 193
Troubleshoot Messenger Chat 196
NetMeeting 197
Set Up and Configure NetMeeting 197
Choose NetMeeting Options 201
Connect with NetMeeting 207
Troubleshoot Connections in NetMeeting 213

Chat with NetMeeting 217
Troubleshoot Chat in NetMeeting 219
Host a Meeting 220
Summary 223

CHAPTER 6   **Make Free Worldwide Voice and Video Conference Calls** **225**
Should You Use Messenger or NetMeeting? 226
Choose and Set Up Audio and Video Hardware 227
Audio Hardware 227
Video Hardware 227
Voice and Video with Messenger 228
Run the Audio and Video Tuning Wizard 228
Hold a Voice Conversation 229
Hold a Voice and Video Conversation 230
Troubleshoot Messenger Audio and Video 232
Make PC-to-Phone Calls with Messenger 233
Voice and Video with NetMeeting 235
Run the Audio Tuning Wizard 235
Hold an Audio Conversation 235
Hold a Video Conversation 235
Record a NetMeeting Call 236
Troubleshoot Audio Problems in NetMeeting 238
Troubleshoot Video Problems in NetMeeting 242
Phone Dialer 246
Run Phone Dialer 246
Configure Phone Dialer 247
Make a Call 249
Take a Call 250
Hide the Phone Dialer Window and Call Panes 250
Create and Use Speed Dial Entries 252
Summary 252

CHAPTER 7   **Enjoy Unrestricted, Untraceable File Sharing** **253**
Understand the Basics of File Sharing 254
The Law 254
Compression and Zip Archives 259
Monitoring and Traffic Analysis 260
XP's Tools for Sharing 261
Transfer Files with NetMeeting 261
Before Receiving Files 261
Send Files via File Transfer 262
Receive Files via File Transfer 263
Troubleshoot File-Transfer Problems in NetMeeting 264

Transfer Files with Messenger 264
    Send a File with Messenger 265
    Receive a File with Messenger 265
    Troubleshoot File Transfers with Messenger 266
Online Storage 267
Transfer Files via E-mail 267
HyperTerminal 268
    Create the Incoming Connection 268
    Create the Outgoing Connection 270
    Establish a Connection 271
    Send and Receive Files with HyperTerminal 271
Share Files via Virtual Private Network (VPN) Connections 271
    Set XP to Accept Incoming Connections 272
    Create the Incoming VPN Connection 277
    Connect via a VPN Connection 279
    Share Files via a VPN Connection 279
Summary 279

CHAPTER 8   **Work with Friends, Family, or Coworkers on Online Projects** **281**
Use Whiteboard with NetMeeting and Messenger 282
    Differences Between Whiteboard in NetMeeting and Messenger ... 283
    Whiteboard Basics 283
    Work with Text 284
    Add, Delete, and Synchronize Pages 286
    Move and Copy Information 287
    Copy a Program Window into Whiteboard 287
    Lock Whiteboard 287
    Save Whiteboard 288
    Open a Saved Whiteboard File 288
    Troubleshoot Whiteboard 288
Share a Program—or Your Desktop—Using NetMeeting or Messenger 290
    Share in True Color 291
    Allow Control of the Shared Program or Desktop 292
    Troubleshoot Sharing Programs 293
    Program Sharing Doesn't Work on Windows Me ICS Host
      or ICS Client 293
Use Remote Desktop Sharing in NetMeeting 297
    Troubleshoot Remote Desktop Sharing 298
Summary 299

CHAPTER 9   **Build Your Own Free Online Communities** **301**
Create and Use MSN Communities 302
    Create an MSN Community with Members 303
    Create a Personal MSN Community 305
    Manage Your Community 305

Alternatives to MSN Communities 306
    Web Sites 306
    Online Drives 306
Access Online Sites 307
Use Network Places to Access Online Sites 307
Use the Web Publishing Wizard to Publish Files or Folders to the Web 308
Access FTP Sites with Internet Explorer 308
Use XP's Command-Line FTP Client 308
Summary 310

Glossary 311

Index 321

Acknowledgments

I'd like to thank the following people for their help with this book:

- Gary Masters for rogue agency
- Roger Stewart for deciding the book was a good idea
- Tana Diminyatz for handling the details that Roger didn't
- Julie M. Smith for coordinating the editing and production of the book
- Felicia Buckingham for reviewing the manuscript for technical accuracy
- Bart Reed for editing the manuscript with a light touch
- Tara Davis for laying out the pages
- Linda Medoff for proofreading the book
- Jack Lewis for creating the index

Introduction

XP offers a great set of tools for communicating, collaborating, and sharing files across the Internet. Without needing to install add-on software, you can make audio and video calls to anyone with a computer anywhere in the world, chat with them, transfer files back and forth, and collaborate on projects—all for the price of your Internet connection.

Unfortunately, Microsoft has hidden some of XP's most powerful communications tools to encourage you to use the tools that Microsoft wants you to use. XP's default communications tool for most purposes is Windows Messenger, which ties in with Microsoft's .NET Passport digital persona to reveal to Microsoft the details of your communications sessions and online habits. To that end, Microsoft has positioned Windows Messenger to eclipse other powerful tools included with XP, such as NetMeeting and Phone Dialer, doing the unsuspecting user a great disservice.

Who Is This Book For?

This book is for anyone using XP Professional or XP Home Edition who wants to fully understand the range of communications tools that XP offers, know the advantages and disadvantages of each communications tool, and use them to the max to communicate effectively and securely across the Internet.

In other words, it's for you.

This book assumes that you're at least moderately comfortable with XP—that you know how to log on, manage your user account, navigate the Start menu, use Windows Explorer and Internet Explorer, and so on. If you're not, you might want to supplement this book with a book that'll get you going on XP basics.

What Does This Book Cover?

This book discusses how to use the communications technologies built into Windows XP to communicate effectively and securely over the Internet. Here's what the chapters cover:

- Chapter 1, "Meet Windows' Hidden Internet Communication Tools," sets the scene for the rest of the book. This chapter explains why XP hides some of its best communications tools, introduces you briefly to each of the tools the book covers, and shows you which tools to use for which task.

- Chapter 2, "Get the Best Internet Connection and Secure It," tells you how to choose the right type of Internet connection for your needs and your budget, how to choose an ISP, and how to set up and configure your Internet connection. This chapter also covers how to share your Internet connection with other users on your home or office network, how to secure the connection against intrusion with a firewall, and how to troubleshoot your connection, sharing, and firewall.

- Chapter 3, "Establish Your Digital Identity—and Protect Your Privacy," discusses the problems of establishing identity in the physical world and online and the tools you can use to prove your identity online. The chapter highlights the threat that Microsoft's .NET Passport scheme poses to your privacy and suggests an approach for minimizing this threat. The chapter also tells you how to get and install a digital certificate for proving your identity.

- Chapter 4, "Create, Manage, and Use Free E-mail Accounts and Outlook Express," shows you how to create, manage, and use e-mail accounts on XP. The chapter covers Hotmail, Microsoft's Web-based e-mail service, in detail, examining its benefits and drawbacks. It then shows you how to use Outlook Express, XP's built-in e-mail client, to access Hotmail or other e-mail services. The chapter ends by mentioning some of the other prominent Web-based e-mail providers that you may want to consider instead of Hotmail.

- Chapter 5, "Chat with Anyone in Public or Private," shows you how to use Windows Messenger and NetMeeting to chat with anybody in public or private on the Internet. The chapter starts by comparing Windows Messenger and NetMeeting to each other and discussing which of them you should use for chat in which circumstances. It then shows you how to configure Messenger and use it as a chat client. After that, it shows you how to set up NetMeeting, configure it, and use it as a chat client.

■ Chapter 6, "Make Free Worldwide Voice and Video Conference Calls," discusses how to make voice and video calls using your PC and your Internet connection. By using Messenger, NetMeeting, and Phone Dialer, you can make PC-to-PC calls that cost you nothing more than the cost of your Internet connection. These calls can be to any computer in the world that has an Internet connection. And by using Messenger with a suitably configured voice service provider, you can also make calls from your PC to a phone anywhere in the world for relatively modest charges.

■ Chapter 7, "Enjoy Unrestricted, Untraceable File Sharing," discusses how to share files using the programs and tools that come with XP. This chapter assumes that you want to share files securely (for example, for business reasons or privacy) and explains which tools let you share files securely and which don't. To help you avoid committing copyright violations that could cost you dearly in money or time, this chapter also runs quickly through the legalities of sharing files of copyrighted content.

■ Chapter 8, "Work with Friends, Family, or Coworkers on Online Projects," shows you how to use the whiteboarding features built into NetMeeting and Messenger to brainstorm or sketch out ideas, and how to use NetMeeting's and Messenger's program-sharing and Desktop-sharing features to work with other people on other kinds of documents (for example, text documents or spreadsheets). It also describes how to use NetMeeting's Remote Desktop Sharing feature for controlling your computer remotely.

■ Chapter 9, "Build Your Own Free Online Communities," discusses how to create MSN communities so that you can share files and hold discussions. It mentions other possibilities for storing and exchanging information online, and it details the tools that XP provides for uploading files to and downloading files from online sites.

■ The Glossary provides a list of terms you may want to refer to while reading the book.

As you can see, this book concentrates on communications: It's anything but a general-purpose XP book. XP has scores of other features, from its graphics-heavy and resolutely shiny new interface, to built-in CD burning and improved support for wireless networking—but many of these features aren't covered in this book. Only when your understanding of one of those features is critical to understanding XP's communications technologies does this book cover them.

Approach of This Book

Because many of the programs discussed in the book have overlapping functionality, this book presents its material task by task rather than program by program. This approach lets you compare the features that the programs offer for completing a given task more easily.

For example, you can make voice and video calls by using Windows Messenger, NetMeeting, or Phone Dialer. Rather than reading a chapter about each of those programs and all the features they offer (for many tasks other than voice and video calls), you probably want to know which of them you're better off using for making calls. The way the chapters in this book are organized, you can find that out easily.

Conventions Used in This Book

To make its meaning clear without using far more words than necessary, this book uses a number of conventions, two of which are worth mentioning here:

■ The pipe character or vertical bar denotes choosing an item from a menu. For example, "choose File | Open" means that you should pull down the File menu and select the Open item on it. Use the keyboard, mouse, or a combination of the two, as you wish.

Most check boxes have two states: *selected* (with a check mark in them) and *cleared* (without a check mark in them). I'll tell you to *select* a check box or *clear* a check box rather than "click to place a check mark in the box" or "click to remove the check mark from the box." (Often, you'll be verifying the state of the check box, so it may already have the required setting—in which case, of course, you don't need to click at all.) Some check boxes have a third state as well, in which they're selected but dimmed and unavailable. This state is usually used for options that apply to only part of the current situation. For example, in Word for Windows, if you select one word that is formatted with strikethrough and one that isn't and then display the Font dialog box, the Strikethrough check box will be selected but unavailable, because it applies to only part of the selection.

Chapter 1

Meet Windows' Hidden Internet Communication Tools

This chapter gives you the big picture of what's covered in the book, introducing you to the communications tools—the communications programs and communications technologies—that Windows XP provides. This chapter is short, and its meat provides a brief description of each tool, a discussion of its purpose, and a summary of its advantages and disadvantages. At the end of the chapter, there's a moderately exciting table listing the communications tasks covered in the book and the communications tools most suited to them.

XP: Built to Take Advantage of the Internet—and of You

Microsoft designed and built Windows XP to take advantage of the Internet. That's no surprise, given how central the Internet has become to most businesses (and organizations) of any size and to hundreds of millions of individual users. And it sounds like unmitigated good news—which it should be. But it's not. Along with helping *you* take advantage of the Internet, XP is designed to help Microsoft take advantage of the Internet—and to take advantage of you as you use the Internet.

In order to take advantage of the Internet while preventing yourself from being taken advantage of—or, more realistically, while limiting the advantage that Microsoft or anyone else takes of you—you need to understand the various tools XP provides for using the Internet; you need to know which of these tools reveal which information about you and your actions; you need to know who might be interested in keeping an eye on you; and you need to know which tools to use and how to use them to get your business (or pleasure) accomplished most quickly and effectively while limiting your exposure to recording, monitoring, surveillance, or worse.

Windows XP (hereafter, "XP," unless we need to be formal) emphasizes some of these communications tools while hiding others. For example, XP nags you relentlessly via notification area pop-ups to add a .NET Passport (a form of digital ID) to your Windows user name. Windows Messenger (XP's shiny new client for chat, audio and video calls, sharing, and collaboration) automatically displays an icon in the notification area. This icon appears with a "broken" symbol (a white X on a red circle) until you add a .NET Passport to XP and configure Messenger. (You can also specifically hide the notification area icon for Messenger, but—human nature being what it is—most people will click the icon to find out what's wrong.)

By contrast, XP also includes a fully functional version of NetMeeting, a multifaceted client for chat, videoconferencing, meetings, sharing, and collaboration that Microsoft used to plug heavily in earlier versions of Windows. In XP, NetMeeting receives no icon in the notification area, no shortcut on the Start menu or Desktop, and in fact no acknowledgment of its presence beyond its program folder (which XP screens from view until you insist on seeing the Program Files folder and its contents) and a few mentions in the Help file.

Likewise, XP includes HyperTerminal and Phone Dialer. HyperTerminal is a program for dial-up communications and Telnet; Phone Dialer is a program for making phone calls (including audio and video if you like) via phone lines or an Internet connection. HyperTerminal gets a Start menu shortcut (on the Accessories | Communications submenu). Phone Dialer gets none.

Strange, huh? Why are some of the communications tools hidden? Could it be that Messenger is the little piggy that went to market; NetMeeting is the one that stayed home; HyperTerminal is the little piggy that had roast beef (in the days before BSE and CJD, you'd hope); and Phone Dialer is the little piggy that had none? And perhaps .NET Passport is a big bad wolf ready for some huffing and puffing?

Well, no. The world being what it is, Microsoft isn't exactly sitting there playing eeny-meeny-miney-mo with shortcuts. This is all very deliberate.

You'll notice, even from these brief descriptions, that the communications tools have overlapping functionality. For example, you can chat (text, audio, or video—or all three) using both Windows Messenger and NetMeeting, and you can make phone calls using Messenger, NetMeeting, Phone Dialer, and HyperTerminal.

Microsoft is positioning Messenger not just as *the* messaging client for Windows (competing with AOL Instant Messenger, Yahoo! Messenger, and so on) but also as a replacement for NetMeeting, which Microsoft seems to view as having served its purpose. Now, Messenger is a nicely designed and well-executed piece of software, and those things it does, it does well. But it's a very different kettle of cod from NetMeeting. NetMeeting has capabilities that Messenger doesn't have—for example, hosting a meeting and limiting the actions that other users can take. And NetMeeting is particularly appealing if you want to make station-to-station computer calls without having the .NET Messenger Service monitor every action you take.

Even Phone Dialer, which is basically just a voice-and-video-over-copper-or-IP program, outdoes Messenger when it comes to audio and video. Phone Dialer lets you videoconference with as many as six people at a time. Admittedly, each video window on Phone Dialer competes with an average-sized postage stamp in the invisibility stakes, and the frame rate on each video window will be lousy—but you can do it. With Messenger, you can only share audio or video with one other person at a time.

Why is Microsoft pushing Messenger at the expense of other tools that it includes? In fact, why did Microsoft include the other tools and then hide them? Well, the other tools are included for backward compatibility with previous versions of Windows, and because power users would scream if they weren't there. But, unlike Messenger, they give Microsoft minimal leverage in its ongoing effort to wrest more control of the Internet from whoever has it at the moment. Whereas Messenger forces you to have or get a .NET Passport, NetMeeting doesn't even force you to use the Internet Locator Server system (a good job, too, because Microsoft has now converted it to the .NET Messenger Service). Whereas Messenger forces you to have an Internet connection and to log into the .NET Messenger Service before you can place a call, NetMeeting, HyperTerminal, and Phone Dialer all let you place calls without an Internet connection in sight and without the .NET Messenger Service having ever heard of you. And whereas the .NET Messenger Service monitors every move you make with Messenger, the other tools let you communicate privately and securely if you so choose.

The overlapping functionality of these different tools gives you fair flexibility, but it can also make things confusing until you get the hang of using the tools. To help you get things straight, the table at the end of the chapter summarizes the communications tasks that this book covers and the tools that are best for them.

Windows Messenger

Windows Messenger is Microsoft's entry in the hot instant-messaging arena. Competing directly with America Online Instant Messenger (AIM), whose many million users Microsoft would dearly love to poach from AOL, and with other platform-independent, instant-messaging programs (such as Yahoo! Messenger), Windows Messenger provides a wide selection of features based on its instant-messaging capabilities: text chat, voice calls and video calls, file transfer, and program sharing and collaboration. And that's just the basic program: Messenger is extensible, so Microsoft and third-party companies can supply extensions that snap into Messenger, appear as tabbed pages in the interface, and deliver .NET Passport–enabled services while riding on Messenger's capabilities.

Messenger is powerful software, and it appears front and center in XP's user interface. But Messenger has a darker side that Microsoft doesn't emphasize. Messenger, the client software, necessarily ties into Messenger Service, the server end of the software. In order to achieve its effects, Messenger Service tracks every move you make online while you're signed in—and Messenger is set up to sign you in the moment you log on to Windows and to keep you signed in until you deliberately sign out. All this solicitude is to help you, of course; however, the net effect is to track your actions.

We'll visit this topic in more depth is Chapter 5, which discusses how to configure Messenger and use it for chat. Chapters 6, 7, and 8 discuss further features of Messenger.

NetMeeting

NetMeeting is a powerful conferencing and collaboration tool that Microsoft has bundled with its software for a number of years—first with Internet Explorer (which, you'll remember, itself came as an add-on product to Windows 95) and then with the versions of Windows that had Internet Explorer bundled with them. NetMeeting's basic repertoire includes text chat; two-person voice and video calls; and multiperson conferencing, whiteboarding, and collaboration. As a coda, it lets you remotely control an application or another computer—or access your own computer remotely.

Microsoft's relationship with NetMeeting over the years has been complex and confusing enough that an incautious analyst would probably have a field day with it. Having bought NetMeeting, Microsoft has distributed it widely for free, at first with Internet Explorer and then with those versions of Windows that included Internet Explorer. Microsoft has intermittently promoted NetMeeting as a business solution for low-end videoconferencing; but most businesses have resolutely refused to pay attention, and instead have bravely bought and struggled with third-party videoconferencing solutions—some of which offer fewer features than NetMeeting and perform worse under difficult conditions, but nonetheless cost impressive amounts of money.

More recently, Microsoft appears to have given up on promoting NetMeeting and to have shifted all its eggs to the Messenger basket. But NetMeeting isn't going wholly unappreciated or unused—it has become a great favorite of Internet pirates, because it offers secure communications and file sharing. In XP, NetMeeting is automatically installed, but it's completely hidden. XP creates no shortcut for it on the Start menu or on any of the Desktop toolbars, so there's no reason for the unsuspecting user to guess that it's there. (Unless, that is, the user is suspecting enough to go spelunking in the Program Files superstructure, where they may notice a NetMeeting folder lurking.)

NetMeeting's boatload of features are discussed extensively in Chapters 5 through 8.

.NET Passport

Microsoft's .NET Passport feature and technology is a kind of ersatz digital identity or digital persona—ersatz because it doesn't necessarily give the holder's true identity. .NET Passport is tied to an e-mail address, such as a Hotmail address, an MSN address (the .NET Passport default at this writing), or the e-mail address you already have with your current ISP. Beyond that—at this writing—it includes information such as the holder's purported name, gender (more accurately, sex, but presumably the word is too charged for Microsoft to feel comfortable using), location, time zone, birth date, and occupation.

Because you can set up a .NET Passport without any verification of the information you provide beyond the e-mail address, the .NET Passport doesn't establish your identity. (Many people create multiple .NET Passports and use them for different purposes.) That doesn't mean .NET Passport is useless—provided the e-mail account to which the .NET Passport is tied hasn't been compromised, the .NET Passport can be useful in identifying the user. For example, Windows Messenger uses .NET Passport to establish the user's digital persona. (That the digital persona may not correspond to the user's real-world identity doesn't necessarily matter.) Without a .NET Passport, you can't use Messenger. Or Hotmail. Or MSN. Or the most immediate type of Remote Assistance, which uses Messenger.

.NET Passport also offers a feature called *Passport Wallet*, in which you can store payment information (for example, your credit card details and billing address) so that you can share them effortlessly with Web sites that have implemented the Passport Express Purchase feature. Passport Wallet provides fairly convincing proof of the user's identity, but consumer advocates have raised serious concerns about the safety of the information stored in Passport Wallet.

Chapter 3 discusses .NET Passport, its uses and its dangers, and how Microsoft is likely to develop the .NET Passport service.

Hotmail and Outlook Express

Hotmail, Microsoft's Web-based e-mail service, should need little introduction. Hotmail has the advantages of being free for light and persistent users and being easy to access either via a browser or by using Outlook Express. If you don't like Hotmail, there are various other Web-based e-mail services—such as HushMail, Yahoo! Mail, and Bigfoot—that you may want to try instead. Chapter 4 discusses Hotmail.

Outlook Express is the free e-mail client and newsreader built into all Microsoft's desktop operating systems. From being a puny program whose features were dragged down to its knees by the gravity of its bugs, Outlook Express has grown into one of the best e-mail clients available. Outlook Express includes support for security features, such as digitally signing and encrypting messages, and user-friendly features, such as easy blocking of unwanted messages.

Of course, Outlook Express isn't restricted to Hotmail—you can use it with just about any ISP and mail server. Chapter 4 discusses how to configure and use Outlook Express.

HyperTerminal

HyperTerminal is a straightforward telephony program you can use for making point-to-point data calls or connecting directly to another computer by IP address via your Internet connection. You can also use it for Telnet operations (though most Windows users find they seldom need Telnet these days).

Chapter 7 discusses how to share files using HyperTerminal.

Phone Dialer

Phone Dialer is a humble telephony program you can use to make point-to-point voice and video calls via regular telephone lines or via the Internet. Phone Dialer's video window is much smaller than Messenger's or NetMeeting's—but with Phone Dialer, you can make voice and video calls with up to six people, whereas Messenger and NetMeeting are limited to two people for voice and video.

If you have access to a directory server, you can also use Phone Dialer to set up conferences and join conferences. In the old days, Phone Dialer used the Microsoft Internet Directory servers that NetMeeting also used—but as mentioned earlier, Microsoft has now converted these servers to .NET Messenger Service servers, and Phone Dialer can no longer use them. Because Phone Dialer's conferencing functionality is little used these days, it's not covered in this book.

Chapter 6 discusses how to make calls with Phone Dialer.

Which Program Should You Use for Which Task?

Because many of the programs discussed in this book have overlapping features, it may sometimes be less than obvious which program to use for which task. To help in the long term, this book takes a task-based approach rather than a program-based approach, with each section presenting the programs that can handle a particular task and explaining the advantages and disadvantages they enjoy and suffer compared to each other. To help in the short term, Table 1-1 (which you'll also find on the inside front cover of the book for easy reference) lists the main tasks covered in the book and the programs most suited to perform them.

Task	Programs (In Order of Preference)
Text chat (insecure)	NetMeeting, Messenger
Text chat (secure)	NetMeeting
File transfer (insecure)	NetMeeting, Messenger
File transfer (secure)	NetMeeting
Voice call (insecure, two to six people, without data)	Phone Dialer

TABLE 1-1   Tasks and the Programs That Perform Them

Task	Programs (In Order of Preference)
Voice call (insecure, two people, with or without data)	NetMeeting, Messenger
Video call (insecure, two people, with or without data)	NetMeeting, Messenger
Video call (insecure, two to six people)	Phone Dialer
E-mail	Outlook Express
Secure e-mail	Outlook Express
Encrypted e-mail	Outlook Express with a digital certificate or Pretty Good Privacy
Web-based e-mail	Hotmail, HushMail, Yahoo! Mail, Netscape Mail
Web-based e-mail to Messenger contacts	Hotmail with Messenger
Encrypted Web-based e-mail	HushMail
File transfer via phone lines or IP	HyperTerminal
Telnet	HyperTerminal
Hosting a meeting (insecure)	NetMeeting
Hosting a meeting (secure)	NetMeeting
Program sharing (insecure)	NetMeeting, Messenger
Program sharing (secure)	NetMeeting
Desktop sharing	NetMeeting, Messenger
Remote control of Desktop	NetMeeting
Whiteboarding (insecure)	Messenger, NetMeeting
Whiteboarding (secure)	NetMeeting
Creating an MSN Community	Add Network Place Wizard
Creating an online storage location	Add Network Place Wizard
Browsing an online storage location	Explorer
Establishing your identity online	Digital certificate

TABLE 1-1   Tasks and the Programs That Perform Them *(continued)*

Summary

This chapter has set the scene for the rest of the book by presenting a bit of background and introducing you briefly to the programs that are covered in detail later in the book.

The next chapter discusses how to get the best Internet connection you can and how to secure it against threats.

Chapter 2

Get the Best Internet Connection and Secure It

This chapter discusses the essential prerequisite to communicating via the Internet with Windows XP—a functional and secure Internet connection. As you'd imagine, there are three steps involved if you're starting from scratch: choosing the best kind of Internet connection for you, implementing the Internet connection, and securing it.

If you already have a satisfactory Internet connection, and if you're confident that you've secured it adequately, feel free to skip this chapter. If your Internet connection is in good shape, but you're not sure it's adequately firewalled, turn ahead to the section "Secure Your Internet Connection with ICF" for a discussion of how to use XP's Internet Connection Firewall feature to lock down your Internet connection.

Choose an Internet Connection Type

If you don't have an Internet connection, you need to get one before you can communicate via the Internet. This section discusses the different connection options, their advantages and disadvantages, and how to choose among them. The next section discusses how to choose an Internet service provider (ISP).

That's assuming, of course, you do have a choice. As you'll have noticed if you've been reading the tech-business headlines over the past year or so, a lot of ISPs have been bought out, have merged, have gone bankrupt leaving scads of furious users, or have taken cover in Chapter 11. Among the big names, Excite@Home went into Chapter 11 in Fall 2001, leaving AT&T, Cox Cable, and other major providers struggling to get their subscribers off Excite's broadband network and onto their own networks before Excite pulled the plug. Many smaller ISPs have been gobbled up by the larger ISPs, who want to increase their customer base (because the rate of Internet adoptions is decreasing now that most people who really want to be online are online) and to reduce competition (with a view to raising access prices, as EarthLink has done). And if you live out in the sticks somewhere, your connection options may be limited even if your local ISPs have stayed clear of the feeding frenzy and are still eyeing one another suspiciously.

Even in this world of change and decay, there are some constants. In the matter of getting an Internet connection, the constants are these:

- Get the fastest connection possible.
- And pay as little as possible for it.

A third constant is—or *should be*—to make sure that the Internet connection is as reliable as possible. Just as you probably wouldn't buy the cheapest fast car you could find if you knew its safety record made the Pinto look good, you probably don't want to stake your communications on an Internet connection that intersperses blazing download speeds with frequent outages.

The following sections discuss the various connection types available as of Spring 2002. If you're very lucky, a dangerously fast new connection type may have been deployed since this book was published. But in the meantime, we'll start with the slowest common denominator—a dial-up connection over regular phone lines—and work our way up to the faster and less-available connections from there. Feel free to stop reading as soon as you hit the last option that's available to you.

NOTE

If you're interested in computers, you're probably familiar with Moore's Law, which in its original form states that the number of transistors per integrated circuit will double every 18 months, and in its extended and better-known form, that computing power will double every 18 months. You probably also know what happens to that computing power—software gets correspondingly more demanding (or more bloated) so that it soaks up the available processor cycles. Roughly the same thing happens with bandwidth— the more bandwidth anyone gets, the more and greedier uses they find for it, leaving them little better off than before. Bandwidth demand seems likely to remain eternally unsatisfied until there's such an absurd amount available that every Internet-connected computer and appliance can stream full-motion, high-quality video and audio at the same time.

Dial-Up Connections via POTS

The basic connection to the Internet remains the dial-up connection over standard phone lines or POTS (plain old telephone service) lines using a modem. Modem connections are available just about anywhere with a phone line—although if the wire from the telco's central office is very long or noisy, you may get very low data rates.

The basic principles of dial-up connections have hardly changed since modems were invented. But modem technology has gradually improved over the years as, in the face of (apparently) ultimately inevitable ubiquitous broadband, telecomm engineers have struggled to coax faster data rates out of existing copper lines. They've succeeded to some extent—though dial-up analog data rates remain slower than every other connection option on the block (bar the less-appealing forms of wireless), they're faster than they used to be. The basic problem remains the same—the modems have to convert the digital data to analog data and send it as sound instead of being able to transmit it digitally.

Modem improvements are a bit like the slow but steady improvements to bicycles while cars become cheaper, faster, and (SUVs excepted) more efficient. Except, of course, that dial-up connections aren't exercise or good, healthy fun; you can't freewheel downhill; and Dean Kamen appears not yet to have developed a compelling interest in modems.

To get the most out of your dial-up connection, you need the fastest modem available and an ISP that supports it. V.90 modems have been around for several years now, offering 56 Kbps downstream (or rather 53.3 Kbps downstream, because of FCC limitations) and 33.6 Kbps upstream. At this writing, the latest dial-up modem standard is V.92, which has the same downstream rate as V.90 but increases the maximum upstream speed to 48 Kbps—a 43 percent improvement that's well worth having if you upload or share files, teleconference, or send video.

V.92 modems offer a couple of other features designed to make Internet connections faster and easier:

■ The Quick Connect feature remembers phone-line conditions from previous calls to the same number in order to cut down the length of time required for the modem to handshake with the ISP's telephone interface. Manufacturers claim that Quick Connect can cut handshaking from about 20 seconds to around 10 seconds. Heavy Internet users will consider this feature worth paying a few bucks extra for.

■ The Modem-on-Hold feature lets the modem sustain an Internet connection while taking an incoming call. The phone line needs call waiting, the ISP's equipment has to work with Modem-on-Hold, and the ISP gets to decide how long the user can hold the connection (if at all)—but if all these conditions are met, the user can put the Internet connection on hold, take an incoming call of modest duration, and then resume their Internet session. Most downloads will time out after a few minutes, of course, so those who regularly perform large downloads over dial-up lines will still need a second line for voice calls. But Modem-on-Hold should be a boon for teleconferencing and audio/video calls—provided the other party or parties have the patience to hold.

Some V.92 modems include the V.44 data-compression standard, which improves on the performance of the current V.42bis data-compression standard by an estimated 20 to 60 percent, depending on the type of data involved. If you're transferring compressible data, compression can speed up transfers dramatically; but if the data is already compressed, there's not much the modem can do to shift it faster than the basic speeds.

Because V.92 is new (at this writing), not all ISPs support it. Before you buy a V.92 modem, make sure your ISP does support V.92.

If you have two or more phone lines available for your Internet connection, consider using multilink. Again, you'll need to make sure your ISP supports it. XP supports multilink right out of the box (as do Windows 2000 and Windows Me), so all you need is a modem for each phone line you intend to use and a few seconds' worth of configuration. (See the section "Set Up a Multilink Modem Connection" for details on setting up multilink.) On older versions of Windows, you may need to get a dual-line modem (or *shotgun modem*—remember the double-barreled shotguns used before the shotgun changed from a country weapon to an urban weapon?) in order to use multilink. This pushes the cost up considerably.

ISDN Connections

The next small notch up the speed scale, and a correspondingly small notch down the availability scale, is Integrated Services Digital Network (ISDN). ISDN is widely available, because exchanges in all but the most remote parts of the U.S. are wired for ISDN, and because ISDN can be implemented over moderate distances from the telephone exchange—significantly further than DSL, anyway.

As its name suggests, an Integrated Services Digital Network is a digital telephone line. There are various implementations of ISDN, but the standard consumer version is called *Basic Rate Interface*, usually abbreviated to *BRI*. BRI has two 64 Kbps bearer (B) channels and one 16 Kbps data (D) channel, so if you hear the techno-literate talking about *2B+D*, rest assured they're probably talking about BRI rather than double bondage and domination. BRI's big brother is Primary Rate Interface (PRI), which in the U.S. and Canada is 23B+D, delivering 1.536 Mbps, or T1 speed. (Europe uses 30B+D, giving 1.920 Mbps, in the hope of getting the euro to catch up with the dollar in value.)

ISDN connects to your computer (or network) using a digital device called a *terminal adapter (TA)*. Terminal adapters come in a wide variety of forms—from stand-alone routers to PC Card cards, PCI cards, USB devices, and even serial port adapters. Because a conventional serial port delivers less bandwidth than BRI, a serial connection isn't a good idea unless you're stuck with using a single bearer channel. All the other connections are fine.

With BRI, you can either run one bearer channel at a time (which allows you to do other things, such as make voice calls, on the other bearer channel) for a modest data rate of 64 Kbps or run both bearer channels to get 128 Kbps, a significant jump on dial-up. ISDN implementations are usually symmetrical, so you get 64 Kbps upstream per channel you have open—nearly twice as much as the 33.6 Kbps you get upstream on a V.90 dial-up connection, but not such a big jump up from the 48 Kbps that you may be able to get with V.92. The data channel lurks unobtrusively in the background, carrying the signals to set up, manage, and tear down the calls, and you can't get it to do much else without phreaking.

> NOTE   *ISDN has been around for a while, but it has never broken through in the residential market in the U.S. (By contrast, ISDN has long been big in Germany, because it was implemented there at a cost closer to that of POTS.) This is largely because it has been much too expensive for anybody but businesses and telecommuting professionals to pay for it. ISDN has been expensive for three reasons: First, because ISDN involved a truck roll (yes, this is what they call it) to install digital equipment at customer premises, the telcos charged for installation. Second, because charging for installation largely restricted demand to businesses, the telcos then charged per minute per channel for connectivity. Third, because the result could cost several hundred dollars a month for twice the speed of a flat-rate dial-up connection, residential consumers largely shunned ISDN, so the telcos didn't try to market it to them, thus sealing the vicious circle. Ah, this age of enlightenment....*

Like dial-up over POTS, most consumer ISDN configurations drop the connection after a specified period of inactivity. (By contrast, DSL and cable modems are always on.) So the next time you take an action that requires the connection, it needs to be reestablished. But because ISDN handshaking is digital rather than analog, it takes only a second or two and is far less annoying than an analog dial-up connection. (You also don't get the squeal of the modems courting each other, which helps further the illusion of staying connected.)

If you're too far from the telco's central office to get DSL, and you can't get cable either, and satellite doesn't suit you, ISDN is a strong contender. But exhaust the other options first, because they offer far greater speed than ISDN.

Wireless Connections

Wireless connections offer a variety of speeds depending on the technology used: A wireless connection via a modem connected to a mobile phone is almost always as wretchedly slow as it is expensive; and 3G (the third-generation of wireless appliances), with its promise of megabit-plus bandwidth over the air, hasn't happened yet.

In the meantime, wireless connectivity is largely unsatisfactory, but halfway-decent solutions are available in some—primarily metropolitan—areas. Unfortunately, one of the better wireless solutions, Ricochet from Metricom, went into Chapter 11 in Summer 2001 and subsequently closed down. But it's worth keeping an eye open to see what's available in your area, especially if you need mobile connectivity to the Internet.

Satellite Connections

Satellite connections, such as DirecPC from Hughes Network Systems (www.direcpc.com), offer broadband pretty much anywhere you can see the sky in the right direction for the satellite. Data rates vary depending on how much you're prepared to pay, but typically they're lower than or comparable to the slower DSL and cable connections. Satellite connections tend to be more expensive than DSL and cable connections, which largely confines their appeal to those out of reach of DSL or cable.

Broadly speaking, there are two kinds of satellite service:

■ In the older-style satellite service, the satellite carries data downstream only. For upstream data, you use your trusty old phone line and modem. You can see the problems with this—your phone line is in use the whole time you're online, and your uploads are limited to modem speeds (and if your location is remote enough for satellite service to appeal, you're probably not getting V.92 speeds upstream). You'll see this type of service described as *one-way* (which seems fair enough) or *dial-return* (which is weasel wording). XP's Internet Connection Sharing doesn't work with this type of service, so you won't be able to use it to share your Internet connection.

■ In the new-style satellite service, the satellite carries data both upstream and downstream. This type of service is usually described as *two-way*, has obvious advantages over one-way service, and (you guessed it) costs much more.

When considering a satellite service, check the pricing, terms, and conditions very carefully. These are the main things to watch out for:

■ How much does the dish cost, and how much is installation? Shop around for special offers if possible. You may be able to get the dish free if you can commit to a minimum length of service.

■ Can you get satellite TV on the same dish? Conversely, is your satellite TV dish upgradeable to data?

■ Does the satellite provider act as your ISP for a one-way service, or do you need a separate ISP? Some satellite providers charge extra to act as your ISP, on the basis that you're going to need another ISP anyway for the dial-up part of the connection.

■ Does the plan give you unlimited hours, or do you have to pay extra for hours above your allotted number? If the latter, how extortionate is the hourly cost?

■ How constricting is the satellite provider's fair access policy (FAP)? Most FAPs allow the service provider to restrict your bandwidth if you use your full ration continuously. Most FAPs aren't intended to be punitive—the point is to prevent heavy users from denying other users the service they've paid for—though they can feel that way if you're a heavy user. But FAPs do mean that you shouldn't expect to get the full bandwidth you're paying for all the time.

■ How many e-mail accounts do you get? As you'll see later in this chapter, this is a standard question for evaluating ISPs—but some satellite providers are so surprisingly miserly about e-mail accounts for their "family" packages that this question is doubly important here.

■ Will you need to use Internet Connection Sharing on your satellite connection? If so, you'll need two-way service rather than one-way service, and you'll need to make sure the type of connection the satellite box uses to connect to your computer is shareable. In particular, some USB satellite connections can't be shared via ICS.

> **TIP**   *If you choose a one-way service with limited hours, invest in a download-scheduling utility so that you can work on your dial-up connection to stack up all the files you want to download and then download them in a short but frenzied session via the satellite.*

DSL Connections

Digital subscriber line (DSL) technology offers high-speed connectivity over standard copper phone wires, which means if you have a phone line that's clean enough, you're not located too far from the telco's central office, and the central office is DSL capable, you should be able to get DSL without having to get an extra phone line installed.

Most implementations of DSL use a splitter device to divide the line into separate frequencies for voice use and data use. This means you can use the phone at the same time as you're using the DSL, without needing to close down a channel. At the central office, a digital subscriber line access multiplexer (usually known by its catchy acronym, DSLAM, pronounced *dee-slam*) connects the other end of the digital line to the telco's network.

The most widely deployed form of DSL at this writing is Asymmetric DSL (ADSL), which delivers up to 6.1 Mbps downstream and 640 Kbps upstream. Most ADSL deployers charge premium prices for this kind of speed; normal speeds for residential DSL offerings tend to be in the range of 384 Kbps to 1.5 Mbps downstream and 128 Kbps upstream.

The main disadvantage to ADSL and other forms of DSL that use splitters, such as Rate-Adaptive DSL (RADSL) and Symmetrical DSL (SDSL), is that it takes a truck roll to the consumer end of the wire to install the splitter. This drives up the installation cost and greatly increases the length of time required to roll out DSL.

To circumvent this problem, several splitterless versions of DSL have also been developed, including Consumer DSL (CDSL) and DSL Lite (also known as G.Lite, Universal ADSL, and splitterless ADSL). Both CDSL and DSL Lite are asymmetrical—they're much faster downstream than upstream. CDSL is limited to 1 Mbps downstream, which falls in the disappointing-but-kinda-good-enough category, but DSL Lite can manage 1.5 Mbps to 6 Mbps downstream, making it a serious contender. With splitterless DSL, in theory, the telco needs only check that the customer's line is clean and short enough for the brand of splitterless DSL they're deploying, sell them a "DSL modem," and wait for them to connect it to their computer, the power supply, and their phone line. In practice, of course, if the customer can't get the service working at their end, they squeal loudly and the truck rolls.

> **NOTE** *"DSL modem" is in quotes because the device isn't really a modem, but people know what modems are and (roughly) what DSL is, and the term is descriptive, so it has stuck. "DSL adapter" would be more accurate. (A DSL adapter isn't a modem because it doesn't modulate or demodulate the data it's transmitting.)*

Unlike ISDN, most implementations of DSL are always on, so there shouldn't be any lag in connecting to the Internet. Likewise, because the connection is always on and (usually) has a fixed IP address, you can run a Web server. However, most residential DSL packages keep upstream data rates slow specifically to dissuade you from running a server—and some of their user agreements prohibit you from doing so.

Chances are that you won't have much of a choice of different types of DSL at reasonable rates. That's fine—even CDSL is fast enough for most purposes, so take what's offered.

If you *do* have the choice of different types of DSL at rates you can afford, count yourself lucky, but remember to factor upstream data rates into the comparison if you plan any activities that involve sending large amounts of data upstream, such as sharing files, teleconferencing, streaming audio or video, Webcasting, or running a Web server. If upstream speeds aren't a major influence on your decision, decide on the cost, the downstream speed, and the provider's reliability.

Cable Modem Connections

Cable modems are widely available in urban areas and provide high-speed Internet access. Depending on your cable provider, a cable connection can offer up to 10 Mbps (the same speed as regular Ethernet networks), 20 Mbps, or sometimes more.

If these speeds seem to promise Internet riches beyond the dreams of Croesus, take three deep breaths and bear firmly in mind that each cable loop is typically shared among an apartment building, a street, or a neighborhood, so you won't get anything like the full bandwidth unless you're the only person using the wire. When evaluating cable against DSL or another high-speed technology, try to find out what the capacity is of the cable loop you're on, how many other households are currently on the loop, what the maximum number of households for the loop is, and whether the cable company guarantees you a certain minimum bandwidth. In the bad old days of cable connections late last century, some cable operators so overloaded their loops with bandwidth-hungry households that some users were getting data rates worse than dial-up connections. When there are too many households on a loop to sustain decent data rates, the cable company should either add bandwidth or divide the loop into two or more smaller loops so that more bandwidth is available per household.

Because the computers on the loop share the wire and in many cases connect to the same server, it's vital to make sure your security's tight enough. If you're using XP Home, this means requiring passwords for all users, keeping the Guest account disabled, being very careful which files you share on the network, and using Internet Connection Firewall. You may also want to refrain from using the default workgroup name, MSHOME, because other people on the wire may be using it, too.

In order to, uh, help you share upstream bandwidth more effectively and overcome the temptation to run a server against the terms of your membership agreement, many cable companies cap the amount of upstream bandwidth you can consume. This is called an *upload cap* or *upload speed cap*. Most upload caps aren't overly onerous as long as you're not trying to upload huge amounts of data, share files, or videoconference. But be aware of any upload cap before signing up with a cable company.

Optical-Fiber Connections

Optical-fiber connections are the latest version of bandwidth nirvana for residential customers. (Business customers can buy absurdly large data pipes for correspondingly absurd sums of money.) Optical fiber delivers 100 Mbps, or the same data rate as Fast Ethernet networks, but so far it's available only in new developments in seriously wired areas, such as the more expensive parts of Silicon Valley. As with Fast Ethernet and cable, you'll almost always be sharing the bandwidth rather than having it devoted to you, but unless you're trying to download the Library of Congress, you probably won't feel the pinch. Again, you'll want to keep your computer as secure as possible— well, you're doing so already, aren't you?

If you can get optical fiber at a reasonable price, go for it. You need hardly consider any of the alternatives.

Choose an ISP

This section suggests criteria to apply to choosing an ISP—assuming you need to choose one. If you've read through the previous sections and established that there's only one provider you're interested in, you've probably chosen your ISP already.

If you have multiple technologies and ISPs contending for your business, use the criteria in the following subsections to help you choose among them.

NOTE   *XP's New Connection Wizard links to the Microsoft Internet Referral Service to automatically provide you with a list of ISPs you might want to use. This service can be useful if you have no recommendations for ISPs and no appetite for investigating ISPs on your own. But in general you'll do much better to choose an ISP as described in this section.*

Cost

Cost and connection speed are key deciding factors for most people. Sure, if you paid enough money, you could have an OC-48 line direct to your residence with 2.5 Gbps of bandwidth, but you probably have better uses for your money, such as eating, paying your rent or mortgage, bribing your accountant to minimize your taxes, and so on.

So cost tends to be the first consideration: Whichever Internet connection option you choose, it has to fall within the basic parameters of affordability. Exactly how much you're prepared to pay—$30 or $300 a month—probably depends on your income and what sacrifices, if any, you're prepared to make in order to be able to download and upload data faster. Most people will figure an amount that won't bust their budget and then get the fastest connection available for that amount.

Connection Speed

Other people will fix on a minimum connection speed and then figure out the least expensive way to get it or a faster speed. For example, if you want to make audio and video calls (and enjoy the experience), you might decide that dual-channel ISDN is the slowest connection you'll tolerate.

When evaluating connection speeds offered by different services and ISPs, keep reliability and the factors discussed in the following sections in mind. For most people, an unreliable fast connection is more frustrating than a slower but dependable connection.

Limited or Unlimited Plan

Another key question is whether the plan you're on provides limited or unlimited access. This question applies mainly to dial-up connections, ISDN connections, and satellite connections, because most DSL, cable, and optical-fiber providers offer always-on plans as standard for their broadband products.

Limited plans are almost invariably more affordable than unlimited plans, but some limited plans offer such a miserly number of hours per month that only the lightest of users can avoid exceeding the limit. If you choose a limited plan, check the cost of additional hours beyond those included in the plan. In particular, make sure you know whether the ISP offers hours at different rates—for example, some offer cheap evening and weekend rates, just like most telcos.

E-mail Accounts and Newsgroups

Make sure that the ISP you're considering gives you as many e-mail accounts as you're likely to need for yourself and anyone else who uses your PC or your connection, and that it provides all the newsgroups you want.

Some ISPs are economical to the point of parsimony with e-mail accounts for no apparent reason. (Sure, if you have more e-mail accounts, you can clutter up more of their precious server space—but you'd think that every ISP would want to stay competitive with other ISPs in their category.) Other ISPs provide a fixed number of accounts, usually from three to five. Other ISPs let you choose a hostname and create as many accounts as you need on it.

Some ISPs filter out newsgroups they deem offensive. If this will bother you, choose an ISP that provides a full feed of newsgroups. Alternatively, you can pay for a newsgroup feed from another ISP.

Web-Based Access to E-mail

Does the ISP let you access its e-mail servers via the Web? For example, you might need to access your e-mail from someone else's computer when you're traveling. You could configure an e-mail client to pick up the mail, but it would probably be much easier to read it using a Web browser if you could. As you can imagine, Web-based access to e-mail has security implications in spades, so many ISPs don't provide it. But if it's important to you, find an ISP that offers this service.

Multilink

For dial-up connections (analog or ISDN), make sure your ISP supports multilink if you have any intention (or hope) of using it. Multilink bonds two or more modems or ISDN channels to create a faster connection. To use multilink with analog modems, you need a separate phone line for each modem.

Backup Connectivity for Failure and Travel

If you choose any type of Internet connection other than dial-up, make sure your ISP provides backup connectivity for when its main service fails or for when you need to access it from anywhere other than your usual location.

Backup connectivity almost invariably means dial-up. First, find out how many points of presence (POPs) the ISP has. Second, make sure one or more of them is within your local calling area. (It helps if you have a flat-rate plan for local calls.) Third, try to get an idea of approximately how well the other POPs are distributed across the regions you're likely to travel in—if you're on the road, you don't want to pay long-distance fees for accessing the Internet. Some ISPs offer 800 numbers that you can access for a relatively modest fee (for example, $6 to $10 per hour)— relatively modest, that is, if the alternative is paying hotel charges for local calls or long-distance calls. (If you stay in hotels greedy enough to charge guests hefty fees for calling 800 numbers, all bets are off.)

Set Up and Configure Your Internet Connection

This section discusses how to set up and configure your Internet connection. Windows XP's New Connection Wizard does a good job of walking you through the process of setting up an Internet connection, so this section concentrates on the key points rather than stumbling along through all the details.

Connect Your Communications Device

If your modem, terminal adapter, router, or other communications device isn't already installed in or connected to your computer, install or connect it.

If the device is internal (for example, a PCI modem or terminal adapter), or connects via USB or a serial cable, XP should notice it the first time you boot after installing it and display the Found New Hardware Wizard to shepherd you through the process of adding the device.

If the Found New Hardware Wizard fails you, run the Add Hardware Wizard by clicking the Add Hardware link in the See Also list on the Printers and Other Hardware screen of Control Panel.

Add a Modem

If the device you're adding is a serial modem, XP asks you to choose which COM port to set it up for, but that's about as difficult as the installation gets. If you want to be able to switch the modem from one COM port to another, configure the modem for all available ports. Otherwise, configure only the port to which the modem is currently attached.

If this is the first modem you've added to your computer, XP displays the Location Information dialog box for you to specify your country (or region), your local area code, and any carrier code number or number to access an outside line that you need to dial. When you dismiss the Location Information dialog box, XP displays the Phone and Modem Options dialog box, in which you can create dialing rules, configure the modem, or choose advanced options for telephony providers. You may not need to take any of these actions at this point, but at least change the new location's name from My Location to something more specific and descriptive before dismissing the Phone and Modem Options dialog box.

Choose Options in the Modem Configuration Dialog Box   XP doesn't encourage you to investigate the configuration options for your modems (because it sets default values), but it's worth understanding the options available to you. To do so, display the Modem Configuration dialog box by selecting the modem on the General page of the Properties dialog box for the Internet connection and clicking the Configure button. Figure 2-1 shows the Modem Configuration dialog box.

The Maximum Speed drop-down list lets you specify the maximum speed XP should allow the modem to use. You'll find that this speed is set automatically when the modem is installed and that it's usually quite ambitious—a serial-port modem usually gets a setting of 115,200 bps and a USB modem is likely to get 460,800. The modems are very unlikely to reach these speeds, even with compression, so normally you don't need to worry about adjusting this setting.

The Modem Protocol drop-down list, if available, lists the protocols you can use. Usually, the choices are Error Control Forced, Standard Error Correction, and Use Error Control.

FIGURE 2-1   The Modem Configuration dialog box provides access to the key configuration options for the modem.

The Hardware Features group box controls whether the modem uses hardware flow control, modem error control, and modem compression. All these features are turned on by default for most modems to improve performance, and you should turn them off only if you have good reason to do so (for example, troubleshooting).

The Show Terminal Window check box controls whether the modem displays a terminal window before connecting to the specified connection. You'd use this terminal window to enter modem setup commands—but for most ISPs, you won't need to use this option.

More relevant is the Enable Modem Speaker check box, which lets you control whether the modem speaker can be used.

Choose Options in the Modem Properties Dialog Box   As you just saw, most of the modem-configuration options appear in the Modem Configuration dialog box—but there are a couple that don't.

From the Network and Internet Connections screen of Control Panel, click the Phone and Modem Options link in the See Also list to display the Phone and Modem Options dialog box. On the Modems page, select the modem you want to configure and click the Properties button to display the modem's Properties dialog box.

Apart from general information about the modem and whether it's working, the General page of the modem's Properties dialog box, shown here, contains the Device Usage drop-down list, which lets you disable the modem if you don't want to use it.

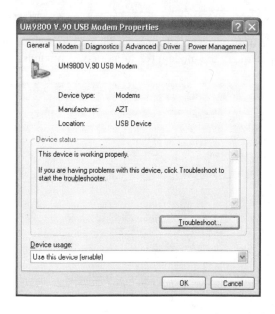

The Modem page of the Modem Properties dialog box, shown next, lets you adjust the speaker volume (in some cases, just on and off), set the maximum port speed for the modem (the speed at which programs can transmit data to the modem), and specify whether the modem should wait for a dial tone before dialing. If you're using an acoustic coupler to attach your modem to a phone handset, or if you're traveling to a country with odd dial tones, it can be useful to tell the modem not to wait for a dial tone.

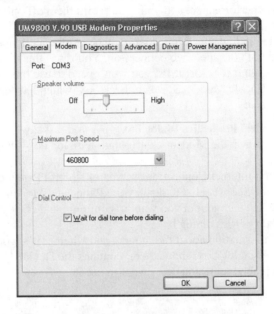

The Diagnostics page of the modem's Properties dialog box, shown next, lets you view the modem's hardware ID and query the modem for supported commands.

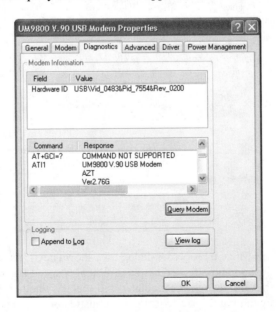

The Advanced page of the modem's Properties dialog box lets you specify extra initialization commands for the modem and change your default preferences for the modem. Unless you're deeply into modems, you probably won't want to bother with initialization commands—most modem drivers do a good job these days for conventional purposes. But you may want to set call preferences and data-connection preferences on the General page of the Modern Default Preferences dialog box, shown here, for the modem. You can access this dialog box by clicking the Change Default Preferences button on the Advanced page.

For USB modems, the Advanced page of the Properties dialog box for a modem also contains the Advanced Port Settings button, which displays the Advanced Settings dialog box, of which the next illustration shows an example. This dialog box lets you specify parameters for the first-in, first-out (FIFO) buffers in the 16550 universal asynchronous receiver transmitter (UART) chipset. (You shouldn't need to mess with this setting.) You can also change the COM port to which the modem is assigned.

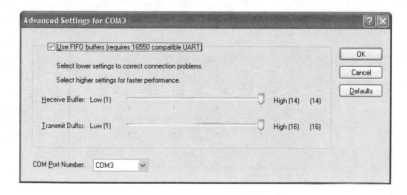

If the modem supports power management, the Properties dialog box for the modem includes a Power Management page, which provides options for allowing the computer to turn the modem off and for the modem to wake up the computer, as appropriate and as necessary.

Add a Terminal Adapter

How you add an ISDN terminal adapter depends on what type it is. Most ISDN terminal adapters are internal (PCI or PC Card) or USB. You can also get serial terminal adapters, but they're not a good idea unless you're running single-channel ISDN, because a serial port's data rate is less than 128 Kbps and so can't deliver the full bandwidth.

TIP   *Another possibility is an ISDN router, which enables you to add ISDN connectivity to your LAN without leaving the connected PC running all the time.*

XP provides the ISDN Configuration dialog box, shown in Figure 2-2, for specifying the line type and whether to use proprietary ISDN protocols (for example, for dialing into DigiBoard servers).

Add a Cable Router or DSL Router

Most cable routers and DSL routers sit between your cable or DSL connection and your network. Some have built-in hubs or switches, so you can use them as the central point of your network (or of a part of your network). Others need to plug into a hub or into the PC that will manage the Internet connection.

Create the Internet Connection

How you create your Internet connection depends on which ISP you've chosen and what kind of setup materials or setup information the ISP has supplied. If your ISP has provided you with a setup CD, run the setup program from its automatically run interface, from Explorer, or from the Run dialog box (Start | Run). Otherwise, use the New Connection Wizard.

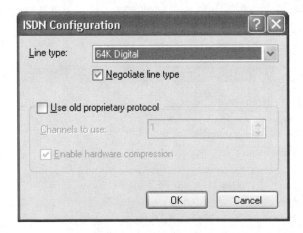

FIGURE 2-2   Specify your ISDN line type in the ISDN Configuration dialog box.

> **NOTE**   *In this book, I assume that you're using XP's regular Start menu, rather than the "Classic" Start menu, and that you're using Category view in Control Panel rather than Classic view. If you've chosen to take either Classic route, you get to find the equivalent procedures yourself.*

Here's the procedure for creating a new connection by using the New Connection Wizard:

1. Start the New Connection Wizard by choosing Start | All Programs | Accessories | Communications | New Connection Wizard. Alternatively, if you have Control Panel open, navigate to the Network and Internet Connections screen and click the Set Up or Change Your Internet Connection link in the Pick a Task list. XP displays the Connections page of the Internet Properties dialog box. Click the Setup button. XP starts the New Connection Wizard.

> **TIP**   *If you have your Internet connection set up on another computer, you can use the Files and Settings Transfer Wizard to transfer the details of the Internet connection to this computer.*

2. On the Network Connection Type page, select the Connect to the Internet option button.

3. On the Getting Ready page, select the Set Up My Connection Manually option button.

4. On the Internet Connection page, select the Connect Using a Dial-up Modem option button, the Connect Using a Broadband Connection That Requires a User Name and Password option button, or the Connect Using a Broadband Connection That Is Always On option button, as appropriate. If you choose the always-on option, the Wizard finishes, telling you that your connection should already be connected.

> **NOTE**   *For a dial-up connection, if you have multiple modems, the New Connection Wizard displays the Select a Device page so that you can specify which modem or modems to use for the connection.*

5. On the Connection page of the New Connection Wizard, the name you assign your Internet connection need have no connection with the ISP's name. This name is for your convenience. So you can call the connection "Shared Internet Connection" or anything that suits you.

6. The Internet Account Information page of the New Connection Wizard, shown next, contains three key options, each of which you can change easily later on.

   - **Use This Account Name and Password when Anyone Connects to the Internet from This Computer**   Controls whether XP uses the account name and password you supply for every user of this computer or just for you.

   - **Make This the Default Internet Connection**   Self-explanatory.

■ **Turn on Internet Connection Firewall for This Connection** Controls whether XP enables Internet Connection Firewall (ICF) for the connection. As you'll see in a couple of pages' time, you can enable ICF manually, but XP enables it by default— which is a good idea in most cases.

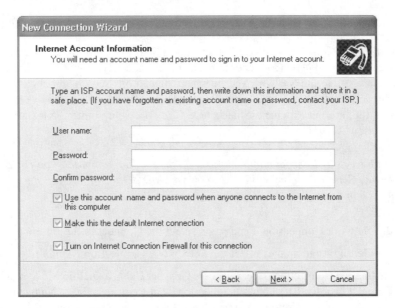

7. The Completing the New Connection Wizard page offers to add a shortcut for the connection to your Desktop. Unless you have such acres of free space on your Desktop that you can afford to leave parts of it visible for quick access to icons, you'll probably do better to access the connection through the Start | Connect To submenu.

Configure Your Internet Connection

Your Internet connection should now be set up and ready for use. But before you use it, check its configuration.

Choose Start | Connect To | All Connections to display the Network Connections window. Then right-click the Internet connection and choose Properties from the context menu. (Alternatively, select the Internet connection and click the Change Settings of This Connection option in the Network Tasks list.) Windows displays the Properties dialog box for the connection with the General page foremost.

Set General Options for Your Internet Connection

If your ISP has supplied you with a variety of different numbers for analog or ISDN dial-up, you'll have entered the first number via the New Connection Wizard. This number appears in the Phone Number group box on the General page of the Properties dialog box for the connection. To add further numbers, click the Alternates button and enter the alternate in the Alternate Phone Numbers dialog box (see Figure 2-3). This dialog box is easy to use, as are the Add Alternate Phone

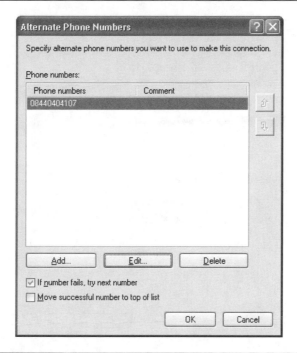

FIGURE 2-3 If your ISP has multiple phone numbers you can use, enter them in the Alternate Phone Numbers dialog box.

Number dialog box, invoked by clicking the Add button, and the Edit Alternate Phone Number dialog box, invoked by clicking the Edit button. For each phone number, you can add a comment (for example, *Second Berkeley number. Never works.*) and choose whether to use dialing rules.

XP selects the If Number Fails, Try Next Number check box by default. In most cases, you'll probably want to leave this check box selected. If appropriate, select the Move Successful Number to Top of List check box as well.

Apart from the alternate-number options, the key choices on the General page of the Properties dialog box for an Internet connection are the Use Dialing Rules check box and the Show Icon in Notification Area when Connected check box.

Whether to use dialing rules depends on your situation—dialing rules can be helpful, or they can be a sharp pain in the neck.

For most Internet connections, it's helpful to display the connection icon in the notification area. The icon gives you quick access to the connection's status, and the screens on the icon's mini-monitors give you a quick visual readout of how much activity is happening on the connection.

Set Dialing Options for Your Internet Connection

The Options page of the Properties dialog box for an Internet connection, as shown in Figure 2-4, contains a slew of options for controlling how XP dials and redials the connection. For these options, XP uses default values that you may well want to change.

FIGURE 2-4   Choose dialing and redialing options on the Options page of the Properties dialog box for the Internet connection.

The Display Progress While Connecting check box controls whether XP displays the informational message boxes while establishing the connection, authenticating your user name and password, and registering the computer on the network. This information is useful for tracking and troubleshooting connections, but it can be an annoyance if your computer needs to frequently redial to reestablish the connection.

The Prompt for Name and Password, Certificate, Etc. check box controls whether XP prompts you for your user name and password in the Connect dialog box for the connection. If you've saved the user name and password for the connection, it's a good idea to clear this check box to remove any temptation to change them.

The Include Windows Logon Domain check box controls whether the Connect dialog box for the connection includes a Domain text box. You can only use this option if you use the Prompt for Name and Password, Certificate, Etc. option.

The Prompt for Phone Number check box controls whether the Connect dialog box for the connection includes the Dial combo box. Unless users will need to enter or select a different phone number for the connection, you may as well clear this check box.

NOTE   *If you turn off the Prompt for Name and Password, Certificate, Etc. option and the Prompt for Phone Number option, XP doesn't display the Connect dialog box at all—instead, it dials the connection when you double-click the connection's icon.*

The options in the Redialing Options group box let you specify the number of automatic redial attempts, the time between them, whether XP should redial automatically if the line is dropped, and how long to let the line languish idle before hanging it up. These settings are easy to understand. If you're paying by the minute for your Internet connection, you may well want to reduce the Idle Time before Hanging Up setting.

The Multiple Devices group box lets you specify the dialing pattern for multiple modems or ISDN channels. We'll examine these in the section "Set Up a Multilink Modem or ISDN Connection," coming up shortly.

Set Security Options for Your Internet Connection

By default, XP implements a "typical" security configuration for dial-up connections. This configuration works for most connections, but you may want to improve on it. To do so, you use the options on the Security page of the Properties dialog box for the connection (see Figure 2-5).

If you choose the Typical option button in the Security Options group box, you can choose Allow Unsecured Password (the default setting), Require Secured Password, or Use Smart Card in the Validate My Identity As Follows drop-down list for an Internet connection. Some ISPs allow you to use a secured password, but others require an unsecured password. As of this writing, very few ISPs use smart cards for consumer Internet connections.

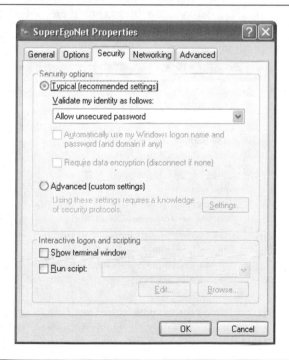

FIGURE 2-5   Use the Security page of the Properties dialog box for a connection to configure security options.

If your ISP supports using a secured password, use the Require Secured Password option. Allow an unsecured password only if you must.

If you choose Require Secured Password, XP makes available the Automatically Use My Windows Logon Name and Password (and Domain If Any) check box but leaves it cleared. This option is more often used in corporate networks than by ISPs.

If you choose Require Secured Password or Use Smart Card, XP makes available the Require Data Encryption (Disconnect If None) check box. You can select this check box to ensure that XP uses encryption for your communications to your ISP. If you leave this check box cleared, as it is by default, XP tries to use encryption but makes the connection even if it can't use encryption. If you select this check box, XP drops the connection if it can't use encryption.

If you eschew the Typical option button and go for the Advanced option button, you can choose security settings in the Advanced Security Settings dialog box (see Figure 2-6). This dialog box gives you more variations and specifics on the same theme as the Typical settings we just examined.

The Data Encryption drop-down list lets you choose whether to refuse encryption, use optional encryption (connect even if your ISP doesn't support encryption), require encryption, or require maximum-strength encryption.

The options in the Logon Security group box let you choose between using the Extensible Authentication Protocol (EAP) and your selection of logon protocols. EAP is used mostly for smart cards (or other certificates) and for systems using MD5-Challenge authentication. You're unlikely to be using these outside a corporate setting, so you'll probably need to select the Allow

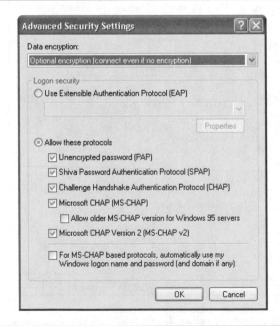

FIGURE 2-6 You can choose custom security settings in the Advanced Security Settings dialog box.

These Protocols option button instead and use the list of check boxes to specify the protocols you want to use. At the risk of stating the obvious, Unencrypted Password (PAP) is the least secure option: The Password Authentication Protocol (PAP, an unfortunately appropriate acronym) uses plain-text passwords, so it should be a last resort. Consult your ISP as to which of the other protocols to use for secure logon, but note that you'll seldom want to use your Windows logon name and password (the lowermost check box in the dialog box).

Set Networking Options for Your Internet Connection

Unless either the Network Setup Wizard has a brainstorm or you have an unorthodox ISP connection (for example, SLIP), you shouldn't need to change the options on the Networking page of the Properties dialog box for a connection (see Figure 2-7). These are the options:

- The Type of Dial-up Server I Am Calling drop-down list offers PPP and SLIP; almost invariably, you'll want PPP.

- The This Connection Uses the Following Items list box lists the network protocols and services available for the connection, with check boxes indicating those in use. By default, the Internet Protocol (TCP/IP) protocol and the QoS Packet Scheduler are used. It's a really bad idea to enable the File and Printer Sharing for Microsoft Networks service for an Internet connection, because it exposes your shared files and printers to the whole wired world. And you're unlikely to need the Client for Microsoft Networks client for Internet connections. (If you have further protocols and services installed, you'll see them listed here as well.)

FIGURE 2-7   In most cases, the Network Setup Wizard chooses appropriate options on the Networking page of the Properties dialog box for a connection.

Choose Advanced Options for Your Internet Connection

■ The Advanced page of the Properties dialog box for a connection, shown in Figure 2-8, contains controls for Internet Connection Firewall and Internet Connection Sharing.

■ The Protect My Computer and Network by Limiting or Preventing Access to This Computer from the Internet check box turns Internet Connection Firewall on and off.

■ The Allow Other Network Users to Connect Through This Computer's Internet Connection check box turns Internet Connection Sharing on and off.

■ The Establish a Dial-up Connection Whenever a Computer on My Network Attempts to Access the Internet check box controls whether Internet requests from other computers start the Internet connection. This check box is selected by default, but you may want to clear it to give yourself tighter control over the connection (for example, for cost reasons).

■ The Allow Other Network Users to Control or Disable the Shared Internet Connection check box controls whether users at other computers can connect or disconnect the connection manually. For example, if you have an analog dial-up connection, someone else may want to disconnect the Internet connection so that they can make or receive a voice call. Like the previous check box, this check box is selected by default, but you may want to clear it to prevent other users from disconnecting the connection when you're using it.

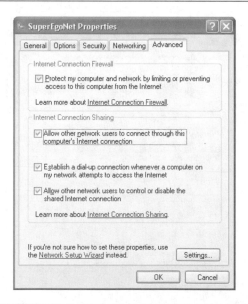

FIGURE 2-8   The Advanced page of the Properties dialog box for a connection lets you turn on and off Internet Connection Firewall and Internet Connection Sharing.

Set Up a Multilink Modem or ISDN Connection

If DSL, cable, or optical fiber isn't available where you live, multilink modems or ISDN channels can make a worthwhile difference to your connection speed. With multilink ISDN, you get the aggregate bandwidth you'd expect. For example, two 64 Kbps channels will give you 128 Kbps. With multilink analog modems, you get a bit less than the aggregate because there's some overhead, but you get a significant increase in speed.

As mentioned earlier, you need a phone line (or ISDN channel) for each device you're using (or an ISDN terminal adapter handling two ISDN channels), and your ISP has to support multilink.

Set Up a Multilink Modem Connection

To set up a multilink modem connection, install and configure each modem involved as usual. Use HyperTerminal or Phone Dialer to make sure each modem and phone line is working. Then open the Properties dialog box for the connection and take the following steps:

1. On the General page, shown here, select the check box in the Connect Using list box for each modem you want to use for the connection. (In most cases, this means using both your modems.)

2. If all the modems will call the same phone number to establish the multilinked connection, leave the All Devices Call the Same Numbers check box selected, as it is by default, and leave the existing phone number and dialing information as it is in the Phone Number group box. If the modems will dial different numbers, clear the All Devices Call the Same Numbers check box, select each modem in turn, and specify the phone number and dialing information for the modem.

3. On the Options page of the Properties dialog box for the connection, shown next, use the Multiple Devices drop-down list to specify how to dial the modems. The default setting is Dial All Devices, which automatically dials all the modems each time you establish the connection. The Dial Devices Only As Needed setting dials the modems according to the conditions you specify (see the next step). The Dial Only First Available Device setting lets you establish a single-line connection using whichever line is available; it's primarily useful when you're sharing phone lines with other people (or with your voice calls).

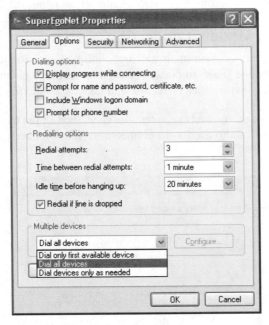

4. If you selected the Dial Devices Only As Needed setting in the Multiple Devices drop-down list, configure automatic dialing and hanging up as described in the section after next.

5. Click the OK button to close the Automatic Dialing and Hanging Up dialog box and then click the OK button to close the Properties dialog box for the connection.

Set Up a Multilink ISDN Connection

To set up a multilink ISDN connection on a BRI, you normally need only configure the connection to use both ISDN channels (by selecting both check boxes in the Connect Using list box on the General page of the Properties dialog box for the connection). In most ISDN configurations, both channels call the same number.

Configure Automatic Dialing and Hanging Up

If you chose the Dial Devices Only As Needed setting for your modems or ISDN channels, click the Configure button to display the Automatic Dialing and Hanging Up dialog box, shown next.

Use its controls to specify the conditions under which XP should automatically dial an extra line and hang up an extra line.

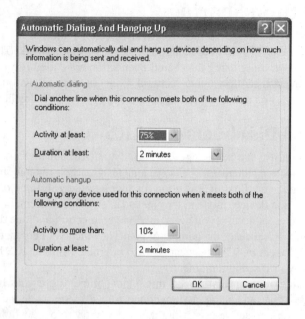

XP's default settings are reasonable for normal use with a modem. Depending on what kinds of operations you typically perform online (for example, frequent downloads or videoconferencing), you may want to adjust the activity thresholds (using the Activity at Least drop-down list and the Activity No More Than drop-down list) to ensure that XP dials and hangs up the extra line or lines at the appropriate times.

Because ISDN can add a second channel almost instantaneously, you may want to sharpen XP's reflexes a bit by reducing the Duration at Least setting in the Automatic Dialing group box. By setting a Duration at Least value of, say, 10 seconds or 30 seconds, you can make the second channel kick in quickly when you're downloading a file of any size while avoiding having the channel added for downloading a typical Web page.

For most people, the key question here is, why aren't you using the extra line or lines all the time? For example, if you have an ISDN BRI, you might want to run only one channel most of the time because you're being charged per minute per channel. (If you've got an all-you-can-eat ISDN connection, you might as well run both channels the whole time.) If you're using a second (or subsequent) analog phone line, is your reason for not using it the whole time that you need to keep it open most of the time for voice calls? If so, you may prefer to dial the extra line manually when it's safe to do so.

TIP *Dial-up connections are stored in the Rasphone.pbk file in the %systemroot%\Documents and Settings\All Users\Application Data\Microsoft\Network\Connections\Pbk folder. You can back up this file for safety or copy it to another computer to install the dial-up connections on that computer. You'll need to restart the computer before the connections show up in Network Connections.*

Share Your Internet Connection with Internet Connection Sharing

As its name suggests, XP's Internet Connection Sharing (ICS) feature lets you share an Internet connection on your computer with other computers on your local network. The computer sharing ICS is called the *ICS host*; those using the shared connection are called *ICS clients*.

To turn ICS on, select the Allow Other Network Users to Connect Through This Computer's Internet Connection check box on the Advanced page of the Properties dialog box for the connection.

Advantages and Disadvantages of ICS

Like almost any feature, ICS has advantages and disadvantages; but for most people in home, home-office, or small-office situations, ICS's advantages greatly outweigh its disadvantages.

These are the advantages: First, ICS is good for saving money. Instead of needing an Internet connection and connection device (modem, terminal adapter, cable modem, or whatever) for each computer that needs Internet access, you need only one connection and one device. Second, ICS is good for security, in that it reduces the number of points at which your computers can be attacked. Third, all Internet traffic sent by ICS clients appears to originate from the ICS host. (This can also be a disadvantage, as you'll see in a moment.)

These are the disadvantages: First, ICS is much less compelling if your Internet connection is slow—for example, if it's an analog modem connection. Analog modem connections tend to be painfully slow with one active user using them. If you try to put a whole house or small office full of active users through an analog modem connection, none of them is likely to enjoy the experience. Each Web page will take about as long to load as acrylic paint takes to dry, and downloading large files will feel like wandering the banks of Cocytus for a century. E-mail may be tolerable as long as it doesn't have attachments.

NOTE *ICS essentially divides the available bandwidth equally among active users. (The process is much more complicated than that, but roughly equal division is the most useful way of thinking of the result.)*

Second, ICS also creates a single point of failure—if you lose your shared Internet connection, none of the computers can access the Internet. But it's easy to set up another computer or another connection to run ICS. For example, say you normally connect to the Internet via a shared cable modem on your study computer, but you also have an analog modem connection on your kitchen computer for emergencies. If the cable connection goes down, you can easily turn off ICS for the cable modem and turn it on for the analog modem so that your study computer can connect through the kitchen computer instead.

Third, some programs don't work fully through ICS. For example, NetMeeting (which we'll examine in detail later in the book) can't send video if it's connecting to the other computer via ICS. Other programs don't work at all through ICS. For example, mIRC uses a complex protocol in which requests go out on one port but replies come back to several ports. ICS can't handle replies coming back on different ports from that used for the request, so it drops the packets. The result: mIRC doesn't work via ICS.

Fourth, ICS doesn't work with one-way connections such as dial-return satellite service.

Fifth, you need to keep the computer providing the ICS connection running all the time that other computers on the network may need to connect. If this is a problem, consider getting a hardware device (such as a cable-sharing router, DSL router, ISDN router, or residential gateway) for sharing your Internet connection rather than ICS. The hardware device needs to be powered on all the time that other computers need to connect, of course, but it'll use far less power than a PC. It's also likely to be more stable and to offer better security features.

Sixth, ICS is intended (and designed) to handle only a relatively small number of clients—say half-a-dozen or so. ICS *can* handle more clients than this—I've had up to a dozen clients connected at once—but performance tends to degrade.

Seventh, and as mentioned before, all Internet traffic sent by ICS clients appears to originate from the ICS host. This means your ISP can't tell that multiple computers are using the Internet connection, so you can pay for a single-user Internet connection and use ICS to connect multiple computers through it. (That said, most ISPs are fully aware of ICS and other NAT software and hardware and charge accordingly for high-speed connections.) It also means that any embarrassing or illegal actions taken by any of the ICS clients gets blamed on the ICS host's ISP account. For example, if a client downloads illegal files via a file-sharing program, it appears from the ISP's records that the action was taken by the ICS host. Similarly, if another ICS client essays a quick denial-of-service attack on a military site, the jackboots of justice come down on the ICS host rather than the ICS client.

What ICS Is and How It Works

Let's take a page or two to get to grips with what ICS is and what it does, because understanding the basics of ICS helps you to troubleshoot it when things don't work smoothly.

ICS uses an *internal* or *private* ICS connection and an *external* or *public* ICS connection. As you'd guess, the internal connection is the interface between ICS and the computers on your internal network, and the external connection is the interface between your computer and the external network (typically, but not necessarily, the Internet). The internal ICS connection always has the IP address 192.168.0.1. (192.168.$n.n$ is a nonroutable TCP/IP subnet.) The external ICS connection has an IP address assigned by the ISP.

ICS combines a Domain Name System (DNS) proxy, or *DNS forwarder*, and a Dynamic Host Configuration Protocol (DHCP) allocator (a simplified DNS server) with Network Address Translation (NAT).

The DHCP server automatically supplies IP addresses to ICS clients on request, making sure there are no conflicts. The DNS forwarder resolves IP addresses for local computers and forwards nonlocal traffic out through the external ICS connection.

ICS uses NAT to broker the Internet requests and replies it receives. When an ICS client on the internal network sends a TCP/IP packet with an address that isn't local to the 192.168.0.n subnet, XP sends the packet to the internal ICS connection on the ICS host. The ICS host examines the packet, replaces the local source IP address (that of the ICS client) with the external ICS IP address, replaces the source port on the ICS client with a source port of its own, and sends the packet out to the ISP via its external ICS connection. To the ISP, the packets appear to come from the ICS host (which they do).

ICS associates the ICS client information for each outgoing request with the new source port and stores them in a port mapping table to track what's going on. So, when a reply comes back to the specified port on the external ICS connection, ICS examines the packets, matches them to the outgoing request, and routes the packets via the internal ICS connection to the ICS client that made the request. NAT is a bit like the mailroom in an office building, providing an external interface for the mail and other delivery services and an internal interface for the people working within the building—with the difference that because the packets being routed are virtual rather than physical, the delay involved is minimal.

In the scenario described in the previous paragraph, each incoming packet of information needs to match a specific outgoing request. Any packets that don't match get discarded, which helps protect your network. So, if you want to be able to receive incoming packets for particular services, you need to notify ICS where the packets will be coming in and what to do with them. As you'll see a bit later in this chapter, ICS comes configured with a range of Internet services you can turn on at will, but you may also want to configure other incoming services in order to receive particular requests.

ICS uses NAT, and NAT itself can use Universal Plug and Play (UPnP—one of the uglier abbreviations of recent years) if you have UPnP installed on your computer. Despite its abbreviation, UPnP doesn't have much to do with hardware Plug and Play (PnP): Microsoft describes UPnP as "an architecture in Microsoft Windows Millennium Edition, and Microsoft Windows XP, that supports peer-to-peer Plug and Play functionality for network devices." Briefly, UPnP lets devices advertise their services on a network to other networked devices and UPnP control points (software that handles UPnP calls) via the Simple Service Discovery Protocol (SSDP). Control points can then send action requests to the device to use a service.

UPnP lets ICS make its presence known on the network and provides a way of dynamically opening and closing ports on NAT so that ICS clients can make connections. In ICS, NAT uses UPnP to send out packets saying, in binary, "Hey, I've got a shared Internet connection here. Anyone interested?" An XP client that doesn't have the advertised service then displays a screen pop-up to let the user know about it.

NOTE *UPnP isn't installed by default in XP or Windows Me, but you can install it manually by using the Windows Component Wizard (Start | Control Panel | Add or Remove Programs | Add/Remove Windows Components). Double-click the Networking Services item to display the Network Services dialog box, in which you'll find the check box for Universal Plug and Play. Earlier versions of Windows, such as Windows 2000 and Windows 98, don't understand UPnP and can't benefit from the UPnP packets.*

UPnP can also implement a complex protocol stack to notify ICS that replies to outgoing packets will use different ports. By including a complex protocol stack, manufacturers can make applications work with ICS that wouldn't otherwise have worked. For example, for games created before UPnP was released and that require an IP address, manufacturers may need to produce UPnP headers (also called *UPnP extensions*) before ICS clients can participate successfully in the games.

 *If you choose to use a hardware router instead of ICS, make sure it supports UPnP out of the box or is upgradeable to support ICS (for example, via a flash upgrade). Otherwise, you won't be able to use UPnP features through the hardware router.*

Because the ICS host always has the same IP address (192.168.0.1, as mentioned earlier), ICS can be enabled on only one computer on any network. That means you can share only one connection on your home or office network via ICS. (You can have as many unshared Internet connections as you want on the ICS clients—you just can't share them via ICS. However, you may be able to share them using other sharing technologies, either hardware or software.)

If you set up a second ICS host on the same network as an existing and active ICS host, you'll get a series of error messages alerting you to the problem. The first error message appears when the second ICS host is booted or connected to the network, and it notifies you of the IP address conflict for the address 192.168.0.1. If you allow the second host to finish booting, you get a message that ICS has been disabled on it. At the same time, the existing ICS host will be displaying error messages about the address conflict.

For ICS to work consistently, the ICS Internet connection and passwords must be available in every user profile that will run the ICS host computer. Otherwise, you can end up with a user running the ICS host computer who doesn't have permission to dial the ICS connection, thus preventing ICS from functioning.

Alternatives to ICS

Given the centrality of the Internet to using a PC these days, and the gradual but (with any luck) inexorable spread of broadband Internet connections through urban areas, ICS is a compelling feature for most home users and many small businesses. But if ICS doesn't suit you, you should have no problem finding NAT hardware or software that will perform a similar function.

In most cases, once you've decided against ICS, you'll be better off with a hardware NAT solution than another software NAT solution. Look for an independent hardware device, such as a cable router, DSL or ISDN router, or residential gateway.

The disadvantage to using another form of NAT is that unless the device or software can handle UPnP, any program that requires UPnP won't work across it. For example, XP's Remote Assistance feature requires UPnP, so you can't use it across a NAT device that isn't UPnP compliant.

Secure Your Internet Connection with ICF

Whether you share your Internet connection with other computers on an internal network or keep it strictly to yourself, you need to secure it in order to keep your data safe. The best way to do so is to use a hardware or software firewall—a hardware device or software program that examines all incoming TCP/IP packets (and in some cases outgoing traffic) and allows to pass only those packets that either match predefined rules (for example, those packets that are requests to a Web server) or are replies to outgoing packets. (More on this in a moment.)

Internet Connection Firewall (ICF) is a software firewall that comes built into XP and integrated with the Network Setup Wizard, making it easy to set up. In fact, the Network Setup

Wizard implements ICF by default on each Internet connection you set up; so unless you chose to turn ICF off, your Internet connection probably uses it. And just as well—if you don't use ICF, all ports on XP are open and vulnerable to threat.

You can use ICF on any network connection—not just on Internet connections.

Before we get into configuring ICF, it'll help for you to have a basic understanding of how firewalls work, what they can do, and what they can't.

A basic firewall is *stateless*—it retains no memory of the connections that have taken place, and therefore treats each connection through it as a new connection. A stateless firewall compares each packet it receives to its rules. This incoming packet on TCP port 80 is destined for the Web server that's listening there: Pass, friend. This other incoming packet on UDP port 139 is sniffing for unprotected file and printer sharing: Halt, dirtbag.

A stateless firewall takes a very Zen view of life (or at least work)—it works strictly in the here and now, without considering the past. Stateless firewalls work well provided you can reduce your Identification Friend-or-Foe (IFF) criteria to a simple set of rules. But for a dynamic environment with constantly changing demands, such as that you'll get on a Windows-based network connecting to the Internet through ICS, a stateless firewall falls short—it doesn't have the flexibility to allow all the traffic necessary for some tools, and so prevents them from working.

Enter the *stateful* firewall—a firewall that retains a memory of connections that have passed through it. A stateful firewall stores this information in dynamic connection tables and uses it to decide which incoming packets should be allowed and which should be blocked. For example, when an ICS client is browsing the Web, it sends requests for Web pages. Back come the packets. The stateful firewall examines its connection tables, establishes from the port to which the packets have come that they match up with an outgoing request, and allows them to pass.

Okay, you've guessed it already: ICF is a stateful firewall. As such, it prevents people outside your firewalled computer from scanning ports and resources, such as file shares and printer shares, while providing enough flexibility to allow most applications to work. As you'll see in a page or two's time, you can configure ICF to pass specified services to designated computers inside the firewall. For example, if you want to run an FTP server on one of the ICS clients, you can do so.

ICF is a powerful and very positive feature—but like most such features, it also has a downside: It prevents some other programs from operating as they're designed to. We'll examine such problems in the section "Troubleshooting Your Internet Connection, ICS, and ICF," later in this chapter.

ICF filters IPv4 (Internet Protocol version 4) traffic only. It doesn't filter IPv6 (Internet Protocol version 6) traffic or traffic using other protocols.

If you decide you don't like ICF, there are plenty of alternatives. Two popular software firewalls are ZoneAlarm (www.zonealarm.com) and BlackICE Defender (www.networkice.com). Many hardware firewalls are also available.

Enable ICF

If you set up a direct Internet connection when installing XP on this computer, ICF should already be enabled. Likewise, if you let the New Connection Wizard use its default settings when you created your Internet connection, ICF should be enabled. (To check that it is, see the second bulleted paragraph.) If not, you can enable ICF either automatically or manually:

- To enable ICF automatically, run the Network Setup Wizard by choosing Start | All Programs | Accessories | Communications | Network Setup Wizard. (Alternatively, click the Setup or Change Your Home or Small Office Network item in the Pick a Task list on the Network and Internet Connections page in Control Panel.) Choose options relevant to your network configuration. The Network Setup Wizard enables ICF when you tell the wizard that the computer is directly connected to the Internet.

- To enable ICF manually, select the Protect My Computer and Network by Limiting or Preventing Access to This Computer from the Internet check box on the Advanced page of the Properties dialog box for the connection.

As you'd imagine, you can turn off ICF by repeating the second process and clearing the Protect My Computer and Network by Limiting or Preventing Access to This Computer from the Internet check box. When you do so, XP displays a dialog box warning you that turning off ICF could expose your computer to unauthorized access and makes sure you want to continue.

> **TIP**
> *The Network Setup Wizard stores log information in the file %systemroot%\Nsw.log. The easiest way to view this information is to choose Start | Run, enter **nsw.log** in the Run dialog box, and click the OK button.*

What ICF Does and Doesn't Block

To protect your computer from intrusions across the Internet, ICF blocks all ports for ICS clients to unsolicited incoming traffic. To receive unsolicited incoming traffic, you need to open ports manually, as described in the section after next.

The ICS host necessarily has a lot more freedom than the ICS clients. On the ICS host, TCP port 135 and UDP port 139 are blocked in order to block server message block (SMB) requests (file and printer sharing requests) on the external ICS adapter. Were these ports not blocked, remote computers would be able to access the shares and printers on the internal network. (In exceptional circumstances, you may want to unblock these ports by using the technique described in the next section so that you can share your printers and shares on the Internet.)

Apart from ports 135 and 139, ports 1 to 1024 on the ICS host aren't blocked, so packets can be sent and received without being translated by ICS. For example, if on your ICS host you're running a Web server that's listening on port 80, it can receive packets directly via port 80 without translation. Ports above 1024 on the ICS host require translation like all ports on the ICS clients.

The result of all this blocking is that the ICS host, while moderately well protected from SMB requests, can communicate directly with much regular Internet traffic, whereas the ICS clients cannot. This causes problems when you want to use a program that needs to use some of the ports in order to work. Unless you open ports in ICF, you won't be able to use these programs on one of the ICS client computers. (Provided the port is between 1 and 1024 and isn't TCP port 135 or UDP port 139, the programs should work fine on the ICS host.)

Poke Holes in Your Firewall

ICF is now set up; your ICS clients are protected from unsolicited Internet traffic, and you know what's blocked and what's not. So things are all well in your connected world.

Well, not quite. In many cases, no sooner do you get your firewall set up than you need to start poking holes in it, for a couple of reasons. First, you may want to use XP's preconfigured services to provide Internet services from an ICS client. For example, if you're running a Web server on an ICS client and want people to be able to access it, you need to tell ICS and ICF where the server is located and how to get the relevant packets to it. Second, you may need to open ports manually on ICF in order to use some programs at all or to use certain features of other programs. The following list gives some examples:

- NetMeeting requires several ports to be opened manually in order for its audio and video features to work. See Chapter 5 for details of the ports that NetMeeting uses.
- Windows Messenger requires certain ports to be opened manually in order for you to receive files and incoming file transfers. See Chapter 5 for a list of the ports that Messenger uses.
- Napster (R.I.P.) required TCP port 6699 and UDP port 6699 to be opened.
- AOL Instant Messenger requires TCP ports 443 and 463 to be opened.

The following sections discuss how to allow incoming services via ICS and ICF and how to open ports manually for other programs.

Allow Incoming Services via ICS and ICF

ICF and ICS use the same interface for configuring the services that you're allowing Internet users to use from outside your network. That this tool is shared isn't immediately apparent from the user interface, which makes it look as though you're configuring ICS rather than ICS and ICF at the same time.

By default, incoming services are directed to the computer that has the Internet connection—much as you'd imagine. But if you're running ICS, you can redirect Internet services to particular computers on the internal network. For example, you could specify that Messenger file transfers be redirected to computer A on the internal network while NetMeeting telephony requests be redirected to computer B.

Obviously enough, you need to be running ICS (or a similar Internet-sharing program) for computers on the internal network to be able to receive redirected services. If you're not running ICS, only the computer directly connected to the Internet can receive Internet services.

Redirecting services to a particular port without ICS running (to redirect the services to the intended computer on the internal network) can represent a security risk, because ICF passes packets through to the specified port even if the specified service isn't running.

Follow these steps to configure incoming services via ICS:

1. Display the Properties dialog box for the Internet connection. For example, choose Start | Connect To, right-click the Internet connection's item in the Connect To submenu, and choose Properties from the context menu for the item.

2. Click the Advanced tab. XP displays the Advanced page.

3. Click the Settings button. XP displays the Advanced Settings dialog box, whose Services page, shown here, provides a list of preconfigured services and lets you define further services as necessary.

4. To start a service, select its check box in the Services list box. The first time you start any given service, XP displays the Service Settings dialog box (shown next) for you to identify the computer running the service and check the ports used. Change the computer identified in the Name or IP Address text box if necessary.

5. To stop a service, clear its check box in the Services list box.

6. Click the OK button to close the Advanced Settings dialog box, and then click the OK button to close the Properties dialog box for the Internet connection.

If the Internet connection is currently connected, XP warns you that some changes may not be applied until you disconnect it and reconnect it. To make sure your changes are applied in good order, disconnect and reconnect the connection as soon as is practicable but without terminating any crucial ongoing session.

Allow ICMP Requests

The ICMP page of the Advanced Settings dialog box, shown here, lets you specify which—if any—ICMP requests to respond to. ICMP, as you'll remember from Internet Abbreviations Boot Camp (IABC), is the Internet Control Message Protocol, a protocol designed to handle errors at the Network layer of the OSI stack.

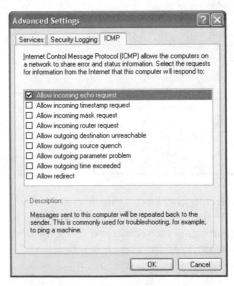

By default, all these check boxes are cleared so that XP doesn't respond to any ICMP requests. Taking the Fifth on ICMP like this is definitely the safest course of action, because it prevents XP saying anything that might incriminate itself. For example, the Allow Incoming Echo Request check box controls whether XP answers ping packets. If you're trying to establish, from a location outside your firewall, whether your ICS host is up, having the computer respond to the ping is positive and valuable. If a malicious teenage hacker in Tijuana is pinging IP addresses at random looking for a computer to attack, you'd probably prefer that your computer not volunteer as a target.

Allowing the echo request is the most obvious example; but the other ICMP services can be useful, too, depending on what you're trying to do. For example, a source quench message is one that ICMP sends when a computer sending data to it is supplying the data at a faster rate than the computer can handle. Given the relative speeds of computers and most Internet connections these days, this is unlikely to be a problem—but you may find a time when it's useful to allow outgoing source quench requests. The point is, you have to balance the benefits that answering these ICMP requests could deliver against the threats they might pose. Proceed delicately.

As you can see, I haven't discussed each ICMP request. That's because the Description box at the bottom of the ICMP page displays a decent explanation of the currently selected item.

Use ICF's Security Logging Feature

If you use ICF—and you should—you should use its security logging feature (on the Security Logging page of the Advanced Settings dialog box, shown here). Select the Log Dropped Packets check box to log incoming and outgoing packets that are dropped. Select the Log Successful Connections check box to log successful inbound and outbound connections.

In the Log File Options group box, you can change the location of the firewall log file and the amount of space it can occupy. The default is 4,096KB (4MB).

TIP   *The easiest way to open the firewall log is to choose Start | Run, enter **pfirewall.log** in the Run dialog box, and click the OK button.*

Open Ports Manually on ICF

Follow these steps to open ports manually on ICF:

1. Display the Advanced Settings dialog box for the Internet connection by following steps 1–3 in the section "Allow Incoming Services via ICS and ICF," earlier in the chapter.

2. Click the Add button. Windows displays the Service Settings dialog box, shown next.

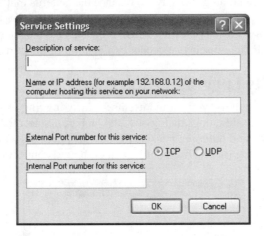

3. In the Description of Service text box, enter a descriptive name for the port. This name is for your benefit, so make it understandable.

4. In the Name or IP Address of the Computer Hosting This Service on Your Network text box, enter the name or IP address of the computer hosting the service. You might want to specify the actual IP address or name of the computer. You can also specify 127.0.0.1, the loopback address used for testing network setups.

5. If you specify the computer's name, it's best to use a fully qualified DNS name. The default domain name for XP using ICS is MSHOME.NET, so your computer's fully qualified DNS name would be *computername*.MSHOME.NET. If you want to check the fully qualified DNS name of a computer, issue an **ipconfig /displaydns** command on your ICS host and read the appropriate entry in the resulting list.

6. In the External Port Number for This Service text box, enter the external port number to use.

7. In the Internal Port Number for This Service text box, enter the internal port number to use. In many cases, this will be the same port number as the external port number.

8. Choose the TCP option button (the default) or the UDP option button, as appropriate.

9. Click the OK button. Windows closes the Service Settings dialog box and adds the port to the list on the Services page of the Advanced Settings dialog box.

To edit a service you've configured in this way, double-click it in the Services list box on the Services page of the Advanced Settings dialog box.

To delete a service you've created, select the port in the Services list box and click the Delete button. Windows deletes the port without confirmation.

Troubleshoot Your Internet Connection, ICS, and ICF

With any luck, you'll never need to read this section.

Okay, who do I think I'm kidding? There are all sorts of problems you may have with your Internet connection, ICS, and ICF. This section provides a brief approach to troubleshooting your Internet connection, a more-detailed approach to troubleshooting ICS connectivity and a couple of other problems, and information on a couple of problems that ICF may cause you.

Troubleshoot Your Internet Connection

How to troubleshoot your Internet connection depends on your connection technology and your ISP, but these are the basic steps:

1. Check your connection device:

   ■ For a dial-up connection, make sure that your modem is working, that it's powered on (if it's an external serial modem), and that it's correctly connected to your computer and to the phone line. If it's an external modem with a power supply and you suspect it of being confused, switch it off for 10 seconds or so and then switch it on again. If possible, turn on the modem's sound by selecting the Enable Modem Speaker check box in the Modem Configuration dialog box. (You can display this dialog box in various ways—for example, by selecting the modem on the General page of the Properties dialog box for the Internet connection and clicking the Configure button.) You'll then be able to hear whether the modem's dialing.

   TIP   *If you have a modem problem, run the Modem Troubleshooter in XP's Help and Support Center.*

   ■ For an ISDN, cable, or DSL connection, make sure your terminal adapter, cable router, or DSL router is correctly plugged in and powered on. Again, if necessary, power it off and on again.

   ■ For another type of connection, such as wireless or satellite, check the connection device for lack of power or unorthodox behavior.

2. Check your communications line (if you're using one):

   ■ If it's a regular phone line, place a voice call to your ISP's number and make sure you get the siren call of modems trying to mate.

   ■ If it's a cable or DSL connection, check the status light on the cable modem or DSL modem.

3. Make sure the network adapters are correctly assigned. If XP has gotten confused and is trying to connect to the Internet through your LAN card rather than through your external connection, it's not going to get far. Reassign the Internet connection if necessary.

4. Make sure your ISP is alive. If it's temporarily down or, uh, *resting*, you can mess with your configuration all you want, and it won't do you any good. Phone the support number and learn what's up. If you have a backup ISP you can use, connect using that connection and check your ISP's Web site for information on problems.

5. If your ISP is alive but you can't browse the Web even from the ICS host, open a command-prompt window and try pinging a host on the Internet by name. For example, you might try pinging Osborne, because Osborne is courteous enough to send a response to ping packets. (Many sites don't respond to ping packets.) Here's an example:

```
D:\>ping osborne.com
Pinging osborne.com [198.45.24.130] with 32 bytes of data:
Reply from 198.45.24.130: bytes=32 time=281ms TTL=238
```

   As you can see in the second line, the ISP's DNS has resolved the name osborne.com to the IP address 198.45.24.130. The third line shows a reply to the ping packet, indicating that the Osborne site is online and alive. But if your ISP's DNS servers are down, as sometimes happens, the name won't be resolved to the IP address, and the command will fail. You'll still be able to access any Internet host by IP address (for example, ping 198.45.24.130 would still work)—if you know the IP address.

6. If none of the preceding helps—in other words, you're sure your communications equipment is fine, your line is fine, they're connected properly, and your ISP is up and running—try running the Network Setup Wizard again.

If you're still stuck, bear in mind that your corner of the Internet might be having a really bad day. If some oaf with a backhoe has ripped up a major communications cable (again, it has happened), it may be a while before you're surfing the Web again.

Interpret Connection Error Messages

This section discusses some of the more common error messages you may see when connecting to the Internet and how to troubleshoot them.

Error 691 or Error 734   If you get Error 691 (either "The computer you are dialing in to cannot establish a Dial-up Networking connection. Check your password, and then try again" or "Access was denied because the username and/or password was invalid on the domain") or Error 734 ("The PPP link control protocol was terminated") when trying to connect via dial-up, check the following:

- First, check that your user name and password are correct for the connection.

- Second, check that you haven't selected the Include Windows Logon Domain check box on the Options page of the Properties dialog box for the connection.

- Third, check that the Validate My Identity As Follows drop-down list on the Security page of the Properties dialog box for the connection doesn't have the Require Secured Password item or the Use Smart Card item selected.

Invalid DHCP Lease   This is an entertaining error message that you may get when using a one-way or two-way cable modem. The problem occurs because XP's Autoconfiguration option automatically assigns an IP address to your cable adapter if it thinks the adapter has failed to get an address itself, whereas, in fact, the adapter may still be requesting an IP address from your ISP's DHCP server. The IP address that Autoconfiguration assigns is valid for your local network rather than for the ISP's network, so it prevents you from accessing the Internet.

The workaround for this problem is to open a command-prompt window and use an ipconfig command to check the IP address assigned to the network adapter for the cable modem. (For a one-way modem connection, you'll need to check the IP address for the PPP Adapter connection as well.) If the number is in the 169.254.*n.n* range, you know that Windows has assigned it automatically. Issue an **ipconfig /release** command for the affected adapter to release the connection and then an **ipconfig /renew** command for the affected adapter to force XP to renew the connection.

Error 633   If you get Error 633 ("The modem [or other connecting device] is already in use or is not configured properly") when you try to establish a broadband Internet connection, it usually means the connection is already open. If you feel you must reconnect the connection, disconnect it first.

Troubleshoot ICS

This section discusses how to troubleshoot ICS. The usual problem is that ICS doesn't work, for any of a variety of reasons. ICS also throws a wrench in the works if you're bridging two network adapters on the ICS host. More positively, ICS works with operating systems other than XP if you configure them correctly; this section covers that, too.

ICS Doesn't Work

So you've set up ICS—but it doesn't seem to be working. Troubleshoot first the ICS host and then the ICS client, as described in the following subsections.

Troubleshoot the ICS Host   Here are the steps to take to troubleshoot the ICS host:

1. Make sure the Internet connection on the host is working. Use Internet Explorer or another browser to access a Web site or ping an external host.

2. Make sure you've shared the correct connection—the one connecting to the Internet.

3. If you've enabled ICF on the internal network interface, disable it before setting up ICS. Alternatively, use the Network Setup Wizard to configure ICS. (The Network Setup Wizard automatically disables ICF on internal network interfaces.)

4. Make sure the ICS host is getting an IP address from your ISP. You can do this in various ways, but one of the easiest ways is to open a command-prompt window (Start | All Programs | Accessories | Command Prompt) and issue an **ipconfig** command. XP displays a list of network connections, as shown here. In the illustration, the PPP Adapter listing shows the IP address, subnet mask, and default gateway for the dial-up connection.

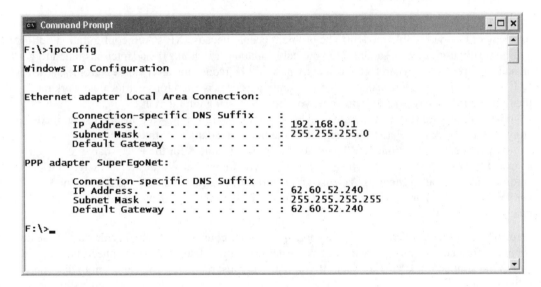

5. Make sure the host's IP address on its internal connection is 192.168.0.1. Again, one of the ways to do this is by issuing an **ipconfig** command in a command-prompt window; again, the previous illustration shows an example (the Ethernet Adapter Local Area Connection entry).

6. Check the Network Setup Wizard log file (Start | Run, enter **nsw.log** in the Run dialog box, and click the OK button) and the System log for ICS configuration errors.

Troubleshoot the ICS Client   Here are the steps to take to troubleshoot an ICS client:

1. Use Internet Explorer or another browser to try to access a Web site that you've verified you can access via Internet Explorer from the host (in other words, make sure the Web site is up and functional before you use it as a test for the ICS client). If you get the Web site, ICS is working.

2. Open a command-prompt window and check the IP address assigned to the ICS client by running the **ipconfig** command. The IP address needs to be in the range 192.168.0.2 to 192.168.0.254, inclusive. If it's not, take the following steps:

■ Choose Start | Control Panel, click the Network and Internet Connections link, and click the Network Connections link to open the Network Connections screen.

■ Right-click the LAN connection and choose Properties from the context menu to open the Local Area Connection Properties dialog box.

■ In the This Connection Uses the Following Items list box, select the Internet Protocol (TCP/IP) item and click the Properties button to display the Internet Protocol (TCP/IP) Properties dialog box.

■ On the General page, make sure the Obtain an IP Address Automatically option button and the Obtain DNS Server Address Automatically option button are selected. If they're not selected, try selecting them and closing the Internet Protocol (TCP/IP) Properties dialog box and the Local Area Connection Properties dialog box, and seeing whether ICS starts working. If these option buttons are already selected, or if selecting them doesn't make a blind bit of difference, try specifying an IP address and DNS server manually. Select the Use the Following IP Address option button and enter an IP address in the range 192.168.0.2 to 192.168.0.254, the subnet mask **255.255.255.0**, and the default gateway **192.168.0.1**. Then select the Use the Following DNS Server Addresses option button and enter **192.168.0.1** in the Preferred DNS Server text box and the Alternate DNS Server text box. Close the two dialog boxes and check for connectivity.

3. Open a command-prompt window (or use the same one you used for **ipconfig**) and ping the ICS host by issuing a **ping 192.168.0.1** command. If you get a series of replies, as shown next, you know that you have a TCP/IP connection between the ICS client and the ICS host. If you get the message "Request timed out" or "Destination host unreachable," use an **ipconfig** command to get the IP address of the client computer and ping it (from itself) to make sure that TCP/IP is working. If you get a response to the ping, there's most likely a problem with the physical connection between the computers (for example, your hub or switch has lost power or is dead, or a cable is disconnected). If you don't get a response to the ping, you have a TCP/IP problem on the ICS client.

```
Command Prompt                                                    _ □ ×

E:\>ping 192.168.0.1

Pinging 192.168.0.1 with 32 bytes of data:

Reply from 192.168.0.1: bytes=32 time<1ms TTL=128
Reply from 192.168.0.1: bytes=32 time<1ms TTL=128
Reply from 192.168.0.1: bytes=32 time<1ms TTL=128
Reply from 192.168.0.1: bytes=32 time<1ms TTL=128

Ping statistics for 192.168.0.1:
    Packets: Sent = 4, Received = 4, Lost = 0 (0% loss),
Approximate round trip times in milli-seconds:
    Minimum = 0ms, Maximum = 0ms, Average = 0ms

E:\>_
```

TIP

To find out further IP configuration information, such as the physical address of your network adapter and the address of your DNS servers, use the ipconfig command with the /all switch: ipconfig /all. You can also see most of the same information from the Details page of the Status dialog box for an Internet connection or the Network Connection Details dialog box for a LAN connection. (To display the Network Connection Details dialog box, click the Details button on the Support page of the Status dialog box for the network connection.)

Bridge Two Internal Network Adapters on an XP ICS Host

You need to turn ICS and ICF off before trying to bridge the internal ICS connection (192.168.0.1) with another internal network adapter on an ICS host. Otherwise, you'll get the error message "An unexpected error occurred when configuring the network bridge," and the bridge won't be created.

Once you've created the bridge (either manually or by using the Network Setup Wizard), turn ICS and ICF back on, and all should be well.

Use ICS with Earlier Versions of Windows

XP's ICS works with earlier versions of 32-bit Windows. All you need to do is configure Windows to use DHCP to obtain an IP address from ICS automatically. (If the version of Windows doesn't have TCP/IP installed, you'll also need to install TCP/IP.)

Windows 98 Second Edition, Windows Me, and Windows 2000 include versions of ICS. If you already have your network set up with ICS running on one of these versions of Windows, you *can* simply patch in XP as an ICS client and get basic connectivity. But because versions of ICS earlier than XP's version don't support UPnP, you won't be able to use any programs or features that rely on UPnP. You also won't have the firewall protection that ICF offers. So it's better to use the computer running XP as the ICS host, unless you have a compelling reason for doing otherwise.

Use ICS with Macs and Linux Boxes

ICS can provide Internet connectivity for Macs and Linux boxes as well as Windows PCs. All you need to do is configure the Mac or Linux box to use DHCP so that it picks up an IP address from ICS. If a Mac won't work with DHCP, hard-code an IP address in the range 192.168.0.2 to 192.168.0.254. (You can do the same with Linux, but all current distributions of Linux grew up with DHCP in the cradle, so it's unlikely you'll need to.) On older versions of Mac OS, you may have to install TCP/IP as well.

Troubleshoot ICF

ICF causes problems with various programs because it attempts to protect your computer from unauthorized intrusions. Some of these problems are soluble. Others are less so.

Problems Involving Dynamic Port Mapping

Problems occur especially with ICF if the program involved uses dynamic port mapping. As you've seen, ICF lets you open specified ports for incoming traffic—but it doesn't let you allow a program to open ports dynamically. This blocking of dynamic ports has effects such as preventing you from hosting Unreal Tournament or Battlezone II games on the Internet, as well as receiving file transfers on ICQ99a.

The only workaround for this problem is to disable ICF for the duration of the game or the ICQ session. Needless to say, disabling ICF to make programs work removes the protection that ICF offers against attacks, so be sure to reenable ICF as soon as possible after you finish using the problem program.

Windows Media Player Can't Play Streaming Audio

When using an ICS client connected through a connection protected by ICF, you may get the following message when trying to listen to streaming media using Windows Media Player: "Windows Media Player cannot find the specified file. Be sure the path is typed correctly. If it is, the file does not exist in the specified location, or the computer where the file is stored is offline." This message doesn't mean what it says; rather, it means that the server requires UDP or you've chosen to use UDP, and UDP is disagreeing with ICS and ICF. You may be able to get around this problem by selecting the check boxes for other protocols (Multicast, TCP, and HTTP) on the Network page of the Options dialog box for Windows Media Player.

The List of Servers for This Workgroup Is Not Currently Available

If you receive a system error 6118 ("The list of servers for this workgroup is not currently available") when you use a net view command to view a computer's shares, it's probably because you've enabled ICF, which has closed the ports for file sharing.

Summary

This chapter has discussed how to choose an Internet connection that suits your pocket, your needs, and your situation; how to set up the connection and configure it; how to share it by using Internet Connection Sharing (ICS) or another form of Network Address Translation (NAT); how to secure it by using Internet Connection Firewall (ICF); and how to troubleshoot it. For you to do just about anything described in the rest of this book, you need to have a satisfactory and secure Internet connection, so if you're reading this paragraph before reading the rest of the chapter and you don't have a functional Internet connection, be good and return to the beginning of the chapter and sort yourself out a connection.

The next chapter discusses how to establish one or more digital identities and protect your privacy online. Turn the page.

Chapter 3

Establish Your Digital Identity— and Protect Your Privacy

This chapter discusses how and why to establish one or more digital identities and digital personas for use on the Internet, and how to protect your privacy online.

That begs several questions—what a digital identity is, and how it compares to a digital persona—why you should want one (or more than one) of each; what kind of privacy you should expect to have online; and what threats there are to you online.

This chapter starts by discussing how we prove our identity in the real world, and how some of those mechanisms translate to the wired world. It then muses briefly on what privacy and anonymity mean and how both are being eroded in both the physical world and online—and by whom and what. That brings us to the point at which we can profitably consider .NET Passport, Microsoft's digital-persona initiative, and its implications. The chapter then concludes by delving into digital certificates, how and where to get them and how to manage them on XP.

In order for this chapter to make sense and convince you of what you should do to establish your digital identity and protect your privacy, I've included a fair amount of background. But you should know a fair amount of the background already, so I think you'll find the chapter easy going. (If not, persevere. It'll do you good.)

Establish Identity in the Physical World

If you happen to find Joe Sixpack's wallet in the street, you'll probably have little trouble working out who it belongs to. Supermarket club cards, medical insurance card, credit cards—any of these will give you Joe's name. Joe's driver's license will give you his address as well—perhaps even his current address. If Joe's a conscientious soul without a finely attuned sense of impending wallet loss, you might find his social security card as well, with its all-important identification number. And if Joe's on his way to the airport for an international trip (who knows?), you might find his passport as well and be able to learn further details about him.

All the documents mentioned in the previous paragraph provide a way of establishing one's identity. As you'll know from your own use of them, they apply in different circumstances and form a rough hierarchy of proof of identity. (Okay, I forced the example. But you didn't notice at first. So sue me.) A supermarket club card is of interest only to the supermarket that issued it and provides meager proof of identity—it's easy to get a club card with a false name on it; but doing so won't do you much good, so few people would bother. Getting a medical insurance card probably involved going through a number of hoops that firmly established your identity to the health insurance company, but the card isn't exactly anything you could use to prove your identity if the cops pulled you over for weaving. A credit card might provide some proof of identity for the cops, especially if it was one of the few that bears a picture of the holder. But really a credit card is meant for financial transactions, and the cops would want your driver's license because, in order to get a driver's license, you'll have had to prove your identity beyond almost any doubt—in fact, you'll have had to prove your identity to almost the extent involved in getting a passport. (In some cases, you may have used your passport to prove your identity to the DMV.)

Okay, so you knew all that. The point is, we're used to establishing our identity in the physical world by using a variety of mechanisms. Roughly speaking, there are three main mechanisms for identification and authentication: biometrics, passwords, and access tokens. *Biometrics*—the use of measurements of parts of the body as a form of identification—include fingerprints, handprints, retinal scans, DNA, and even mappings of the configuration of the crucial points of the bone structure in the face (these mappings can identify people even if they've added or removed facial hair or if they're wearing disguises). *Passwords* involve demonstrating specific knowledge that will discriminate between those in the know and those that aren't. *Access tokens* can be physical or virtual and run the gamut from keys and credit cards to digital certificates and other identifying chunks of code—having the right key will let you into your house or car, while the locks will deny access to holders of other keys; having the right credit card (and signature) lets you borrow money at the drop of a wallet; and having the right digital certificate lets you into your company's accounting system.

> **NOTE**   *Technically, photographs and signatures are biometric forms of identification. But because they're so much less precise than other biometric forms of identification (in particular, signatures are highly amenable to forging), I'm not considering them as hardcore biometrics for the purposes of this discussion.*

Typically, the mechanisms we use for establishing our identity in the physical world tend to be roughly appropriate to the situation we're in. For example, one of the simplest ways of establishing identity is by physical presence. Suppose you and your significant other agree to meet outside King Street Station so you can go for a meal. (I don't know why. Maybe you've been watching old movies.) You both turn up on time, authenticate each other visually and perhaps tactilely, and fade off together into the sunset. *Rain*set. Whatever.

If you've been significant for a while, and recently, biometric authentication shouldn't be difficult. Your significant other looks the same as before; sounds the same; feels the same; smells…even better than usual. Stories and movies have long played the theme of twins and ringers in this type of situation, and more recently of clones and androids—but that's entertainment. In the world that we know in 2002, you're unlikely to be fooled by a stand-in for someone you know intimately.

But suppose your Aunt Mildred cables you that she's coming into town for a Mariners game and a ceremonial reading of her latest will. You haven't seen Aunt Mildred since she moved to Tupelo 25 years ago, and you're not especially interested in inheriting half a field and three chicken coops, but you agree to show up at SeaTac anyway out of familial loyalty.

How are you and Aunt Mildred going to authenticate each other? You both look different after 25 years—assuming you both can remember what the other looked like back then. Even your heights have changed—you've grown, while she's shrunk. Tactile authentication is kinda out, so scratch the biometrics. At the same time, you probably don't feel like demanding ID, because she's not going to react positively to your request for a physical access token. (You might lose those chicken coops and be stuck with half a field.) Instead, chances are that you and Aunt Mildred will authenticate each other by testing for expected knowledge and establishing connections. You'll talk to her and draw on family history and shared knowledge until you're pretty sure that it's her. If you like, this will be a form of stateful authentication, in that you're drawing on your knowledge of what has happened in the past in order to make a valid judgment in the present. This represents a complicated use of passwords for identification.

Photographs tend to be used as a basic check of identity in documents such as driver's licenses, passports, and even some credit cards. But a plain photograph, biometric though it be, provides weak proof of identity. Many people look like other people, and many people don't resemble their passport photograph very closely—especially when the passport is the best part of ten years old. Some documents use photographs that show more than the face—for example, a photo that shows the subject's right ear, the ears being not only distinctive in themselves but also much less amenable to plastic surgery than most facial features. Other documents, such as U.S. Resident Alien cards, combine photos (with or without the right ear) with further proof of identity, such as a fingerprint or thumbprint.

The fingerprint (or thumbprint) forms the most acceptable face of hardcore biometrics. Biometric identification systems can establish identity beyond any reasonable doubt—depending on the system used, the likelihood of error can be anything from one in a few million to one in more than a billion. But because most biometric identification systems either are invasive or are perceived to be invasive (the ultimate biometric identification, DNA fingerprinting, is also one of the most invasive), biometrics tend to be reserved for situations where strong or irrefutable proof of identity is required, such as high-security corporate, government, or military premises. Assuming that the body part used by the biometric is still attached to the original owner, biometric systems give irrefutable proof of identity.

The humble fingerprint has been used for identification for so long, and with such success, that people are well used to fingerprinting, perhaps even to the extent of barely recognizing it as a biometric. This blurriness (so to speak) is encouraged by the popular image of the traditional technology—ink smudges on a sheet of cardboard. Although this low-tech method is still used for taking some fingerprints, most fingerprints these days are taken with electronic scanners that dump the results directly into databases. Even fingerprints taken on cardboard are routinely scanned.

In the last few years, some companies have tried using biometrics for consumer transactions. Customer reaction tends to range from grudging acceptance to outright refusal. For example, some banks require a fingerprint or thumbprint for some high-value transactions. Customers tend to accept that, because they can see that it benefits them to be sure that nobody else can perform such transactions on their accounts without producing a matching fingerprint. By contrast, when in 2001 Dollar Rent A Car ran a trial requiring fingerprints when customers rented a car, some customers resented the requirement and refused it.

The problem that Dollar experienced (and other companies have experienced in similar situations) is twofold. First, most people also feel that the degree of authentication should be proportionate to the transaction involved. Take a DNA test to settle a paternity suit or clear yourself of murder? No problem. Take a DNA test to get a supermarket club card? No way. Second, data taken by biometric identification systems is likely to be stored, either temporarily (for example, for the duration of your car hire) or forever. For example, if you give your fingerprints to Dollar, they're likely to end up in a corporate database linked to your record. That database may well be shared with other companies.

Establish Identity Online

Establishing identity online is quite a different matter from establishing identity in the physical world. The old joke about "on the Internet, nobody knows you're a dog" cuts both ways. Sure, nobody knows you're a dog. But if you *are* a dog, you'll have a hard time proving it. (There's a market for an enterprising certification authority here....)

Some of the mechanisms for establishing our identity in the physical world work over the phone as well. For example, suppose you call Lands' End and order a half-dozen fleece-lined deerskin moccasins for your Pekingese to hunt around the couch. Lands' End checks that you've given the correct credit card information (including the all-important billing address); that the card is still valid, not on any revocation list, and that funds are available; and accepts the order.

Notice that Lands' End hasn't really authenticated *you* here—they've just authenticated the payment information. That's all they're really interested in. (In passing, notice also that *you* haven't really authenticated *them*. They answered the phone number you called, said they were Lands' End, and claimed to have deerskin moccasins. They could have phreaked the phone system in order to steal your credit card information. You probably wouldn't know until the bailiffs arrived for your furniture rather than UPS arriving with your moccasins.)

Similarly, you can pay for goods online by using a credit card. You can even apply for a credit card online by supplying an impressive variety of sensitive identifying information. If you do so, you'll want to be very sure that it's a bona fide credit card company you're sharing information with rather than a cunningly camouflaged identity-theft operation.

Again, the authentication on each side is very weak. Because visual identification isn't an option, most of the proofs of identity used in the physical world are little use. Instead of using a likeness to establish proof, you need to use knowledge: credit card numbers, the billing address, your mother's maiden name, someone's place of birth, a password, a secret question. These are all passwords in the general sense.

Clearly, biometrics offer one of the best ways—perhaps *the* best way—of authenticating a user beyond doubt over a network. And it's probably inevitable that biometrics will eventually be built into or bolted onto most computers that are connected to networks and that need to be able to authenticate users beyond doubt. At this writing, various biometric devices are available for computers. For example, you can get keyboards that include a built-in fingerprint scanner, digital cameras that double as face-mapping devices, and serial port or USB scanners that hook into Windows logon procedures. Such devices are in use in settings that need them—again, typically in corporate, military, and government offices that require high security—but they haven't moved into the consumer realm.

Until biometric devices are widespread, we're stuck with using knowledge (passwords) or a digital access token to prove our identity online. Knowledge usually involves passwords and codes, which work adequately for many environments but tend to prove unwieldy when the user is required to enter them often. Passwords and codes can, of course, be shared by the holder and used by others.

The digital access token currently in favor is the *digital certificate*, an encrypted chunk of code intended to prove the user's identity by applying a digital signature to an item (for example, an e-mail message or a document) or by presenting the digital certificate to an Internet site as an access token. Because the certificate is encrypted, it's very hard to forge—likewise, the digital signature applied using the certificate. So, if the issuers of digital certificates take sufficient care authenticating the people and companies to which they issue digital certificates, digital certificates can be very secure.

But like passwords and codes, digital certificates can be shared. A digital certificate can be installed on a number of different computers and applied by any user who can access it. Such flexibility can be useful in a corporate environment in which various people are authorized to use the digital certificates for agreed purposes, such as signing code. In this case, the digital signature resulting from the application of the certificate would establish the corporate identity, but it wouldn't establish the identity of the individual who applied it.

Digital certificates are gradually becoming more widely used, especially by technology companies and software developers; but at this writing, they're far from widespread. Getting a digital certificate that proves your identity takes more effort than most consumers are prepared to put in without the promise of clear and immediate benefits. (I'll discuss how to get a digital certificate later in this chapter.) So the day when every home computer user has a digital certificate and routinely applies it to the messages they send and the documents they create (or modify) is a long way off—and indeed might never arrive.

With biometrics and digital certificates unlikely to achieve mass-market penetration in the short term, it might seem that the Internet is crying out for a type of identification that can be used easily, quickly, and without awkwardness or embarrassment over the wires.

Microsoft's .NET Passport is one of several attempts at such identification. We'll examine .NET Passport in detail a little later in the chapter. Other types include the Liberty Alliance project (http://www.projectliberty.org—*not* http://www.libertyalliance.org, which is the gateway to Jerry Falwell Ministries), which is backed by Sun Microsystems but is still in development. AOL Time Warner has an identity service called Magic Carpet, which is also in development—so at the moment, .NET Passport is leading the field and threatening to become the default identity service.

If, that is, any of the identity services really catch on. At this writing, users aren't exactly slavering for digital identities. In fact, a survey carried out by Gartner, Inc., in August 2001, took the temperature of just over 2,100 adult American Web users on Passport-style services. The survey found that most of those who shopped online preferred to register separately at each Web site rather than use a central service for handling their financial information. Here are the details: 54 percent of the users registered because they had to, 22 percent registered to save time, 17 percent registered to receive tailored sales pitches (these guys sound like a marketer's dream, but maybe there were extenuating circumstances we don't know about), and the remaining 5 percent didn't register— mostly to avoid receiving spam and to avoid sharing their private financial data with the sites.

So, establishing identity online is currently a problem. Let's move on to the questions of privacy and anonymity online. At the end of the chapter, I'll show you how to get, install, and manipulate digital certificates on XP.

Privacy and Anonymity Online

Before we discuss exactly what Microsoft .NET is and how it threatens your privacy online, we need to talk a bit about what privacy means in our modern world, about how privacy and anonymity differ from each other, and about why online anonymity is largely an illusion.

The Erosion of Privacy in the Modern World

When the founders drew up the Constitution, the privacy of the individual was clearly a major concern. In particular, the Fourth Amendment ("the right of the people to be secure in their persons, houses, papers, and effects, against unreasonable searches and seizures, shall not be violated," etc.) and the Fifth Amendment ("nor shall [any person] be compelled in any criminal case to be a witness against himself") define areas of privacy that have proved very effective for the best part of 200 years. If you were feeling unreasonable, you might choose to take exception with the founders for not having anticipated electronic monitoring and eavesdropping, but in general they displayed remarkable precision and prescience in what they wrote.

In the last century, the Supreme Court made a number of decisions that lopped large limbs off the tree of privacy. Jeffrey Rosen traces this process clearly in *The Unwanted Gaze*, so I'll content myself with a couple of examples here. First, in 1928, the Supreme Court ruled in Olmstead v. United States that wiretaps implemented on phone lines outside a person's private property didn't violate the Fourth Amendment, thus opening the way for all kinds of monitoring of communications. (Previously, in 1877, the Supreme Court had maintained that the government needed a warrant to open mail in transit.) Then, in 1967, the Supreme Court messed up the Fourth Amendment by deciding that the "Fourth Amendment protects people, not places," with Justice Harlan suggesting that a person must have a reasonable, subjective expectation of privacy in any given place or situation. Subsequent Supreme Court decisions have taken the bizarre line that when you share information with anybody else—even with a friend in a private conversation—you implicitly assume the risk that they may disclose that information to the government.

In the last ten years, developments in technology and court decisions have substantially eroded privacy in the United States. In particular, efforts to minimize or stamp out sexual harassment in the workplace have led to legal decisions that have caused employers to implement preventative workplace surveillance. I'll discuss this subject in more detail later in this chapter.

The Differences Between Privacy and Anonymity

Many people confuse anonymity with privacy, but it's important to understand the distinctions between the two.

Anonymity

Anonymity basically means that you can take an action, seen or unseen, without other people knowing your name. For example, you might post a message anonymously to a newsgroup: Because the message bears neither your name nor anything that links it to you, nobody knows you posted it, and nobody saw you post it either. By contrast, you might choose to streak at the next Red Sox game to demonstrate your artistic spontaneity, your tan, or your tattoos. If nobody who knows you is among the thousands to witness your art, you'll remain anonymous if you escape getting caught by security and Miranda'ed by the cops. Both those actions would be anonymous. The first would be private; the second wouldn't.

Anonymity is under threat from modern technology. For example, the First Amendment provides the right to read anonymously, but new copyright-protection technologies for digital works essentially remove your ability to do so. For example, some copyright-protection technologies require you to prove your identity before you can access the digital work—each time you want to read part of it, you need to identify yourself by password or digital certificate. Other technologies prevent you from passing your copy of the work along to someone else by locking it to your PC or to your identity. Limiting customers' rights like this is a violation of the First Sale Doctrine, so such copyright-protection technologies may face stiff legal challenges.

Privacy

So, when you're anonymous, others don't know your name. Privacy is substantially different. You can be private when people know who you are, or even know everything about you, but they aren't directly observing you at the time in question.

Before the advent of modern technology, observing someone essentially involved being physically present and close enough to see what that person was doing (perhaps from a distance, using a telescope) or to overhear what they were doing. People who wanted privacy could remove themselves from eyeshot and earshot of all others and be reasonably certain that they weren't observed.

Modern technology has changed all that. Even when no person is physically present to keep an eye or an ear on you, people may be watching you remotely, or you may be under surveillance by automated mechanisms. And any information gathered about you, your actions, or your movements can be stored for future examination.

In *The Unwanted Gaze*, Jeffrey Rosen writes: "Privacy can be conceived along two dimensions. There is the part of life that can be monitored, or directly observed, and there is the part of life that can be searched, because it leaves permanent records." Rosen points out that many of the decisions that have influenced the legal conception of privacy come from earlier times when relatively little information was stored and thus searchable, but these days it's possible for large chunks of a person's life to be stored and searchable. For example, closed-circuit television systems track both pedestrians and vehicles in many cities and on major roads, meaning that you may well be under observation all the way from leaving home to arriving at work. At work, as you've already seen, you stand a good chance of being under some form of surveillance: your computer usage, e-mail messages, Web surfing, and telephone calls may be monitored, and many workplaces are constantly swept by video cameras.

As I'll discuss in the next section, more or less every action you take on the Internet can be monitored unless you take steps to prevent monitoring. Under U.S. law, once you've surrendered a piece of information to a company, you've essentially lost control of it, and the company can do more or less what it likes with this information. This is because corporations have strongly opposed efforts to pass legal protection for privacy, since they want to be able to use people's personal information for marketing. By contrast, under European law, information that you release to a company in one context cannot legally be used in another context. (At this writing, the U.S. and Europe are having an ongoing battle—uh, *negotiation*—about the implications of data protection.)

In the U.S., some particular categories of information are protected, usually by piecemeal legislation haphazardly passed in response to a well-publicized incident that caused outrage or horror. For example, the Video Privacy Protection Act was passed in response to journalists investigating Robert Bork's video-rental habits during the confirmation hearings for the Supreme Court—so other people shouldn't be able to access your video rental records now. Similarly, most states have laws that protect records of library usage: others shouldn't be able to learn which books you've checked out of the library. The Driver's Privacy Protection Act (passed in 1990) was inspired by the murder of the actress Rebecca Schaeffer (star of the sitcom *My Sister Sam*) in 1989, so others shouldn't be able to get your address from the DMV anymore. By contrast, your medical records aren't protected, because of vested interests that oppose their protection. If asked, most people would want their medical records to be even more private than their library records and their video rental records, because medical information tends to be more sensitive—but the law is the other way around.

As David Brin memorably put it in *The Transparent Society*, "Matters of privacy, accountability, and freedom are often judged first and foremost on the basis of whose ox is being gored." If it's *your* ox, then there's a problem. So we might conclude on current evidence that the Supreme Ox hasn't been gored anything like enough in the last 10 or 15 years, given the anti-privacy and pro-surveillance decisions the Supreme Court has been handing down.

The Illusion of Anonymity Online

When you're online, particularly when browsing the Web, it's easy to get the feeling that you're more or less anonymous. Your ISP knows that you're online, of course, because you've established a connection through them using your account. And any Web sites at which you enter any personal information (for example, your name, address, and payment information when ordering an item) know who you are. But that's about it; the rest of the time, you flit from site to site anonymously, leaving no trace…

…or so it feels. In fact, you're stomping about wearing size-13 clodhoppers. Just about any action you take online leaves electronic footprints that can be stored and tracked.

Who's Watching You Online?

Various parties can monitor what you do online—anyone from government agencies to companies to private individuals with enough motivation and determination. This section discusses the main contenders.

Your ISP

Your ISP can track every action you take online. Depending on the country you're in and the country in which the people you're communicating are, and possibly which other countries the packets of information you receive and generate happen to run through, your ISP may store records of all your online activities for a short time (such as the duration of a billing cycle, in case you dispute the charges) or for a long period mandated by the government. For example, in December 2001, the U.K. passed anti-terror laws that required ISPs to maintain logs of all connections, browsing, and e-mail for a year—so if you've communicated electronically with someone in the U.K., their ISP will have a record of it. The U.K. and European police forces can access an ISP's records to pursue their enquiries of any crime (yes, *any* crime).

Even if you have a fine, upstanding ISP who respects your privacy, and you do nothing to get Europol on your case, you scatter a huge amount of information while browsing the Web. Your *click-stream*—the data that you generate while browsing—can contain information about the sites you visited, how long you were there, which pages you looked at and for how long, what you downloaded, what you bought, and even how you paid. (Although any e-commerce site worth its salt uses encryption to secure all transactions, some smaller sites still implement poorly designed shopping-cart and checkout systems that don't secure transactions effectively.)

The Web Sites You Visit

Each Web site you visit can, of course, track the actions you take on their site. Most sites of any size use cookies to track what you're doing (for example, adding items to a shopping cart or wish list) and to present you with information that'll be useful to you. A site can usually also learn the last site you visited before you accessed their site, and the site to which you go when you leave their site.

Most of the sites that collect your personal data have little interest in using it to assemble a fuller picture of you. For example, if you create a customer account at an online clothing store and make several purchases of men's clothes, they'll develop an idea of your size, taste in clothes, and the amount you're prepared to spend for particular items. All this information will be in their database and will let them put together tempting special offers customized for the preferences you've demonstrated. But they probably won't feel the need to find out whether you like products that they don't sell themselves. For example, the fact that you also buy high-end hunting knives and fired-clay Dutch ovens is probably irrelevant to them. And to you it's not a matter of serious concern that the online clothing store knows what types of clothes you buy.

The Companies That Work with the Web Sites You Visit

But if multiple Web sites were to band together to assemble the information that each has gleaned about you, they could put together a much more comprehensive profile—perhaps enough of a profile to sell to direct marketers, or enough of a profile to cause you concern.

This aggregation of information caused a firestorm of controversy when the news emerged that DoubleClick, Inc., a major coordinator of banner ads, was planning to cross-reference its extensive database of purchase records, surfing habits, and e-mail addresses with the real-world identities and addresses of people. DoubleClick, Inc., was in a position to do this because its cookies were able to track surfers' movements from site to site on which its banner ads appeared. The explosion of bad press when this news broke caused DoubleClick, Inc., to drop its plans for cross- referencing the data.

The Companies That Were Monitoring You Anyway

But even DoubleClick, Inc., and similar companies that can track you from site to site on which they advertise can only dream of the quantity of precise and valuable information that flows to

Assess the True Cost of an Action or a Transaction

This monitoring, surveillance, and storing of information means you must balance the convenience of getting something done online (for example, making a purchase or simply visiting a site to learn some information) against the possible problems that may be caused by other people being able to link the transaction back to you. Of course, this has always been the case in the real world as well—for example, people tend to try to make sensitive purchases as discreetly as possible, from making sure they're not observed by people they know when ordering embarrassing items at a drugstore to paying with cash rather than check or credit card for illegal items such as drugs or stolen goods.

In passing, the embarrassment that can be caused by various perfectly legal transactions has provided a great boost to Internet sales of the products in question. Ordering via the Internet is discreet in that it prevents your neighbors from seeing what you're buying—but it requires your real name, address, and payment information, all of which go into a database that the Internet store can easily share with other businesses.

the credit card companies and the credit agencies (such as Equifax, Inc.; TRW, Inc.; and Experian). In most cases, these companies aren't specifically tracking you online, because they don't need to. Each time you use your credit card to make a purchase—be it online, via telephone, or in person—a nugget of data rolls automatically into your record.

You're probably already aware of roughly what a credit report reveals about you, so we shouldn't need to get into that here. But if you're worried about being tracked online, it's worth remembering the detailed trail you leave in the physical world as well.

Government Agencies

Government agencies may be—probably *are*—monitoring you as well. For example, if you're in the U.S., you may draw the attention of friendly government agencies from the Federal Bureau of Investigation (FBI; www.fbi.gov) to the Internal Revenue Service (IRS; www.irs.gov) to the National Security Agency (NSA; www.nsa.gov). Or an agency may get someone else to monitor you, as you'll see in a page or two.

Depending on which of your (real or putative) sins they're focusing on, government agencies are mostly interested in different ends than businesses are. But both government agencies and businesses would love to have the means to know everything about you by having all your information in the mother of all databases: your full name, address, date and place of birth, parentage, and race; your fingerprints, your DNA fingerprints, your photos (as many as possible), and a mapping of your facial bone structure (so that computer scanning can recognize you in disguise); and all your financial details, and information on every transaction you commit.

Supra-Government Security Agencies

Government agencies can be pretty scary, especially when it's *your* six they're locked onto. But most government agencies are more or less confined to the nation whose government supposedly oversees them. Scarier are the supra-government security agencies, which can monitor online actions in much of the world.

As a breed, supra-government security agencies tend to duck publicity—and to be able to do so, unlike some of their less fortunate brethren. For example, at this writing, the European Union is wrangling over the creation of a European Police Office—*Europol* for short—that would "improve police cooperation between the Member States to combat terrorism, illicit traffic in drugs and other serious forms of international crime." Because Europol is (or will be) essentially a police force, as opposed to a security agency, the wrangling is taking place in the limelight of international conferences. Many citizens of would-be participating countries are concerned about the scope of Europol and how it will extend the European Union's reach into each of the member states, so there should be some lively discussions to come. And, in any case, Europol will largely be limited to acting in the countries that belong to the European Union, though it will naturally coordinate with other police forces in pursuit of the forms of crime mentioned earlier. Europol looks set to be one of the "police archipelagos" that Didier Bigo refers to—but it should remain clearly in public view.

By contrast, consider ECHELON. ECHELON managed to operate from the 1970s until the late 1990s almost entirely unheard of by the public—and, apparently, by many leading politicians as well. Established and operated in secrecy, ECHELON is the code name for an automated global interception and relay system run by the NSA, the U.K.'s General Communications Headquarters (GCHQ), Canada's Canadian Security Intelligence Service (CSIS), Australia's Defence Signals Directorate (DSD), and New Zealand's Government Communications Security Bureau (GCSB). GCHQ is the same entity as starred (in an earlier incarnation) in *Enigma* and the true story behind it; three generations later, it has processing power enough to make your Pentium 4 monster look like a pocket calculator, storage enough to eat the Library of Congress as a canapé, and bandwidth enough to cause minor telecoms to drool at the canines. CSIS, DSD, and GCSB fulfill similar functions in Canada, Australia, and New Zealand, respectively, to those that the NSA and GCHQ fulfill in the U.S. and the U.K., only with fewer resources, fewer targets, and usually less publicity.

ECHELON specializes in sigint (signals intelligence) and comint (communications intelligence) and has monitoring stations at a number of known locations. The biggest ECHELON station— in fact, the biggest monitoring station in the world—is at Menwith Hill near the picturesque town of Harrogate in North Yorkshire, U.K., and it deserves a few moments of your attention for its capabilities, which are best described as fearsome.

As of 1997, Menwith Hill was known to be connected with fiber optics capable of carrying more than 100,000 calls at the same time. This information leaked out after the trial of two peace campaigners protesting at Menwith Hill; by now, these capabilities have probably been upgraded. Menwith Hill is also connected to Hunters Stone Tower, a nearby British Telecom microwave transmitter that just happens to relay hundreds of thousands of calls a day. Some sources suggest that ECHELON may intercept and monitor up to three billion communications (phone calls, faxes, text messages, e-mail messages, satellite transmissions, file downloads, and file transfers) every day. (As you'll appreciate, ECHELON chooses not to correct these figures if they're inaccurate, so the number might in fact be far greater.)

NOTE   *Intercepting e-mail is much easier and more effective if all e-mail is fed through an interception system. Britain's Regulation of Investigatory Powers (RIP), passed after a firestorm of controversy in 2000, forces all U.K. ISPs to be connected to an e-mail interception center run by MI5, the British security service. RIP (an appropriate acronym: E-mail privacy,* requiescat in pace*) is part of a push by the NSA to, uh, encourage other ECHELON members and European governments to adopt a standardized framework for intercepting communications more efficiently. RIP makes intercepting communications and hacking into computers illegal, but it exempts the security agencies and the police from the law.*

Most of the monitoring of this seething mass of communications is done by computer, which sift the wheat from the chaff and the mutant grains from the wheat. This sifting process identifies keywords of interest (particularly in combination), voices that match the voiceprints of surveillance subjects, and any encryption that seems worthy of cracking. Humans then examine the mutant grains and determine which (if any) of it merits further examination by higher-ups.

As mentioned earlier, some of the monitoring done by ECHELON happens at one logical remove. That's because most countries have written or unwritten constitutional restrictions on their intelligence services that forbid them from putting their subjects under surveillance without explicit authorization. (For example, the FBI is supposed to get explicit authorization before tapping your phone lines.) But the countries in ECHELON can get around this limitation by implementing the surveillance from another ECHELON country or by having it carried out by (or under the auspices of) foreign nationals employed in the country in question.

Inquisitive Individuals

As mentioned earlier, most of the snooping that goes on is by companies and government agencies, because they have the motivation and the money to implement monitoring and surveillance on a grand scale. But the Internet has also been a great boon to inquisitive individuals—everyone from journalists to private eyes to people curious about their neighbors. Apart from searching for information manually, either by using Internet resources or by using the instructions in any of various books that tell you how to track down assorted types of public and semi-public information, you can also get programs that automatically search online databases for commonly requested types of data.

Surveillance in Everyday Life

Before you get too paranoid about being spied on via the Internet, consider to what extent you're spied on in your everyday life. The U.S., like most other first-world countries, is bristling with closed-circuit television (CCTV) cameras in public places. (If you're unaware of the extent of camera surveillance, take a look at sites such as the NYC Surveillance Camera Project: www.mediaeater.com/cameras.) Most use of CCTV is not only legal but encouraged by the government concerned. For example, the U.K. is estimated to have more than 1 million CCTV cameras as of the end of 2001, and the government has earmarked £150 million of additional funds for more cameras.

Some CCTV systems are intended to increase security, usually by helping discourage crime through the threat of the criminal's being easily identified after the fact. (Even your friendly neighborhood watch group may be using CCTV or Webcams.) Face-recognition software is already widely used in public places such as airports, bus stations, and sports stadiums to identify convicted criminals and suspected malefactors. Some face-recognition systems are capable of recognizing hundreds of faces per second and matching them with great accuracy against a database of faces. As usual, the information gained can be stored immediately and forever. If you attended a sports game, paid cash, and behaved yourself impeccably, that fact might be stored forever in a surveillance register.

Other CCTV systems are intended to decrease fraud: Every time you fill up your gas tank, chances are that the gas station is recording all license plates to help it cut down on theft. So even if you pay cash, there's a record of your being there.

Yet other CCTV systems are intended to help keep vital infrastructure functioning. For example, many countries use cameras to monitor roads, intersections, and bridges to keep traffic flowing, identify problems as early as possible so that they can be resolved, and warn people when they're en route to gridlock. Few people object to this monitoring, because it benefits them either directly or indirectly. But as soon as these systems, or their near relatives, are used to identify speeders or those who run red lights, public perception of them changes substantially.

CCTV is very widely used, sometimes with audio as well as video recording, but it's far from the only game in town. Most people in first-world societies use devices every day that provide information about where they are and what they're doing. In the home, cable or satellite TV devices track the shows you watch, either for advertising or to establish your preferences and feed you further shows. Credit cards closely track their users: every time you make a credit card transaction via a swipe-card system, your credit card is validated in real time, and your card's location can be pinpointed. And many people freely choose to carry mobile phones wherever they go so that they can make or receive calls. The mobile phone seems so benign that the fact that its network tracks the phone everywhere tends to be glossed over. Although this tracking is necessary for the phones to work effectively, it means that the location of the phone is known with fair accuracy at any given time.

Surveillance in the Workplace

It's no secret that many companies in the U.S. are using surveillance on their employees in the workplace. A 1999 study by the American Management Association reported that 45 percent of the nearly one thousand companies surveyed routinely monitored their workers' phone calls, e-mail messages, and computer usage. This monitoring ranges in scope and intrusiveness from the mild (for example, checking Web logs to make sure nobody's visiting porn sites) to the very intrusive (for example, using e-mail–checking software such as Assentor to scan all incoming and outgoing mail, and using computer-monitoring software such as WinWhatWhere Investigator or Spector, which can record every keystroke the employee entered during a session). Some companies specifically notify employees of the surveillance; others prefer to bury it in general terms of an employment agreement.

Be As Anonymous and Private As Possible Online

If you want to avoid your usage of the Internet being monitored, you have to take active steps, such as those mentioned in this list:

- For browsing, you can go through a service such as Anonymizer.com (www. anonymizer.com) or Zero Knowledge Systems, Inc. (www.zero-knowledge.com). These services use various encryption and redirection techniques to remove identifiers from your requests, prevent cookies from landing on your computer while letting you enjoy the benefits of cookies during surfing sessions, block scripts, and sanitize downloads.

- For e-mail, you can use a Web-based service that offers encrypted e-mail, such as HushMail (www.hushmail.com), use encryption technology such as Pretty Good Privacy (PGP) with Outlook Express or another conventional client, or use a digital certificate to encrypt e-mail using Outlook Express or another client. Anonymizer.com also offers anonymous e-mail.

- For secure document transfer, you can use a point-to-point solution, such as NetMeeting, or a Web-based secure-transfer solution, such as ZipLip (www.ziplip.com). Your ISP will have details of the connections you've made, so it'll know that, for instance, you've spent three hours each day at Anonymizer.com, sending this number of bytes and receiving that number of bytes, but it won't be able to tell what those bytes contained.

Companies monitor their employees for several reasons—to track and improve performance (for example, in a tightly managed call center), to protect confidential or otherwise sensitive information, and, most of all, to prevent sexual harassment suits. That's because the law places liability for sexual harassment in the workplace on the employer rather than the harasser.

Understand .NET and Neutralize Its Threat

If you were feeling cynical, you might say that .NET is Microsoft's latest attempt to rule the e-world. If you were feeling a little less cynical, you might say that .NET is a framework intended to leverage Microsoft's dominance of desktop computing and its strength in servers to gain control of and influence over the Internet. And if you were feeling more or less wholly naïve, you might say that .NET is an impressive new technology that makes it easier for Windows users to stay connected via the Internet.

Each of these views has more than a little truth. Let's try to assemble a more balanced picture.

What Is .NET?

Microsoft pronounces .NET as *dot-net* and describes it as "Microsoft's platform for XML services." XML is the abbreviation for Extensible Markup Language, a markup language for presenting and distributing content on the Web. Like HTML (Hypertext Markup Language), the language used for the first Web pages, XML uses tags and can be used to describe the layout and formatting of a document. But unlike HTML, XML tags also describe the structural elements of a document, thus enabling the transfer of information from one application to another. And because XML is extensible, you can create new markup elements, rules, and markup languages for different types of content. Markup languages built using XML are sometimes referred to as *XML applications*.

Microsoft divides .NET into five areas: .NET experiences, .NET clients, .NET services, .NET servers, and .NET tools. The following subsections discuss briefly what these areas are.

.NET Experiences

.NET experiences are the user end of .NET—how users experience .NET. The highest-profile .NET experiences at this writing are .NET Passport, MSN, and .NET Alerts. .NET experiences are the end of .NET that we're most interested in for the purposes of this chapter, but it's a good idea for you to know a bit about the other areas of .NET as well.

.NET Clients

.NET clients are devices that can access .NET services across the Web. To be able to access .NET services, a device needs to be running software that supports XML. As you'd expect, PCs of various descriptions (from laptops to desktops to workstations) are .NET clients. So are handheld computers, mobile phones, game consoles, and tablet PCs that can run XML. For example, the Xbox game console is a .NET client.

.NET Services

.NET services are building-block services of functionality, on top of which developers can create programs. For example, as you'll see in Chapter 5, Messenger provides user-to-user communications. Developers can build programs that use Messenger's functionality to deliver extra services.

.NET Servers

.NET servers are the server software used to create the infrastructure for deploying, managing, and using XML Web services. If you're familiar with Microsoft's server products, it'll come as no surprise to learn that .NET servers include Microsoft bastions such as Windows 2000 Server, Exchange Server, and SQL Server (together with other servers such as BizTalk Server, Commerce Server, and Content Management Server).

.NET Tools

.NET tools are the tools for building, deploying, and running XML Web services. .NET tools include Visual Studio .NET and the Microsoft .NET Framework.

What Is .NET Good For?

.NET is designed to appeal to several very different groups: users, service providers, and service developers. The following subsections discuss what .NET offers to those groups.

.NET's Appeal to Users

.NET is intended to appeal to users by making it easier for them to take certain actions and use certain services online. That phrasing is a bit vague because of the scope of .NET, so let's consider three key components.

.NET Passport   The .NET Passport initiative is designed to make it easier for users to establish their identity on the Internet. As you'll see a little later in this chapter, you can get a .NET Passport with minimal effort by supplying a modest amount of information. You can then use that .NET Passport to sign into Web sites affiliated with .NET Passport Service, to use Windows Messenger, and as the basis of your Passport Wallet—a feature for storing your credit or debit card information online so that you can apply it easily to an online transaction.

.NET Alerts   .NET Alerts lets you receive real-time alerts through Windows Messenger when you're online and signed in. These alerts come from service providers and supposedly only at your request. For example, an online auction site might use .NET Alerts to let you know the status of your bids, thus saving you from having to log into the auction site repeatedly (or check for e-mail notifications) to find out if anything has happened. Likewise, an online merchant might use an .NET Alert to let you know that an item you've ordered has come into stock, that a price has come down to a level you've specified interests you, or that an order you've placed has shipped. If you're signed into Messenger, you get alerts instantly. Otherwise, they stack up until you sign in and check for them.

.NET My Services   .NET My Services is the centralized framework into which .NET Passport and .NET Alerts tap. At this writing, .NET My Services comprises a slew of services, including .NET Profile (a personal profile, from name to optional photos), .NET Contacts (contact management), .NET Inbox (for managing e-mail and voicemail), .NET Calendar (you guess), .NET Documents (document storage), .NET Presence (whether you're online, offline, busy, faking being busy, or whatever), and .NET Wallet (payment information, receipts, coupons, and more; currently called Passport Wallet at the user end). These services are often used in combination. For example, Messenger relies on .NET Passport for identity; NET Contacts for the list of contacts; and .NET Presence for information on whether the protagonist and their contacts are online, offline, or under another status.

NOTE   *If you've been following buzzwords, .NET My Services is the new name for what Microsoft had been calling by the code name HailStorm for several years. .NET My Services uses industry-standard protocols, including XML, HTTP, SOAP (Simple Object Access Protocol), and UDDI (Universal Description, Discovery, and Integration).*

At this writing, some of the services are much more convincing than others. Microsoft is forcing users of Messenger, Hotmail, and MSN to use .NET Passport, so .NET Passport is useful. Once you're using Messenger, .NET Alerts can be very useful, because it enables you to receive time-sensitive information in real time. And as mentioned earlier, some services use other services. But some services look dubious at this stage. For example, .NET Documents, which provides document storage in a secure location on the Internet, is staggeringly uncompelling if you don't have the bandwidth to save and open documents on the Internet quickly and you don't want to use a service such as MSN communities for backup.

.NET's Appeal to Service Providers

To service providers, .NET offers a chance to ride the Microsoft technology wave and a standardized way to deliver services to what should be a growing market of .NET users. In particular, .NET Passport offers an easy way to establish a user's identity and to track their actions, and technologies built on Messenger let businesses communicate cheaply and effectively with their customers in real time.

Microsoft says .NET My Services "offers businesses the opportunity to achieve deeper customer relationships and to translate those relationships into increased revenue." In other words, if a business can track your actions and supply you with more information about products and services you might be interested in, it's likely to be able to relieve you of more money than it would otherwise have been able to.

The downside to .NET is that it requires the service provider to use Microsoft software and to pay Microsoft licensing fees for using the .NET technology.

.NET's Appeal to Developers

In the early days of Webmania (the mid 1990s), many companies built their Web applications from scratch, using either their favorite programming languages (even the venerable COBOL) or programming languages that were being developed at breakneck speed for building Web applications. Writing applications from scratch proved to have several disadvantages, foremost among them being that it took forever and a day, the resulting applications didn't always do what they were supposed to (or the requirements had changed, or both), and the applications tended to be even fuller of holes than the average person's understanding of the Vietnam War.

Bearing this history in mind, you can see that .NET should have a strong appeal to developers, because it offers them a way of building applications faster and more easily.

If you're familiar with the Microsoft Office programs—Word, Excel, PowerPoint, Access, Outlook, and so on—you'll probably have heard of Visual Basic for Applications (VBA). VBA provides a way of manipulating the objects that make up the programs and a way of creating new objects to extend the programs. For example, VBA provides userforms, which you can use to create anything from a minor dialog box to a complete program running from the host program (for example, Word or Excel). VBA is essentially a subset of Visual Basic (VB), a programming language for building standalone applications.

In much the same way that VBA and Visual Basic provide the tools for building hosted programs and standalone programs, .NET provides the building blocks for building Web applications. Instead of building from scratch, developers can use the functionality that .NET Services offer to quickly put together the core for their applications. Instead of struggling with not wholly suitable or not wholly developed programming languages, developers can use the familiar languages in Visual Studio .NET.

In theory, the resulting applications should not only be quicker to create and easier to update, but also more reliable and more secure.

.NET Detriments

At this writing, and looking from a user's point of view, it's hard to see .NET in an entirely positive light.

It's undeniable that some .NET services—particularly Messenger and .NET Alerts—already deliver benefit to some (perhaps many) users. And other .NET services will no doubt be developed that benefit users in ways I can't imagine right now. But at the same time, you'd be hard pushed not to notice that Microsoft is forcibly generating demand for .NET by requiring Hotmail, MSN, and Messenger users to use .NET Passport. Users aren't exactly screaming for .NET, but it's being shoved down their throats.

From the user's point of view, the problem with .NET is that it essentially acts as a user-tracking mechanism, shredding some of the last vestiges of privacy that users have enjoyed on the Internet by removing their anonymity in an ever-increasing number of transactions.

As the Internet moves from being the great free-for-all of the end of the millennium to more of a controlled and formalized pay-as-you-go model, more and more sites that offer valuable content will require users to establish accounts and to log in on each visit. Logging in can be done with cookies, but cookies don't have the same portability (from computer to computer) that .NET Passport can offer. So it seems likely that .NET Passport will catch on as a quick-and-easy way to log in automatically to these sites—especially since Microsoft has taken steps to ensure that all Hotmail, MSN, and Messenger users must use .NET Passport. If Passport Wallet gains enough users to marshal critical momentum, more sites will implement Passport Express Purchase, thus driving users to use Passport Wallet and to divulge their financial details to Microsoft. Sooner or later, more and more .NET services will require subscriptions, and you can be sure that the payment structures won't allow anonymous payments.

As discussed earlier in this chapter, Web sites have been tracking users for several years now—ever since they figured out how to do it. This tracking has been increasing recently as the dotcom crunch has cut off advertising funds and driven sites to search for new sources of revenue by exploiting visitors more directly. Most Web users are aware that they're being tracked to some extent—though many were surprised to learn of the amount of specific data that DoubleClick, Inc., had managed to amass—and regard it as one of the less desirable but inevitable consequences of using the Web. If you like, the tracking is the price people are prepared to pay for free content.

What's different about .NET is the centralization and degree of the tracking. In .NET, Microsoft has constructed a structure for gradually drawing ever more information from users. Starting with the modicum of information needed to get a .NET Passport (none of which need be true, apart from the e-mail address), users will gradually need to reveal more and more information—and more and more true information—to fully use the .NET services. The strategy uses XP, the shiny new operating system, and the pan-Windows messaging client, Windows Messenger, to snare people in .NET. It's beautifully done. And it's very Microsoft. Bunches of tasty carrots proffered, with sticks swishing pianissimo in the background.

Microsoft is using .NET Passport and .NET Alerts to suck users into buying the whole .NET My Services package and gradually storing more and more data online under Microsoft's auspices. Each user's data, we're assured, is kept in a "digital safe deposit box" where it's "private, secure, and available," and from which the user can choose to share the information with family, friends, companies, and so on. But the net (okay, okay, pun more or less inevitable) effect of these digital safe deposit boxes is to build up a massive database of information on millions of online users and shoppers. Even if Microsoft keeps the .NET My Services data secure (as it has pledged to do), having this database will give Microsoft extra leverage in propelling itself to the forefront of electronic commerce. If .NET Passport and Passport Wallet are used by millions of prime online shoppers, no online merchant of any size will be able to resist incorporating .NET Passport in their Web site. If .NET Passport and Passport Wallet become global standards for identification and commerce over the Web, no business will be able to avoid using .NET My Services.

Remember that quote a couple of pages ago about achieving deeper customer relationships and translating them into increased revenue. Does that sound great for the customers?

Protect Yourself from .NET

Because .NET threatens both your anonymity and your privacy, you may well want to use .NET with care. In fact, having read the previous description, you may feel you don't want to touch .NET even with a ten-foot bargepole.

If you're using Windows, and particularly if you're using XP, the bargepole is an option, but it doesn't seem a great one. Shunning .NET means dispensing entirely with the features offered by Messenger, which are appealing right out of the box and seem destined to grow more appealing as more .NET services are deployed. It's probably better to get yourself one or more .NET Passports, possibly in names other than yours, and use them carefully as outlined here so that you can enjoy some of the benefits of .NET while avoiding its rapacious data-gathering tentacles and surrendering as little true information about yourself as possible. (If you're using another operating system, such as Linux or Mac OS, you should be able to insulate yourself much more thoroughly from .NET. You might not even need to touch the bargepole.)

Here are suggestions for limiting the amount of information that Microsoft can gather about you using .NET:

- For each .NET Passport you create, use a free e-mail account (for example, Hotmail or MSN) that you can abandon if it becomes contaminated. Don't pay for the account, because doing so requires your real information.

- If you create a .NET Passport using your real identity, don't use it by default. Use it only when necessary to accomplish something.

- Create as many .NET Passports as you need. At this writing, there's no limit on the number of .NET Passports you can create. Even Microsoft recognizes that people may want to have multiple .NET Passports rather than just one.

- If you use multiple .NET Passports with the same XP user account, avoid associating any of the .NET Passports with your user account.

- If you want to maintain various identities while enjoying the benefits of .NET Passport, create multiple user accounts in XP, one for each .NET Passport. You'll need to switch user accounts more often, but it will help you keep your identities and your cookies straight.

- When there's a sensible alternative to using a .NET service, use it. For example, as you'll see in Chapters 5 through 8, NetMeeting duplicates much of Messenger's basic functionality and allows you to perform those functions (for example, chat, voice and video conversations, and program sharing) in a more secure way than Messenger does. So when possible, use NetMeeting rather than Messenger.

■ Avoid using .NET Passport to log into any .NET Passport–enabled sites if possible. Unless and until .NET Passport crushes all competition, most sites will maintain other ways of authenticating users. Use those ways, even if it means maintaining a plethora of separate accounts and passwords.

■ Don't let Messenger, Internet Explorer, or any other .NET Passport–using program log you in automatically.

> CAUTION   *.NET Passport–enabled sites can associate your .NET Passport with your true identity if you log in using .NET Passport and then make a purchase using your true identity*

Understand .NET Passport

Passport was introduced in 1999 and renamed .NET Passport in 2001 to fit more neatly into Microsoft's .NET initiative. .NET Passport is one of the key ".NET experiences" that end users will have, and it's what Microsoft calls a *platform service*: .NET Passport acts as a way of authenticating users over the Internet without any of those handy identifying documents and without biometrics.

The numbers for .NET Passport accounts are a tad shaky—okay, I'll be honest: they vary wildly—but they're certainly in the tens or hundreds of millions. Here's one data point: As of August 2001, .NET Passport had 25 million users enrolled in the U.S. (and more in other countries). Interestingly, only 7 million of those 25 million actually knew (or, perhaps more accurately, *understood*) that they had a .NET Passport. Fewer than 1 million of those 7 million had used their .NET Passport at a Web site other than one of Microsoft's. In other words, most of the .NET Passport holders are Hotmail and MSN users, and 18 million of them probably use their .NET Passport strictly for e-mail and perhaps Windows Messenger. As of November 2001, 2 million .NET Passport users had signed up for Passport Wallet.

Here's another data point: Shortly before the launch of XP (in October 2001), Microsoft was claiming that there were over 165 million .NET Passport accounts and more than 36 million active MSN Messenger users. (Those figures are worldwide.)

Consumer and civil-liberties groups, including the Electronic Privacy Information Center (EPIC), Consumers Union, and the Consumer Federation of America, have claimed that Microsoft doesn't adequately protect .NET Passport users' data. As you would expect, Microsoft denies this. But as you'll see shortly, problems with .NET Passport—especially with Passport Wallet—have been demonstrated, so it's difficult to accept Microsoft's bland assurances that all is well.

One of the consumer groups' complaints was that .NET Passport doesn't have a mechanism for you to cancel your account and remove your personal information from the .NET Passport servers. You can check in any time you want, but you can never leave. Microsoft claims to have resolved this issue. But at this writing, there's no easily visible link on the Passport Web site for canceling a .NET Passport, and there's nothing in the Help files about canceling anything other than a Kid's Passport—Microsoft seems to have followed AOL's brand of customer service, which made it as difficult and discouraging as possible to cancel an AOL account. (In passing, Kid's Passport is a get-'em-while-they're young version of .NET Passport.)

Consumer groups also have complained about the uses to which Microsoft might be putting .NET Passport users' data. Microsoft has said that "this information is completely private, secure, not mined, sold, rented, or ever used for secondary purposes. It's not mined at all, period." If this is true, it's remarkable, because .NET Passport will give Microsoft a huge database of information about people's Web browsing preferences, shopping habits, and means of payment.

In March 2001, privacy advocates noticed that the Passport Terms of Use agreement gave Microsoft the right to (among other things) "use, modify, copy, distribute, transmit, publicly display, publicly perform, reproduce, publish, sublicense, create derivative works from, transfer, or sell" any of the communications or files you transmitted via Passport services (for example, Hotmail or Messenger). As you can imagine (or perhaps remember), this made the headlines. Since then, Microsoft has withdrawn sweeping claims to your information from the Passport Terms of Use.

As I mentioned earlier, you may want to get two or more identities—your real one for communicating securely with your friends and family, and one or more fake identities for using Microsoft's .NET features for purposes that you don't want to be tracked back to your real identity.

Not surprisingly, Microsoft realizes that many users have multiple .NET Passports. But interestingly, Microsoft has been relatively upfront about it, rather than maintaining the line that you might expect—that one .NET Passport should be good enough for any user. Here's a quote from Microsoft about Passport:

> …nothing prevents any user from having multiple Passports for this very purpose and many users do have more than one. This does not defeat the value of single sign-in, because users are likely to have many applications for which each Passport can be used.

At this writing, the .NET Passport registration form performs no check of identity beyond checking that your ZIP code is valid for the state you specify and that your e-mail address works. Assuming you can supply a valid ZIP code for the state you claim to be in, .NET Passport registration doesn't check on you any further. So your unvarnished .NET Passport offers zero proof of identity.

That said, Microsoft is planning to bolster Passport by adding multifactor authentication. For example, some uses of Passport may require Secure Key. In Secure Key transactions, you will need to enter a secondary PIN for each transaction you perform. The PIN will never be stored on your computer in the way your Passport sign-on information is stored, and the authentication token generated by validation of the PIN will be transmitted over Secure Channel, an SSL channel. (SSL is the abbreviation for Secure Sockets Layer, an interface for encrypted data transfer between a client and a server.) Further out, Microsoft plans for future versions of Passport to support smart cards and software certificates.

Get a .NET Passport and Add It to XP

If you want to use Windows Messenger, Hotmail, or MSN, you'll need to get a .NET Passport and add it to XP so that XP knows about it.

An increasing number of other Web sites now use .NET Passport as well. For example, eBay uses .NET Passport to let users sign on to their accounts quickly, and Prudential Banking's Egg.com online bank is switching from another authentication system to .NET Passport.

At this writing, the process of getting a .NET Passport is trivially simple. In fact, XP almost forces you into it by displaying a Messenger icon in the notification area that bears a "broken" symbol that just begs you to click it. Clicking this icon fires up Messenger, which, in turn, cranks up the .NET Passport Wizard that walks you through the steps of getting a .NET Passport and applying it to XP. (If the notification area isn't displaying the Messenger icon, you can run the .NET Passport Wizard by clicking the Set Up My Account to Use a .NET Passport link on the What Do You Want to Change About Your Account? page of User Accounts in Control Panel: choose Start | Control Panel, click the User Accounts link, and then select your account.)

If you have an e-mail address already, you can use that as the basis for your .NET Passport. If you don't have an e-mail address, the .NET Passport Wizard points you to MSN.com to get a free e-mail account. You may want to take up this offer, but think carefully before you do: you may well do better to get an e-mail account with another provider (such as your ISP or one of the free e-mail services) and use that to get your .NET Passport (at the Passport Web site, www.passport.com) rather than being bound to a Microsoft solution.

By default, the .NET Passport Wizard associates your .NET Passport with your XP user account. If your .NET Passport represents the same identity as the XP user account you're currently using, this may be a good move. If not, be sure to clear the Save My .NET Passport Information in My Windows XP User Account check box on the Type Your .NET Passport Password page of the wizard.

> **TIP** *To change the .NET Passport associated with your XP account, click the Change My .NET Passport link on the What Do You Want to Change About Your Account? page in Control Panel.*

Edit Your .NET Passport's Profile

You can specify what information to share with .NET Passport–enabled Web sites by following the Edit My .NET Passport Profile link on the Passport Web site. At this writing, you can choose to share your e-mail address, your first and last names, and your other registration information (date of birth, gender, country or region, language, time zone, and occupation).

Although there may be good reasons for sharing more information about yourself than is required for any given transaction, I can't think of any. I suggest you share as little information as possible.

Should You Use Passport Wallet?

When you bite the bullet and get a .NET Passport, you have an important choice to make— should you use Passport Wallet or avoid it like the plague?

Briefly, Passport Wallet lets you store credit card and debit card information together with your billing address and shipping address. You can store the information for multiple credit cards or debit cards and choose which one to use for any given transaction. Once you identify yourself via your .NET Passport and enter the password for your Passport Wallet, your card number, billing address, and so on, all snap into place.

Passport Wallet's appeal is essentially that of features such as One-Click Ordering at Amazon.com—once you've entered your financial information into Passport Wallet and had it authenticated, you'll be able to apply that information easily or automatically for transactions. But Passport Wallet is on a far grander scale than One-Click Ordering—Passport Wallet is intended to work seamlessly across all sites that use the .NET Passport service and have implemented the Passport Express Purchase feature. Once your Passport Wallet is operational, you can make purchases at any of these sites easily and (in theory) securely.

The most obvious consideration here is that Passport Wallet requires your real name, address, and credit card information. No authenticated credit card, no Passport Wallet. So if you're the type of person who has multiple .NET Passports for different roles or identities, you'll need to choose which of them is your permanent and verifiable .NET Passport (or create a new .NET Passport under your real name). Alternatively, you can set up multiple Passport Wallets with your real name, address, and credit card information if you'll somehow benefit from doing so.

Provided you're comfortable with a .NET Passport in your real name, and you're prepared to accept Microsoft's assurances about Passport Wallet's security (see the next section), Passport Wallet can offer real convenience. But it has drawbacks as well. The first problem is the amount of data that .NET Passport and Passport Wallet between them give to Microsoft and its .NET Passport partners about your surfing and shopping habits. The second problem is the security of the Passport Wallet service and, by extension, the data in it. The next section discusses this topic.

> **NOTE**   *One quick note here: When you make a payment by using Passport Wallet, the .NET Passport service doesn't receive information about what you purchased, how much you paid, or whether the transaction succeeded or failed. Similarly, the online merchant to whom you've made the payment doesn't have access through the .NET Passport service to information about transactions you've made with other companies using Passport Wallet. Of course, the merchant knows the details of this transaction, and the .NET Passport service knows that you've used that Passport Wallet to make a purchase at the site in question at that time. But overall, your greatest exposure when using Passport Wallet is with your credit card issuers, who know about every transaction you make using their card. This is the same risk you assumed when you applied for a credit card from them, and it underlines the importance of shopping around for a reputable credit card company rather than succumbing to the wiles of whichever company throws plastic in your general direction with the most generous credit limit.*

How Secure Is Passport Wallet?

If you're considering using Passport Wallet, you'd probably like to be sure that it's secure before you sign up. Otherwise, some of your most sensitive data—your credit card number, expiry date, and billing address—can be compromised.

As you know, identity theft is on the rise, partly because it's relatively easy to do and partly because the law hasn't really gotten to grips with it yet. Credit card fraud has long been significant if not massive (it accounts for a goodly chunk of that APR your credit card company likes to charge you), and one of the most popular targets for malicious hackers on the Internet has been the credit card information that ISPs and merchants have stored in supposedly secure locations. If you've even skimmed the headlines over the last few years, you'll probably recall that there have been many successful break-ins, in some of which the hacker has netted hundreds of thousands of credit card numbers. And those have been just the break-ins that have been publicized for one reason or another. As when dealing with employee fraud, companies have a strong incentive to keep quiet about attempted break-ins that appear not to have caused a major problem.

Microsoft claims that Passport Wallet stores your address and credit card information "in a secure, online location," adding that "Only you have access to the information in your .NET Passport wallet." You'd have to take this with a pinch of salt because Passport Wallet has had a number of security problems already.

Passport Wallet's worst known security problem as of this writing occurred in November 2001, when Marc Slemko, a software developer and a founding member of the Apache Software Foundation, wrote a demonstration script that exploited browser bugs and flaws in Passport's authentication system to steal a Passport Wallet and the victim's credit card number. All the victim had to do was open a message sent to their Hotmail account—an action most Hotmail users perform daily.

Microsoft disabled Passport Wallet temporarily while it patched the bugs and tweaked a software timer so that Passport Wallet users had to enter their password every time they accessed Passport Wallet. Microsoft then declared that everything was fine again.

Slemko's exploit demonstrated real flaws in .NET Passport and Passport Wallet. Before that, .NET Passport itself (earlier called *Microsoft Passport*) had suffered plenty of theoretical criticism. In particular, in 2000, two AT&T researchers slated Passport, saying it had to be "viewed with suspicion" and that it "carries significant risks to users." Microsoft issued a response suggesting that the researchers had parked their heads where the sun didn't shine by working with white papers and the Passport client rather than with the Passport Wallet Software Development Kit. Some of Microsoft's responses to the AT&T researchers' concerns and objections are convincing. Others are less so. A couple are worth examining here, together with some peripheral information that you may find interesting if you're considering using .NET Passport yourself and putting any sensitive data into it.

Like many Internet programs, .NET Passport uses cookies. .NET Passport uses session cookies to store information on your computer during the time that you're signed into .NET Passport. Windows deletes these session cookies when you log out of .NET Passport. .NET Passport uses permanent cookies to store your Passport name and (if you choose to store it) your password on your local computer. Saving the password enables Messenger and Internet Explorer to log you onto .NET Passport automatically, but it can compromise your security. Microsoft recommends that you don't use the Sign Me In Automatically option on a public terminal, and you'd be very ill advised to do so. If you share your XP username with other people (which you shouldn't— they should have their own usernames), be sure not to use the Sign Me In Automatically option.

A malicious hacker could, in theory, attack the .NET Passport servers, but they probably represent one of the toughest points of the .NET Passport system. Microsoft has stated that the servers are located in "a secure data center with restricted access and constant supervision." The servers aren't connected directly to the Internet, being cordoned off with heavy-duty hardware and software firewalls and filters. The information in the servers is stored in access-controlled databases. The security is audited by both Microsoft security experts and external security experts. Etc., etc. But when you know that in 1999 intruders managed to hack Microsoft's internal systems and spend a month rummaging through the Windows source code before being detected, Microsoft's security claims for .NET Passport ring more than a little hollow.

To protect passwords, .NET Passport doesn't share user passwords with .NET Passport–enabled sites. When a site uses .NET Passport to authenticate a user, the authentication takes place at the .NET Passport servers, which give the user the thumbs-up or thumbs-down.

.NET Passport uses triple-DES encryption with 168-bit keys. 168-bit keys in theory provide heavy-duty security—more than anybody except perhaps the NSA, GCHQ, or perhaps Mossad could crack without undue effort by brute force. (And if any of those organizations is on your case, you've got more to worry about than the security of your Passport Wallet.) But, as you'll see in Chapter 4, many keys are far less secure than the key length (the number of bits in the key) would suggest. Be that as it may, each .NET Passport–enabled site has a separate key and can use key versioning to rotate its keys to decrease the likelihood of their being compromised.

One of the flaws that the AT&T researchers suggested was that an attacker could spoof the user by creating a fake site into which the user would trustingly enter their .NET Passport username and password. Microsoft's response to this was interesting in its obliqueness: "Spoofing the credential UI is an attack to which all authentication systems are vulnerable. When a user is asked to enter his password, he needs to be certain that the party asking is trustworthy. On the Web, that party is represented by the DNS address of the servers and the visual appearance of the pages." In other words, the system is secure as long as the user is careful enough not to use it on a site that's only pretending to be a bona fide .NET Passport site.

That could be a little painful. Microsoft's next assurance, that "The visual appearance of Passport's credential UI includes a protected icon that makes reproduction a violation of a federal law," isn't much of a balm. Stealing credit card information is a violation of a federal law as well. Everyone knows that. But lots of people find it worth their while.

This concern with spoofing was for versions of Windows before XP. In these versions, the Passport credential UI is served as part of a Web page, making it (in theory) relatively easy to spoof. In XP, things are a bit better because Microsoft moved the .NET Passport sign-on system out of the browser and into the operating system: XP has a secure Credential Manager to manage the process, and .NET Passport users enter their usernames and passwords directly into the Credential Manager user interface client rather than into a Web page. The Credential Manager UI *could* be spoofed, but it'd be much more difficult than spoofing a Web page.

Another possible attack is a man-in-the-middle attack, in which the attacker would alias the .NET Passport Web site (www.passport.com) to the address of a server they controlled, thus putting themselves in a position to grab information as it passed in either direction. Microsoft admits that .NET Passport, like other Web-based authentication systems, is theoretically vulnerable to this type of attack. The protection against it is that "All large ISPs are well aware of this issue and take the appropriate measures to ensure the integrity and security of their DNS servers." In other words, it's not Microsoft's problem. Again, you could be forgiven for interpreting this response as buck-passing and deeming it less than reassuring.

Passport Wallet: What Is It Good For?

I've been quite negative about Passport Wallet, haven't I? You can probably tell that I don't feel enthusiastic enough about it to entrust it with my own financial data, so I can hardly recommend that you do so.

Time and determined hackers (or crackers) will show whether Passport Wallet is secure enough to trust. If it is, it probably has a bright future with some consumers. If you do a lot of shopping on the Web, Passport Wallet can save you some time entering your address and payment information at sites on which you don't have an account. Perhaps more valuable, it can save you from making mistakes in your address and payment information and thus messing up a vital order. Passport Wallet might also be extended so that, for example, your employer could authorize your work-related Passport Wallet to make certain types of business-to-business (B2B) transactions up to a certain limit on behalf of the company using company funds or purchase orders.

NOTE   *One thing to be clear about is that using Passport Wallet doesn't mean sharing your Wallet information the moment you sign into a Passport–enabled Web site. During a Passport Express purchase, you get to specify which pieces of information to send to the merchant.*

As it stands, though, many people feel they don't need the type of service that Passport Wallet offers. These people have probably established accounts at the online stores they use frequently, so they can order quickly without needing Passport Wallet. For example, once you've set up One-Click Ordering on Amazon.com, buying anything they sell is easier and faster than falling off a tightrope. And for anyone who can type reasonably fluently and who has memorized their credit card number, filling out billing and payment information at a new site isn't exactly onerous. It takes a couple of minutes, but you should need to do it only once.

Besides site-based accounts such as Amazon.com's, there are more widely usable payment schemes as well. For example, one payment solution that's finding considerable favor at this writing is PayPal (www.paypal.com), which lets you store money in an online account from which you can transfer money to other PayPal users. PayPal is mostly a solution for consumer-to-consumer (C2C) transactions; the canonical example of a PayPal transaction is eBay, because PayPal lets two parties who have minimal trust in each other transfer money quickly and safely without needing the recipient to have facilities for accepting credit cards. But some e-commerce sites are also using PayPal for B2C (or, more accurately, C2B) transactions, and this number may well grow.

What Happens When You Use .NET Passport

Let's consider briefly what happens when you associate your .NET Passport with your XP user account and use it the way that Microsoft intends you to.

If you don't change Messenger's defaults, it attempts to connect to Messenger Service as soon as you log onto Windows. If you have a persistent Internet connection, or if you've configured your dial-up Internet connection to connect automatically to the Internet whenever any program requests a connection, Messenger initiates the connection (if necessary) and then holds it open until you quit Messenger and the connection times out or until you close the connection manually. That means you're signed into Messenger Service—and into .NET Passport—until you deliberately sign out of Messenger Service or log off Windows.

CAUTION *If you switch users rather than log off Windows, Messenger remains connected to Messenger Service by default.*

For obvious reasons, being signed into Messenger for the duration of each computing session is less than desirable if you don't have a persistent Internet connection—for example, if you have a dial-up connection with a limited number of hours per month. But even if you have a persistent Internet connection, you may not want to use Messenger the whole time. In particular, you may be spooked by the idea that Messenger Service is tracking you the whole time, and that any action you take at a .NET Passport–enabled site is telling Microsoft's tracking mechanisms exactly where you are. If you've chosen to allow .NET Passport to share your details with sites that request them, you're leaving a trail from site to site like a tank charging across cornfields.

The problem isn't so much that the .NET Passport–enabled sites can see where you're going, because each site sees only what concerns it and any sites that it's directly affiliated with. The problem is that the .NET Passport Service learns all your movements as each .NET Passport–enabled site, in turn, authenticates you. If you use Passport Wallet as well, the amount of information you leave behind is that much greater.

The upside of being signed in is, of course, that you can use Messenger Service at any point and that you can receive instant messages, calls, files, and more from any of your contacts who are online. The upside of using .NET Passport to access enabled sites is that you can prove your identity seamlessly without needing to enter a username and password manually. The upside of using Passport Wallet is that you can make purchases at sites that support Passport Wallet without having to enter your payment information manually.

When you sign out of .NET Passport, Windows deletes all .NET Passport–related session cookies from your computer. (Permanent cookies remain on your computer to track your sign-in preferences in Messenger.) This deletion is reassuring in that it means malicious programs can't attempt to access the session cookies after you've signed out. But most people feel that because Messenger Service has already gotten and stored the relevant information, this is a case of razing the stable after the horse has departed.

Use Digital Certificates to Prove Your Identity and Protect Yourself

As you saw earlier in this chapter, one of the currently popular ways of proving your identity online is to use a digital certificate—a collection of identity information that's encrypted and signed with the digital signature of the certification authority that issued it. You can use a digital certificate for various purposes, such as adding a digital signature to e-mail messages, encrypting messages and attachments so that only the specified recipient can read them, and making sure that signed messages you receive haven't been tampered with.

As you also saw earlier in the chapter, the digital certificate has some of the same problems as other nonbiometric proofs of identity. Although a digital certificate is (theoretically, at least) more or less impossible to forge, it can be borrowed, stolen, or shared easily. Microsoft describes the benefit of digital certificates as follows: "you can use digital certificates to verify that another person has a right to use a given identity." Note the phrasing: You don't know that the other person *is* who the certificate says they are, but that they have the right to *use* that identity—that is, if they haven't stolen the digital certificate.

A digital certificate typically contains at least the holder's name and e-mail address, and it may often contain much more information, such as age, address, and citizenship. The digital certificate includes details of the type of encryption used and of the holder's cryptographic keys.

NOTE *One problem with digital certificates at this writing is that they bundle a number of separable items of information that you may not want to share with other people. For example, a digital certificate might contain your full name, e-mail address, physical address, age, and other details. You can't use the digital certificate to prove your identity without divulging the other information at the same time. There's a strong argument for developing digital certificates that contain lesser amounts of information, or digital certificates from which you can choose to expose only a specific subset of information for any given transaction. For example, if you choose to gamble online, you might need to prove that you are over 18 or over 21. With a more flexible digital certificate, you could prove this without giving out your name, e-mail address, and so on.*

In case you're not familiar with the basics of public key cryptography, let's take a minute to run through them. Each key holder—for example, *you*—has a key pair that consists of a public key and a private key that are used to encrypt and decrypt data securely. You share your public key with the whole wired world, either directly (by sending the key to the recipient) or indirectly, via a public key infrastructure (PKI) that lets people look up your public key (or that of any other person or organization). The public key is used to encrypt messages and documents coming to you and to authenticate and decrypt messages coming from you—anything encrypted with your public key can only be decrypted using your private key, which you keep to yourself and use to encrypt outgoing messages and documents. Those messages and documents can be decrypted only by using your public key.

Described this simply, public key cryptography is improbable enough to require a Bambleweeny 57 Sub-Meson Brain and a really hot cup of tea—but if you plunge into the details (which we won't do here), you'll find that it stands up to scrutiny. For mathematical reasons, neither key can be inferred from the other key, so it's safe to publish your public key worldwide—nobody will be able to derive your private key from it. Assuming you keep your private key safe, anyone sending you a message encrypted with your public key can be sure that you're the only person who will be able to decrypt it. But because *anyone* can get your public key, they need to encrypt the message with their private key in order to prove to you that it comes from them. You then decrypt the message using their public key (followed by your private key), and you've authenticated each other and communicated securely. Again, this description is a simplification, but a forgivable one.

The essence of digital certificates is that both parties involved in a transaction secured by digital certificates have to trust the issuer of the digital certificates to have authenticated the other party closely enough for the needs of the transaction. As discussed earlier in the chapter, the degree of authentication varies depending on the transaction being carried out—in order to read an e-mail from a friend, you might want a digital certificate that gives only a modest degree of certainty that it is your friend; whereas if you are selling them depleted uranium, you'd probably want a high degree of certainty (or perhaps a shipload of unmarked bills).

Digital certificates can, of course, be used within closed systems—for example, within a sealed corporate, military, or government system—but they're more widely used for authentication on the Internet. For digital certificates to work, a PKI needs to be in place for accessing public keys. Certification authorities need to supply digital certificates to individuals and organizations that they've satisfactorily authenticated. Those individuals and organizations can then trust each other because both trust the certification authorities—either the certification authority that has issued their own certificate or a different certification authority that their certification authority trusts.

In XP, Internet Explorer acts as the primary interface for digital certificates. As you'll see in a moment, you use Internet Explorer's Certificates dialog box to install and manage digital certificates. Internet Explorer stores the digital certificates in the Registry, from where other programs can use them as well. For example, Outlook Express uses digital certificates both to sign outgoing messages (verifying that they're coming from you—or rather from someone with your digital certificate) and to encrypt and decrypt e-mail messages (preventing your outgoing messages from being read by someone who doesn't have the required private key and your incoming signed messages from being read by anyone who doesn't have your private key).

Address Book includes a Digital IDs page in the Properties dialog box for a contact that you can use to associate a digital certificate with an e-mail address for a contact. (In one of Microsoft's endearing efforts to simplify matters that turn out to make them more complicated, Address Book and Outlook Express refer to digital certificates as *digital IDs*.)

Get a Digital Certificate

The process of getting a digital certificate varies depending on the type of certificate you decide you want and the company you get it from, so this section discusses the general steps involved rather than crunching through all the details. It includes screenshots of a couple of the steps in the process.

Where to Get a Digital Certificate

There are three ways to get a digital certificate:

- *From a commercial certification authority*. These include VeriSign, Inc. (www.verisign.com), GlobalSign NV (www.globalsign.net), Thawte Certification (www.thawte.com), or BT Ignite (www.ignite.com). For the latest list of certification authorities that Microsoft favors, click the Get Digital ID button on the Security page of the Options dialog box (Tools | Options) in Outlook Express. Outlook Express opens a browser window to the Microsoft Office Assistance Center's list of certification authorities.

NOTE
A certification authority is sometimes also called a certificate authority. *Both terms abbreviate to CA.*

- *From the company you work for.* If your company runs its own digital certificate server, it can issue digital certificates to its employees.

- *By using a program that allows you to create a digital certificate yourself.* For example, some versions of Microsoft Office ship with a program named SELFCERT.EXE, which you can use to create a digital certificate bearing any name you choose. Such a certificate is next to useless for authenticating identity—if *you* can create a certificate without any verification, so can anyone else—but it can be useful for practicing importing, exporting, and deleting digital certificates.

Types of Digital Certificates

As you'd imagine, various kinds of digital certificates are available, including corporate certificates, software developer certificates, and personal certificates. In this section, I'll assume you're interested in personal certificates that you can use over open networks for purposes such as signing and encrypting e-mail, rather than, say, private digital certificates that work only for a company's internal applications and are used for restricting users' access on a network.

Get a Personal Certificate

The steps for getting a personal certificate usually go roughly as follows, though not necessarily exactly in this order:

- Complete an online enrollment form. The complexity of the form and the information you need to complete it depend on the type of certificate you're trying to get.

- Confirm your e-mail address. As a preliminary check of the lines of communication, in response to the form you've submitted, the certification authority sends you an e-mail message containing a URL specific to your application for a certificate. By following this link, you confirm that your e-mail address is valid.

- Verify your identity, either via a big-name agency (TRW, Equifax, or Experian for a personal certificate, and Dun & Bradstreet Financial Services or something similar for a business) or by submitting verifiable information such as the details of your passport, driver's license, or identity card (if your country uses them).

- Pay for the digital certificate (in most cases), preferably via a nice verifiable credit card in your own name.

- You may need to submit paper documents containing your signature and photocopies of your means of identification (for example, a copy of the details page of your passport).

■ For some certificates, you may have to visit a representative of the certification authority in person, bearing your proof of identity. This check of your physical identity provides the strongest authentication that most certification authorities use.

■ Once the certification authority has authenticated your identity to the degree required for the type of digital certificate, you get an e-mail to the address you supplied, containing a personal identification number (PIN) for picking up your certificate from the provider. Using the same computer from which you submitted your enrollment form, paste in the PIN (or type it with great care), and the certification authority generates the certificate. Some certification authorities install the certificate on your computer automatically, whereas with others, you download the certificate to a file and then install it manually. (I'll discuss the procedure for installing a certificate manually in a minute or two.)

■ You may need to create a new RSA Exchange key. See the next section for an illustration of the process.

CAUTION *The certification process may offer to protect your private key. You probably don't want to accept this offer because it will prevent you from exporting your private key to archive it or to install it on another computer. In other words, you'll be able to use the digital certificate only on the computer on which you initially install it.*

If you didn't encrypt your private key, you should export a copy of the certificate to a floppy disk or other handy removable medium immediately and store it in a safe location off your premises. If you don't have a secure deposit box at your bank, now might be the time to get one. You might also choose to further encrypt the file containing the digital certificate and store it in a secure online locker that you will be able to access easily even if your computers are destroyed or stolen.

There's one interesting exception to the confirmation-of-identity step. Instead of relying on a top-down authentication approach run from one or more central offices, Thawte Certification uses a bottom-up authentication approach in its Web of Trust. Thawte describes the Web of Trust as a "community-driven certification system based on face-to-face ID validation on a peer-to-peer basis." In the Web of Trust, each member can become a notary who can help certify other people. To become a member, you accumulate 50 points by meeting in person with existing members, who assert to Thawte that they've met you and checked your ID. Different members are worth different numbers of points, depending on the number of trust assertions they've made so far, so you'll typically need to meet anywhere from two to five people to accumulate enough points to certify you as being authentic. (If there aren't any Web of Trust notaries in your area, Thawte has a Trusted Third Party program that involves getting signed proof of identification from fine upstanding business folk such as bank managers and lawyers.)

Once you've become a member of the Web of Trust, you can gain further points by meeting further notaries. When you accumulate 100 points, you become a notary yourself, which means you can start authenticating new members.

Create a New RSA Exchange Key

As mentioned a few moments ago, the procedures for creating a digital certificate vary depending on the certification authority you're using, so I can't really presume to show you what you might see. But if the digital certificate–creation process involves creating a new RSA exchange key, as well it might, you're likely to see the Creating a New RSA Exchange Key Wizard spring into action. First, you'll see the Creating a New RSA Exchange Key dialog box shown in Figure 3-1.

Here, you can change the security level by clicking the Set Security Level button and using the second Creating a New RSA Exchange Key dialog box, shown in Figure 3-2, to specify the level of security.

A High security level means you have to enter a password before Internet Explorer can supply the certificate when a site requests it. A Medium security level means that Internet Explorer asks your permission before supplying the certificate, but you don't need to enter the password. A Low security level (not an option in the dialog box shown in Figure 3-2) means that Internet Explorer supplies the certificate without consulting you when a site requests it.

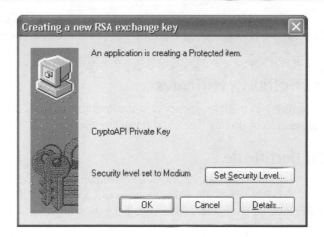

FIGURE 3-1   The First Creating a New RSA Exchange Key dialog box

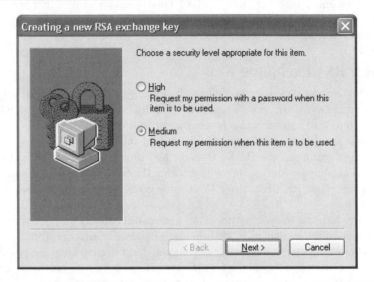

FIGURE 3-2 In the second Creating A New RSA Exchange Key dialog box, specify the level of security you want.

If you choose the High security level, when you click the Next button, you see another screen of the Creating A New RSA Exchange Wizard, prompting you for the password. Enter it and click the Finish button.

Manage Your Digital Certificates

This section runs you quickly through the maneuvers you're likely to perform with digital certificates: installing them, scrutinizing them, and removing them.

Install a Digital Certificate

As mentioned earlier, some certification authorities automatically install the certificate on your computer when you download the certificate. Other times, you'll need to install the digital certificate on your computer (or on another computer) manually. Take the following steps:

1. In Internet Explorer, choose Tools | Options to display the Internet Options dialog box.

2. On the Content page, click the Certificates button to display the Certificates dialog box, shown here.

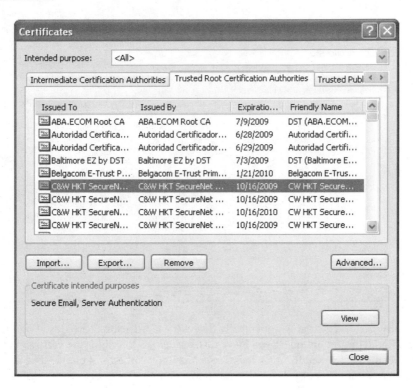

3. Click the Import button to start the Certificate Import Wizard; then click the Next button to get to the File to Import page of the wizard.

TIP   *If you have the certificate on your Desktop or in an open Explorer window, you can start the installation process by double-clicking the certificate and then clicking the Install Certificate button on the General page of the resulting Certificate dialog box.*

4. Enter the filename of the certificate in the File Name text box, either by using the Browse button or by typing the path and filename manually. Note that the Files of Type drop-down list in the Open dialog box accessed from the Browse button defaults to X.509 Certificate (*.CER, *.CRT), and that you'll have to change the setting if you want to import a type of certificate other than one of those types.

5. Click the Next button to get to the Certificate Store page of the Certificate Import Wizard, shown here.

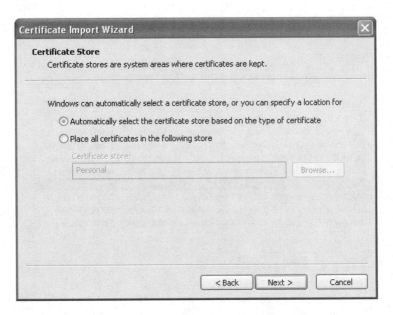

6. Usually, XP selects the Automatically Select the Certificate Store Based on the Type of Certificate option button. If you leave this selected, XP assigns the certificate to the store that seems best suited for it. In most cases, XP makes the right choice; but in some cases, you may want to specify the certificate store manually. To do so, take the following steps:

■ Select the Place All Certificates in the Following Store option button. XP enables the Certificate Store text box, with its default value of Personal, and the Browse button.

■ Click the Browse button to display the Select Certificate Store dialog box, (shown here in its two manifestations—with and without the physical stores displayed.

■ To specify the store by category, select the store in the list box.

■ To specify the physical store, select the Show Physical Stores check box. XP displays the physical stores (as in the preceding version of the dialog box on the right). Expand the appropriate branch of the tree and select the subfolder. For most of the branches, your choice is Registry, Group Policy, or Local Computer.

■ Click the OK button to close the Select Certificate Store dialog box and return to the Certificate Store page of the wizard.

7. Click the Next button to move on to the Completing the Certificate Import Wizard page of the wizard, shown here, which summarizes the choices you've made.

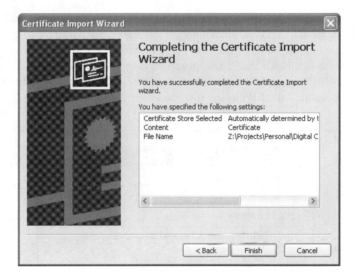

8. Double-check the information. If it's right, click the Finish button. The Certificate Import Wizard completes the import procedure and, if it's successful, displays a message box saying so.

TIP *If Internet Explorer is unable to import the certificate, the cause may be that you're running a version of Internet Explorer with less that 128-bit encryption and the certificate has a key length of 1,024 bits or more. To solve the problem, upgrade to the 128-bit version of Internet Explorer.*

Scrutinize a Digital Certificate

One of the steps you're likely to take with many certificates is to examine them to see whether they're current and what they're supposed to be for.

For a brief list of a certificate's intended purposes, select the certificate in the list box in the Certificates dialog box and look at the purposes listed in the Certificate Intended Purposes group box. For more detail, double-click the certificate in the list box, or select it and then click the View button. XP displays the Certificate dialog box, which contains details of the certificate on its three pages: General, Details, and Certification Path.

General Page Information   The General page, shown in Figure 3-3, contains information about the issuer of the certificate, the person or entity to which the certificate was issued, and the period for which the certificate is valid. If all is well with the certificate, the General page also lists the purposes for which the certificate is intended—for example, "protects e-mail messages," "ensures the identity of a remote computer," or "protects software from alteration after publication." If there may be a problem with the certificate, the General page gives a message such as "Windows does not have enough information to verify this certificate." If the Issuer Statement button on the General page is available, you should be able to display information about the issuer of the digital certificate by clicking it.

Details Page Information   The Details page, shown in Figure 3-4, contains details about the certificate: everything from its version, serial number, and algorithm to its public key and thumbprint. You can reduce the amount of information shown by making a selection— <All>, Version 1 Fields Only, Extensions Only, Critical Extensions Only, or Properties Only—from the Show drop-down list. To view the details of a field that won't fit in the Value column of the upper list box, select the field to make XP display it in the lower list box.

FIGURE 3-3   The Certificate dialog box lets you examine a certificate to see whether it's current and what it's for.

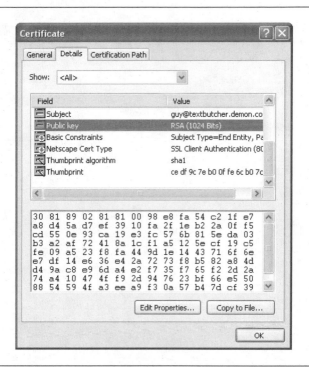

FIGURE 3-4   The Details page lets you examine the details of the certificate, including its thumbprint, thumbprint algorithm, and public key.

Certification Path Information   The Certification Path page, shown in Figure 3-5, displays the hierarchy of certificates—from the certification authority ultimately responsible for this certificate to the holder of the certificate. You can view the certificate for one of the bodies higher in the hierarchy by selecting it and clicking the View Certificate button.

The Certificate Status box on the Certification Path page displays the current status of the certificate—for example, "This certificate is OK" or "This certificate has expired or is not yet valid."

Remove a Digital Certificate

In the natural course of events, many people who use digital certificates actively tend to install more certificates than they remove. But just as you might lose trust in a family member, an acquaintance, or a company, you may want to stop trusting a digital certificate that you used to trust. And like family members, acquaintances, and many companies, most digital certificates eventually expire. So it's a good idea to go through your certificates every now and then and weed out those that have expired or are no longer trustworthy.

If a certificate has expired or become untrustworthy, you'll usually want to remove it, as described in this section. If a certificate has become less trustworthy than it used to be, instead of removing it, you may want to change the purposes for which you use it. The next section describes how to do that.

FIGURE 3-5 The Certification Path page lets you examine the certification path from the certification authority to the holder of the certificate.

CAUTION *Before you remove a digital certificate, be aware of the consequences of doing so. If you remove one of your personal certificates, you'll no longer be able to decrypt data that you encrypted using that certificate. For example, you won't be able to read any e-mail messages to others that you encrypted using that digital certificate, nor will you be able to read any e-mail messages that others encrypted for you to read securely using that certificate. If you've used the digital certificate to authenticate yourself for Web sites, you won't be able to access those sites without authenticating yourself again (presumably using a different certificate). And if you remove the digital certificate for a certification authority, XP won't trust any digital certificates issued by lower-level certification authorities or by companies that, in turn, are authorized by that certification authority.*

To remove a digital certificate, display the Certificates dialog box as described in steps 1 and 2 of the section "Install a Digital Certificate," earlier. Navigate to the appropriate page, select the certificate, and click the Remove button. XP displays a Certificates dialog box to warn you of the consequences of removing the certificate and to confirm that you want to proceed. Click the Yes button if you're sure you want to remove the certificate.

Change a Digital Certificate's Friendly Name, Description, and Purposes

If you use digital certificates a lot (as is increasingly a good idea), you'll probably accumulate a goodly number of digital certificates before too long. When you do, the plethora of digital certificates can become confusing.

To clarify things, XP lets you edit the friendly name (the descriptive name) and the description for a certificate. To do so, click the Edit Properties button on the Details page of the certificate's Certificate dialog box to display the Certificate Properties dialog box. On the General page, shown in Figure 3-6, you can change the text in the Friendly Name text box and add a description in the Description text box.

On this page, you can also specify the purposes for which you want to use the certificate by using the Enable All Purposes for This Certificate option button, the Disable All Purposes for This Certificate option button, or the Enable Only the Following Purposes option button. For the third option, use the check boxes to specify which purposes to use. As you might imagine, you're usually limited to those purposes for which the certificate has been issued—you can't add purposes that the certificate doesn't cover, unless the certificate is extensible, in which case the Add Purpose button will be available.

FIGURE 3-6   The General page of the Certificate Properties dialog box for a digital certificate lets you edit the friendly (descriptive) name and description for the certificate and specify the purposes for which you want to use the certificate.

Export a Digital Certificate

To export a digital certificate, select it in the Certificates dialog box and click the Export button. XP launches the Certificate Export Wizard, which walks you through the process of exporting the certificate. The key steps are as follows:

1. The Export Private Key page, shown here, may or may not offer you the choice of exporting the private key with the certificate. If the private key associated with the certificate is not marked as exportable, XP won't let you export it. If you choose to export the private key, you have to enter a password to protect the private key. (You enter the private key later in the wizard, not immediately.) Make sure the password is strong if you need to protect it against being cracked. (If you feel you're entering the password only because you must, be sure your appraisal of your security risks is accurate.)

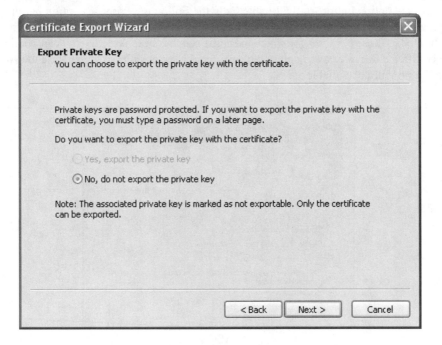

2. The Export File Format page of the Certificate Export Wizard, shown next, lets you specify the format in which to export the digital certificate. Internet Explorer typically offers these four formats for exporting digital certificates:

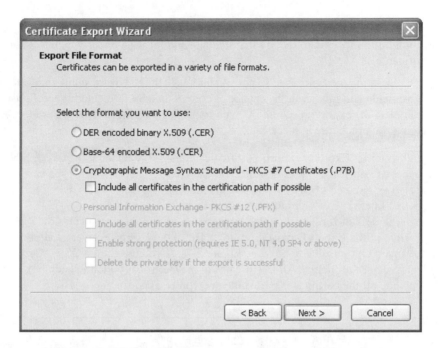

- **DER Encoded Binary X.509**   A binary format best used for exporting a single certificate (rather than all the certificates in a certification path). The file uses a CER extension.

- **Base64 Encoded X.509**   A textual representation of a DER-encoded certificate. Use this format when you need to send a certificate to a computer running an OS other than Windows (for example, Linux). Like the DER Encoded Binary X.509 file, this file uses a CER extension.

- **PKCS #7**   A file that contain all the certificates in the certification path. The file meets the Cryptographic Message Syntax Standard PKCS #7 created by RSA Security, Inc. The file uses a P7B extension.

- **PKCS #12**   A file that contains all the certificates in the certificate path. The file meets the PKCS #12 standard, again created by RSA Security, Inc. With PKCS #12, you can use strong protection, and you can choose to delete the private key after successfully exporting the certificate. Microsoft uses the extension PFX for PKCS #12 data, whereas Netscape uses the extension P12.

3. The File to Export page (which isn't worth showing here) provides a text box and a Browse button for you to specify the filename and location under which to save the certificate file.

4. The Completing the Certificate Export Wizard page of the wizard summarizes the choices you've made and gives you the chance to correct them before clicking the Finish button to complete the export procedure. As with importing a certificate, the wizard lets you know whether the procedure is successful.

By default, Internet Explorer exports certificates in the DER Encoded Binary X.509 format. When you use the Certificate Export Wizard, you can change the certificate type easily enough. But you can also export a certificate by dragging its file from the Certificates dialog box to a folder. When you do so, Internet Explorer automatically uses the default format.

To change the default format, click the Advanced button in the Certificates dialog box and choose the format in the Export Format drop-down list in the Export Format group box in the resulting Advanced Options dialog box (see Figure 3-7). If you use the PKCS #7 Certificates format, select or clear the Include All Certificates in the Certification Path check box to specify whether to include all the certificates or just the one you're exporting.

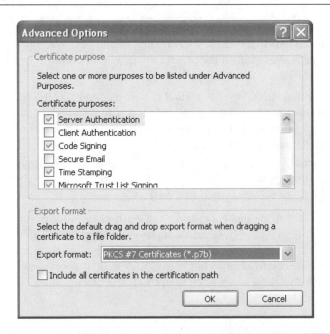

FIGURE 3-7   Choose a default format for certificates you export in the Export Format drop-down list in the Export Format group box in the Advanced Options dialog box.

Summary

This has been a long chapter, and we've covered a lot of ground in it. We started by discussing the different mechanisms for establishing our identity in the physical world and the problems in translating these mechanisms to the wired world to prove our identity there. We then considered how privacy and anonymity differ from each other, what they mean, and how privacy has been substantially eroded during the last ten years—both in the physical world and online.

After that, we moved on to understanding what Microsoft's .NET initiative is; what it's for, good for, and bad for; and how it threatens your privacy in a new and cunningly implemented way. I then gave you a couple of reasons why you should probably use .NET Passport anyway, and I showed you how to get a .NET Passport and associate it with your user account in XP.

By the time we reached the final third of the chapter, I feared you were wilting, but you pulled yourself together gallantly and learned what digital certificates are, how to get one, and how to install and manage certificates on XP.

In the next chapter, I'll discuss how to create, manage, and use free e-mail accounts and Outlook Express.

Chapter 4

Create, Manage, and Use Free E-mail Accounts and Outlook Express

E-mail is the life-blood of the Internet, and almost every Internet user needs one or more e-mail accounts. Your ISP probably provides you with some e-mail accounts as part of your Internet service; but sooner or later, you may well need further accounts—particularly ones that aren't directly linked to your real-world identity.

This chapter discusses how to create, manage, and use e-mail accounts on XP. As you'll soon see (if you don't know already), various Web sites provide free e-mail accounts. This chapter concentrates on Hotmail, Microsoft's industry-leading Web-based e-mail site, but it also mentions some of the other prominent Web-based e-mail providers that you may want to consider instead.

The whole point of Web-based e-mail is, of course, that you can access it via the Web using just a Web browser—whichever one you happen to have convenient to the computer you're using. But for greater power and flexibility with Hotmail, you'll probably want to use the Outlook Express e-mail client that comes built into XP. This chapter shows you how to configure Outlook Express for security, efficiency, and ease of use and how to use it to send and receive e-mail with HTTP, POP3 (Post Office Protocol), and IMAP (Internet Message Access Protocol) accounts. (Outlook Express also includes a powerful newsreader, but I don't discuss that in this book.)

> NOTE
>
> *In talking about POP3 and IMAP accounts, I go a bit off the assumption that you're using just Hotmail—but given that you may well want to use Outlook Express with a POP3 or IMAP account as well as with Hotmail, I doubt you'll object to getting the extra information.*

A Brief History of Hotmail

If you've been computing for a while, you'll probably remember that Hotmail, Microsoft's Web-based e-mail service, hasn't always belonged to Microsoft: Hotmail started off as an independent entity offering free e-mail accounts—an entity fueled in theory by advertising revenues from the banner ads inflicted on all the eyeballs drawn in by the free e-mail accounts.

Hotmail quickly became popular because it was free and easy. You didn't need to prove your identity in any way for a Hotmail account—when you signed up for an account, you had to provide some supposedly personal information; but because Hotmail checked none of this, many people felt no compulsion to be honest, particularly if they were using Hotmail for messages that they were embarrassed to have associated with e-mail accounts that bore their real names.

When Microsoft bought Hotmail, droves of Hotmail users threatened to quit Hotmail because they didn't like Microsoft or feared that it would exploit Hotmail users. Many probably did quit, but, overall, the service has grown impressively over the years. By and large, Microsoft hasn't exploited Hotmail users—but now it's starting to.

If you see any number quoted for Hotmail users, take it with a couple of good shakes of salt. First, many Hotmail accounts have been forgotten, deactivated, and expired, or have had the hammer dropped on them for misuse. For many users, forgetting the password to a Hotmail account counted as no great misfortune: If they weren't able to recover the password through Hotmail's secret-question mechanism, they would abandon the account and create another. They'd need to let their contacts know their new e-mail address, of course, but even that had an upside—they could omit any contacts who were no longer worthwhile from the e-mail giving the new address. There's a strong suspicion that these deleted accounts still show up to swell the user numbers. Second—and arguably even more of a distortion—many Hotmail users have multiple accounts: some for good reasons, and some for, well, not such good reasons. The good reasons include keeping different categories of e-mail separate—for example, keeping your personal e-mail separate from your business e-mail. The less-good reasons include being able to receive more messages or (more likely) more attachments without exceeding one's space allocation, and maintaining alternate personalities for anything from cyber-romance to stock manipulation to digital piracy.

Many Hotmail users haven't exactly forgotten that Microsoft owns Hotmail, but they don't treat it as a major issue except when something exciting occurs. In 2001, something exciting *did* happen: Microsoft tried to implement new language in the Hotmail user agreement that gave Hotmail (and thus Microsoft) the right to use the contents of any message or attachment sent via Hotmail. So, if you wrote a business plan in a Hotmail message, Microsoft could use it; if you sent the manuscript of your new novel as an attachment, Microsoft could publish it.

It seems likely that the new language was caused by an attack of *lawyeritis*—a lawyer applying legal language to a topic he or she doesn't understand—like the lawyers who proposed that downloading any Web page should constitute an infringement of copyright because downloading a page makes a copy of it. (That unvisited Web sites and pages obviated the point of the Web seems to have escaped them.) But whatever the intent, the ensuing user reaction and press coverage was spectacular enough to persuade Microsoft to drop this language.

Combining as it does a user-friendly interface and very wide accessibility via both e-mail clients and Web browsers, Hotmail has had some major security scares. In particular, in 1999, hackers discovered a bug in a CGI script that let any user access any other user's account without providing a password. And, as mentioned in Chapter 3, in 2001, a white-hat hacker put together a script that exposed flaws in Hotmail that allowed the hacker to steal a Passport Wallet by sending a Hotmail member an e-mail message and having them do nothing more than open it. Both these security holes have been patched, but concerns remain.

In early 2001, Microsoft started to integrate .NET Passport with Hotmail and MSN, its other free e-mail service. Although Microsoft notified Hotmail users about .NET Passport, many users seem to have missed or ignored the e-mail: As you saw in the previous chapter, the statistics suggest that most Hotmail and MSN users don't know that they're using .NET Passport when they sign into Hotmail or MSN.

In late 2001, Microsoft started to up the ante on getting people to take Hotmail seriously and provide real information that could be tied to their .NET Passport information.

Hotmail's account limit had remained a stingy 2MB for quite a while, with individual attachments limited to 1MB, even though competitors such as Yahoo! offered accounts with 10MB or more. The 2MB limit was carefully calculated to be usable but problematic. If you received plain-text messages, you could keep just about any amount of messages in your Inbox and folders without problems. If you received HTML messages, you could keep correspondingly fewer in your Inbox and folders, but enough to be useful. But if you received attachments, all bets were off. For example, if your maiden aunt sent you a handful of JPEGs of her Siamese's latest brood, they might well bump you beyond your account allowance. You'd then get a brisk little message from Hotmail Member Services telling you that your account was stuffed beyond the gills, and further messages sent to you would get bounced back to their senders with the message "Mail delivery failed: returning message to sender" and the error (if they looked into the ugly message) "552: Requested mail action aborted: exceeded storage allocation." If the sender didn't look quite that far, they would see an announcement that "the following address(es) failed" and your address—an error that you might be forgiven for considering deliberately misleading in that it suggested the e-mail address wasn't valid.

Even if your maiden aunt spared you the Siamese, spam (particularly with attachments) could easily balloon your Hotmail account beyond bursting. This limitation changed your Hotmail account from being a universally accessible wonder to being a business liability. Sure, you could access it from anywhere via the Web—but any large attachments might have bounced. Anyone who read only the first part of the bounce message might think that your Hotmail address was no longer valid (or that they'd gotten it wrong).

Then there was the problem of keeping your account active. In the early days, Hotmail allowed you to go for 45 days without accessing your account. Then—presumably, as the number of lightly used accounts grew—they tightened things up. By 2001, you needed to access your account every 30 days. If you didn't, Hotmail deactivated your account and deleted all your messages, folders, and contacts. If you came back within 90 days after deactivation, you could get the account back, but all the messages, folders, and contacts stayed gone. So, if you planned, say, a six-week hike around the foothills of Annapurna, you could kiss your e-mail history goodbye. That was marginally tolerable for casual use, but not for serious use—either for personal e-mail or for business.

Hotmail then began offering paid accounts that allowed 10MB of storage and attachments of up to 1.5MB each for the meager fee of $12.95 per year (plus applicable taxes). Paid accounts also removed the bugbear of having to sign in every 30 days or have your account deactivated (with all its attendant unpleasant consequences).

But for you to pay $12.95—aye, there's the rub. You don't get to pay through an anonymous account—nor even through PayPal. No: To pay for a Hotmail account, you need to supply a real name, real address, real phone number, and real credit card information. The free-and-easy accounts had come home with a vengeance

At this writing, it seems safe to say that most Hotmail users haven't taken up Microsoft's Hotmail offer with a rush of enthusiasm. For those who use Hotmail as their main e-mail account with their true identity, it makes sense to pay, because 10MB and no deactivation makes Hotmail more practical than the free version. But for anyone using Hotmail as a pseudonymous service, putting up with the restrictions tends to make much more sense than paying. In any case, the $12.95 turned into a special offer, with the price then rising to $19.95 for those who had missed the deadline.

Get a Hotmail Account

Signing up for a Hotmail account is so simple that you'd be insulted if I walked you through the process. Point your favorite browser at the Hotmail site, www.hotmail.com, and follow the registration process. As mentioned earlier, you need to supply some information and create a secret question (and answer) that you can use, in combination with your username, country, and ZIP code (if that country is the U.S.), to retrieve your password if you forget it. If the details you supply are less than wholly truthful, memorize them well, because you'll need to supply them if you forget your password and secret question. (Write them down if you must, but be clear that writing down any sensitive information like this compromises its security.)

The process is easy, but a couple of things are worth mentioning here. The first thing is that when you sign up for a Hotmail account, you automatically create a .NET Passport. There's no way around it. (Again, this is one of the reasons that there are so many million .NET Passports.)

> TIP   *When you create a Hotmail account and its associated .NET Passport by using the Hotmail Web site registration form, your .NET Passport doesn't automatically get associated with your XP user account. But if you allow the .NET Passport Wizard to sign you up for a free e-mail account (which, at this writing, is at MSN rather than Hotmail), you'll need to prevent the .NET Passport Wizard from associating the new .NET Passport with your XP user account, since it does so by default.*

Second, a couple of Hotmail's suggestions for creating a secret question are way out of line. Hotmail suggests using the last five digits of your social security number or credit card. *Ouch.* Although these numbers are ones you should always be able to access easily (if you don't have them memorized), and the former at least shouldn't change unless you suffer an identity transplant, it's not a good idea to associate them with a Hotmail account—even (or perhaps especially) if it's an account that you intend to use with your real name and for business purposes.

For one thing, social security numbers are widely used these days—everything from a rental application to your paycheck probably carries your social security number. It may not be easy for someone else to learn your social security number, but it's not exactly a secret. So anyone who knows your Hotmail address (at least all the people to whom you've ever sent an e-mail from Hotmail) and your social security number can get at your password. That's bad.

Much the same goes for your credit card numbers. These days, most people who have computers seem to have multiple credit cards so that they can contribute to the national debt, help the country escape recession, or whatever. So, even if you followed this misguided suggestion, you'd need to remember which credit card you used for Hotmail.

But you don't really want Hotmail to have even part of your credit card number, anyway. Various e-businesses use the last five digits of your credit card number as a quasi-harmless identifier. The message is, this is enough to identify the credit card you used; but because we've given only five of the 16 digits, nobody can guess the rest. But you don't have to be paranoid to see even five-sixteenths of a vital number as quite a threat to your security. At the very least, it provides enough information to easily match you up with another credit card transaction using the same card.

In any case, you need to keep your password and secret question secure. If anyone can derive your secret question from your credit card number or social security number, your security level is miserable. And once someone knows your password, they can use your .NET Passport—and your Passport Wallet, if you have one.

Second, instead of a Hotmail account, you may want to get an MSN account. An MSN account is Microsoft's preference at this writing—if you ask the .NET Passport Wizard to sign you up for a free account, it leads you through creating an MSN account, which includes accepting the Hotmail and .NET Passport user agreements. MSN uses a similar approach as Hotmail, giving you a barely adequate free e-mail account to encourage you to upgrade to the paid service.

This shift from Hotmail (which the .NET Passport Wizard used to use) to MSN is perhaps because Microsoft is trying to encourage the adoption of its MSN Explorer software with its simplified interface. By default, the .NET Passport Wizard sets you up to use MSN Explorer to access your e-mail account. If you want to use Outlook Express instead, clear the Use MSN Explorer to Access My E-mail Account check box on the Create Your MSN.com E-mail Address page of the .NET Passport Wizard. (If you're reading this book of your own volition, chances are you'll prefer the power of Internet Explorer and Outlook Express to the colorful simplicity of MSN Explorer. If you prefer MSN Explorer, you're on your own....)

The shift is also certainly related to MSN's ambitions to take on AOL in the online-service business. You don't have to squint too hard to see MSN Explorer as providing an online experience not entirely dissimilar from AOL's—even if most MSN Explorer users are using another ISP than MSN to access MSN.

Access Hotmail via the Web

At first, Hotmail was accessible only via the Web, and this remains the classic way to access it. The advantage is that you can access your e-mail from any computer connected to the Internet, no matter which operating system it's running. For example, you can log in from an Internet café in McMurdo using BeOS or halfway up Krakatoa using Linux and deal with your e-mail just as easily as if you were slopping a double skim latte dangerously near your keyboard in Berkeley.

The main disadvantage of accessing Hotmail via the Web is that you need to be online the whole time you're working with e-mail. You can get around this to some extent by writing e-mail offline in a text editor or word-processing program and then pasting it into the Hotmail window when you go online. But this remains a less than satisfactory solution because it introduces an extra step of complication into each message you send—you need to get the text out of the file in which you've created it and paste it into the composition window. Be sure that the Rich Text Editor feature is on before pasting in any text that includes formatting, and be aware that moving from the Compose page to another page loses the text you've entered so far, unless you've saved the draft.

The other disadvantage to writing e-mail in Hotmail is that, because of the inflexibility of the Web-based interface, you get only a relatively small composition window.

Configure Hotmail to Suit Your Needs

Hotmail offers a variety of configuration options you should at least be aware of, even if you choose not to use them. Some of the options, such as your personal profile and password, apply whether you access Hotmail via the Web or via Outlook Express. Other options, such as sent-message confirmation and session expiration, apply only if you access Hotmail via the Web.

To choose Hotmail configuration options, click the Options link to display the Options page, and then use the links it contains to access the page for the option you want to set.

Update Your Personal Profile, Password, and Secret Question

Use the Personal Profile link, the Password link, and the Secret Question link to update your personal profile (your name, address, country or region, state [if the country is the U.S.], ZIP code, time zone, gender, birthday, and occupation), password, and secret question and answer, respectively.

Choose Whether to Be Listed in the Hotmail Member Directory

Use the Member Directory link to specify whether to be listed in the Hotmail Member Directory.

The Hotmail Member Directory is implemented quite neatly to encourage people to be listed and prevent them from harvesting e-mail addresses. Anyone listed in the Directory can search it for other members by name and location. The Directory displays the name and general location (state or country) but not the e-mail address of people who match. The searcher can then send messages to these people, again without seeing their e-mail addresses.

Choose Free Newsletters and Special Offers

If you want to receive an exciting amount of e-mail in a short time, use the Free Newsletters link or the Special Offers link to sign up for free newsletters or special offers. The free newsletters can contain useful information. The special offers are spam by any other name, except that you've requested them.

Be warned that both the free newsletters and the special offers can get old fast. When they do, turn them off again by using the Free Newsletters link or the Special Offers link on the Options page again.

Filter and Delete Junk Mail

Spam—junk mail—has long been a problem on Hotmail, with offers of Viagra, suppositories, mail-order brides, and worse showing up in rather too many mailboxes for comfort. (Okay, because you ask—the "worse" there are things like DIY spamming software, which sets *you* up to spam other people with offers of brides, suppositories, and spamming software.) As a result, Microsoft has developed anti-spam tools for Hotmail. These tools are a bit crude at first, but work reasonably well if you persist with them and tweak them.

The next sections detail the several steps for filtering and deleting junk mail. First, you choose a Junk Mail Filter setting. Then you build a Safe List of addresses that Hotmail has mistaken for junk but that are actually okay. Then you need to check your Junk Mail Folder for messages that have been incorrectly identified as junk mail and tell Hotmail that they're not junk mail. If you receive messages from mailing lists, you should probably add them to your Mailing Lists list to make sure they don't get filtered as junk mail either.

Apart from that, you can manually block senders from whom you don't want to receive messages, whether they're sending junk mail or not.

Choose a Junk Mail Filter Setting

To choose a Junk Mail Filter setting, click the Junk Mail Filter link on the Options page to display the Junk Mail Filter page, then choose the option button for the amount of filtering you want to apply: Off, Low, High, or Exclusive. Low filtering is likely to allow a fair amount of junk mail into your Inbox, whereas High filtering is likely to catch most junk mail but also some innocent messages. Exclusive filtering treats every message that isn't from someone in your Address Book or someone on your Safe List as junk mail, and it's best kept in reserve until you find yourself besieged by junk mail.

Create a Safe List

Your Safe List is a list of e-mail addresses that aren't junk mail. Essentially, putting an e-mail address on your Safe List tells the Junk Mail Filter never to put messages from that address in the Junk Mail Folder, regardless of whether the contents of the messages may resemble spam.

To maintain your Safe List, click the Safe List link on the Options page. Hotmail displays the Safe List page (see Figure 4-1). To add an entry to the Safe List, enter an e-mail address (for example, bill@acmewidgets.com) or a domain (for example, acmewidgets.com) in the text box and click the Add button. To remove an entry, select the item in the Safe List box and click the Remove button. When you've finished adjusting the Safe List, click the OK button.

NOTE *Adding a domain to your Safe List causes the Junk Mail Filter to pass all messages from that domain. Be cautious with this option. For example, because many Hotmail users use Hotmail to send spam (in contravention of the user agreement), it'd be a mistake to put hotmail.com on your Safe List. That said, even if you put a domain on your Safe List, you can block specific e-mail addresses from that domain by adding them to your Block Sender List.*

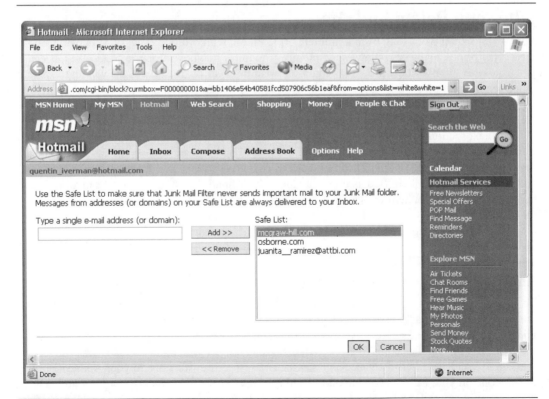

FIGURE 4-1   Hotmail lets you maintain a Safe List of addresses that aren't spammers.

Manage Your Junk Mail Folder

Hotmail automatically deletes all messages in your Junk Mail Folder after seven days, so it's a good idea to check the folder a couple of times a week so you can salvage any messages that Hotmail has consigned to the Junk Mail Folder in error.

Use the Put in Folder drop-down list to move a message from the Junk Mail Folder to another folder. Once you've finished salvaging any worthwhile messages, click the Empty Folder button to remove all the remaining messages from the Junk Mail Folder.

Specify That a Message Isn't Junk Mail

To specify that a message in your Junk Mail Folder isn't junk mail, select its check box and click the This Is Not Junk Mail button.

Make Sure Your Mailing Lists Aren't Treated As Junk

Because most mailing lists send messages using a To address that isn't your (or other recipients') e-mail address, the Junk Mail Filter is likely to decide they're spam and consign them to the Junk Mail Folder. To avoid this happening, click the Mailing Lists link on the Options page and use the text boxes on the resulting Mailing Lists page (which resembles the Safe List page) to maintain a list of the e-mail addresses from which you want to receive mailing list messages.

Block a Sender

If you don't want to receive any more e-mail from a particular sender or domain, you can block them by adding the sender or domain to your Block Sender List. To do so, click the Block Sender link on the Options page and use the text boxes on the resulting page, shown in Figure 4-2, to maintain the Block Sender List using the same techniques as for your Safe List.

When you block a sender, they don't get any notification that you've done so. Any message they send to you is deleted automatically without being delivered to you and is not bounced back to the sender.

You *can* use your Block Sender List to filter junk mail, but, in general, it's best to rely on the Junk Mail Filter as a first line of defense and keep the Block Sender List for blocking specific e-mail addresses or domains that send you mail you don't want to receive. If you don't use the Junk Mail Filter and rely solely on your Block Sender List, the Block Sender List will grow uncomfortably long and unwieldy.

 Addresses on your Block Sender List take precedence over domains on your Safe List. If you add to your Block Sender List an entry that conflicts with one or more entries on your Safe List, Hotmail deletes the conflicting Safe List entries and notifies you that it has done so.

Filter Mail to Specific Folders

If you receive a lot of mail, you may want to have Hotmail sort it for you so that you can approach it more efficiently. For example, you might want to filter all your incoming newsletters into a Newsletters folder so that you could keep them separate from your e-mail; or you might want to cordon off family messages to protect your business messages or delete any message whose subject line includes "free" or "sex."

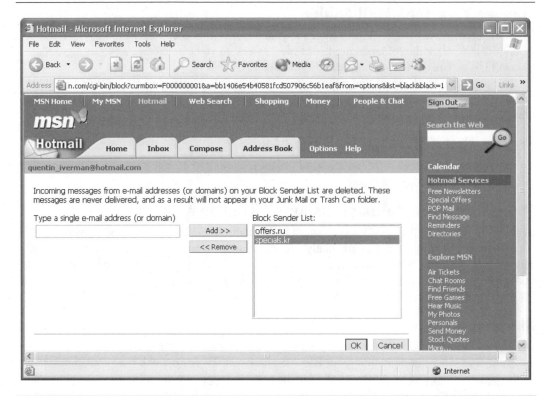

FIGURE 4-2 The counterpart to the Safe List is the Block Sender List, which you use to specify e-mail addresses and domains from which you don't want to receive e-mail messages.

To apply filtering to your messages, click the Custom Filters link on the Options page and use the resulting Filters page, shown in Figure 4-3, to specify the details of the filters.

You can set up to 11 filters. For each filter you create, take these steps:

1. Select the Enabled check box to enable the filter.

2. In the first drop-down list, choose the appropriate item: Subject, From Name, From Addr, or To or Cc Lines.

3. In the second drop-down list, select the appropriate item: Contains, Does Not Contain, Contains Word, Starts With, Ends With, or Equals. (The first five comparisons are self-explanatory. *Equals* means "is the same as"—in other words, the whole of the field has to match the text you specify.)

4. In the text box, enter the text with which the specified item is to be compared.

5. In the Then Deliver To drop-down list, select the folder into which you want Hotmail to put messages that meet this criterion.

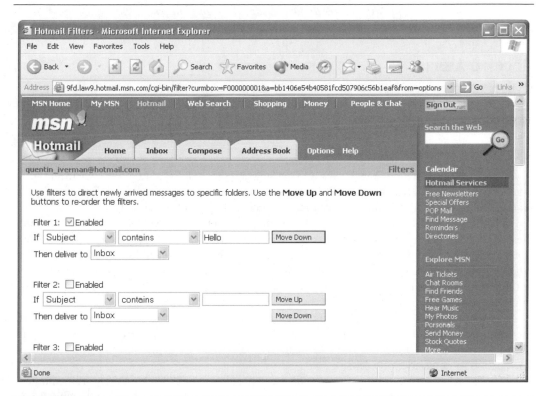

FIGURE 4-3 Use the Filters page to apply filtering to your incoming mail.

Here are a couple of examples:

- To move mail from a particular person to a folder, choose From Addr in the first drop-down list and Equals in the second drop-down list. Then enter that person's e-mail address in the text box and select the folder in the Then Deliver To drop-down list.

- To dispose of all mail that has a certain word in the subject line, choose Subject in the first drop-down list and Contains in the second drop-down list. Then enter the offending word in the text box and select the folder (for example, Trash Can) in the Then Deliver To drop-down list.

Once you've created several filters, you may need to rearrange the order in which they apply. For example, you might find that Filter 3 is catching the messages you had intended to catch with Filter 5—in which case, you'd probably want to rearrange the filters so that Filter 5 is before Filter 3. To rearrange the filters, use the Move Up and Move Down buttons beside each filter. (For obvious reasons, the first filter has no Move Up button and the last filter has no Move Down button.)

When you've finished specifying the details of your filters, click the OK button. Thereafter, Hotmail applies those filters to new incoming mail you receive.

TIP   *If you want to apply the filters to the messages currently in your Inbox, click the Apply Filters Now button at the bottom of the Filters page.*

Receive Alerts

If you have a pager or cell phone on which you want to receive alerts when you get new e-mail messages at Hotmail, click the Alerts button and use the resulting page to create an MSN Mobile account and specify settings.

Get Your POP Mail via Hotmail

If you want, you can have Hotmail pick up your messages from a POP server at your ISP or at work. You can do this for up to four POP accounts, which gives you great flexibility for using Hotmail to access POP accounts that you're not in a position to access directly.

When you use Hotmail to access a POP account, you can choose whether to download the messages on the POP server to your Hotmail account or leave them on the server. Either choice is reasonable, depending on the circumstances. Leaving the messages on the server can be useful when you want to use Hotmail to get a sneak preview of the contents of your POP mailbox without removing the messages from the POP server—for example, when you're using Hotmail to check your POP account from work but you want to be able later to retrieve all the e-mail messages on your POP account using your regular e-mail client. Using Hotmail to download the messages from the POP server tends to be more useful when you're using Hotmail in the longer term—for example, if you want to use Hotmail to access your POP mailbox when you're away on vacation for a number of weeks.

The disadvantage to leaving messages on the POP server when checking them from another account used to be that each time you used the other account to check the POP mail, you got *all* the messages waiting for you, not just the ones you hadn't yet read from the other account. If you received a lot of e-mail, your sessions would get longer and longer as you downloaded all messages, from the earliest to the latest. And, unless you were diligent about deleting all the copies of the messages from the second account before checking for new messages, you could get multiple copies of the same message in your second account. This could be confusing, particularly if the messages were in conversations and had similar subject lines.

Fortunately, Hotmail has a setting specifically designed to deal with this problem.

To use Hotmail to view your POP mail, click the POP Mail Retrieval Settings link on the Options page. Hotmail opens the POP Mail Retrieval Settings page, of which the top part is shown in Figure 4-4.

In the Settings for First POP Account area, enter the POP server name, your username for the account, and your password for the account. If necessary, change the server timeout from the default setting of 90 seconds and the port number from the default and standard setting of 110. Then select the Leave Messages on POP Server check box if you want to leave the messages on the POP server and download only copies of them. Clear this check box if you want to download the messages from the server to your Hotmail account. (This check box is cleared by default.) If you want to download only new messages from the POP account, leave the Download New Messages Only check box selected, as it is by default. If you want to download all messages from the POP account, clear this check box and, in the New Mail Indicator area, select the icon you

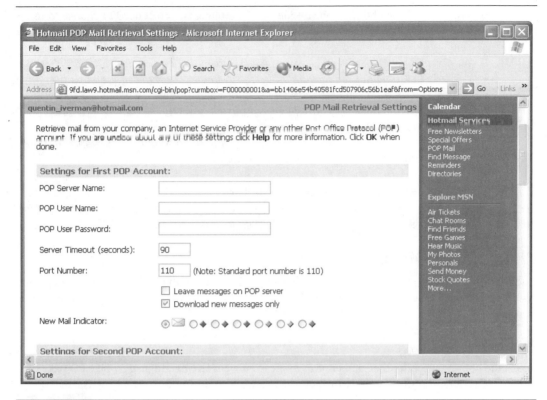

FIGURE 4-4   You can use Hotmail to retrieve mail from up to four POP mail servers
(for example, from your ISP or from your company).

want Hotmail to use in your Inbox for messages from this POP account. By using different icons,
you can give yourself a visual cue as to which messages come from which account.

If you have more than one POP account from which you want to download messages to your
Hotmail account, choose settings in the Settings for Second POP Account area, Settings for Third
POP Account area, and Settings for Fourth POP Account area, as appropriate.

Click the OK button when you've finished choosing POP settings.

Apply a Signature to Your Messages

If you want, you can apply to your messages a *signature*—not a signature in the conventional sense,
but a file of information that's automatically added to the end of a message. Traditionally, e-mail
signatures have been used to provide information about the sender (for example, contact information
or position); to include a thought, an aphorism, or a quote; or both. Also traditionally, e-mail
signatures have been short (to keep the message size down) and in plain text (with no formatting).

These days, many people use long signatures that include formatting and hyperlinks. Hotmail
supports complex signatures like this, but it lets you use only one signature at a time. (As you'll
see later in this chapter, Outlook Express lets you create multiple signatures and switch among

them as necessary.) To avoid boring your frequent correspondents, you'll need to change your signature often.

If you want to switch between signatures frequently without having to re-create them laboriously in Hotmail, keep them in a file (for example, a text file or rich-text file) on your Desktop or somewhere else handy so that you can quickly paste a different signature into Hotmail's Signature page—or paste it directly into a message. There's nothing magical about the signature once it's in the message, so you can paste it in from a local source if you have one handy. The point of the signature is simply to avoid having to retype boilerplate text for each message.

To create a signature, click the Signature link on the Options page and compose your signature in the text box on the resulting Signature page. If you want to use formatting in your signature, select the Show the Rich-Text Toolbar check box and use its buttons to apply the formatting.

Choose Mail Display Settings

The Mail Display Settings page, which you can access by clicking the Mail Display Settings link on the Options page, lets you specify the following settings for how Hotmail displays your mail in folders.

Messages per Page

Select the option button for the number of messages you want Hotmail to display on each page of a folder. The default setting is 100, which may take a while to download over a slow connection.

Line Width

Select the appropriate option button to specify the line width in characters. Your choice will probably depend on your screen resolution and the size at which you usually display the Hotmail window on it.

Message Headers

Select the appropriate option button to specify the extent of message headers to display. A message header is the block of marginally comprehensible text that appears at the beginning of a message. These are your choices:

- The default setting, Basic, displays the sender's name, the recipient's name, the date, and the subject.

- The None setting displays no headers and tends to make messages harder to read (because you can't see who they're from).

- The Full setting displays extra routing information that's useful primarily when you need to check the machines through which the message passed.

- The Advanced setting displays the full detail of MIME headers, which you should seldom need.

Choose Reply-Related Settings

Hotmail offers three important options for the replies you compose using its Web interface. Click the Reply-Related Settings link on the Options page to access the Reply-Related Settings page (see Figure 4-5).

Include Original Text When Replying

Specify whether to include the text of the message to which you're replying. Select the Auto option button (the default) or the Manual option button, as appropriate. Auto causes Hotmail to include the full text of the message. Manual causes Hotmail to include only that part of the text you've selected before clicking the Reply button or Reply All button.

Original Text Indicator

Choose the type of indicator to use for original text in replies. The default setting is the Begin Each Line with ">" option button, the greater-than sign (>) being the traditional indicator in

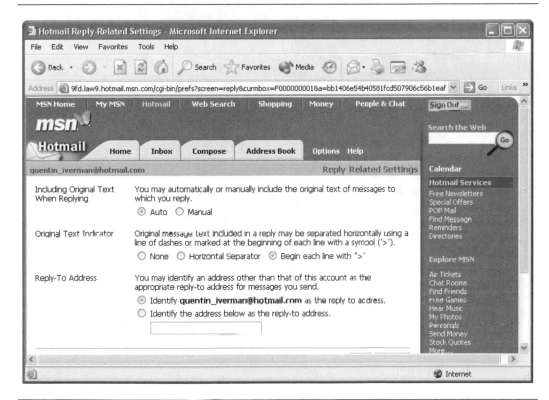

FIGURE 4-5   The Reply-Related Settings page contains three key options for the replies you write.

plain-text e-mail. You can also choose the Horizontal Separator option button (to separate the original text with a horizontal line of dashes) or the None option button (to have the original text appear without marking). In most cases, having original text appear without marking is visually confusing because the recipient will have a hard time distinguishing what you wrote from the original text. But it can be useful if you're using e-mail to work together on text (for example, on a draft) when what's important is to get the whole text right rather than to preserve distinctions between original and subsequent parts of it.

Reply-to Address

The Reply-To Address option buttons let you specify a different address to use as the reply-to address for your messages—the address that will be used when the recipient of one of your messages replies to it. By default, your reply-to address is your Hotmail or MSN address. But you may want to set a different reply-to address—for example, if you're writing messages from work using Hotmail or MSN but you want replies to go to your POP account. To do so, select the Identify the Address Below As the Reply-to Address option button, enter the address in the text box, and then click the OK button.

Turn Off Sent Message Confirmation

By default, Hotmail confirms the act of sending each outgoing message. This feature was useful in the early days when the Hotmail Web interface was, let's say, *shaky*. These days, it tends to be an irritant once you've used Hotmail for more than a few messages.

To turn off Sent Message Confirmation, click the Sent Message Confirmation link on the Options page, select the No Confirmation Is Needed option button on the Sent Message Confirmation Setup page, and click the OK button. (To turn Sent Message Confirmation back on, choose the Yes, Receive Confirmation option button on the Sent Message Confirmation Setup page.)

Choose to Have Hotmail Expire a Session After a Given Time

By default, Hotmail allows you to remain logged in as long as your Internet connection remains connected—so if you have a permanent Internet connection, you can stay connected to Hotmail for an uncomfortably long time.

Many people don't actually want to remain connected to Hotmail while they're away from their computer because this can represent a security risk. To make Hotmail expire your sessions automatically a certain number of hours after you sign in, click the Session Expiration link on the Options page and choose the appropriate option button on the Session Expiration page: 2 Hours, 8 Hours, 16 Hours, 24 Hours, or Never. (The default is Never.) Better yet, sign out manually before leaving your computer.

Access Hotmail via Outlook Express

Although accessing Hotmail via the Web is great for casual use, particularly when you need to use a computer other than your own, its disadvantages soon stack up. Foremost among these, as mentioned earlier, are that you need to be online when creating and reading e-mail and that Hotmail's Web-based interface, although impressive and flexible for a Web application, is necessarily far clunkier and more awkward to use than Outlook Express, which gets to use the latest Windows widgets in its interface. So if you use Hotmail extensively, and you have regular access to a computer that has XP (or an earlier version of Windows) installed, you'll probably do better to use Outlook Express to access Hotmail, as described in the rest of this chapter.

Start Outlook Express

The easiest way to start Outlook Express is to choose Start | E-mail. If you've assigned the E-mail shortcut to another program, choose Start | All Programs | Outlook Express instead.

TIP

To reassign the E-mail shortcut on the Start menu, display the Start menu, right-click the E-mail shortcut, and choose Internet Properties from the context menu. XP displays the Internet Properties dialog box. On the Programs page, choose Outlook Express in the E-mail drop-down list. Then click the OK button to close the Internet Properties dialog box.

Set Up Your E-mail Account

The first time you run Outlook Express on a computer for which you haven't already configured e-mail, Outlook Express launches the Internet Connection Wizard, which walks you through the process of setting up an e-mail account. The process is described in the following list, which shows only the more complex pages of the wizard:

1. On the Your Name page, enter the name you want to use for the From field of messages you send.

2. On the Internet E-mail Address page, enter your e-mail address.

3. On the E-mail Server Names page, shown next, select the type of incoming mail server in the My Incoming Mail Server Is a *NNN* Server drop-down list. The choices are POP3, IMAP, and HTTP. If you don't know which your ISP uses, check with it. Generally speaking, POP3 (Post Office Protocol 3) is more widely used than IMAP (Internet Message Access Protocol) at this writing—partly because POP3 is older than IMAP, but perhaps more because IMAP is more demanding for ISPs to implement. Many ISPs include *POP* or *POP3* in the names for their POP3 servers; so if you see a name such as pop3.acmeisp.net, you can be pretty sure it's a POP3 server.

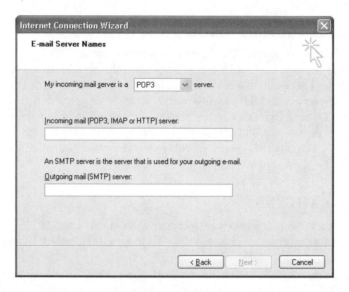

4. If you choose HTTP in the My Incoming Mail Server Is a *NNN* Server drop-down list, the Internet Connection Wizard displays the My HTTP Mail Service Provider Is drop-down list and makes the Outgoing Mail (SMTP) Server text box unavailable, as shown here. (If you enter a Hotmail address on the Internet E-mail Address page, the wizard automatically selects HTTP and Hotmail on the E-mail Server Names page.)

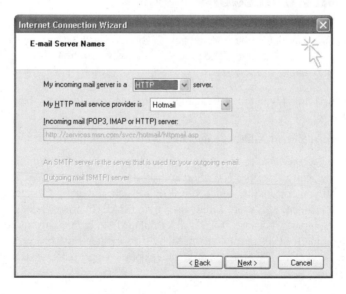

5. On the Internet Mail Logon page of the Internet Connection Wizard, enter your account name and password. Your account name may be the same as your e-mail address, but it may not. (Again, check with your ISP if you're not sure.) If you want Outlook Express to store the password so that you won't need to enter it manually when checking e-mail, leave the Remember Password check box selected. Saving a password like this reduces your security; so, if you have the patience to enter your password manually when checking e-mail, you'll be more secure.

6. If your ISP uses Secure Password Authentication (SPA) to secure passwords, select the Log On Using Secure Password Authentication (SPA) check box.

7. Click the Finish button on the Congratulations page to close the Internet Connection Wizard.

Configure Outlook Express for E-mail

Outlook Express offers a boatload—maybe even a shipload—of configuration options. Some are easy to understand; others are more complex. Some make a big difference to your experience to e-mail; others are trivial or obscure.

So, rather than trail through all these options in turn and bore you rigid, this section focuses on the options you're most likely to need. As a result, instead of presenting the options in order, it presents them in logical groups by the benefit or difference they can offer you. Therefore, I suggest you browse the headings and read the sections that seem relevant, rather than battering grimly ahead like an icebreaker up the St. Lawrence.

As usual with Microsoft programs, all the Outlook Express settings come with defaults that may or may not suit your needs. You *can* just proceed using the default settings, but you'll almost certainly benefit from spending a little time configuring Outlook Express. After all, if you're going to use it extensively for e-mail, you might as well make the experience as easy, efficient, and enjoyable as possible, mightn't you?

NOTE   *This section doesn't discuss the Outlook Express newsreader options. Reading news involves security considerations, but these are adequately treated in most basic XP books and therefore are not discussed here.*

Make Outlook Express the Default Mail Handler

The Default Messaging Programs area at the bottom of the General page of the Options dialog box shows whether Outlook Express is the default mail handler and default news handler for your XP user account. (The default *mail handler* is the program that XP uses when a program requests a mail action.) If Outlook Express isn't the default handler for mail or news, you can make it so by clicking the appropriate Make Default button.

Prevent Outlook Express from Signing You into Messenger

By default, Outlook Express automatically signs you into Messenger when you start Outlook Express. To prevent it from doing so, clear the Automatically Log On to Windows Messenger check box in the General area of the General page of the Options dialog box.

If your Outlook Express account involves a .NET Passport, signing into Messenger automatically makes a kind of sense. For example, if you're signing onto Hotmail or MSN, you may want to sign into Messenger as well to see what's happening. But if you're using

Outlook Express with another ISP, chances are you'll prefer to sign in to Messenger only when you want to use it.

Set Up the Outlook Express Window for Easy Reading

This section discusses the assorted options for setting up the Outlook Express window for reading e-mail. Figure 4-6 shows the components of the Outlook Express window with the Inbox open.

Choose Whether to Use the Preview Pane

The first choice to make is whether to use the Preview pane to display the contents of the currently selected message in the current mail folder.

Most users find that the Preview pane is a helpful tool for triaging their e-mail quickly into categories—so unless you're one of the few people who doesn't like the Preview pane, you've probably got a strong incentive to use it. But the Preview pane has a downside too: Displaying

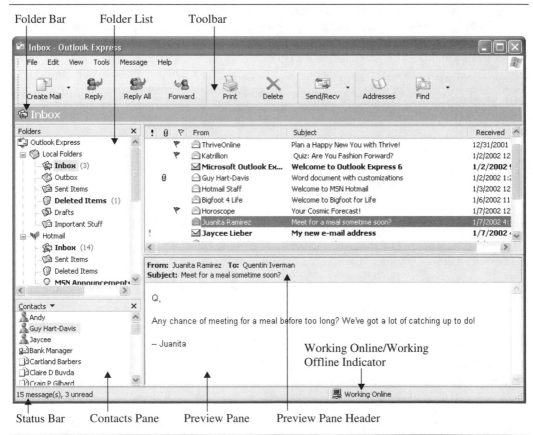

FIGURE 4-6 The components of the Outlook Express window with the Inbox open

a message in the Preview pane can start a script based on the Read action (which is triggered when Outlook Express decides you've "read" a message; more on this in a moment) that can take actions on your computer without your authorization. In other words, using the Preview pane can unleash a script on your computer. Most scripts and viruses use less sophisticated methods than this—for example, giving the user an apparently enticing file to open, as the Anna Kournikova virus did—but the attack has been demonstrated in the real world, and you may want to guard against it.

At this point, you're probably saying, "Wait! Isn't a Read event triggered when you open a message in a message window without using the Preview pane?" Indeed it is. The problem with the Read event in the Preview pane is that Outlook Express can trigger it automatically by deciding that you've read a message. But Outlook Express doesn't open a message in a message window without you telling it to do so. So, if you see a message header that looks suspicious in your Inbox, you can delete the message without reading it.

Toggle the Preview Pane On and Off

To toggle the display of the Preview pane on and off, choose View | Layout and select or clear the Show Preview Pane check box in the Preview Pane area of the Window Layout Properties dialog box (see Figure 4-7).

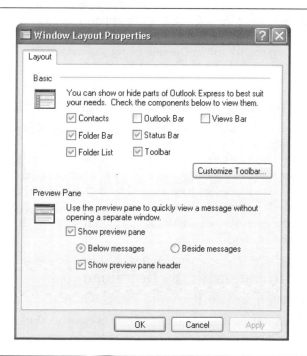

FIGURE 4-7 The Window Layout Properties dialog box contains options for toggling the display of the Preview pane and the other configurable elements of the Outlook Express interface.

Configure the Preview Pane

If you choose to use the Preview pane, specify its position by choosing the Below Messages option button (the default) or the Beside Messages option button in the Preview Pane area of the Window Layout Properties dialog box. Also, specify whether to display the Preview pane header (the gray bar that appears at the top of the Preview pane with the From, To, and Subject fields) by selecting or clearing the Show Preview Pane Header check box.

Toggle the Display of Other Components

You can toggle the display of most of the other components shown in Figure 4-6—the Contacts pane, the Folder bar, the Folder list, the toolbar, and the status bar—by selecting or clearing their check boxes in the Window Layout Properties dialog box. You get to balance the advantage that a component's functionality provides against the amount of screen space it consumes. For example, because the Contacts pane shows you which of your Messenger contacts are online and offline, and lets you contact those online, all without displaying the Messenger window, you may find it useful. But if you're using a low screen resolution, you may want to reclaim the space it takes up so that you can see more of your messages.

If you've quizzed the Window Layout Properties dialog box closely, you'll notice a couple of items that aren't accounted for in Figure 4-7: the Outlook bar and the Views bar. The Outlook bar displays another representation of the list of local folders and, as its name suggests, is more suited to Outlook than to Outlook Express. The Views bar provides a graphical representation of the View | Current View submenu, letting you navigate quickly between different views and groupings of messages. Figure 4-8 shows Outlook Express with the Outlook bar and the Views bar displayed.

Choose Whether to Mark Previewed Messages As Read

If you use the Preview pane, you can choose whether displaying a message in the Preview pane for a certain length of time causes Outlook Express to mark the message as having been read (thus triggering a Read event). To do so, select or clear the Mark Message Read After Displaying for *NN* Second(s) check box in the Reading Messages area of the Read page of the Options dialog box. If you select the check box (which is selected by default), set an appropriate number of seconds in the text box. For most people, "appropriate" in this case means a number of seconds more than they'll spend deciding to keep the message for later scrutiny and fewer than they'll need to decide that they've read the message to their satisfaction.

Choose Whether to Automatically Download a Message Displayed in the Preview Pane

If you're reading messages using a Web-based service such as Hotmail, Outlook Express downloads the message headers for you but not the message bodies (which can be much larger). This allows you to delete messages after seeing just the message header, which can save you downloading a bunch of data. This setting is good for when you're working online because Outlook Express can download the

Outlook bar   Views bar

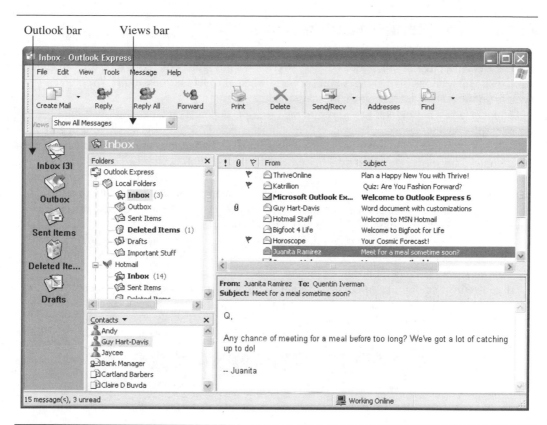

FIGURE 4-8   Outlook Express with the Outlook bar and the Views bar displayed

body of the message when you need it. But if you're not online, you'll need to go online before you can read the rest of the message.

To enable Outlook Express to download just the headers, select the Automatically Download Message When Viewing in the Preview Pane check box in the Reading Messages area of the Read page of the Options dialog box. If you use this option, you can force Outlook Express to download the body of the selected message by pressing the spacebar. (Alternatively, you can open the message in a new window, which also forces Outlook Express to download the body.)

Display ToolTips for "Clipped" Headers

The Show ToolTips in the Message List for Clipped Items check box controls whether Outlook Express displays a tooltip when you hover the mouse pointer over a message header item (the From text or the Subject text) that's too long to be fully displayed in the column. This option is turned on by default, and most people find it useful. The only downsides are that the tooltips can be visually distracting and that displaying them requires a few extra processor cycles.

Request and Return Read Receipts

(Sorry about the alliteration in the heading.)

The Receipts page of the Options dialog box, shown in Figure 4-9, lets you specify whether to request read receipts on messages you send and whether to let Outlook Express send read receipts on messages you receive that request them.

Whether you want to request and return read receipts depends on what you use e-mail for (for example, business or social purposes), how time-critical your messages are, your degree of patience or impatience, and other things I probably shouldn't speculate about here. Read receipts are often used for intracompany e-mail because many people find it can be a great help to know that someone has read a message before they bug them about its subject. For Internet mail, read receipts tend to be less widely used, particularly because many people are reluctant to return them—some because of the extra bandwidth the receipts require and some because the people don't like to feel they're being monitored by their correspondents.

You can request read receipts on all the messages you send by selecting the Request a Read Receipt for All Sent Messages check box in the Requesting Read Receipts area. Alternatively, you can request a read receipt manually on any message you send.

If you're using a digital certificate to digitally sign your messages, click the Secure Receipts button to display the Secure Receipts Options dialog box, shown in Figure 4-10, and verify that

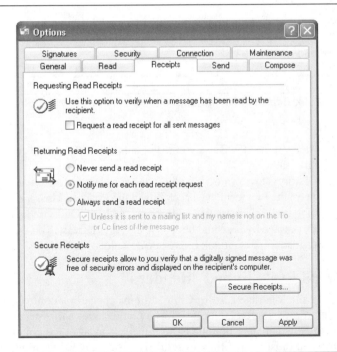

On the Receipts page of the Options dialog box, specify whether to ask for read receipts on outgoing messages and whether to give read receipts when they're requested.

its settings suit you. These settings mirror those on the Receipts page of the Options dialog box, except that they apply only to secure receipts—those for digitally signed messages. Select the Request a Secure Receipt for All Digitally Signed Messages check box to request a receipt by default on digitally signed messages. In the Sending Secure Receipt area, select the Never Send a Secure Receipt option button, the Ask Me If I Would Like to Send a Secure Receipt option button, or the Always Send a Secure Receipt option button, as appropriate.

Send and Check for Messages

This section discusses the options that Outlook Express offers for sending outgoing messages and checking for new incoming messages.

Send Messages and Check for Messages Automatically

Outlook Express offers two options for sending and receiving messages automatically:

- You can set Outlook Express to check for messages when you start it by selecting the Send and Receive Messages at Startup check box in the Send/Receive Messages area on the General page of the Options dialog box.

- You can set Outlook Express to check for new messages automatically at a specified interval by selecting the Check for New Messages Every *NN* Minutes check box in the Send/Receive Messages area of the General page of the Options dialog box and specifying the interval in the text box. When this check box is selected, Outlook Express makes available the If My Computer Is Not Connected at This Time drop-down list, which lets you choose Do Not Connect, Connect Only When Not Working Offline, or Connect Even

FIGURE 4-10   If you're sending and receiving digitally signed messages, use the options in the Secure Receipt Options dialog box to specify whether to request and send secure receipts.

When Working Offline, as appropriate. Do Not Connect is good for dial-up connections that you want to manage yourself. Connect Only When Not Working Offline is useful for mobile computers that may not have an Internet connection available when Outlook Express needs to check for mail. Connect Even When Working Offline is useful for dial-up connections that you're happy to have Outlook Express establish at will—for example, flat-rate connections.

Send Messages Immediately or Queue Them

If you want to send each new message the moment you click the Send button (or otherwise issue a Send command), select the Send Messages Immediately check box in the Sending area on the Send page of the Options dialog box (see Figure 4-11).

Sending messages immediately is great for situations in which you've got a persistent Internet connection (for example, cable, DSL, or a connection at work), but don't use this option with a dial-up modem connection because Outlook Express will try to dial the connection each time you send a message. Instead, you'll do better to queue messages for sending (which is what

FIGURE 4-11   The Send Messages Immediately check box on the Send page of the Options dialog box controls whether Outlook Express sends messages immediately or queues them when you issue a Send command.

happens when you clear the Send Messages Immediately check box) and then either send them in a batch at a time that suits you (for example, when you go online for other purposes) or use the Check for New Messages Every *NN* Minutes option to check for incoming messages and send outgoing messages at regular intervals.

Choose Fonts, Stationery, and Business Cards

The Compose page of the Options dialog box, shown in Figure 4-12, provides a number of mostly self-explanatory options for formatting the messages you compose:

- The Compose Font area lets you choose the fonts to use for e-mail messages and news items.

- The Stationery area lets you select, create, or download stationery to use for HTML messages. Use stationery only when it will enhance a message, not just because Outlook Express makes it easy to do so.

- The Business Cards area lets you select a business card to attach to new outgoing messages. In this case, a *business card* is a text representation of one of the records contained in your Address Book. If you decide to send a business card with your messages, edit it first to make

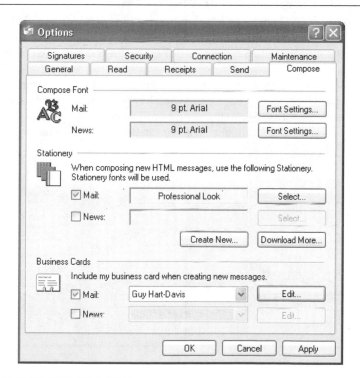

FIGURE 4-12   Use the options on the Compose page of the Options dialog box to specify fonts, stationery, and business cards for your outgoing messages.

sure the information is correct and that you're not sharing any secrets unintentionally. If you want to add your business card manually to messages, select the Mail check box, use the drop-down list to choose the business card, and then clear the Mail check box again.

Choose an E-mail Format: HTML or Plain Text

One of the big decisions you need to make when sending e-mail is whether to use HTML e-mail or plain-text e-mail. HTML messages, like HTML Web pages, can contain a wide variety of formatting, including styles, graphics, and hyperlinks. Plain-text messages can contain only plain text, as the term suggests. HTML messages have the advantage of being more visually impressive and including more information, but the disadvantage of using HTML messages is that some older or less capable e-mail clients can't display them accurately (or at all). Plain-text messages can be read by any e-mail client, no matter how simple or decrepit.

That said, these days, most e-mail clients *can* read HTML messages—which is why Outlook Express defaults to sending HTML messages. If you want to send plain-text messages, select the Plain Text option button instead of the HTML option button in the Mail Sending Format area of the Send page of the Options dialog box.

Choose Formatting for HTML or Plain Text

You can choose settings for the type of mail you're sending by clicking the HTML Settings button or the Plain Text Settings button in the Mail Sending Format area and working in the resulting HTML Settings dialog box, or the Plain Text Settings dialog box, both shown in Figure 4-13.

Of the settings in these dialog boxes, the one you're most likely to want to change is the Indent the Original Text with [character] When Replying or Forwarding check box and drop-down list in the Plain Text Settings dialog box. The default character for indentation is the greater-than sign (>), which is traditional, but you can use an exclamation point (!) or colon (:)

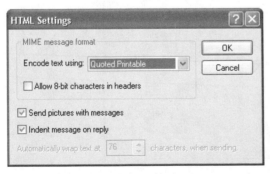
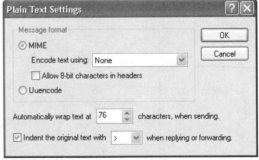

FIGURE 4-13   The HTML Settings dialog box and the Plain Text Settings dialog box offer formatting options for your messages.

instead if you prefer—or you can remove indentation if you don't want the original text to be distinguishable from your additions.

Use Plain Text or HTML As Appropriate for Replies

Choosing HTML or plain text for your messages is the first step, but Outlook Express offers another option on this front that gives you more flexibility than the bald choice.

To make sure your replies use the same format—plain text or HTML—as original messages, select the Reply to Messages Using the Format in Which They Were Sent check box in the Sending area on the Send page of the Options dialog box. Selecting this check box makes sure you don't send an HTML-formatted message to someone who has written to you in plain text.

Include the Original Message in the Reply

To include the original message in your reply, select the Include Message in Reply check box in the Sending area on the Send page of the Options dialog box.

Add Correspondents to Your Address Book Automatically

To have Outlook Express automatically create Address Book entries for people to whose messages you reply and who are not already in your Address Book, select the Automatically Put People I Reply to in My Address Book check box in the Sending area on the Send page of the Options dialog box. Many people find this option useful; but if you use it, take a weekly turn through your Address Book and prune any entries that you don't want to keep.

Turn AutoComplete On and Off for E-mail Addresses

Like just about any other Microsoft program, and like many other e-mail programs, Outlook Express offers an AutoComplete feature. In this case, the feature is for automatically completing e-mail addresses as you type them. This feature is turned on by default, but it's not to everyone's liking. The reason is that a misplaced keystroke can cause it to enter the wrong e-mail address, possibly without you noticing.

To turn AutoComplete on or off, select or clear the Automatically Complete E-mail Addresses when Composing check box in the Sending area of the Send page of the Options dialog box.

Get Notification of New Messages

To receive notification of incoming messages, select the Play Sound When New Messages Arrive check box in the Send/Receive Messages area of the General page of the Options dialog box.

> **TIP**
>
> *You can change the sound that Outlook Express plays when new mail arrives by changing the sound for the New Mail Notification event in the Windows category in the Program Events list box on the Sounds page of the Sounds and Audio Devices Properties dialog box. (To display this dialog box, choose Start | Control Panel; click the Sounds, Speech, and Audio Devices link; and then click the Change the Sound Scheme link in the Pick a Task list.)*

If the e-mail account in question is a Hotmail or MSN account, you'll also receive notification of new mail through Messenger when you're signed into Messenger Service. You can change the sound that Messenger plays for new mail by changing the sound for the New Mail event in the Windows Messenger category in the Program Events list box on the Sounds page of the Sounds and Audio Devices Properties dialog box.

Apply Signatures to Your Messages

As mentioned earlier in the chapter, a *signature* is a short file you can add automatically to the end of messages you send. The conventional use for a signature is to provide extra information about the sender or a pithy quote, but you can essentially put any information you want in one— at the risk of annoying the recipients of your messages.

As you saw, Hotmail supports only one signature at a time, so you need to change your signature file manually each time you want to make a change. Outlook Express provides better signature features: you can create multiple signatures and manage them easily by using the controls on the Signatures page of the Options dialog box (see Figure 4-14).

FIGURE 4-14   Outlook Express provides strong features for creating and managing multiple signatures for your outgoing messages.

Create a Signature

To create a signature, take the following steps:

1. Click the New button. Outlook Express creates a signature named Signature #1 in the Signatures list box, selects Signature #1, and puts the insertion point in the Edit Signature text box with the Text option button selected.

2. To create the signature using text, type the text in the text box. To create the signature from an existing text file or HTML file, select the File option button and then use the Browse button and the resulting Open dialog box to specify the file. By default, the Open dialog box's Files of Type drop-down list is set to show text files. To open an HTML file, choose HTML Files in the Files of Type drop-down list.

3. Click the Rename button to display an edit box around the Signature #1 name in the Signatures list box. Type the name for the signature and click an empty space in the dialog box or press ENTER.

You can delete a signature by selecting it in the Signatures list box and clicking the Remove button. Be warned that Outlook Express doesn't confirm the deletion of signatures. (If you delete a signature by mistake, you can recover it by immediately clicking the Cancel button to dismiss the Options dialog box before applying the change.)

Change Your Default Signature

To change your default signature, select the signature you want to make the default and click the Set As Default button. Outlook Express displays *Default signature* to the right of the current default signature in the Signatures list box.

Add a Signature to Your Outgoing Messages

Depending on what you use e-mail for and whom you're writing to, you may want to automatically add a signature to all your outgoing messages or add signatures manually only when you feel a message needs one.

To add a signature to all your outgoing messages, select the Add Signatures to All Outgoing Messages check box in the Signature Settings area of the Signatures page of the Options dialog box. When you select this check box, Outlook Express makes available the Don't Add Signatures to Replies and Forwards check box available. By default, this check box is selected, preventing Outlook Express from adding a signature to replies you send and to messages you forward. If you want to add a signature to replies and forwards, clear this check box.

NOTE *Outlook Express doesn't add signatures to read receipts, even if you clear the Don't Add Signatures to Replies and Forwards check box.*

You can also add a signature manually to any given message by choosing Insert | Signature from the New Message window and choosing the signature you want to insert from the resulting submenu.

If you choose to add a signature to all your outgoing messages, Outlook Express enters the signature when you create a message, so you can easily edit it or delete it if necessary.

Associate a Signature with a Particular E-mail Account

If you're using Outlook Express to check multiple e-mail accounts, you may want to associate different signatures with different accounts—for example, a formal signature for work-related e-mail, and a looser signature for social e-mail.

To do so, select the signature in question. Then click the Advanced button to display the Advanced Signature Settings dialog box (see Figure 4-15). Select the check boxes for the accounts and then click the OK button. Repeat the procedure for other signatures, as appropriate.

Choose Virus-Protection Options

Outlook Express offers three disparate virus-protection options in the Virus Protection area of the Security page of the Options dialog box.

The Select the Internet Explorer Security Zone to Use list lets you choose which of the Internet Explorer–defined security zones Outlook Express should use. The default setting is the Restricted Sites Zone option button, which increases your security but may prevent Outlook Express from taking some actions. (The Restricted Sites zone consists of a list of sites you've designated as being a potential or real security threat.) Instead, you can choose the Internet Zone option button, which reduces your security but makes it less likely that you'll lose any functionality.

The Warn Me When Other Applications Try to Send Mail As Me check box controls whether Outlook Express displays a warning when another program tries to send e-mail using your Outlook Express identity. There are a couple of times when this is likely to happen: First, when you use Remote Assistance to send an e-mail invitation. Second, if you use an automated mailto form from Internet Explorer (for example, a form on a Web page) that piggybacks on your e-mail program.

The Remote Assistance action is harmless—beneficial, even—and the automated form's action should be harmless, too. The reason for the warning is that many macro viruses use Outlook Express or Outlook itself to send e-mail, controlling Outlook Express or Outlook from another program via the

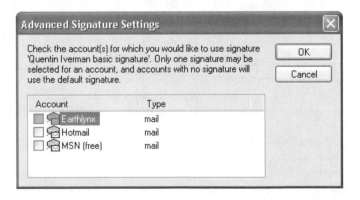

FIGURE 4-15   Use the Advanced Signature Settings dialog box to associate a signature with one or more e-mail accounts.

Windows Automation feature. For example, the Melissa macro virus and the I Love You virus used Microsoft Word to control the e-mail program.

The Do Not Allow Attachments to Be Saved or Opened That Could Potentially Be a Virus check box controls whether Outlook Express refuses attachments that might be viruses or contain viruses. This option is well intended but only marginally effective. The problem is that although this feature undeniably protects you from some viruses, it has a high ratio of false positives. For example, if someone sends you a Word document or Excel workbook with even the tiniest of toolbar, menu, or keystroke customizations, Outlook Express treats the document or workbook as if it contains macros that might indeed threaten your computer. Even if you know that the document is harmless, Outlook Express prevents you from using it—which might well drive you up the wall.

Choose Options for Sending Secure Mail

If you have a digital certificate, you can use it to encrypt your outgoing messages and attachments and to digitally sign outgoing messages.

> **NOTE**   *See Chapter 3 for a discussion of digital certificates and where to get them. As discussed in that chapter, Outlook Express uses the term "digital ID" instead of "digital certificate."*

Encrypt All Messages and Attachments

You can choose to encrypt all outgoing messages and attachments by selecting the Encrypt Contents and Attachments for All Outgoing Messages check box on the Security page of the Options dialog box, or you can apply encryption manually to some messages when you want to use it.

Because you have to have a digital certificate for every recipient to whom you want to send encrypted messages, you may prefer to apply encryption manually. However, if you have digital certificates for a good number, or perhaps most, of your correspondents, this option is viable because Outlook Express warns you when you're sending a message (or attachment) to someone for whom you don't have a digital certificate. You can then choose whether to send the message without encryption or cancel sending it.

Digitally Signing All Outgoing Messages

To apply a digital signature to all your outgoing messages so that the recipients can be sure it's you that messages come from, select the Digitally Sign All Outgoing Messages check box on the Security page of the Options dialog box. There's no downside to this option if you have a digital certificate.

Choose Advanced Security Settings

If you're planning to send encrypted messages or digitally signed messages, it's a good idea to examine the settings in the Advanced Security Settings dialog box (see Figure 4-16). The defaults may suit you—they're at least halfway sentient—but then again, they may not.

FIGURE 4-16   If you're encrypting or digitally signing messages, check that the options in the Advanced Security Settings dialog box have suitable settings.

How Much Encryption Do You Need, and How Secure Is It?

At this writing, most people don't use encryption for day-to-day e-mail, just as they don't use scramblers for regular telephone calls. As a result, encryption is largely left to security-sensitive companies, government agencies, the military, and the paranoid. The public's *laissez-lire* attitude toward security benefits the security services, who can of course read unencrypted e-mail with far greater ease than encrypted e-mail, and malicious hackers, who can intercept and read unencrypted e-mail and glean information they can use (for example, for social-engineering attacks).

But with more and more computers worldwide being networked, and with no ultimately satisfactory way of reliably establishing identity online, there's an ever-increasing need for security. If you want to keep your messages secure so that only the intended recipient can read them, you should encrypt them. And, if you want to enable the recipient to be sure a message comes from you, you should apply a digital signature to it. This means getting a digital certificate, as discussed in Chapter 3.

In order to make sensible decisions about encryption, you should understand the basics of encryption and what different encryption key lengths mean.

Briefly, a *cryptographic key* is a secret value used to make a cryptographic algorithm for the people using the key. Very loosely speaking, the longer the encryption key, the harder it should be to crack via a brute-force attack—an attack that tries every possible key until it gets a match. The number of possible keys is 2 to the power of the number of bits, producing around a trillion possible keys for a 40-bit key and 72,057,594,037,927,936 possible keys for a 56-bit key. The progression is exponential: Add one bit to the key length, and the key is twice as hard to crack. Add another bit, and it's twice as hard again. So, when you add 112 bits to that impressive number for a 56-bit key (to give a key length of 168 bits), cracking it becomes very tough indeed—in theory, anyway.

That said, computational power is increasing all the time. In 1998, the Electronic Frontier Foundation built a computer called DES Deep Crack that performed a brute-force attack on the DES algorithm and could break a 56-bit DES key in an average of four-and-a-half days. DES Deep Crack could plow through 90 billion keys a second. Distributed.net, a distributed Internet key-search program set up in 1999, could process 250 billion keys a second. You can only imagine how many keys a second the NSA's computers can process—though you might get an idea from this: In January 2002, American intelligence services broke the encryption on a laptop computer that had belonged to Dr. Ayman al-Zawahiri, reportedly Osama bin Laden's right-hand man. Breaking the encryption took a cluster of high-speed computers five days, so the encryption must have used a fair number of bits.

The number of possible keys for, say, a 168-bit key might make it seem virtually impossible to track, but there are a couple of things to bear in mind. First, unless the attacker is very unlucky, the key isn't going to be the last possibility tried. A brute-force attack may stumble on the key after just a few tries (or a few billion). For an average, experts suggest figuring that trying half the number of possible keys will turn up the key. Second, if the key has low entropy, it'll be much easier to crack than if it has high entropy.

Entropy? Isn't that, like, the world going to pot in a handcart?

In cryptographic terms, *entropy* is a measure of how "uncertain" something is. For an English speaker, a five-letter password that's a standard English word is far more likely than a five-character jumble of letters, numbers, and symbols, and so has lower entropy. So most brute-force attacks start by exhausting the words in the standard dictionary before moving on to combinations. (More accurately, most brute-force attacks actually start with the hundred or so most frequently used passwords because these will often do the trick.)

So, to make your encryption tough to crack, you need to use a password or pass-phrase that has high entropy. There are several possibilities for this:

- ■ **Use a long pass-phrase**   In *Secrets and Lies*, expert cryptographer Bruce Schneier estimates that an eight-character password in standard English has about the same entropy as a 32-bit key and that a 98-character pass-phrase in standard English would be required to give sufficient entropy for a 128-bit key. A 168-bit key would require a correspondingly longer pass-phrase—but very few people could be expected to enter a pass-phrase of even 25 characters for regular use.

- ■ **Don't use standard English (or standard words in any language)**   Mix letters, numbers, and symbols to create a password of moderate length that's not too difficult to type.

■ **Get mathematical assistance**   One way to create an unguessable pass-phrase is to use a random method of picking words. Diceware (www.diceware.com) has an interesting method involving dice.

Because any encryption can be broken by a determined and sustained enough attack, it's best to think of encryption as being like a safe—it doesn't necessarily give you safety forever, but it buys you time against a determined assault, and it will likely deter casual thieves and snoopers.

Encrypted Messages Area Options

In the Encrypted Messages area of the Advanced Security Settings dialog box, you can use the Warn on Encrypting Messages with Less Than This Strength drop-down list to adjust the minimum level of encryption you'll tolerate. The default setting is 168 bits, which should provide strong security, as you saw earlier. If you find yourself frequently getting warnings that you're using a shorter key length—for example, "only" 128 bits—you may want to lower this setting so that you don't get warnings unnecessarily.

Select the Always Encrypt to Myself When Sending Encrypted Mail check box if you want to keep an encrypted copy of the message. This copy is encrypted with your digital certificate, *not* with the message recipient's digital certificate, so that you can read it later.

Digitally Signed Messages Area

The Include My Digital ID When Sending Signed Messages check box controls whether Outlook Express sends your digital certificate with each digitally signed message you send. Sending the digital certificate is useful because it means a recipient who doesn't have your public key already can verify that the message is from you (and subsequently encrypt messages they send to you) without having to cavort through the public-key infrastructure to find your public key. If the recipient already has your public key, sending the digital certificate is redundant. But because digital certificates are very small, sending one unnecessarily isn't a major bandwidth tragedy.

The Encode Message Before Signing (Opaque Signing) check box controls whether Outlook Express encodes your digitally signed messages in such a way as to protect the digital signature from tampering. This is generally a good idea, except that if the recipient's e-mail program doesn't support S/MIME, they won't be able to read the message. So use this option with care.

The Add Senders' Certificates to My Address Book check box controls whether Outlook Express automatically adds to your Address Book the certificates of people who send you digitally signed messages. For most people, it's a good idea to use this option, which is selected by default.

Revocation Checking Area

The two option buttons in the Revocation Checking area—the Only When Online option button and the Never option button—let you specify when to check whether the digital IDs other people are using are still valid and haven't been revoked. If you're feeling security conscious, select the Only When Online option button.

Choose Spelling Options

If you have Microsoft Office or Microsoft Word installed, the Spelling page of the Options dialog box, shown in Figure 4-17, offers a half-dozen self-explanatory options for checking spelling in your messages, specifying which words to ignore, and so on. You can also specify the language to use for spell-checking your messages, as well as edit your custom dictionary.

Make Outlook Express Ask Before Changing the Dial-Up Connection

If you have multiple dial-up connections, and you've configured Outlook Express to establish a dial-up connection when it needs one, it'll try the connections in turn, starting with the default, until it finds one that works.

If all your dial-up connections are flat-rate, you may want Outlook Express to be free to use them all. But if they're not, you may want it to get your permission before it uses any connection other than the default. To do so, make sure the Ask Before Switching Dial-Up Connections check box in the Dial-Up area of the Connection page of the Options dialog box is selected (see Figure 4-18). To let Outlook Express use the connections without permission, clear this check box.

FIGURE 4-17   If you have Word or Office installed on your computer, you can choose spelling options on the Spelling page of the Options dialog box.

FIGURE 4-18   The Connection page of the Options dialog box offers two settings for controlling Outlook Express's use of your dial-up connections.

Make Outlook Express Hang Up the Internet Connection After Sending and Receiving Messages

If you want Outlook Express to hang up your Internet connection after sending and receiving messages, select the Hang Up After Sending and Receiving check box in the Dial-Up area of the Connection page of the Options dialog box.

This setting is most useful when you choose to allow Outlook Express to establish a connection, but there's no reason why you shouldn't use it for a connection you establish manually if you so wish.

Empty the Deleted Items Folder Automatically

By default, Outlook Express puts messages you delete into the Deleted Items folder and leaves them there until you empty the folder. If you want Outlook Express to empty the Deleted Items folder automatically when you close Outlook Express, select the Empty Messages from the "Deleted Items" Folder on Exit check box in the Cleaning Up Messages area of the Maintenance page of the Options dialog box (see Figure 4-19).

FIGURE 4-19   The Maintenance Page of the Options dialog box contains options for
automatically compacting and deleting old messages.

Remove Deleted Messages from IMAP Folders

If your ISP has an IMAP server, you can purge from your account those messages you've
deleted during a session by selecting the Purge Deleted Messages When Leaving IMAP Folders
check box in the Cleaning Up Messages area of the Maintenance page of the Options dialog box.

Compact Old Messages to Save Space

Deleting the messages (and attachments) from your Deleted Items folder can save you a good
deal of space, but you can usually recover a good amount more space by compacting old messages
that you don't want to delete. Outlook Express offers options for compacting messages automatically
(which this section discusses) and manually (discussed later in this chapter).

To make Outlook Express compact messages automatically in the background as you work,
select the Compact Messages in the Background check box in the Cleaning Up Messages area of
the Maintenance page of the Options dialog box.

When you select this check box, Outlook makes available the three controls under it:

- **Delete Read Message Bodies in Newsgroups check box**   This check box controls
  whether Outlook Express deletes the bodies of newsgroup messages you've read while

leaving the headers there. This deletion takes place when you quit Outlook Express and can recover a good deal of space, but you'll need to redownload any message you want to read again. (Bear in mind that most news servers expire messages after a certain age, so you may not be able to download the message again.)

- ■ **Delete News Messages *NN* Days After Being Downloaded check box**   This control provides an easy way of disposing of old news messages. Adjust the number of days to suit your needs. But if you want to save those news messages you haven't deleted, be sure to turn this option off, because it's on by default.

- ■ **Compact Messages When There Is *NN* Percent Wasted Space text box**   This control lets you adjust the threshold for compacting messages. The default setting is 20 percent wasted space.

The Clean Up Now button lets you perform a cleanup manually. I'll discuss this option later in this chapter.

Change the Location of Your Message Store

As you'd guess, your *message store* is the folder in which Outlook Express stores your messages. By default, the message store folder is located deep within a hidden system folder in your \Documents and Settings\ folder. You can move it (for example, to a different drive) by clicking the Store Folder button in the Cleaning Up Messages area of the Maintenance page of the Options dialog box, clicking the Change button in the resulting Store Location dialog box, and using the resulting Browse for Folder dialog box to specify the new folder. After doing so, exit Outlook Express and restart it to effect the change.

Add an E-mail Account to Outlook Express

As you've seen, Outlook Express automatically runs the Internet Connection Wizard to set you up with an e-mail account the first time you run Outlook Express. If you have multiple e-mail accounts, you'll probably want to add them to Outlook Express so that you can manage them all from a central location.

To add an e-mail account to Outlook Express, choose Tools | Accounts to display the Internet Accounts dialog box (see Figure 4-20). Then click the Add button and choose Mail from the context menu to start the Internet Connection Wizard. Follow through the steps of the wizard as discussed in "Set Up Your E-mail Account," earlier in this chapter.

Configure an E-mail Account

In addition to its many global settings (of which we examined most earlier in this chapter), Outlook Express provides a large number of settings for each e-mail account, news account, or directory service account. This section discusses the key configuration options for an e-mail account. As before, it presents the configuration options arranged by what they can offer you rather than plowing through them all in turn.

To start configuring an e-mail account, select it in the Internet Accounts dialog box (Tools | Accounts) and click the Properties button. Outlook Express displays the Properties dialog box for the account.

FIGURE 4-20 Use the Internet Accounts dialog box to create new mail and news accounts and to manage your existing accounts.

The number of pages in the Properties dialog box for an e-mail account varies depending on the type of server used: HTTP, POP3, or IMAP. The Properties dialog box for an HTTP account has four pages: General, Server, Connection, and Security. The Properties dialog box for a POP3 account has five pages: General, Servers, Connection, Security, and Advanced. The Properties dialog box for an IMAP account has those five pages and an IMAP page as well. Beyond this, the Advanced page for an IMAP account has several more controls than the Advanced page for a POP3 account.

Rename the E-mail Account

The Internet Connection Wizard manages to name any Hotmail account "Hotmail," but any other type of account it names simply by the server's name. To change this, enter the new name in the Mail Account text box on the General page of the Properties dialog box (see Figure 4-21).

Change Your User Information

You can change your user information—your display name and organization, your e-mail address, and your reply address—on the General page of the Properties dialog box for an account.

Include or Exclude the Account When Checking for Mail

To control whether Outlook Express checks for mail on this account when you click the Send/Recv button, select or clear the Include This Account When Receiving Mail or Synchronizing check box on the General page of the Properties dialog box for the account.

FIGURE 4-21   The General page of the Properties dialog box for an e-mail account lets you change the account's name, your name and organization, your e-mail address and reply address, and whether to check the account when sending and receiving mail.

Change Your Mail Server Information

To change your mail server information, use the controls on the Server page of the Properties dialog box for an HTTP account or the Servers page for a POP3 account or an IMAP account. Figure 4-22 shows the Server page on the left and the Servers page on the right.

For an HTTP account, enter the server URL in the Server URL text box, your login name in the Login Name text box, and your password in the Password text box. To save the password (and reduce your security), select the Remember Password check box.

For a POP3 account or an IMAP account, make sure the My Incoming Mail Server Is a *NNNN* Server text box is showing the appropriate server type. (If not, see the upcoming Note.) Enter the details of the servers in the Incoming Mail text box and the Outgoing Mail text box, as well as your account details in the Account Name text box and the Password text box. Select the Remember Password check box if appropriate. To use Secure Password Authentication (SPA) for logging on, select the Log On Using Secure Password Authentication check box.

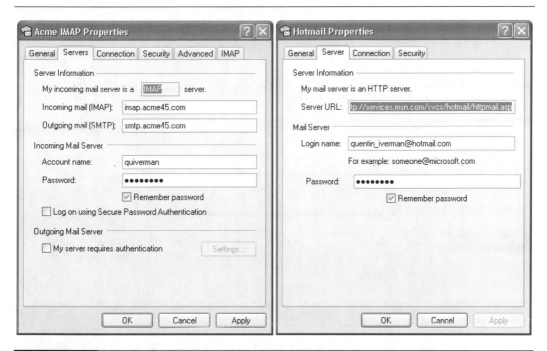

FIGURE 4-22   You can change your mail server information on the Server page of the Properties dialog box for an HTTP account or the Servers page for a POP or IMAP account.

NOTE   *You can't change the server type of an account once you've created it. For example, if your ISP changes from POP3 to IMAP servers, you can't change the server in the mail account from POP3 to IMAP. Instead, you need to create a new account with the new server information (and all the other existing information) and then delete the old account.*

Authenticate with a POP3 or IMAP Server

If your POP3 server or IMAP server requires you to log on (for example, if you're using a mail server other than that of the ISP through which you're connecting to the Internet), select the My Server Requires Authentication check box in the Outgoing Mail Server area of the Servers page of the Properties dialog box for the account. Then click the Settings button to display the Outgoing Mail Server dialog box (see Figure 4-23). Select the Log On Using option button and specify the details in the Account Name text box and the Password text box. Select the Remember Password check box and the Log On Using Secure Password Authentication check box, if appropriate, and then click the OK button.

Specify a Specific Connection for Checking E-mail on This Account

By default, each account uses your regular Internet connection. But you can set a specific connection by selecting the Always Connect to This Account Using check box on the Connection

FIGURE 4-23 Use the Outgoing Mail Server dialog box to specify logon information for an SMTP server that requires you to log on separately from your ISP's logon procedure.

page of the Properties dialog box for the account and choosing the account in the drop-down list (see Figure 4-24).

Specify a Certificate for Digitally Signing Messages

To specify a certificate for digitally signing messages on this account, click the Select button in the Signing Certificate area on the Security page of the Properties dialog box for the connection, shown in Figure 4-25, and use the resulting Select Default Account Digital ID dialog box to choose the certificate to use with the account.

Specify a Certificate for Encrypting Messages and Attachments

To specify a certificate for encrypting messages and attachments sent from this account, click the Select button in the Encrypting Preferences area of the Security page of the Properties dialog box for the connection and use the resulting Select Default Account Digital ID dialog box to choose the certificate to use with the account. If necessary, change the encryption algorithm specified in the Algorithm drop-down list. (Usually, Outlook Express chooses the correct encryption algorithm for the certificate you chose, so you shouldn't need to change this setting once you've specified the certificate.)

Specify Server Port Numbers and Timeouts

If necessary, you can change the ports used by your SMTP server and the POP3 server or IMAP server by using the options in the Server Port Numbers area of the Advanced page of the Properties dialog box for a POP3 account or an IMAP account. The left screen in Figure 4-26 shows the Advanced page for a POP3 account, and the right screen shows the Advanced page for an IMAP account.

Also, if necessary, you can change the server timeout interval by moving the Server Timeouts slider control along its Short/Long axis.

FIGURE 4-24   If you need to use a specific Internet connection for this e-mail account, specify it on the Connection page of the Properties dialog box.

Break Apart Longer Messages

If your POP3 server or IMAP server refuses messages larger than a certain size, you can set Outlook Express to break your large messages (or, more likely, large attachments) into smaller pieces by selecting the Break Apart Messages Larger Than *NN* KB check box in the Sending area of the Advanced page of the Properties dialog box for the account and specifying the appropriate value for the resulting fragments in the text box. For example, if you're sending MP3 or AVI files, you might break them into pieces of 1MB or less in order to keep the mail servers from rejecting them.

Leave a Copy of Messages on the Server (POP3 Only)

For a POP3 server, you can choose to leave a copy of messages you download via Outlook Express on the server by selecting the Leave a Copy of Messages on Server check box in the Delivery area of the Advanced page of the Properties dialog box for the account. If you do so, Outlook Express makes two further options available to you:

- To make the messages expire from the server after a specified number of days, you can select the Remove from Server After *NN* Days check box and specify the number of days in the text box.

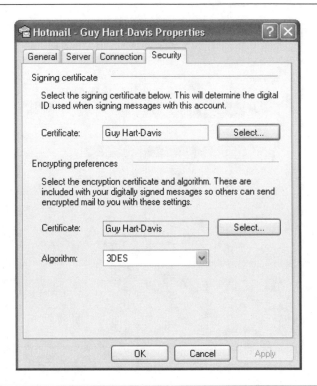

FIGURE 4-25   On the Security page of the Properties dialog box for a connection, specify the certificates for digitally signing messages and encrypting messages and attachments.

■ To make Outlook Express delete the messages from the server when you delete them and then empty your Deleted Items folder, select the Remove from Server When Deleted from "Deleted Items" check box.

Choose IMAP Options

The IMAP page of the Properties dialog box for an IMAP account, shown in Figure 4-27, lets you specify the root folder path, whether to check for new messages in all folders when checking e-mail, and whether to store the Outlook Express folders Sent Items and Drafts on the IMAP server (and, if you do, where to store them).

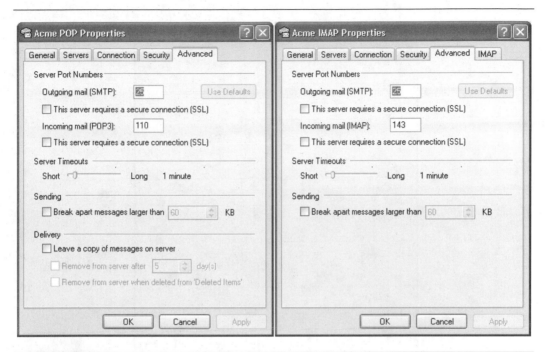

| FIGURE 4-26 | On the Advanced page of the Properties dialog box for a POP3 account (left) or an IMAP account (right), adjust the server port numbers and specify whether to use an SSL connection. |

Send and Receive E-mail

This section runs you through the basics of sending and receiving e-mail with Outlook Express. In order to keep you at least moderately challenged and the book portable, this section skips over the easiest maneuvers so as to spend time on the less intuitive actions you may want to take with e-mail. For example, formatting an e-mail message is about as difficult as eating toast, whereas applying a digital signature to a message has some complexities.

Create a Message

You can create an outgoing message by starting a new message from scratch, forwarding a message you've received (or previously sent), or replying to a message you've received.

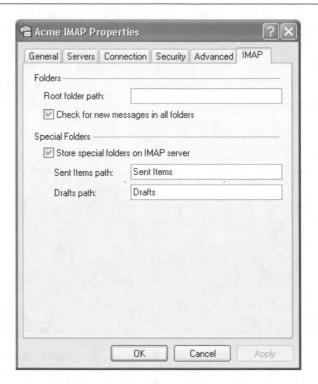

FIGURE 4-27   Choose paths for folders and special folders on the IMAP page of the Properties
dialog box for an IMAP account.

Create a New Message

Outlook Express offers several ways to create a new message:

- To create a blank message, click the Create Mail button, press CTRL-N, or choose File |
  New | Mail Message. The following illustration shows a new message in the New Message
  window, with the signature added by default.

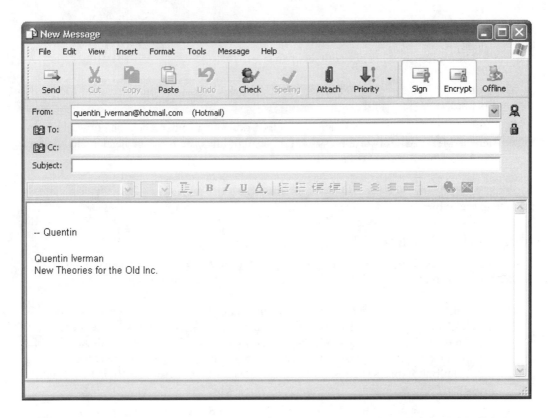

■ To create a new message addressed to a contact in your Address Book, right-click the contact's entry in the Contacts pane and choose Send E-mail from the context menu.

CAUTION   *You can also create a new message addressed to a contact by double-clicking the contact's entry in the Contacts pane—but only if the contact isn't a Messeger contact who's currently online. If the contact is a Messenger conact and is currently online, double-clicking their entry starts an instant message to them instead.*

■ In Address Book, select the contact, click the Action button, and choose Send Mail from the resulting menu. Alternatively, right-click the contact and choose Action | Send Mail from the context menu.

Forward a Message

You can forward a message in either of these ways:

- With the message open in a message window, click the Forward button, choose Message | Forward, or press CTRL-F.

- With the message header selected in the Inbox or another folder, click the Forward button, choose Message | Forward, press CTRL-F, or right-click the message header and choose Forward from the context menu.

When you forward a message, Outlook Express enters the subject line from the original message in the Subject text box, preceding it with "Fw:."

Address the Message

If you've created a new message that isn't to a contact, or if you've forwarded an existing message, you'll need to address it. As you'd expect, there are various ways to do so:

- Type the address of the recipient or recipients in the To text box and the address of any "Cc" recipients in the Cc text box. If you chose to allow Outlook Express to use its AutoComplete feature (by selecting the Automatically Complete E-mail Addresses When Composing check box in the Sending area of the Send page of the Options dialog box), Outlook Express suggests matching entries from your Address Book as you type. Press ENTER to accept the suggestion and double-check that it's the right address.

- Click the To: button or the Cc: button to display the Select Recipients dialog box (see Figure 4-28). Select the Address Book category to use in the drop-down list (for example, Main Identity's Contacts or Shared Contacts). Then select recipients in the list box and use the To button, the Cc button, or the Bcc button to copy the recipient to the appropriate box. Click the OK button when you've finished. (To remove a recipient from a box, select their entry and press DELETE, or right-click their entry and choose Remove from the context menu.)

NOTE   *By default, the New Message window doesn't display the Bcc text box until you add a Bcc recipient by using the Select Recipients dialog box, as described in this section. But you can toggle the Bcc text box on and off by choosing View | All Headers.*

Create a Reply

You can create a reply to a message in any of these ways:

- To reply to the sender of a message open in a message window, click the Reply button, choose Message | Reply to Sender, or press CTRL-R.

- To reply to the sender *and* all other recipients of a message open in a message window, click the Reply All button, choose Message | Reply to All, or press CTRL-SHIFT-R.

- To reply to the sender of a message, select its header in the Inbox or another folder, click the Reply button, choose Message | Reply to Sender, press CTRL-R, or right-click the message header and choose Reply to Sender from the context menu.

- To reply to the sender and all other recipients of a message, select its header in the Inbox or another folder, click the Reply All button, choose Message | Reply to All, press CTRL-SHIFT-R, or right-click the message header and choose Reply to All from the context menu.

When you create a reply, Outlook Express enters the subject line from the original message in the Subject text box, preceding it with "Re:".

Enter the Subject

For a new message, enter the subject in the Subject text box. Because the recipient will likely use the subject line to triage their e-mail, try to make the subject line as informative but concise as possible.

Enter the Body Text

Now you need to enter the body text for the message. If you're sending an HTML message, use the controls on the Formatting toolbar to apply any formatting you want the message to include.

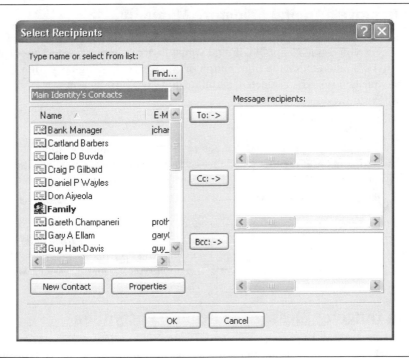

FIGURE 4-28   The Select Recipients dialog box lets you quickly set up your To, Cc, and Bcc recipients for a message.

You can switch a message from plain text to HTML by choosing Format | HTML. Likewise, you can switch a message from HTML to plain text by choosing Format | Plain Text. When you do so, Outlook Express displays an eponymous message box warning you that by switching to plain text, you'll lose any formatting in the message. Choose the OK button if you want to proceed or the Cancel button if you don't.

Attach Any Attachments

Next, attach any files you want to send with the message. Click the Attach button on the toolbar or choose Insert | File Attachment to display the Insert Attachment dialog box. Then select the file and click the Attach button.

You can start a new message with an attachment by right-clicking the file in an Explorer window (or the Desktop) and choosing Send To | Mail Recipient from the context menu. (If you prefer not to right-click, select the file and click the E-mail This File link in the File and Folder Tasks list.) XP causes Outlook Express to start a new message with the file attached.

> **CAUTION** *If you're using Hotmail, remember there's a limit of 1MB per message. Because wrapping up an attachment for transmission via e-mail entails some overhead, and because the message itself takes some space, any attachments you send need to be 900KB or less. If the file is uncompressed, you may be able to compress it (for example, by using XP's File | Send To | Compressed Folder command) to reduce its size before transmitting it.*

Apply or Remove a Digital Signature Manually

Earlier in this chapter, I discussed how to set the option to apply a digital signature to all the outgoing messages you send. To apply a digital signature to a message or to remove a digital signature due to be applied, click the Sign button or choose Tools | Digitally Sign. (The Sign button appears "pushed in" when selected, and the Digitally Sign item on the Tools menu has a check mark next to it.)

When you digitally sign a message, XP displays the Signing Data with Your Private Exchange Key dialog box (see Figure 4-29).

In most cases, it should be pretty clear that you're the person causing the application to request access to a protected item (your digital certificate). But if you want to check which application is making the request, click the Details button. XP displays a second Signing Data with Your Private Exchange Key dialog box (see Figure 4-30).

> **NOTE** *You might expect Outlook Express to make the Sign button and the Digitally Sign command unavailable if you don't have a digital certificate—but it doesn't. Instead, it lets you specify that you want to sign the message and then pulls you up with the message "You cannot send digitally signed messages because you do not have a digital ID for this account" when you try to send the message.*

Encrypt an Outgoing Message or Remove Encryption

If you haven't set Outlook Express to encrypt all outgoing messages, you can encrypt any message by clicking the Encrypt button on the Message window toolbar or choosing Tools |

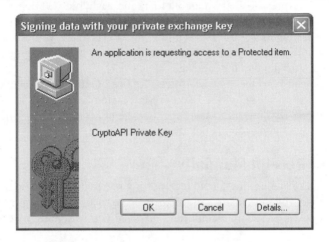

FIGURE 4-29   XP displays the Signing Data with Your Private Exchange Key dialog box when you digitally sign an outgoing message.

Encrypt. Similarly, if you *have* set Outlook Express to encrypt all outgoing messages, you can remove encryption from an unsent message by clicking the Encrypt button or choosing Tools | Encrypt.

FIGURE 4-30   The second Signing Data with Your Private Exchange Key dialog box identifies the application that's requesting access to a protected item.

If you tell Outlook Express to encrypt an outgoing message, but you don't have a digital certificate with which to encrypt the copy that Outlook Express keeps for you, Outlook Express displays a Security Warning dialog box, shown in Figure 4-31, to tell you that you won't be able to read the copy in your Sent Items folder. Click the Yes button to send the message anyway, or click the No button to stop sending the message.

If Outlook Express can't find the digital certificate for one or more of the recipients of a message you're encrypting, it displays the Outlook Express Mail dialog box, shown in Figure 4-32, to warn you of the problem. If you want to send the message unencrypted, click the Don't Encrypt button. To cancel sending the message, click the Cancel button.

Request a Read Receipt Manually

You can toggle on and off requesting a read receipt for a message by choosing Tools | Request Read Receipt. Likewise, if you're using a digital certificate to sign outgoing messages, you can toggle on and off requesting a secure receipt for a message you're signing by choosing Tools | Request Secure Receipt.

Add a Business Card to a Message

Once you've specified a business card in the Business Cards area of the Compose page of the Options dialog box, you can add a business card to a message manually by choosing Insert | My Business Card.

You can remove a business card that has been added to a message (automatically or manually) by choosing Insert | My Business Card again or by clicking the business card icon (to the right of the Cc box) and choosing Delete from the resulting menu.

Send the Message

To send the message you've created immediately, click the Send button, press ALT-S (to click the Send button by using the keyboard), or choose File | Send Message. If you've set Outlook Express to send messages immediately (by selecting the Send Messages Immediately check box in the Sending area on the Send page of the Options dialog box), the message will go immediately; if not, it'll be placed in the Outbox until the next scheduled check for mail or the next time you check for mail manually on this account.

FIGURE 4-31   You'll see this Security Warning dialog box if you try to encrypt a message you're sending without having a digital certificate yourself.

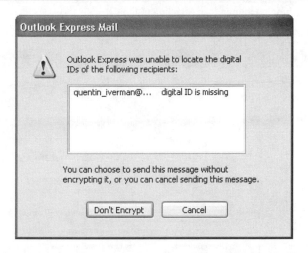

FIGURE 4-32   If Outlook Express can't find the digital certificate for a recipient of a message you've asked to encrypt, it displays the Outlook Express Mail dialog box to let you choose between sending the message unencrypted and not sending it.

If you have configured Outlook Express to send messages immediately, you can cause this message to be placed in the Outbox instead of sent immediately by choosing File | Send Later.

Read E-mail

Reading e-mail in Outlook Express is mostly pretty straightforward—you display or open the message you're interested in and then let your eyeballs do the walking. After you've gotten the hang of the assorted icons that pepper the Inbox, most of the excitement centers around messages with unusual features, such as encryption, digital signatures, and attachments.

Figure 4-33 shows the Inbox, with labels indicating the icons you'll see most often: priority icons, attachment icons, flag icons, and icons for read messages and unread messages.

As you can see if you peer at the figure, Outlook Express displays an unread-message icon (a closed envelope) for each unread message and a read-message icon (an open envelope) for each read message. (You can change a message's read status by right-clicking its header and choosing Mark As Read or Mark As Unread from the context menu.) If the message has an attachment, a paperclip icon appears in the Attachments column. And if the sender has marked the message as high priority, an exclamation point appears in the Priority column.

In Outlook Express as in real life, a *flag* is a marker calling for attention. You can apply a flag to a message by clicking in the Flag column beside the message header (or choose Message | Flag Message). Click again (or choose Message | Flag Message again) to remove a flag.

You can also drag a message from one folder to another. For example, you can drag a message from your Hotmail Inbox to your Local Folders Inbox.

You can delete a message by selecting its header and clicking the Delete button on the toolbar or by clicking the Delete button on the toolbar in a message window. In the fine Apple/Microsoft

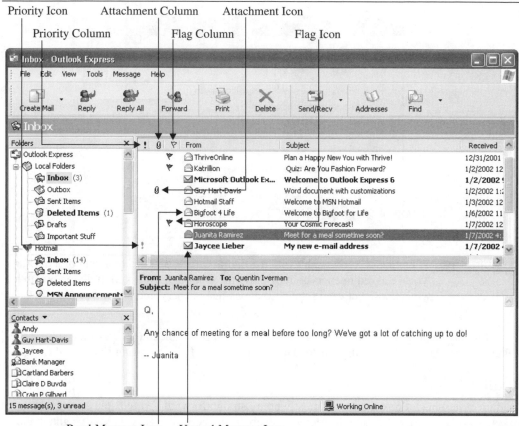

FIGURE 4-33 The Inbox

tradition, "deleting" a message doesn't actually get rid of it right away—it just places the message in the Deleted Items folder, which is the Outlook Express equivalent of the Recycle Bin. As you saw earlier in this chapter, you can configure Outlook Express to empty the Deleted Items folder automatically at the end of a session (by selecting the Empty Messages from the "Deleted Items" Folder on Exit option in the Cleaning Up Messages area of the Maintenance page of the Options dialog box). You can also empty the Deleted Items folder by right-clicking it and choosing Empty "Deleted Items" Folder from the context menu or by selecting it and choosing Edit | Empty "Deleted Items" Folder.

You can open a message in its own window by double-clicking its header. The message window, of which an example is shown in Figure 4-34, has easy-to-use controls, including Previous and Next buttons for navigating from message to message without closing the message window.

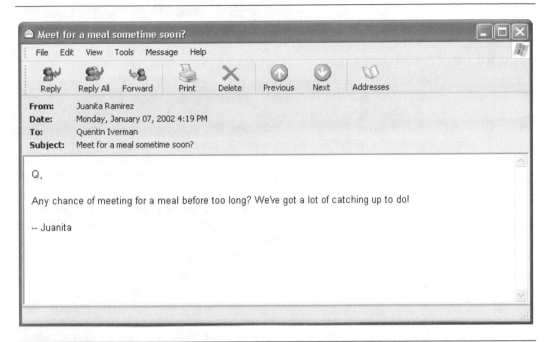

| FIGURE 4-34 | You can open a message in its own window to display more of it or to view multiple messages at the same time. |

Receive an Attachment

Outlook Express makes receiving an attachment straightforward. The Inbox displays an attachment icon in the message header for a message that has an attachment, so you can see at a glance which messages have attachments.

If you're working in the Preview pane, the Preview pane header (if you have it displayed) contains an Attachment button (again, bearing the paperclip). Click the Attachment button to display a menu of actions you can take with the attachment. Usually, you'll want to issue the Save Attachments command, specify a location in the resulting Save Attachments dialog box, and click the Save button. If you don't have the Preview pane header displayed, you can save the attachment by choosing File | Save Attachments.

The message window for a message with an attachment includes the Attach text box, which appears below the Subject line and contains details of the attachment. To save the attachment, choose File | Save Attachments.

Grant a Read Receipt

When you open a message on which the sender has requested a read receipt, Outlook Express checks your setting for returning read receipts. If you've chosen the Notify Me for Each Read Receipt Request option button (on the Receipts page of the Options dialog box), Outlook Express displays a message box asking whether you want to return the receipt. Choose the Yes button or the No button, as appropriate.

Open an Encrypted Message

When you tell Outlook Express to decrypt an encrypted message, XP displays the Using Your Private Exchange Key to Decrypt dialog box, shown in Figure 4-35.

If you want to see which program is requesting access to a protected item, click the Details button. XP displays another Using Your Private Exchange Key to Decrypt dialog box, of which Figure 4-36 shows an example, identifying the program. In this case, we know that the program is Outlook Express, so there's not much point in displaying this dialog box. But if you see the Using Your Private Exchange Key to Decrypt dialog box unexpectedly, you may want to know which program is responsible.

The first time you open a signed or encrypted message in the Preview pane, Outlook Express displays a Security Help message about digitally signed and encrypted messages. To prevent Outlook Express from displaying this message again, select the Don't Show Me This Help Screen Again check box and click the Continue button. Outlook Express then displays the decrypted message.

CAUTION
If you choose the Cancel button in the Using Your Private Exchange Key to Decrypt dialog box when trying to decrypt an encrypted message, Outlook Express displays the message "Outlook Express encountered an unexpected problem while displaying this message. Check your computer for low memory or low disk space and try again." The problem is, of course, that you prevented Outlook Express from decrypting the message, not that you're low on memory or disk space—so ignore this red herring, however juicy it may seem.

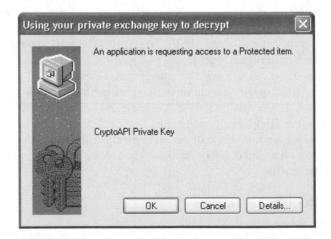

FIGURE 4-35 XP displays the Using Your Private Exchange Key to Decrypt dialog box when Outlook Express starts to decrypt an encrypted message.

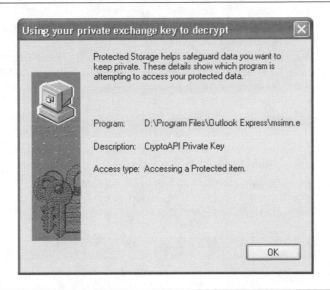

| **FIGURE 4-36** | Clicking the Details button in the first Using Your Private Key to Decrypt dialog box displays a second Using Your Private Key to Decrypt dialog box with details of the program involved. |

Work Offline with Outlook Express

One of the most appealing features of Outlook Express is that you can use it to work offline if you don't have a persistent Internet connection.

To work offline, double-click the Working Online indicator in the status bar or choose File | Work Offline. Double-click the resulting Working Offline indicator in the status bar or choose File | Work Online to start working online again.

> **NOTE** *If you have a dial-up Internet connection, Outlook Express offers to hang it up when you go offline.*

Create Rules to Protect Your POP3 Mailbox from Spam

As you saw earlier in this chapter, Hotmail provides a Junk Mail Filter feature and custom filters that you can use to reduce the amount of spam that lands in your Hotmail account. You can use the Junk Mail Filter whether you're using Hotmail's Web interface or Outlook Express to access your Hotmail account. (In either case, you need to administer the Junk Mail Filter through Hotmail's Web interface.)

Most POP3 mail providers don't give you filtering capabilities like Hotmail's, so you need to apply filtering at the e-mail client instead. If you're using Outlook Express to access your POP3 account, you can use the sophisticated filtering features we'll examine in this section. You can create any number of filters to catch mail that matches criteria you specify. A filter can take any of a variety of actions on a message: move it or copy it to a folder; delete it; forward it; flag it; highlight it; mark it as read, watched, or ignored; send an automatic reply; not download it from the mail server; or delete it from the server.

The following list describes the generic steps for creating a rule for filtering incoming messages. Because the procedure is a little involved (though easy enough to follow once you've tried it), I've provided three specific examples in the following section.

1. From the main Outlook Express window, choose Tools | Message Rules | Mail. If you haven't created any mail rules yet, Outlook Express displays the New Mail Rule dialog box directly; if you have created a mail rule, Outlook Express displays the Mail Rules page of the Message Rules dialog box, from which you can click the New button to display the New Mail Rule dialog box. The illustration here shows the New Mail Rule dialog box as you'll see it when you first display it. (In the next section, I'll show you how it looks as you add information to it.)

2. Specify the conditions for the rule in the Select the Conditions for Your Rule list box by selecting one or more of the check boxes. Outlook Express adds these conditions to the Rule Description list box. You can filter by any of the following, or you can set a filter for all messages:

   ■ By specific people being in the From line, the To line, the Cc line, or either the To line or the Cc line

- By specific words being in the Subject line or the message body
- By the message being high priority
- By the message being bigger than a certain size
- By the message having an attachment
- By the message being sent to a specified e-mail account of yours
- By the message being secure

3. Specify the action for the rule in the Select the Actions for Your Rule list box. Outlook Express adds the actions to the Rule Description list box.

4. Click each link in the Rule Description list box in turn and choose appropriate values for it in the resulting dialog box and any associated dialog boxes. (Yes, I know that's a bit vague. I'll show you specifics on this step in the upcoming examples.) Check the And links and Or links and change them as necessary.

5. Enter the name for the rule in the Name of the Rule text box.

6. Click the OK button. Outlook Express creates the rule and displays it on the Mail Rules page of the Message Rules dialog box.

Examples of Creating a Mail Rule

The description in the previous section was necessarily a little generic, so this section provides three specific examples of creating mail rules. All three examples are of types of rules widely used in the real world. Although you won't necessarily want to implement any example exactly on your mail accounts, the three together illustrate how to use the controls on the Mail Rules page of the Message Rules dialog box to construct rules that meet your needs.

To avoid boring you to death—I mean, *for concision*—each of these examples assumes you've read the previous section enough to be familiar with the basic steps of the process of creating a rule to filter incoming mail messages.

The first example shows a full suite of dialog boxes to illustrate the process. The second and third examples show only additional screens where they'll be helpful.

Create a Mail Rule to Move Messages from Specific People to a Particular Folder

This example shows you how to create a mail rule that moves incoming messages with specific From addresses (names or e-mail addresses) to a particular folder. For example, you might create a few rules like this to move all your work-related messages to a particular folder or to get messages from different clients sorted into folders for the projects for those clients.

Here we go:

1. In the Select the Conditions for Your Rule list box, select the Where the From Line Contains People check box. Outlook Express adds this condition to the Rule Description list box.

2. In the Select the Actions for Your Rule list box, select the Move It to the Specified Folder check box. Again, Outlook Express adds this information to the Rule Description list box. The illustration here shows the New Mail Rule dialog box with the rule as it stands.

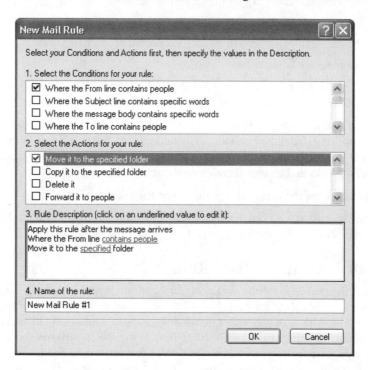

3. In the Rule Description list box, click the "contains people" link to display the Select People dialog box, shown here with two people added already and a third underway.

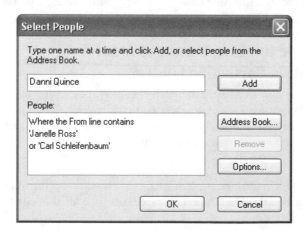

4. Populate the People list box by typing each name or e-mail address into the text box and clicking the Add button or by clicking the Address Book button and selecting people from the Address Book.

5. If necessary, click the Options button to display the Rule Condition Options dialog box (shown here). As you'd imagine, the contents of this dialog box vary depending on the details of the rule you're constructing. In this case, you can choose for the rule to apply to the message containing the people listed (the default) or not containing them. You can also choose between the message matching any of the people (the default) and matching all the people. For the rule we're constructing, we'll go with both default settings so that the rule applies to any of the people listed.

> **Rule Condition Options**
>
> You can further customize this condition by setting the options below.
>
> Apply rule if:
> 1. ⦿ Message contains the people below
>   ◯ Message does not contain the people below
> 2. ◯ Message matches all of the people below
>   ⦿ Message matches any one of the people below
>
> Rule Condition:
>
> Where the From line contains
> 'Janelle Ross'
> or 'Carl Schleifenbaum'
> or 'Danni Quince'
>
> [OK]   [Cancel]

6. Click the OK button to close the Select People dialog box. Outlook Express adds the people specified to the Rule Description list box in the New Mail Rule dialog box. The illustration here shows the Rule Description list box with the updated rule.

> 3. Rule Description (click on an underlined value to edit it):
>
> Apply this rule after the message arrives
> Where the From line contains 'Janelle Ross' or 'Carl Schleifenbaum' or 'Danni Quince' or 'nmd@trinitrotolerance.com'
> Move it to the specified folder

7. In the Rule Description list box, click the "specified" link (in the "Move it to the specified folder" line) to display a Move dialog box (which is a renamed Browse for Folder dialog box).

8. Select the folder to which you want to move the messages (if necessary, use the New Folder button to create a new folder), and then click the OK button. Outlook Express adds the folder's name to the Rule Description list box (shown here with the final rule).

> 3. Rule Description (click on an underlined value to edit it):
>
> Apply this rule after the message arrives
> Where the From line contains 'Janelle Ross' or 'Carl Schleifenbaum' or 'Danni Quince' or 'nmd@trinitrotolerance.com'
> Move it to the Important Stuff folder

9. Enter the name for the rule in the Name of the Rule text box.

10. Click the OK button. Outlook Express closes the New Mail Rule dialog box and adds the rule to the list on the Mail Rules page of the Message Rules dialog box. (I'll discuss what happens next in "Apply Your Mail Rules," a little later in the chapter.)

Quickly Create a Mail Rule to Delete Messages from Someone Who's Spamming You

The easiest way to create a new rule is from an existing message from the person you want to block. Open a message from the irritant in its own message window (yes, you have to look at it, but only for a moment), and choose Message | Create Rule from Message to have Outlook Express start a rule based on information in the message. By default, Outlook Express selects the Where the From Line Contains People text box and adds the person's address to the Rule Description text box.

Select the Delete It check box in the Select the Actions for Your Rule list box, enter a name in the Name of the Rule text box, and click the button. The rule is now ready.

Create a Mail Rule to Delete Assorted Messages Containing Specific Text

This example shows you how to create a rule to delete messages containing specific words that you've deemed offensive. These words don't have to be George Carlin's seven dirty words you can't say on television—just any that you've found indicate junk mail heading in your direction.

Here are the steps to take:

1. In the Select the Conditions for Your Rule list box, select the Where the Subject Line Contains Specific Words check box and the Where the Message Body Contains Specific Words check box. Outlook Express enters those items in the Rule Description text box and applies an And condition between them, meaning both conditions must be met for the rule to apply.

2. Click the And link to display the And/Or dialog box (shown here).

3. Select the Messages Match Any One of the Criteria option button and then click the OK button. Outlook Express closes the And/Or dialog box and changes the condition to an Or.

4. In the Select the Actions for Your Rule list box, select the Delete It check box.

5. Click the first Contains Specified Words link and use the resulting Type Specific Words dialog box, shown here, to specify the offending words or a phrase for the Subject line.

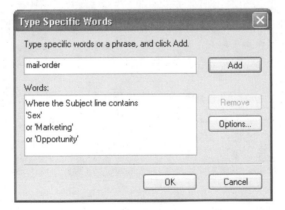

6. Once you've typed two words or a phrase, Outlook Express makes available the Options button. You can click this button to display the Rule Condition Options dialog box and change the conditions under which the rule should apply.

7. Click the second Contains Specified Words link and use the Type Specific Words dialog box to specify the offending words or a phrase for the message box.

8. Enter the name for the rule in the Name of the Rule text box.

9. Click the OK button. Outlook Express closes the New Mail Rule dialog box and adds the rule to the list on the Mail Rules page of the Message Rules dialog box.

Arrange Your Mail Rules into Order

Once you've created your mail rules, use the Move Up button and Move Down button on the Mail Rules page of the Message Rules dialog box to arrange the rules into the order in which you want them to apply.

Apply Your Mail Rules

To apply your mail rules, take the following steps:

1. Choose Tools | Message Rules | Mail to display the Mail Rules page of the Message Rules dialog box (shown here).

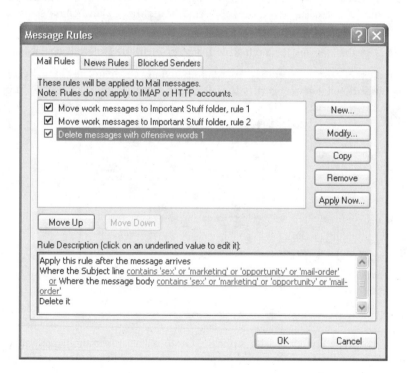

2. Click the Apply Now button. Outlook Express displays the Apply Mail Rules Now dialog box (shown here).

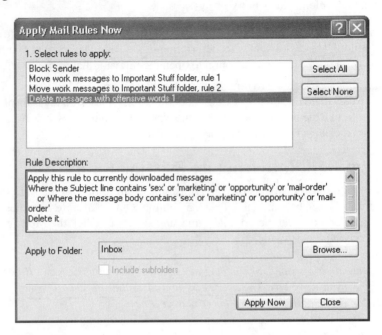

3. In the Select Rules to Apply list box, choose the rules you want to apply. (Use the Select All button to select all the rules.)

4. Check the folder selected in the Apply to Folder text box. If necessary, use the Browse button and the resulting Apply to Folder dialog box to change the folder.

5. If applicable, select or clear the Include Subfolders check box to include or exclude subfolders of the folder you chose.

6. Click the Apply Now button. Outlook Express applies the rules to the folder or folders and then displays a message box telling you that it has done so. When you dismiss this message box, Outlook Express returns you to the Apply Mail Rules Now dialog box.

7. Apply further rules to further folders, as necessary, and then close the Apply Mail Rules Now dialog box and the Message Rules dialog box.

Modify a Mail Rule

You can modify a mail rule in either of two ways:

■ To tweak the rule a bit, select it on the Mail Rules page of the Message Rules dialog box so that Outlook Express displays its description in the Rule Description text box. Then click one of the links in the description to open the relevant dialog box.

■ To make bigger changes or to rename the rule, select it on the Mail Rules page of the Message Rules dialog box and click the Modify button. Outlook Express displays the rule in the Edit Mail Rule dialog box, which is the New Mail Rule dialog box by another name. You can then change the rule to your heart's content.

Derive a New Mail Rule from an Existing Rule

To derive a new mail rule from an existing rule, select the existing rule on the Mail Rules page of the Message Rules dialog box and click the Copy button. Outlook Express creates a copy of the rule, naming it "Copy of" and the original name, and selects it. Click the Modify button and change the rule to create the new rule.

TIP
You can create news rules for filtering newsgroups by using the News Rules page of the Message Rules dialog box. The process is similar to that for creating mail rules, but it's outside the scope of this book, so I don't cover it here.

Maintain a Blocked Senders List

Like Hotmail (and many e-mail programs), Outlook Express lets you maintain a list of e-mail addresses from which you don't want to receive e-mail. Outlook Express calls this list the *Blocked Senders list.*

NOTE
The Blocked Senders list applies only to POP3 accounts. You can't use the Blocked Senders list with an HTTP account (for example, your Hotmail account) or an IMAP account. So to block senders of messages to your Hotmail account, you need to use Hotmail's blocking features (discussed in the section "Block a Sender," earlier in this chapter).

The easiest way to add a sender to the Blocked Senders list is by choosing Message | Block Sender from a message window containing a message from the offending sender. Outlook Express displays a dialog box telling you that the sender has been added to your Blocked Senders list and asking whether you want it to remove all messages from the sender from the current folder.

You can also add a sender to your Blocked Senders list by using the Blocked Senders page of the Message Rules dialog box, shown in Figure 4-37, which you display by choosing Tools | Message Rules | Blocked Senders List. Here are some tasks you can perform from this dialog box:

■ To create a new entry, click the Add button and use the resulting Add Sender dialog box to specify the details.

■ To change the e-mail address or domain name that's blocked for an existing entry, select it, click the Modify button, and work in the resulting Edit Sender dialog box.

■ To change the categories for which a sender is blocked (Mail, News, or Both), use the check boxes on the Blocked Senders page or the option buttons in the Edit Sender dialog box.

■ To remove a blocked sender from the list, select their entry in the list box and click the Remove button. Outlook Express confirms the removal in case you've had a rush of blood to the head.

Perform a Local File Clean Up

If you use Outlook Express actively, especially if you read a lot of newsgroups, the number of messages on your hard disk is likely to increase dramatically and to consume ever more hard disk space. Hard disks have grown so much in capacity in the last few years that if you have a modern computer, you may well have storage to burn—but even so, it's a good idea to reduce the amount of space that messages are taking up on your hard drive so that you can more easily back it up.

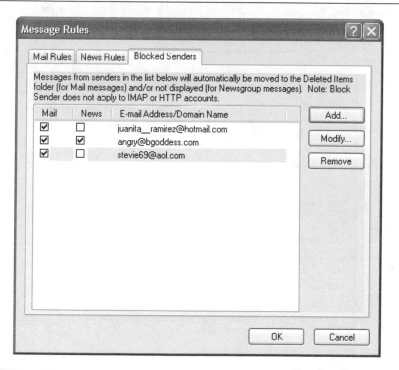

FIGURE 4-37   Use the Blocked Senders page of the Message Rules dialog box to add offenders to, edit offenders on, and remove forgiven transgressors from your Blocked Senders list.

To slim down the footprint of Outlook Express, click the Clean Up Now button on the Maintenance page of the Options dialog box (Tools | Options) to display the Local File Clean Up dialog box (see Figure 4-38).

Check the account specified in the Local File(s) For text box. If necessary, click the Browse button and use the resulting dialog box to select the right account. (Selecting the Outlook Express account compresses all the accounts configured for Outlook Express.) The Total Size of File(s) readout and the Wasted Space readout show you the account's footprint and the amount of wasted space you can reclaim by compacting the account.

Now choose the action you want to take. These are your options:

■ To compress the files but retain all the information, click the Compact button.

■ To remove message bodies but keep the headers, click the Remove Messages button. You might want to do this for a news account in which you can retrieve message bodies from the server for a while, but it's usually not a good idea for a mail account on which you're downloading messages (as opposed to leaving copies on the server).

■ To remove message bodies and their headers, click the Delete button.

■ To remove message bodies and their headers and to reset the folder so that it'll download the message headers again, click the Reset button. You won't usually want to do this unless your folder for an account has gotten trashed.

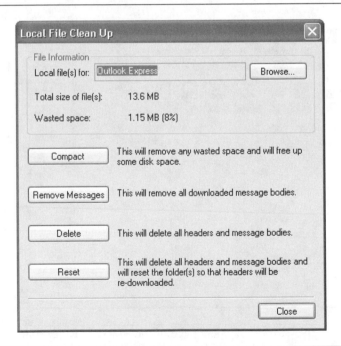

FIGURE 4-38   Use the options in the Local File Clean Up dialog box to reduce the amount of space that messages in Outlook Express are taking up on your hard drive.

When you've finished compacting or deleting, click the Close button to close the Local File Clean Up dialog box.

Other Free E-mail Services

If you don't like the thought of Microsoft knowing (through .NET Passport) the timings of your logons, logoffs, and e-mail usage, you may prefer to use another Web-based e-mail service instead of Hotmail or MSN. This section discusses several of the biggest and most appealing services: Yahoo! Mail, Hushmail, Netscape Mail, and Bigfoot. As you'll see, the features they offer are quite varied.

The advantage of non-Microsoft Web-based e-mail services is, by definition, that Microsoft doesn't run them, and therefore can't track your actions so easily. The disadvantage is that the non-Microsoft services offer less integration with XP and with Outlook Express than do the Microsoft services.

Yahoo! Mail

If you've been on the Web, you're probably familiar with the Yahoo! site (www.yahoo.com). Combined with its many other offerings (from the search engine to shopping), Yahoo! offers both free and paid e-mail services. To sign up for Yahoo! Mail, steer your browser to mail.yahoo.com and follow the link to sign up for an account.

At this writing, Yahoo! Mail offers three grades of service, which they term *editions*: Free Edition (an address at yahoo.com, 4MB of storage space, spam protection, and virus protection), Custom Edition ($35 per year for a personalized e-mail address with up to five accounts on top of what the Free Edition offers), and Business Edition ($9.95 per month for a domain address with advertisement-free messages and an advertisement-free interface).

If you want an account that doesn't require verifiable identity information, you need to go for the Free Edition. As with Hotmail, once Yahoo! has got you, it goes for the "upsell," trying to persuade you to upgrade to a larger amount of space in order to, let's say, cement the relationship with a formal introduction involving a credit card.

If you choose to pay for your Yahoo! Mail account, the signup procedure leads you through the process of signing up for a Yahoo! Wallet, which contains the details of the credit card with which you pay for your Yahoo! Mail account. This Yahoo! Wallet is then used for any Yahoo!-based shopping you succumb to.

If you sign up for the Yahoo! Delivers feature (which entails being bombarded with special offers, promotions, and discount offers for the interests you claim to have), you can use a POP3 client such as Outlook Express, Eudora, or Netscape to manage your mail. If you can't face using Yahoo! Delivers, you're stuck with Yahoo!'s Web-based interface, which is functional but suffers from the generic defects of the species (you need to be online to use it, and the interface is clumsy compared to those of local clients).

Yahoo! also offers mail forwarding from your Yahoo! Mail account to another e-mail account—but, again, only if you're signed up for Yahoo! Delivers. Cute.

Mail sent from free Yahoo! Mail accounts comes with an advertisement tacked onto it.

Hushmail

Hushmail.com (www.hushmail.com) offers you the ability to send secure Web-based e-mail to other Hushmail users and nonsecure e-mail to other e-mail addresses. Hushmail offers both a free service and a slew of paid services designed for security-conscious users and for businesses that have decided to use Web-based e-mail solutions.

A free Hushmail account gives you 2MB of storage space—as with Hotmail, an amount that's pretty much designed to encourage you to upgrade to a paid account. As usual, you need to provide verifiable billing information for a paid account. Hushmail's current offering is a Hushmail Premium account, which costs you $19.99 for setup and then $2.49 a month thereafter. A Premium account provides 32MB of space, giving you the ability to send and receive large attachments (including, say, MP3 files of average size but only the tiniest of AVI files), as well as keep a good number of messages. A Premium account also buys you freedom from the banner ads that inflict themselves on free accounts.

To keep a free account active, you need to access it at least once every three weeks— otherwise, it gets deleted. Hushmail Premium accounts don't get deleted as long as the money keeps rolling in.

Hushmail uses OpenPGP (the freeware version of the Pretty Good Privacy program, PGP) to encrypt messages. As I mentioned, you can encrypt messages only to other Hushmail users— users with regular e-mail accounts get unencrypted messages.

That's not much of a limitation, but Hushmail does have several limitations worth mentioning that result directly from its encryption.

- First, you have to install the Hush Encryption Engine and your key pair on your computer in order to use Hushmail. If you use just one computer to access your account, that's not a big deal. If you want to be able to access your account from other computers, installing the Encryption Engine and key pair may get tedious.

- Second, you can access Hushmail only through its Web interface. (Hushmail offers a secure client for Outlook but not for Outlook Express.) This puts Hushmail at a disadvantage compared to some of its competitors. This limitation is somewhat offset by Hushmail's ability to page you at another e-mail address when mail arrives—either with the sender's e-mail address or (for security) without.

- Third, Hushmail is noticeably slower to use over a non-broadband connection than most of the other Web-based e-mail services.

If you need security for your Web-based e-mail, Hushmail's limitations pale into insignificance compared with its capabilities. If you need security for only some of the messages you send, you may choose to use Hushmail only for those messages and use a regular account with a local e-mail client for your nonsecure correspondence.

NOTE   *Besides offering secure e-mail, Hushmail can automatically generate a username for you, thus helping preserve your anonymity.*

Netscape Mail

Netscape Mail (www.netscape.com) offers free and paid accounts. A free account gives you 5MB—substantially more than a free Hotmail account. At this writing, Netscape Mail is also more patient about abandonment than Hotmail, requiring you to log in only once every 120 days to prevent Netscape from wiping out your mail. So you can take that three-month tour of the Peruvian Andes without worrying that your Netscape Mail account will have been obliterated by the time you find an Internet café in Lima.

A free e-mail account requires your first name, last name, ZIP code, country, and age range. If you're feeling expansive, you can supply further information as well, but I don't recommend doing so. If you don't want to receive special offers and product information, be sure to clear any preselected check boxes lurking around the nether regions of the registration form before you submit it.

Netscape Mail is plain text only, and has a clumsy but effective interface. Netscape Mail's preferences include letting you create and apply a single signature for all your messages.

Messages sent from free Netscape Mail accounts come with not one but multiple advertisements at the end.

Access Netscape Mail Using Internet Explorer

If you're using Internet Explorer to access Netscape mail and you've set a Medium High or higher level of security for the Internet Zone, you may find the Netscape login page rejects your valid username and password and simply redisplays the login page.

If this happens, you'll need either to reduce your security level to Medium or lower (on the Privacy page of the Internet Options dialog box in Internet Explorer) or to manually allow cookies for the login server before the login procedure will run.

To allow cookies for the login server, take the following steps:

1. With the Netscape login page displayed, select the URL in the Address Bar and copy it (for example, press CTRL-C).

2. Choose Tools | Internet Options to display the Internet Options dialog box.

3. Click the Edit button in the Web Sites group box on the Privacy page to display the Per Site Privacy Actions dialog box.

4. Paste the URL of the Netscape login page into the Address of Web Site text box (for example, press CTRL-V).

5. Click the Allow button to add the URL to the Managed Web Sites list box.

6. Click the OK button to close the Per Site Privacy Actions dialog box.

7. Click the OK button to close the Internet Options dialog box.

When you've done that, try logging into the server again.

Bigfoot

Somewhat different from the other three services just discussed, but worth knowing about, is Bigfoot (www.bigfoot.com). Bigfoot is a forwarding service that provides what it calls a Bigfoot for Life address and mail-filtering and management tools. You can use a Bigfoot address to forward e-mail to any other e-mail address, including Hotmail or other Web-based e-mail accounts.

The advantage of Bigfoot is that you can keep the same Bigfoot address even if your other e-mail accounts change. For example, if you change ISP, you'll need to change any e-mail address at that ISP; likewise, if you move from one company to another. But your Bigfoot address can remain the same, and you can quickly configure it to forward messages to the new account. (If you have your own domain name, you're essentially doing the same thing on a grander scale and with more complex administration.)

Bigfoot offers three grades of account: Premium, Ultra, and Basic. Basic is free and lets you forward up to 25 e-mail messages a day to one e-mail address (which you can change at any time). Premium costs $19.95 per year and lets you forward up to 150 e-mail messages a day to up to five different accounts. Ultra costs $39.95 per year and lets you forward up to 500 e-mail messages a day to five different accounts. Premium and Ultra both offer filtering capabilities that you can use both to kill junk mail (without forwarding it) and to specify to which account to forward particular messages. For example, you could filter work-related messages from other messages and forward them to your work account.

Registration for all types of Bigfoot accounts involves a detailed questionnaire about your computer use, income, hobbies, interests, and so on. You also have to provide a name that's supposedly yours, together with a mailing address that includes a valid ZIP code.

Summary

In this chapter, we've been through what Hotmail is and does, and we've discussed how to use Hotmail both through its Web interface and through Outlook Express. Along the way, you've seen how to configure Outlook Express for e-mail; how to use it to send, receive, and manage e-mail; and how to create filters to automatically process incoming mail on POP3 accounts. To prevent you from claiming that I'm Microsoft obsessed, the last section of this chapter discussed several other Web-based e-mail services you might want to use instead of Hotmail, and it pointed out the advantages and disadvantages they each have.

E-mail is a fine form of communication, but it's always asynchronous. If you want to get in sync with someone, you need to chat with them, as discussed in the next chapter.

Chapter 5

Chat with Anyone in Public or Private

This chapter discusses how to use Windows Messenger and NetMeeting to chat with anybody in public or private on the Internet. By "chat," I mean text-based chat—we'll get to voice and video chat in the next chapter.

The chapter starts by discussing the advantages and disadvantages that Windows Messenger and NetMeeting bring to the party and discussing which of them you should use for chat in which circumstances. It then shows you how to configure Messenger and use it as a chat client. After that, it shows you how to set up NetMeeting, configure it, and use it as a chat client.

Should You Use Messenger or NetMeeting for Chat?

Windows Messenger (hereafter plain "Messenger," unless we need to be formal) and NetMeeting provide overlapping functionality—so much so that you might wonder why Microsoft includes both of them in XP. If you *are* wondering, Microsoft officially intends Messenger to be a replacement for NetMeeting. Messenger provides most of the functionality of NetMeeting, but at a heavy price of security. (More on this in a moment.) But both Messenger and NetMeeting provide text chat, voice and video calls, file transfer, whiteboarding, program sharing, and remote control of a shared program or computer. NetMeeting provides further features, such as hosted meetings and remote control of your own computer. Messenger provides some extra chat features, such as the display of emoticons and the monitoring of when someone in a conversation with you is typing in the conversation.

Actually, you probably *weren't* wondering that. If you've used a new installation of XP, you'll know that Messenger features so prominently in the XP interface that you have to put in some effort to get it out of your face, whereas NetMeeting is buried until you run it manually by its executable or create a shortcut for it. If you've seen this difference, and you were aware that XP included NetMeeting, chances are you had little doubt that Microsoft intended you to use Messenger rather than NetMeeting. But is that really in your interest? Or is it just in Microsoft's interest?

You'll see in due course. (Or, if you read Chapter 1 and remember it, you already know.) But for the moment, let me mention that Messenger and NetMeeting can't talk directly to each other, though they're blood-siblings under the skin and come from the same stable. (Another delicate shove by Microsoft to persuade you to transfer your allegiance from NetMeeting to Messenger? Why, sure.) However, NetMeeting can access the Messenger contact listing, and you can use Messenger to send a Messenger contact an invitation to start using NetMeeting.

Messenger tracks you and your actions the whole time you're online. NetMeeting lets you connect securely to other users, without being monitored. Chances are, if you have even a usual healthy interest in privacy, you'll prefer NetMeeting to Messenger, except where Messenger offers features and performance that NetMeeting can't match.

Messenger

This section discusses how to configure Messenger and use it for chat. Before that, though, it talks about how Messenger works, because understanding this is critical to deciding when to use NetMeeting and when to use Messenger for chat.

How Messenger Works: The Lay Version

In its basic form, Messenger is essentially an instant-messaging service. As such, it competes directly with instant-messaging services such as AOL Instant Messenger (which had more than 100 million users as of Winter 2001) and Yahoo! Messenger, as well as with Internet-based chat programs such as Eyeball Chat (www.eyeball.com). It outdoes AOL Instant Messenger at this writing by providing not only one-to-one audio chat but also one-to-one video chat, but it's outdone in both capabilities by Yahoo! Messenger, which offers multiparty audio and video chat.

Like most of its competitors, Messenger is a server-based service. Most of its features are coordinated through a central server network that performs essential tasks, including coordinating users' signing in and out of the service, tracking their IP addresses, managing their status information (Online, Offline, Away, Out to Lunch, and so on), storing their contact lists and blocking lists, and so on. (As you'll recall from Chapter 3, these features use various .NET services to accomplish their ends.)

Compared to the server, the local client is almost dumb (in the computer sense). It stores your user preferences and accepts your input, of course, but its main function is to pass information to and receive information from the server.

When you sign into the Messenger Service (and sign into your .NET Passport at the same time), the local client connects with the server, starting your Internet connection if necessary. Messenger Service then checks your database of contacts and updates the local client with details of each contact's status (Online, Offline, Be Right Back, On the Phone, and so on). It also checks for Messenger users who have you listed as a contact and who are online, and it updates their local clients with the information that you're online.

When Jane sees that you're online and requests a conversation with you, the Messenger server checks to see whether you're otherwise engaged and then tells the Messenger client to display a screen pop telling you that Jane is hot to chat with you. If you choose to take up the invitation, Messenger establishes a direct channel between your computer and Jane's but continues to monitor the conversation (so that it knows that you and Jane are busy). This reduces the amount of bandwidth required for the communications between you and Jane. Text doesn't take up much bandwidth, but audio takes up a good amount, and video takes up much more, so it's important that the traffic go directly from sender to recipient. Likewise, when you're transferring a fat file to Jane, the data goes directly from you to Jane without clogging the .NET Messenger Service servers the way a triple bacon cheeseburger clogs your arteries. This is why you can send a file to only one person at a time in a Messenger file-transfer operation. (You can run up to ten file-transfer operations at the same time if you want, sending ten files, each to a different person.)

That's what the basic form of Messenger does. But as I mentioned in Chapter 3, Messenger is one of the platform services of Microsoft's .NET initiative (you remember: .NET experiences for the users, .NET clients running them,., .NET clients, .NET servers, .NET tools   right, you remember). Into Messenger snap other services, such as .NET Alerts (which provides notification of time-sensitive offers and so on), CNBC on MSN Money, Expedia, MSN CarPoint, and others, all designed to shove information at your online persona in real time with the goal of causing you to spend more money with the associated companies than you would otherwise have done.

Understand the Privacy Implications of Messenger

Before you start using Messenger, you must understand its privacy implications. Messenger is a very slickly executed piece of software that provides strong instant-messaging and collaboration features out of the box, with more to come as more .NET services are released that snap into it. But the way Messenger is implemented, it tracks your actions the whole time you have it running and are signed into the service.

Here's what happens: In order to use Messenger, you must have a .NET Passport. At first, that seems reasonable, because most instant-messaging services require some kind of login using a username and password. But because the .NET Passport is tied both into the XP operating system and into all .NET Passport–enabled sites (such as Hotmail, MSN, Expedia, and other high-traffic Web sites), it provides user tracking on an unprecedented scale. Worse, you can check into Messenger any time you want, but you can't always leave: Because .NET Passport–enabled sites are using .NET Passport as well, you can't sign out of Messenger Service if you're logged into another .NET Passport–enabled site at the same time. For example, if you're using Hotmail (either directly or by using Outlook Express online), you'll need to sign out of Hotmail before you can sign out of Messenger Service.

All the time you're signed into Messenger Service, your Messenger client keeps in touch with the server about what you're doing: whether you're in a conversation (and if so, with whom); if you *are* in a conversation, whether you're typing in the Messenger window (so that it can let the other people in the conversation know); whether you're making an audio or video call; whether you're transferring a file (and if so, what file it is); and whether you're collaborating with other users (for example, via program sharing). The way Messenger is designed, such user tracking is essential to the service, but it results in a huge amount of information that Messenger gathers about you as you use it.

Moreover, unlike NetMeeting, Messenger offers neither encryption nor any useful authentication. In theory, Messenger's use of .NET Passport means you can be sure of the identity of the person you're chatting with. But in practice, as you saw in Chapter 3, .NET Passport offers no even halfway-reliable evidence of identity unless the user has taken the extra step to get a Passport Wallet (or another .NET Passport feature that requires the applicant to prove their identity) or is paying for their Hotmail or MSN account. Even then, there's not necessarily any correlation between the person's e-mail address and their real identity. For example, various people have Hotmail addresses with variations on "Bill Clinton": bill_clinton@hotmail.com, bill_ _clinton@hotmail.com (that one had two underscores), bill_clinton_@hotmail.com, and so on. Most of these people aren't called Bill Clinton. Some of them may have proved their real-world identity for Passport Wallet, or Hotmail, but their e-mail address won't reflect that. So you need to be very careful about believing what you're told. Providing that the .NET Passport's security hasn't been compromised (and, as you saw in Chapter 3, there are concerns on that front as well), you can be pretty sure of the .NET Passport that's communicating with you. But that's about it.

Configure Messenger

This section discusses how to configure Messenger. Many of the configuration options are straightforward, but others are more subtle than they appear. So this section discusses each of the options briefly to make sure you understand them. To make the information easier to find, it presents the options in categories by function.

NOTE
Microsoft is developing Messenger rapidly, so the Messenger interface may have changed since this book went to press. However, the basics described in this section seem likely to remain the same.

You can configure some of Messenger's options while offline, but in order to choose other options, you need to sign into Messenger Service using your .NET Passport.

CAUTION
If you choose to store your .NET Passport in your XP user account, Messenger automatically uses that .NET Passport to sign in. After you sign out, Messenger then presents that .NET Passport's e-mail address as the suggested sign-in for the next Messenger session, so anyone can see which account you're using. The only way to avoid this is not to store your .NET Passport in your XP user account, which means you'll need to enter your .NET Passport manually each time you use Messenger or another .NET Passport–enabled service. It also means XP will bug you incessantly to get a .NET Passport, even though you already have one. At this writing, there's no way to remove a .NET Passport from a user account other than to associate a different .NET Passport with the account. (Another possibility is to change the name of your existing XP account, create a new XP account with the original name, and then use that instead. Use the Files and Settings Transfer Wizard to transfer your files and settings from the old account to the new account.)

Change Your Display Name

The first thing to check is what name Messenger is displaying for you. By default, Messenger uses the contents of the First Name field of your .NET Passport as your display name. You can change this in the My Display Name text box (or the My .NET Messenger Service Display Name text box, depending on the version of Messenger) on the Personal page of the Options dialog box (see Figure 5-1). For example, you might want to add your last name to your first name or use a nickname instead.

Publish Your Phone Numbers

If you choose, you can have Messenger display up to three phone numbers for you: home, work, and mobile. Enter these numbers on the Phone page of the Options dialog box (see Figure 5-2). You can display this page of the dialog box directly by choosing Tools | Publish My Phone Numbers. Make sure the My Country/Region Code drop-down list is showing the correct country or region.

These phone numbers then appear in the Properties dialog box that you can display for a contact by right-clicking the contact and choosing Properties from the context menu.

Change the Font and Font Size Messenger Uses for Your Text

You can change the font for your display text (the text that you write) by using the Change My Message Font dialog box, which you can display by clicking the Change Font button on the

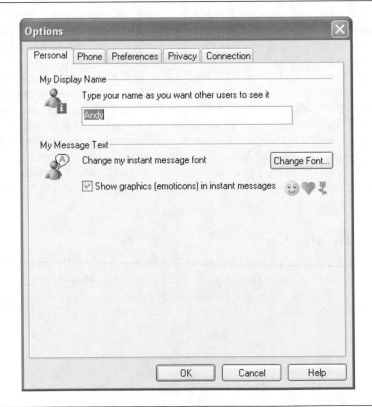

FIGURE 5-1   First, make sure your display name is correct on the Personal page of the Options dialog box.

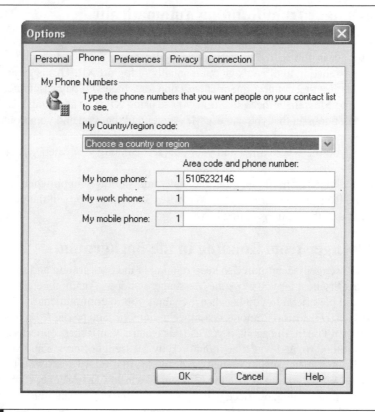

FIGURE 5-2   If you want to make your home, work, or mobile phone numbers accessible to your contacts, enter them on the Phone page of the Options dialog box.

Personal page of the Options dialog box or by clicking the Font button in a Conversation window (or choosing Edit | Change Font).

The Change My Message Font dialog box limits you to a small selection of "sensible" font sizes—between 8 points and 16 points. Each Messenger user can change the relative size of text they're seeing by choosing View | Text Size and selecting the size (Smallest, Smaller, Medium, Large, or Largest) from the submenu. Small script fonts still tend to be illegible even at the Largest setting, so it's best to avoid using them.

Show or Suppress Emoticons

By default, Messenger displays emoticons (graphical symbols such as ☺) when you type the appropriate text sequence. To toggle them on and off, select or clear the Show Graphics (Emoticons) in Instant Messages check box in the My Message Text area of the Personal page of the Options dialog box.

Prevent Messenger from Running Automatically and Opening Your Internet Connection

By default, Messenger is configured to sign you into Messenger Service as soon as you log onto XP and to keep you signed in until you sign out manually or log off XP. This is great provided (a) you have a persistent Internet connection, or at least one for which you pay a flat rate, and (b) you *want* to be signed into Messenger the whole time you're using XP. The advantages of being signed into Messenger are, of course, that you can use Messenger and that you and your contacts can see when each other is online. The disadvantages are that Messenger Service and any contacts of yours online can monitor you the whole time, and your contacts can bug you when you're trying to get things done.

To prevent Messenger from running automatically and signing you on when you log onto Windows, clear the Run This Program When Windows Starts check box in the General area of the Preferences page of the Options dialog box.

Prevent Messenger from Running in the Background

Also by default, Messenger is configured to keep running in the background and to keep you signed into the Messenger Service after you close the Messenger window. Again, this feature is ostensibly well-intentioned and beneficial to you because it enables you to communicate with your contacts and receive messages, calls, files, Remote Assistance invitations, and so on, from them even if the Messenger window isn't open. But again, if you use this feature, you'll stay connected to the Internet even if you didn't intend to, and you'll be monitored by Messenger Service and your contacts.

The danger of running Messenger in the background is that many users won't spot what Messenger is doing. When you first close the Messenger window, Messenger displays a pop-up to warn you that it's still running; but once you've dismissed the pop-up and told it not to reappear, it's easy to forget. If you have a dial-up Internet connection, Messenger either will hold it open or will make XP keep trying to establish the Internet connection for no apparent reason—which might make less experienced users suspect that XP has caught a virus.

To prevent Messenger from running in the background, clear the Allow This Program to Run in the Background check box in the General area of the Preferences page of the Options dialog box.

Prevent Messenger from Signing You In When You Connect to the Internet

Even if you've manually signed out of Messenger and then closed your Internet connection, Messenger automatically signs you in the next time you establish the Internet connection.

By default, Outlook Express causes Messenger to sign you in when you run Outlook Express. This is deeply antisocial behavior that you'll probably want to change. To do so, choose Tools | Options in Outlook Express to display the Options dialog box, clear the Automatically Log On to Windows Messenger check box in the General area on the General page, and then click the OK button.

Choose the Interval Before You're Marked As "Away"

By default, Messenger changes your status from Online to Away after you've been inactive for five minutes. You can adjust the length of time by changing the value in the Show Me As "Away" when I'm Inactive for *NN* Minutes text box on the Preferences page of the Options dialog box. Alternatively, you can clear the Show Me As "Away" when I'm Inactive for *NN* Minutes check box to turn this option off. If you do so, Messenger changes your status to Away when you've been inactive for the number of minutes specified in the Wait text box on the Screen Saver page of the Display Properties dialog box—the length of inactivity required for your screen saver to kick in. (To display the Display Properties dialog box, right-click your Desktop and choose Properties from the context menu.)

If you use no screen saver and clear the Show Me As "Away"… check box, Messenger never changes your status to Away. There's no particular advantage to this unless you like to keep your friends in suspense as to whether you're actually there or just pretending at any given moment.

Choose Alerts for Contacts, Messages, and E-mails

The four options in the Alerts section of the Preferences page of the Options dialog box let you choose whether to display alerts when contacts come online, when you receive an instant message, when you receive an e-mail message on your Hotmail or MSN account, and when contacts sign in or send you a message. Whether you find such alerts useful or an annoyance depends on how you work and (sometimes) how much screen real estate you have.

If you use the alerts, you can specify the sounds used for each of the alerts by clicking the Sounds button and working with the Messenger events in the Program Events list box on the Sounds page of the Sounds and Audio Devices Properties dialog box (see Figure 5-3). Either choose another sound from the Sounds drop-down list or click the Browse button and use the resulting Browse for Sound dialog box to specify the sound file.

Change the Folder into Which Transferred Files Are Placed

By default, Messenger places files you receive via file transfer in your \My Documents\ My Received Files\ folder—a fair enough location for default use. If you want Messenger to put the files somewhere else, click the Browse button in the File Transfer area of the Preferences page of the Options dialog box and use the resulting Browse for Folder dialog box to specify the folder. Bear in mind that, even if you're using a hotshot antivirus program that monitors your downloads and file transfers, it's a good idea to check all incoming files carefully for viruses—so you may want to put all incoming files into a quarantine zone until you check them rather than lumping them in with files you know to be safe.

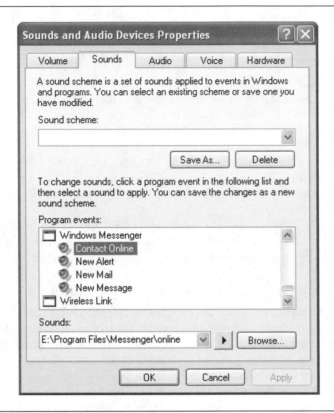

FIGURE 5-3   Use the Program Events list box on the Sounds page of the Sounds and Audio Devices Properties dialog box to specify different sounds for contacts, messages, and e-mail messages.

Maintain Your Allow List and Block List

The Privacy page of the Options dialog box, shown in Figure 5-4, provides a My Allow List list box and a My Block List list box for keeping your lists of those contacts who may and may not see your online status and send you messages. You can shift one or more selected contacts from one list box to the other by using the Allow button or the Block button. The key entry here is the All Other Users entry, which appears by default in the My Allow List list box, letting all Messenger users other than those listed check your status and send you messages. If you need privacy from everyone except the contacts you specifically allow to contact you, move the All Other Users item to the My Block List list box.

Check Whose Contact Lists You're On

To see which other users have added you to their contact lists, click the View button on the Privacy page of the Options dialog box. Messenger displays a dialog box showing an unadorned list of the contact lists on which you appear. Use this information to identify forgotten friends or

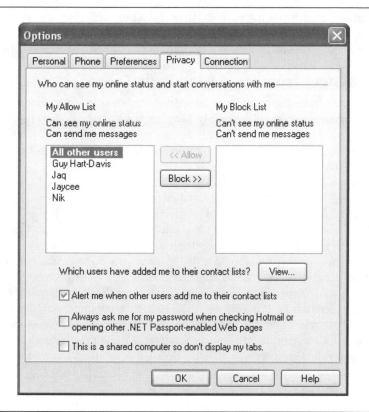

FIGURE 5-4   On the Privacy page of the Options dialog box, use the My Allow List list box and the My Block List list box to specify which of your contacts may and may not view your status and contact you.

to block users as appropriate. You can also right-click a user's name and choose Add to Contacts to add that user to your contact list or choose Properties to display information about the user. (If the user is already one of the your contacts, the Add to Contacts item will be unavailable.)

To make sure Messenger always warns you when another Messenger user adds you to their contact list, verify that the Alert Me when Other Users Add Me to Their Contact Lists check box on the Privacy page is selected. (This check box is selected by default.) I'll show you what happens as a result of this setting in "Add a Contact when They Add You to Their Contact List," later in this chapter.

Keep .NET Passport Under Control

One of .NET Passport's features is to automatically log you into .NET Passport–enabled Web sites once you've successfully logged into .NET Passport during an XP session. If you're in the habit of leaving your computer running and accessible to other people while you're still logged in, it may be a good idea to select the Always Ask Me for My Password when Checking Hotmail or Opening Other .NET Passport–Enabled Web Pages check box on the Privacy page of the Options dialog box. (This check box is cleared by default.) When this check box is selected, each time you try to access a .NET Passport–enabled page, Internet Explorer will demand your password.

Prevent Messenger from Displaying Your Tabs

To prevent Messenger from displaying your tabs along the left side of the window, select the This Is a Shared Computer So Don't Display My Tabs check box on the Privacy page of the Options dialog box. After you sign out and sign back in again, or someone else signs in using Messenger from your XP user account, Messenger doesn't display the tabs, and it removes the Show Tabs command from the Tools menu so that the user can't display tabs that way.

The benefit of removing tabs is that it prevents other users who are using Messenger from your XP account from seeing which tabs you have installed and which tabs you're using. At this writing, the services available on the tabs are few and relatively uncontroversial. But as more companies (and perhaps government departments) provide services via extensions that appear as tabs in Messenger, hiding the tabs to prevent other users from accessing them will become more important.

That said, nobody other than you should really be using your XP user account in the first place. If someone will be needing to use your computer regularly, you'll be much better off creating a separate user account for them so that they can associate their .NET Passport with their account and use Messenger more easily. If the person needs to use the computer only temporarily, have them use the Guest account instead of your account. You'd expect Guest account users not to be able to save their .NET Passport in XP—but they can (at least, at this writing). But suppressing the display of tabs for the Guest account should help keep guest users from interfering in each other's business.

NOTE *By default, XP disables the Guest account until you choose to enable it. To do so, choose Start | Control Panel, click the User Accounts link, and then click the Guest Account link to display the Do You Want to Turn On the Guest Account? screen. Click the Turn On the Guest Account button, and the Guest account will be in business.*

Connect via a Proxy Server

If you connect to the Internet via a proxy server, you'll need to check your configuration on the Connection page of the Options dialog box (see Figure 5-5). (If you connect to the Internet directly from the computer you're using, or if you connect via a small network that uses Internet Connection Sharing, you shouldn't need to worry about the controls on this page.)

The key control on this page is the I Use a Proxy Server check box. Once you select this check box, Messenger makes all the other controls on this page available. Specify the type of proxy server in the Type drop-down list. Enter the server's name in the Server text box. Correct the port number from the default that Messenger enters in the Port text box if applicable.

If you specify a SOCKS Version 5 proxy server, you'll need to enter your username in the User ID text box and your password in the Password text box.

NOTE *Connecting to the Internet through ICS (with or without ICF, correctly configured) is considered a "direct connection (no firewall)" by Messenger.*

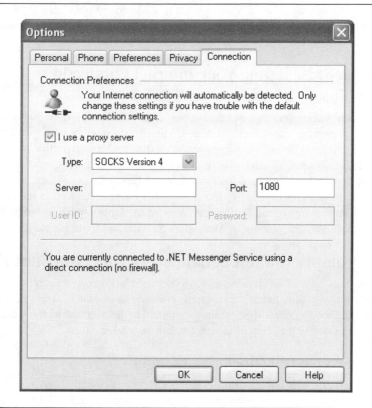

FIGURE 5-5   If you use a proxy server to connect to the Internet, specify the details on the Connection page of the Options dialog box.

Display Messenger Always on Top of Other Windows

If you want Messenger always to appear on top of other applications so that it's always visible when you're working in Windows, choose Tools | Always on Top from the main Messenger window.

Troubleshoot Messenger Configuration and Connection Issues

This section discusses how to troubleshoot several of the more frequent configuration and connection issues that surface with Messenger.

The Display Name You Chose Was Invalid

If you get the error message "The display name you chose was invalid. Please choose another display name and try again," it usually means you've stepped on a trademark or another word that Microsoft is sensitive to on its own account or has been sensitized to by another company. For example, if you try to call yourself "Microsoft," Messenger will object. When you dismiss the error message box, Messenger resets your display name to its previous value.

You might also have entered an offensive word that Microsoft has decided to block. At this writing, the list of words is a little uneven, but you can probably guess most of them. (If not, you can have some fun discovering them by trial and error message.)

Messenger Keeps Redialing Your Internet Connection after You've Closed the Messenger Window

If Messenger keeps redialing your Internet connection after you've closed the Messenger window with the intention of exiting Messenger, chances are that Messenger is configured to run in the background. Because it's not immediately apparent either that it's Messenger that's doing the dialing or that Messenger is still running after you've closed the Messenger window (the notification-area icon isn't all that easy to interpret), this problem can be confusing at first.

To prevent this from happening, clear the Allow This Program to Run in the Background check box in the General area of the Preferences page of the Options dialog box. Closing the Messenger window then signs you out of Messenger Service and exits Messenger.

Messenger Prompts You to Upgrade Every Time You Start It

If you start Messenger by double-clicking an icon on your Desktop, and each time you start Messenger, it prompts you to upgrade the program, you may have pasted a copy of the Messenger executable file to the Desktop rather than creating a shortcut to the executable. If so, create a shortcut to the executable and delete the copy of the executable on the Desktop.

ICF or Another Firewall Blocks Messenger

If you find that Internet Connection Firewall (ICF) or another firewall is blocking Messenger connections, you may need to open ports manually through the firewall. These are the ports that Messenger uses for communicating:

Service	TCP Port	UDP Port
Incoming voice call (computer to computer)	6901	6901
Voice (computer to phone)	—	6801, 6901, 2001–2120
Receiving files	6891–6900	—

In most cases, ICF doesn't cause Messenger any problems because the two have been taught to communicate with each other: Messenger negotiates with ICF the ports that it needs open, and ICF opens them up by implementing the appropriate services. If you want to examine the ports, display the Advanced Settings dialog box for the external ICS interface and look at the services called *msmsgs* running on the Services page. Figure 5-6 shows an example in which several computers are connecting via ICS and using Messenger through ICF.

NOTE   *Turn back to Chapter 2 for a discussion of how to configure ICF and open ports in it.*

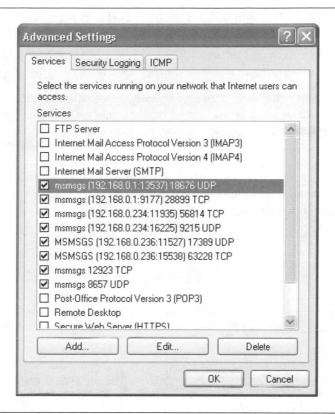

FIGURE 5-6   Messenger automatically gets ICF to open ports for Messenger communications.

Create and Manage Your Contact List

Before you can easily establish a conversation with anyone in Messenger, you need to add one or more contacts to your contact list. You can do this in any of three ways: by using their e-mail address or .NET Passport sign-in name, by searching for them in a directory, or by adding them to your contact list when they add you to their list. The next three subsections discuss these possibilities. The subsections after those discuss how to block, unblock, and delete contacts when they become troublesome or pass their sell-by date.

Add a Contact by Their Sign-in Name

To add a contact by their sign-in, take these steps:

1.   Run the Add a Contact Wizard by clicking the Add a Contact item in the I Want To list or choosing Tools | Add a Contact.

2. On the first page of the wizard, select the By E-mail Address or Sign-in Name option button and click the Next button.

3. On the Please Type Your Contact's Complete E-mail Address page of the wizard, enter the contact's e-mail address and click the Next button.

If the person has a .NET Passport, Messenger displays a page like the one in Figure 5-7, telling you that the contact has been added to your contact list and that, if the person isn't using Messenger, Messenger Service will send them an e-mail encouraging them to start using it. If the person doesn't have a .NET Passport, Messenger displays a page telling you that it couldn't add the person to your contact list but offers to send them an e-mail encouraging them to sign up for a .NET Passport and start using Messenger. In either case, you can add a message of your own to the boilerplate message to encourage the person to take the message seriously. You've just participated in viral marketing for Microsoft, so you might as well make the most of it. (More seriously, you might want to add your real name and other identifying information in case they don't recognize your e-mail address.)

Add a Contact by Searching for Them

If you don't know the e-mail address or .NET Passport sign-in name of the contact you want to add to your contact list, run the Add a Contact Wizard and choose the Search for a Contact option button on its first page. The wizard displays the Type Your Contact's First and Last Name page

FIGURE 5-7   If a contact has a .NET Passport, you can add them to your contacts list in Messenger with minimal effort.

(see Figure 5-8). Enter as much accurate information about the contact as possible, including city or state if they're in the U.S., and choose which directory to search through in the Search for This Person At drop-down list. (At this writing, your choices are limited to the Hotmail Member Directory and your local Address Book, with the Hotmail Member Directory being the default.)

If the search is successful, the wizard displays a Search Results list, from which you can choose the person who seems to match. So far so good—but if you searched using the Hotmail Member Directory, the wizard next displays a page apologizing for not being able to add the person to your contact list because of the Hotmail privacy policy and telling you that it will send them an e-mail instead. Again, you can customize the e-mail so that they (perhaps) have more motivation to respond positively to it—or at least know who your e-mail address represents.

Add a Contact when They Add You to Their Contact List

The third way of adding a contact pops up when another Messenger user adds you to their contact list. If you have the Alert Me when Other Users Add Me to their Contact Lists check box on the Privacy page of the Options dialog box selected, Messenger displays the Windows Messenger dialog box shown in Figure 5-9 when another user adds you to their contact list.

From here, you can select the Allow This Person to See when You Are Online and Contact You option button or the Block This Person from Seeing when You Are Online and Contacting You option button, if appropriate. If you choose to allow the person to add you as a contact, select or clear the Add This Person to My Contact List check box, if appropriate, before clicking the OK button to close the dialog box.

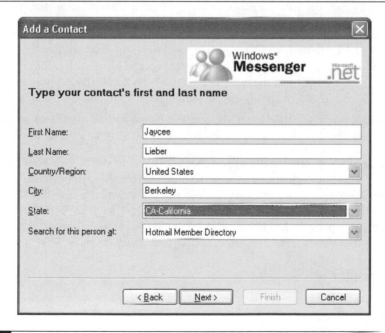

FIGURE 5-8   You can search for a contact by name, country, and (for the U.S.) city and state.

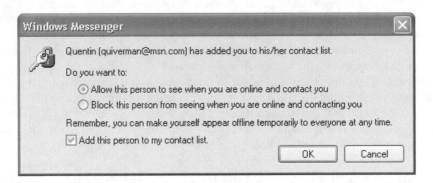

FIGURE 5-9   The Windows Messenger dialog box offers you the chance to add to your contact list somebody who is trying to add you to their list.

If you choose to block the person, Messenger clears the Add This Person to My Contact List check box—but you can select it if you want to add the person to your contact list but block them at present. Whether you add the person to your contact list or not, you get added to their contact list, but you appear permanently in the Not Online group. In order to contact the contact, you'll need to unblock them—you can't send messages to a contact you've blocked

Block or Unblock a Contact

You can block a contact by issuing a Block command from a Conversation window or the main Messenger window:

- Click the Block button in a Conversation window. If the conversation contains multiple people, Messenger displays a menu of people you can block; select the right one. If the conversation contains just the two of you, there's no doubt about whom to block, and your conversation is effectively ended, although the Conversation window remains open.

- Right-click a contact in the main Messenger window and choose Block from the context menu.

When you've blocked someone, they can't check your online status, view your phone numbers, or send you messages until you unblock them. To unblock someone, you can use one of three options— click the Unblock button in a Conversation window in which you've blocked that contact; right- click the contact in the main Messenger window and choose Unblock from the context menu; or display the Privacy page of the Options dialog box (Tools | Options), select the contact in the My Block List option button, click the Allow button, and close the dialog box.

Delete a Contact

You can delete a contact by right-clicking their entry in the main Messenger window and choosing Delete Contact from the context menu. Messenger displays a message box to confirm the deletion in case you've clicked hastily.

Connect with Messenger

You can establish a connection with another Messenger user from the main Messenger window in any of the following ways:

- Double-click the contact's name in the Online category.

- Right-click the contact's name in the Online category and choose Send an Instant Message from the context menu.

- Click the Send an Instant Message link in the action pane (the I Want To list). Messenger displays the Send an Instant Message dialog box (see Figure 5-10). Select the contact on the My Contacts page and click the OK button. (This way of establishing a connection is so much more clumsy than the others that it's barely worth using.)

- If the Messenger user isn't one of your contacts, click the Send an Instant Message link in the action pane to display the Send an Instant Message dialog box. Click the Other tab to display the Other page and enter the person's e-mail address in the text box. If, by the time you're reading this, Messenger has been made interoperable with other instant-messaging services, select the appropriate service in the Service drop-down list. Then click the OK button. Messenger opens a Conversation window addressed to that user.

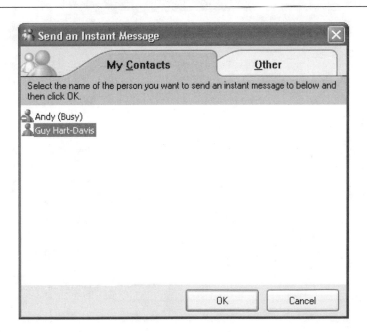

FIGURE 5-10   The My Contacts page of the Send an Instant Message dialog box provides an unnecessarily complex way of starting a conversation with a contact.

CAUTION *When you use the Other page in the Send an Instant Message dialog box, Messenger doesn't verify the address until you try to send a message. If you've made a mistake with the address, or if the person isn't online at the time, Messenger tells you that the message couldn't be delivered to the recipient.*

In the Conversation window that Messenger has opened, enter your opening message in the text box and click the Send button to send it. Messenger transmits the message to your contact.

If they're receiving alerts, Messenger displays a pop-up telling them your display name and the text of the message (or the first part of it, if the message is long). If they're not receiving alerts, Messenger opens a minimized Conversation window and flashes its Taskbar button in a contrasting color to their color scheme to entice them to click it.

Once they do, the conversation is up and running. Figure 5-11 shows the beginning of a conversation in a Conversation window.

Full of nice clickable buttons and links as it is, the Conversation window is easy to use. We'll examine most of the features in subsequent chapters, so for now the only relevant link in the I Want To list is the Invite Someone to This Conversation link. When you click this link, Messenger displays the Add Someone to This Conversation dialog box, which is the

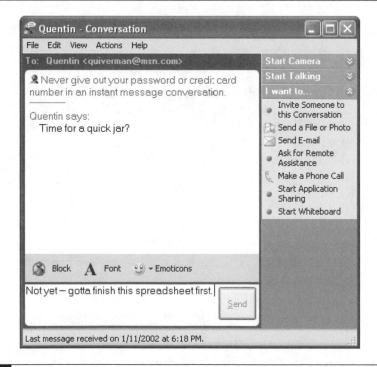

FIGURE 5-11 A conversation starting in a Conversation window

Send An Instant Message dialog box in drag. As before, you can specify an existing contact or take a chance at remembering the e-mail address of another contact (and a further chance that they're online at the time).

The status line at the top of the Conversation window displays any warnings. For example, it may tell you that "Andy may not reply because his or her status is set to Busy" if Andy has set his status to Busy. The status bar at the bottom of the window tells you when someone in a conversation with you is typing a message in the Conversation window so that you can avoid getting your chat out of sync.

Enter Emoticons in Your Messages

You can enter emoticons in your messages using either the mouse or the keyboard:

- With the mouse, click the Emoticons button in the Conversation window and choose the emoticon from the drop-down pane. This pane shows the most common emoticons, but not all that Messenger supports.

- With the keyboard, type the text sequence for the emoticon. If you can remember the text sequence, entering it in a message is much quicker than using the mouse. For a list of the text sequences for emoticons, click the Emoticons button in the Conversation window and choose the ... button to display an Internet Explorer window with the Messenger Help screen listing the text sequences.

End a Conversation

To end a conversation, click the Close button in the Conversation window or choose File | Close from the Conversation window.

End a Messenger Session

How you can end a Messenger session depends on whether you've left Messenger configured to keep running in the background or you've decided to take control over it.

If you've prevented Messenger from running in the background (by clearing the Allow This Program to Run in the Background check box in the General area of the Preferences page of the Options dialog box), you can close Messenger by clicking the Close button on the Messenger window or by choosing File | Close.

If you've allowed Messenger to run in the background, you can close Messenger only by clicking (or right-clicking) the Messenger icon in the notification area and choosing Exit from the context menu.

Regardless of whether you've allowed Messenger to run in the background, you can sign out of Messenger Service by choosing File | Sign Out from the main Messenger window or by clicking (or right-clicking) the Messenger icon in the notification area and choosing Sign Out from the context menu. You can then sign back in by clicking the link in the main Messenger window (if you have it displayed) or by clicking (or right-clicking) the Messenger icon in the notification area and choosing Sign In from the context menu.

Change Your Status

By default, Messenger sets your status to Online once you connect to Messenger Service; changes it to Away after the length of inactivity specified on the Preferences page of the Options dialog box (if you've selected the Show Me As "Away" when I'm Inactive for *NN* Minutes check box) or the length of inactivity it takes for your screen saver to kick in; and changes it to Offline when you sign out of Messenger Service.

When you're signed into Messenger Service, you can change your overt status by clicking your entry at the top of the main Messenger window and choosing the status you want (Online, Busy, Be Right Back, Away, On the Phone, Out to Lunch, or Appear Offline) from the resulting menu. You can also change your status by clicking (or right-clicking) the Messenger icon in the notification area, selecting the My Status item on the menu, and choosing the status from the submenu.

Use Groups to Sort Your Messenger Contacts

If you have a lot of contacts, you may find that Messenger's default Online/Offline grouping doesn't show you all the contacts you need to see at any given time. Instead, you can create and populate custom groups so that you can sort your contacts by categories as needed.

To work with groups, choose Tools | Sort Contacts By | Groups from the main Messenger window. Messenger displays your hitherto unsuspected groups, which at this writing are Coworkers, Family, Friends, and Other Contacts. You can then drag your existing contacts into the appropriate group or create new groups for your contacts by using the Add a Group command on the Tools | Manage Groups submenu. Messenger adds a new group that you can then rename.

Alternatively, you can use the Rename a Group submenu to rename one of the existing groups or the Delete a Group submenu to dispose of a group.

When you tire of admiring your groups and want to return your contacts to the Online and Offline categories, choose Tools | Sort Contacts By | Online/Offline.

Troubleshoot Messenger Chat

Text chat in Messenger is usually pretty straightforward once you've connected to your protagonists. This section discusses a couple of minor issues that might trouble you briefly.

Can't See Emoticons

If you can't see emoticons when you or your contacts type the appropriate text sequences, make sure the Show Graphics (Emoticons) in Instant Messages check box on the Personal page of the Options dialog box is selected.

Messenger Removes Participants from the Conversation

Messenger tends to be happiest with two-person conversations because these can be established as a direct link between two Messenger clients (monitored by Messenger Service, of course) and left running—active or in limbo—for as long as the participants remain online and choose to carry on the conversation.

But as soon as you add further participants into a conversation, it has to be coordinated centrally, with all the messages being relayed through the Messenger Service servers. As a result, Messenger Service has a strong incentive to close down inactive conversations that have three or more participants. It does so by removing people from the conversation after a certain period of inactivity.

Here's a quick example of what happens, using three people: Andy, Billie, and Charlie. Andy places a call to Billie and then adds Charlie to the resulting conversation, creating a three-way conversation. After an initial flurry of chat, they let the conversation languish, so Messenger Service decides to reclaim the bandwidth. What happens then is a little peculiar: Messenger Service announces to Andy that "This conversation has been inactive; some participants will be removed." It then tells Andy that Billie has been removed. But then it tells Billie and Charlie that Andy has left the conversation, leaving Billie and Charlie conversing with each other—having removed the originator of the conversation. Because the resulting conversation has only two parties, Billie and Charlie can leave it inactive for more or less as long as they like without having Messenger Service hassle them.

So far, so moderately understandable. But what's not immediately obvious is that Andy is still connected to Charlie. This connection isn't in the previous three-way Conversation window for Charlie, but if Andy types a message in *his* three-way Conversation window (from which Billie has been removed), Charlie gets a new Conversation window starting a fresh conversation with Andy.

This behavior is…well, *odd*…and I wouldn't be surprised if Microsoft changed it. But you can see what they're trying to do—break up the centrally hosted conversation into two-party, point-to-point components to reduce the load on their servers.

NetMeeting

Default installations of XP include the NetMeeting files but don't set up NetMeeting for use. So, before you can use NetMeeting for chat, you probably need to set it up on your computer and configure it as described next.

Set Up and Configure NetMeeting

This section describes how to set up and configure NetMeeting. Like Messenger and Outlook Express, NetMeeting has a fair number of configuration options that you need to understand in order to use NetMeeting most effectively and most securely. As with Messenger, we'll go through these options by topic in roughly the order in which you're likely to need to set them.

Start NetMeeting Configuration

To start configuring NetMeeting, enter **conf** in the Run dialog box (Start | Run) and click the OK button. XP extracts the NetMeeting files from storage and launches the NetMeeting setup routine. After an introductory page too boring to show here, the setup routine displays the page shown in Figure 5-12, on which you have to enter some text in the First Name, Last Name, and E-mail Address fields. (The Location and Comments fields you can leave blank.) Each of these

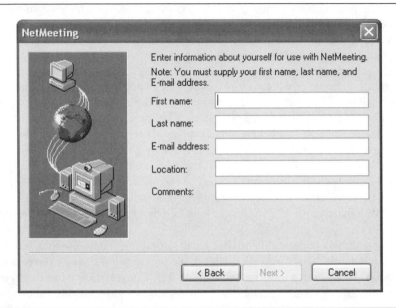

FIGURE 5-12 On this page of the NetMeeting setup routine, enter the first name, last name, and e-mail address that you want NetMeeting to display for you.

three fields requires text, but it can be as short as a single character. NetMeeting displays the first name and last name to identify you to other users, so it's worth making them memorable even if you choose not to use your real names.

The next page of the setup routine, shown in Figure 5-13, lets you specify whether to log onto a directory server (and if so, which server) and whether to list your name in the directory. Unless you're connecting NetMeeting to a third-party directory server, these options are largely superannuated because Microsoft has transformed the Microsoft Internet Directory service that the setup routine encourages you to use into the .NET Messenger Service, which NetMeeting can't access the way it wants to. In most cases, you're best served by clearing the Log On to a Directory Server when NetMeeting Starts check box and ignoring the Do Not List My Name in the Directory check box (but you might choose to select this check box for good measure).

The next page (which isn't worth showing) lets you specify the speed of the network connection over which you'll be making NetMeeting calls. Your choices are 14400 bps Modem (in other words, 14.4 Kbps); 28800 bps or Faster Modem (in other words, 28.8 Kbps or faster); Cable, xDSL or ISDN; and Local Area Network. Choose the speed that's closest to your connection speed because NetMeeting uses this setting to stream audio and video at the correct rates. There's no point in selecting a misleading speed the way there is with some peer-to-peer technologies (to encourage or discourage other users to contact you for files).

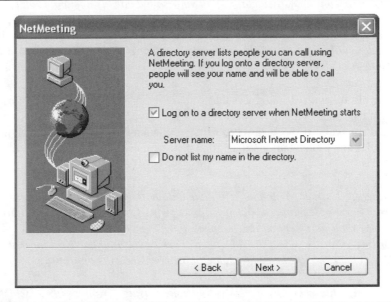

FIGURE 5-13   On this page of the NetMeeting setup routine, choose directory server options if you'll be using a directory server.

The next page (which isn't worth showing either) lets you choose whether to let NetMeeting put shortcuts on your Desktop and on your Quick Launch toolbar. Choose freely according to your preferences.

After this, the NetMeeting setup routine runs the Audio Tuning Wizard, which is discussed briefly in the next section, because you may also need to run it again after setup.

Run the Audio Tuning Wizard

As I just mentioned, when you set up NetMeeting, it runs the Audio Tuning Wizard automatically, but you may also need to run the Audio Tuning Wizard at other times to tweak your NetMeeting configuration. For example, if you get a new microphone, or if your environment becomes consistently noisier than it was (or, better, becomes consistently quieter), you'll probably want to run the Audio Tuning Wizard to adjust the microphone's sensitivity.

The Audio Tuning Wizard starts with an introductory page and then walks you through testing the volume (to make sure your speakers or headphones are working), checking the microphone, and setting the recording volume. The page for setting the recording volume contains text for you to read while the wizard sets the recording level. Now that speech recognition is a reality, it's worth mentioning that the wizard isn't using speech recognition—it's just looking for some vocal input. So you can say whatever you want, provided it lasts for the few seconds the wizard needs to get a fix on the input volume. Speak at your normal volume.

NOTE

If the Audio Tuning Wizard claims that your sound card is unsupported, it doesn't necessarily mean the sound card won't work with NetMeeting. It can mean the sound card driver won't let NetMeeting automatically configure the microphone sensitivity (via the Audio Tuning Wizard). If this is the case, configure the microphone sensitivity manually by using the Volume Control applet (or whatever this applet is called for your sound card).

If all goes well, the wizard announces that you've tuned your settings. If the wizard doesn't get any input on the recording volume page, it tells you the problem and suggests you check your microphone and try again. If the wizard can't find your sound card, it'll tell you about that, too.

Once you click the Finish button on the final page of the Audio Tuning Wizard, NetMeeting starts.

NOTE

NetMeeting 2.x had trouble detecting the automatic gain-control features or microphone-boost features of some sound cards. If you're still using NetMeeting 2.x (and you shouldn't be) and this happens, open the Volume Control applet; display the recording controls; select the Advanced check box; and then select the Automatic Gain Control check box or the Microphone Boost check box, as appropriate.

TIP

To find out which version of NetMeeting you're using (or, more likely, which version someone else is using), choose Help | About. NetMeeting displays the About Windows NetMeeting dialog box, which includes a version number (for example, Version 3.01) and a build number (for example, 4.4.3400).

Start NetMeeting

If you just configured NetMeeting, it should be running by now. Otherwise, run NetMeeting by using either of the shortcuts you created or by entering **conf** in the Run dialog box again. Alternatively, create a shortcut manually to conf.exe (you won't need to specify the path) and place it wherever on the Start menu or in your folder structure you find most convenient.

Start NetMeeting from the Command Line

You can also run NetMeeting from the command line—for example, if you need to start NetMeeting from a batch file or script. To do so, use whichever of the following commands is appropriate:

Call Type	Command
IP address call	rundll32.exe msconf.dll,CallToProtocolHandler *IP_Address*
DNS name call	rundll32.exe msconf.dll,CallToProtocolHandler *DNS_Name*
ILS call	rundll32.exe msconf.dll,CallToProtocolHandler *ILS/username*

Choose NetMeeting Options

So you've set up NetMeeting. You *could* start using it straight away. But you'd do better to check its configuration first, as described in this section. As with Messenger, I'll describe the options by function rather than plowing through them all precisely in order.

Change Your Directory Information

You can change your directory information by using the text boxes in the My Directory Information group box on the General page of the Options dialog box (see Figure 5-14). As mentioned before, the First Name, Last Name, and E-mail Address text boxes require an entry of at least one character. The Location and Comments text boxes are optional.

| FIGURE 5-14 | The General page of the Options dialog box for NetMeeting contains options for specifying your directory information, choosing whether to log into a directory, and specifying whether to run NetMeeting when Windows starts. |

The Directory Settings group box lets you specify whether to log onto a directory server when NetMeeting starts, which directory server to use, and whether to list your name in the directory. As mentioned earlier, these options are now redundant unless you're logging into a third-party directory server, because the Microsoft Internet Directory system is no longer in place. So, unless you're using a third-party directory server, make sure the Log On to a Directory Server when NetMeeting Starts check box is cleared—otherwise, NetMeeting will try to log you on.

Make NetMeeting Start Automatically

If you use NetMeeting frequently, you may want to set it to start each time you start Windows. To do so, select the Run NetMeeting in the Background when Windows Starts check box on the General page of the Options dialog box.

Provided you haven't selected the Log On to a Directory Server when NetMeeting Starts check box in the Directory Settings area of the General page of the Options dialog box, NetMeeting will just start up and be ready for use once Windows has finished loading.

Control the Display of the NetMeeting Icon in the Notification Area

To control whether NetMeeting displays an icon in the notification area, select or clear the Show the NetMeeting Icon on the Taskbar check box, as appropriate.

Change Your Bandwidth Setting

To change the bandwidth you specified during the setup routine, click the Bandwidth Settings button on the General page of the Options dialog box and adjust the setting in the resulting Network Bandwidth dialog box.

Set Up Calling Through a Gateway or a Gatekeeper

If your computer connects to the network through a gateway or through a gatekeeper computer, click the Advanced Calling button on the General page of the Options dialog box and specify the details of the gateway or gatekeeper in the Advanced Calling Options dialog box (see Figure 5-15).

Choose the Certificate for Encrypting and Authenticating Communications

NetMeeting lets you encrypt data-only calls and conferences (calls and conferences that don't include audio and video) by using either NetMeeting's built-in digital certificate or a digital certificate of your own. You can't encrypt audio and video calls, so they're always insecure. If you use a digital certificate of your own, you can use authentication as well as encryption. If you use NetMeeting's digital certificate, you can use only encryption (because NetMeeting's digital certificate doesn't identify you).

FIGURE 5-15   Use the Advanced Calling Options dialog box to specify any gatekeeper or gateway computer through which your computer connects to the network.

To use NetMeeting's digital certificate, select the Use Privacy (Encryption) Only option button in the Certificate group box on the Security page of the Options dialog box (see Figure 5-16).

To use a digital certificate of your own, select the Use This Certificate for Privacy and Authentication option button. NetMeeting selects the first certificate listed in your private certificate store and displays its details in the text box on the Security page. If this isn't the right certificate, click the Change button and use the resulting Select Certificate dialog box to choose the right certificate. Then click the OK button.

Specify Security for Incoming and Outgoing Calls

To encrypt data calls with the digital certificate you specified, use the two check boxes in the General group box on the Security page of the Options dialog box:

■ Select the I Prefer to Receive Secure Incoming Calls. Accept Only Secure Calls when I'm Not in a Meeting check box if you want to receive only secure incoming calls other than when you're in an insecure meeting. When you select this option, it's important to understand that NetMeeting simply ignores insecure incoming calls—it doesn't notify you of them, and it's not reliable about telling the insecure caller that you're accepting only secure calls. Sometimes it notifies them immediately, as it should; but other times, it lets the call ring until they give up on it, instead of timing out the unanswered call as it normally would.

■ Select the I Prefer to Make Secure Outgoing Calls check box if you want to make secure outgoing calls by default. (NetMeeting's default is to make insecure outgoing calls.) You'll still be able to place insecure calls (for example, voice or video calls) manually if you need to.

Tweak Your Microphone Setup

The Audio page of the Options dialog box, shown in Figure 5-17, contains several options for controlling your microphone. They're related, so I discuss them all in this section.

FIGURE 5-16   On the Security page of the Options dialog box, specify the digital certificate to use for encryption and authentication, and choose whether to make secure calls.

FIGURE 5-17   Choose audio options on the Audio page of the Options dialog box.

The most important option here is the Enable Full-Duplex Audio So I Can Speak while Receiving Audio check box. *Full duplex* means that you can send and receive an audio signal at the same time; the opposite, *half duplex*, means that you can send and you can receive, but not at the same time—for example, when you speak, you can't hear anything the other person is saying. Almost all recent sound cards can handle full duplex; so if your doesn't, it might be time for a quick upgrade. Half-duplex voice calls are miserable unless you actually like saying "Over" at the end of each turn speaking. So, if this check box is available, make sure it's selected. (If XP thinks your sound card doesn't support full duplex, the check box will be unavailable.)

The Enable Auto-Gain Control check box lets NetMeeting adjust the sensitivity of your microphone to compensate for changes in volume. It's usually a good idea to select this check box if it's available.

The Automatically Adjust Microphone Volume while in a Call check box also lets NetMeeting adjust the microphone sensitivity to compensate for changes in volume. This option is mostly useful for sound cards that don't support auto-gain, but you can leave this check box selected even if your sound card does support auto-gain.

The Enable DirectSound for Improved Audio Performance check box controls whether NetMeeting uses DirectSound. If your computer supports DirectSound, use this option; if it doesn't support DirectSound, this check box will be unavailable.

The option buttons in the Silence Detection group box let you specify whether NetMeeting should adjust silence detection itself or whether you want to adjust it manually. Usually, NetMeeting does a good job of detecting silence; but if you find otherwise, select the Let Me Adjust Silence Detection Myself option button and move the slider to an appropriate position.

Choose Whether to Send and Receive Video

In the Sending and Receiving Video group box on the Video page of the Options dialog box, shown in Figure 5-18, specify whether you want to send and receive video automatically. As you'd imagine, the Automatically Send Video at the Start of Each Call check box is available only if you have a functioning Webcam attached to your computer. The Automatically Receive Video at the Start of Each Call check box is always available, because you don't need to have a Webcam

FIGURE 5-18   The Video page of the Options dialog box lets you specify the size and quality of video you send and receive.

to receive video. But, of course, you'll receive no video—regardless of whether this check box is selected—if the person at the other end of the (virtual) wire doesn't have a Webcam or if they've chosen not to send video for the call in question.

CAUTION   *Remember that a call that includes video can never be secure in NetMeeting.*

Specify Video Size and Quality

To specify the image size NetMeeting sends, select the Small option button, Medium option button, or Large option button in the Send Image Size group box. (In some cases, the Large option button or Small option button may not be available. I'll discuss why in the section "Troubleshoot Video Problems in NetMeeting" in Chapter 6.)

The image size you receive depends on the setting chosen by the person who's sending you video. But you can choose the relative quality of the video at that size by moving the I Prefer to Receive slider in the Video Quality group box along its axis from Faster Video to Better Quality. You're trading frame rate (the speed) against image quality here. We'll discuss this issue a bit more in the next chapter.

Specify a Video Capture Device

To specify the video camera for NetMeeting to use, select it in the The Video Capture Device I Want to Use Is drop-down list in the Video Camera Properties group box. If you have only one video camera attached to your computer, NetMeeting selects it by default. Depending on the type of video camera, you may be able to choose further options by clicking the Source button and the Format button to display configuration dialog boxes for it.

Display Your Video Preview As a Mirror Image

As you'll see in the next chapter, NetMeeting lets you display a preview window of the video image you're sending, which can be useful for checking that your camera position and lighting are acceptable, that your makeup is straight, and that you haven't got spinach stuck between your incisors. If you want to display your video preview as a mirror image (with left and right reversed, as it were), select the Show Mirror Image in Preview Video Window check box on the Video page of the Options dialog box. This option doesn't do much for me—but if you find that your image in the preview window seems to move the wrong way, this option may solve all kinds of problems for you.

Connect with NetMeeting

Establishing a connection with NetMeeting isn't quite as easy as with Messenger, because NetMeeting doesn't have a contacts list that requires you to be perpetually logged into a server. But you can place calls easily either manually or by using SpeedDial entries—or even Messenger, if the person you want to call with NetMeeting is a Messenger contact of yours. And you can call anybody who's using NetMeeting, not just anybody who's using Messenger.

Place a Call

The most direct way to place a call with NetMeeting is by using the Address box in the main NetMeeting window or the Place a Call dialog box. The advantage of the Place a Call dialog box, shown in Figure 5-19, is that you can choose which means of connection to use (Network, Directory, or Automatic) and you can specify whether to use security for the call by selecting or clearing the Require Security for This Call (Data Only) check box. The advantage of the Address box is that it's right there in the main NetMeeting window.

You can specify an address using an IP address, a DNS name, or an Internet Locator Server (ILS) name. If you're connecting to a home user, you'll most likely use their computer's IP address now that Microsoft has closed down the main ILS network. If you're connecting to a user on a company network, you'll probably use their computer's DNS name.

To place a call to an address or a number you've called recently, use the drop-down list in the main NetMeeting window or in the Place a Call dialog box. This list, which is called the History Call Log, stores the last 100 addresses or numbers you've called successfully.

The easiest way to find out your IP address is to choose Help | About Windows NetMeeting to display the About Windows NetMeeting dialog box and read the external IP address shown. If you're on a local network using nonroutable IP addresses, you'll also see one or more addresses on the 192.168.*n.n* or 169.254.*n.n* subnets. These addresses are internal addresses (the "nonroutable" bit means that they can't be routed, so they can't be used on the Internet), so they won't be the right ones unless you're using NetMeeting on an internal network.

You can also find out your IP address by opening a command-prompt window and running the **ipconfig** command. The advantage of this method is that **ipconfig** lists the IP addresses by network connection, so it's easy to tell which address is that of your Internet connection. (The disadvantage is that you have to open the command-prompt window.)

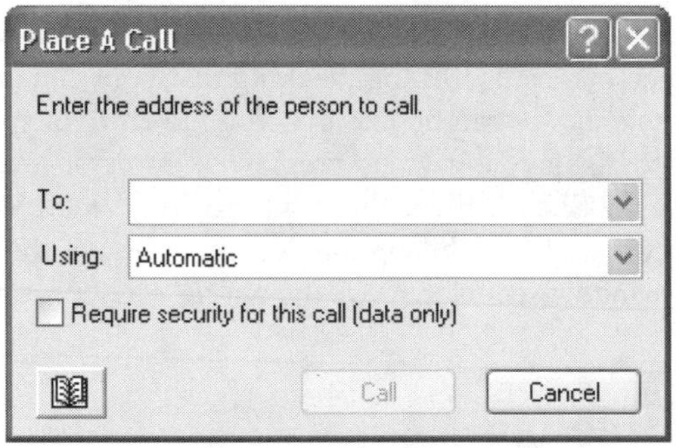

FIGURE 5-19   The Place a Call dialog box lets you specify the connection method and choose whether to require security for the call.

Create and Use SpeedDials

If you call the same people frequently, you can create SpeedDial entries for them. To create a SpeedDial entry, choose Call | Create SpeedDial and enter the information in the Create SpeedDial dialog box (see Figure 5-20). By default, NetMeeting suggests an address at logon.netmeeting.com, the old server network. Change this to an IP address, a DNS name, or an ILS address using a third-party ILS. In the Call Using drop-down list, specify whether to call via a directory or (more likely) a network. Leave the Add to SpeedDial List option button selected if you want to add the SpeedDial entry to your SpeedDial list (which we'll look at in a moment). Otherwise, select the Save on the Desktop option button to save the SpeedDial entry on your Desktop. Click the OK button to close the Create SpeedDial dialog box and create the SpeedDial entry.

To use a SpeedDial you've created, choose Call | Directory to display the Find Someone dialog box; then select SpeedDial in the Select a Directory drop-down list. Select the SpeedDial entry, select or clear the Make This a Secure Call (Data Only) check box, as appropriate, and click the Call button.

Use Messenger to Invite a Contact to Start a NetMeeting Session

Another way to start a NetMeeting session is to use Messenger to invite one of your Messenger contacts to use NetMeeting. The process is a little convoluted—but once you see how it works, it more or less makes sense. The problem is that, at this writing, it *doesn't* quite work, but I'm assuming that Microsoft will fix the problem (which I'll mention when we get to it).

FIGURE 5-20   You can create SpeedDial entries for people you need to contact often.

As you'd imagine, you and your contact both need to be signed into Messenger in order to make the connection—so as far as that goes, you might as well be using Messenger instead of NetMeeting, except for the security and file-transfer features that NetMeeting provides that Messenger doesn't.

NOTE   *Early versions of Windows Messenger (for example, the version provided with the original release of XP in 2001) included a command for inviting someone to start NetMeeting directly from the Messenger interface. Subsequent versions of Windows Messenger don't provide this functionality.*

To invite a Messenger contact to start a NetMeeting session, take these steps:

1. Run NetMeeting.

2. Choose Call | Directory to display the Find Someone dialog box.

3. If the Select a Directory drop-down list is showing anything other than Microsoft Internet Directory, select the Microsoft Internet Directory entry. The Find Someone dialog box displays a list of your Messenger contacts, sorted into Contacts Currently Online and Contacts Not Online groups.

4. Click the name of the contact you want to invite to a NetMeeting session. Messenger prompts the contact with a Conversation window that tells them you're inviting them to start using NetMeeting. They get to choose between an Accept link and a Decline link, as for other Messenger invitations.

5. If your contact clicks the Accept link, Messenger launches or activates NetMeeting on their computer. In theory, it should patch through the call so that NetMeeting accepts it automatically (or gives your contact the chance to accept it manually). But at this writing, NetMeeting just sits there on your contact's computer without taking the call, a bit like Sleeping Beauty waiting for the kiss of True Love, while NetMeeting on your computer waits forlornly for an answer that doesn't come.

To make this work, ask your contact (via Messenger) for their IP address; then cancel the automated NetMeeting call, enter the IP address, and call manually.

Accept a Call

When someone places a call to you, NetMeeting displays the NetMeeting – Incoming Call dialog box, of which Figure 5-21 shows three examples. The topmost example shows a call without security; as you can see, the dialog box shows an Accept button and an Ignore button. The middle example shows a call with security; the dialog box shows a Details button as well. The bottom example shows the information you see when you click the Details button: the information from the certificate used for encryption or authentication.

Click the Accept button to accept the call or the Ignore button to reject it. If the call is secure, you can click the Details button to display details of the digital certificate that the caller is using for encryption and authentication.

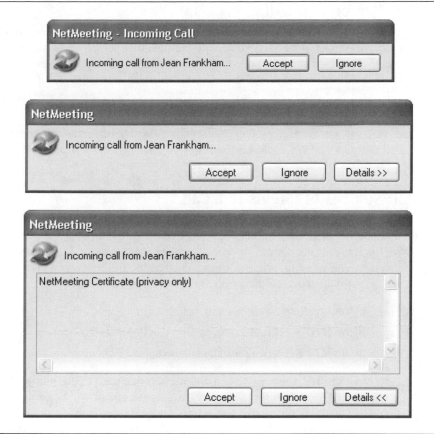

FIGURE 5-21   The NetMeeting – Incoming Call dialog box tells you who's calling and whether they're using security.

So far, so obvious—but two things are worth mentioning:

- First, if another meeting participant has control of your Desktop when you receive an incoming call, you need to take back control in order to accept the call. (Chapter 8 discusses how to use NetMeeting's remote-control features.)

- Second, if another meeting participant has control of a program you're sharing when you receive an incoming call, the Incoming Call dialog box may be hidden behind the shared program's window. When this happens, you'll need to coolswitch (press ALT+TAB) to NetMeeting to display the Incoming Call dialog box. (If you're using audio, you should be able to hear the ringing.)

You can set NetMeeting to answer calls automatically by choosing Call | Automatically Accept Calls. In most recent versions of NetMeeting, you need to choose this setting afresh in each session you start; whereas in older versions, the setting stuck from session to session.

Add Another Person to a Call

You can add another person to a NetMeeting call by placing a call to them once you've established the first call. Unlike Messenger, which lets you create multiple two-person text-chat calls at the same time, NetMeeting lets you have only one ongoing call. Any further people you call during a call are added to it.

Remove Someone from a Call

If you started the call, you get to enforce order. You can remove a participant from the call by right-clicking their entry in the Participant List and choosing Remove from Meeting from the context menu.

Increase the Number of Clients in a Call

So, how many people can you get together in a NetMeeting call? The short answer is that there isn't a specific number, but there are a number of factors you need to consider.

First, there's a limitation on the number of simultaneous connections that TCP/IP can support on the operating system you're using. Microsoft has published the figures shown here (note that these figures aren't exactly up to date, but they do provide some guidance):

- TCP/IP running on Windows 98 can usually handle eight clients.
- TCP/IP running on NT 4 Workstation can usually handle up to 16 clients.
- TCP/IP running on NT 4 Server can usually handle up to 26 clients.

Windows XP is most like NT 4 Server, so one might guess that the TCP/IP numbers for Windows XP are similar to the numbers for NT Server. Twenty-six clients will be enough for many people—it's more people than you get in most chat rooms, and you know how chaotic a chat room can be with even a dozen or so people pursuing different conversations or trying to discover who's worth hitting on. But if it's not enough for you, you can get more people in by cascading calls. Instead of having everyone call you, have the first group of people call you and then have other participants call those people in the first group. That way, you stay below the limitation on TCP/IP connections by spreading the load, but you get all the people into the call. Unless everyone has a blazingly fast connection, bandwidth then becomes the limitation rather than the number of TCP/IP connections.

If you choose to set up large calls (conferences, if you prefer) this way, make sure you don't select the Only You Can Accept Incoming Calls check box in the Meeting Settings group box in the Host a Meeting dialog box when setting up a meeting you're hosting.

The other thing to bear in mind is bandwidth. Even if you're only chatting with people, having a large number of people connected to the same call will start to soak up bandwidth. So, if your bandwidth is limited, you probably don't want to try to host the biggest free-for-all in the wired world.

TIP   *If you're using Windows 98 or NT 4, you can increase the number of TCP/IP connections in Windows 98 and NT 4 by editing the Registry. See Q243116 in the Microsoft Knowledge Base for details.*

Hang Up a Call

To end a call, click the End Call button or choose Call | Hang Up. If you started the call, hanging up ends the whole call, so NetMeeting displays a confirmation dialog box to that effect before it hangs up. If you're just one of the participants in the call, NetMeeting hangs up your connection immediately, leaving the other participants in the call to continue without you.

Troubleshoot Connections in NetMeeting

This section discusses some of the most common problems with connections in NetMeeting. As before, this section includes information on earlier versions of NetMeeting because the people with whom you're trying to communicate may be using them. This section closes with a discussion of how to let people connect to you from a Web page with NetMeeting. This isn't exactly a problem, but you may find the information helpful. (If you don't, you're—of course—free to skip it.)

Unable to Connect to the User

When trying to establish a connection to another NetMeeting user, you may get the message "User did not accept your call" or "User is unable to accept NetMeeting calls."

Normally, these messages mean pretty much what they say: "User did not accept your call" means either the user explicitly rejected your call or they didn't respond to it (for example, because they weren't there) and NetMeeting timed it out. "User is unable to accept NetMeeting calls" typically means that the user either isn't connected to the Internet or that they are connected but not running NetMeeting.

However, these messages sometimes indicate that your installation of NetMeeting has become damaged. If you get these messages consistently for every user you try to connect to, try uninstalling and reinstalling NetMeeting.

"The Conference Host Is Unable to Accept NetMeeting Calls" Error Message

If you get the message that the conference host is unable to accept NetMeeting calls, but you're pretty sure that they're online and waiting to hear from you, try again. These days, this error message typically indicates delays on the network. (In NetMeeting 2.1, it sometimes meant that two people were calling the conference host at the same time, which confused that version of NetMeeting.)

"There Was a Problem Connecting to the Directory Server" Error Message

If you get the message "There was a problem connecting to the directory server. You may not be connected to the network or the server may be busy," you should check your connection to the network and try the server at another time. But this message may also indicate that the ILS has an acceptable-use policy that considers inappropriate one or more of the words in your directory information (in the My Directory Information group box on the General page of the Options dialog box). For example, if you've used offensive words in the name, location, and comments fields, the ILS may take exception with you and refuse to log you on.

Wrong IP Address Registered with ILS

Sometimes you may find that an IP address registered with an ILS doesn't work. This can happen for either of two reasons:

■ First, the user has shut down Windows (or dropped their Internet connection) without quitting NetMeeting. When this happens, NetMeeting doesn't tell the ILS to remove the IP address registered for the user, even though the user can no longer be reached at that address.

■ Second, NetMeeting automatically registers the IP address of the first network adapter bound to TCP/IP in the computer. If that network adapter isn't the one with the IP address for contacting the computer, the IP address registered with the ILS will be wrong. For example, if you have a network adapter for your LAN as well as a dial-up connection or a broadband connection to the Internet, and TCP/IP is bound to both, NetMeeting may register the IP address of the LAN with the ILS instead of registering the IP address of the dial-up adapter or broadband card.

Can't Reconnect Quickly after Dropping the Connection

NetMeeting 2.*x* sometimes fails to detect when a connection has been dropped—for example, if your ISP times you out, or if there's another problem on the phone line. If you then try to reconnect immediately, NetMeeting tells you that "the person you called is currently in a meeting"—yes, the meeting you just dropped out of—and invites you to join it. If you try to accept this invitation, NetMeeting tells you the person is in *another* meeting and invites you to send a message. If you try again, NetMeeting may tell you that "the person you called accepted the call, but is not able to use Microsoft NetMeeting's audio features."

This is a known problem. If it happens, have everyone quit the conference and rebuild it from scratch.

Unable to Accept a Call Because the Directory Dialog Box or Advanced Calling Dialog Box Is Displayed

If you can't accept a call by pressing ENTER because the Directory dialog box or the Advanced Calling dialog box is open, try pressing the spacebar to accept the call. This problem occurs because the Directory dialog box and the Advanced Calling dialog box are system-modal dialog boxes rather than application-modal dialog boxes. (You have to dismiss a system-modal dialog box before you can continue to work with the system; whereas with an application-modal dialog box, you can continue to work in any program other than the one displaying the dialog box.)

Automatically Accept Calls Setting Doesn't Stick

As mentioned a few pages earlier, the Automatically Accept Calls setting doesn't stick in later versions of NetMeeting (whereas it did stick in earlier versions). Microsoft presumably intends this change to be a security enhancement, but it can trip you up if you choose the setting, then have to restart NetMeeting for whatever reason, and forget to reapply the setting in order to automatically accept incoming calls.

If you're using this setting to enable yourself to access your computer remotely, try using Remote Desktop Sharing instead. (Chapter 8 discusses how to configure and use Remote Desktop Sharing.)

WinFax Pro Answers Incoming NetMeeting Calls

Perhaps not entirely surprisingly, if you have WinFax Pro installed and configured to answer incoming calls, it tries to answer incoming NetMeeting calls. The solution, even less surprisingly, is to quit WinFax Pro or configure it not to answer incoming calls.

Can't Find Users via the Internet Locator Server

As mentioned earlier in this chapter, Microsoft has dismantled the Microsoft Internet Directory server network of ILS machines to shunt people toward using Messenger rather than NetMeeting. But there are various third-party ILS servers on the Internet, and some companies that use NetMeeting run their own ILS machines to provide user address–finding services for their clients.

> TIP   *You can run your own ILS on Linux if you have the equipment, the OS, and the determination. See the Linux NetMeeting HowTo (www.freesoft.org/software/NetMeeting/) for details.*

If you've found an ILS still in operation, there are various reasons why you may not be able to see another user on the ILS: First, the user may have told NetMeeting not to list them on the ILS. Barring that, the user may be there, but the ILS might not have been refreshed with the information; if so, try pressing F5 to refresh your listing. Then again, the ILS may be too busy to deal with your request; if so, log off, wait a few minutes, and log back on.

Alternatively, you may be looking on the wrong ILS. It's not immediately apparent that, unlike some other Internet services, ILS directory servers are independent and don't feed each other with user information.

If you're on the right ILS, but you're still not seeing anything, you may be looking in the wrong user category. Check which filter you're using (if any) and select the All category in the Category drop-down list to make sure you're seeing all users.

To remove or change your default ILS, run the Registry Editor, navigate to the HKEY_ CURRENT_USER\Software\Microsoft\Conferencing\UI\Directory key, and delete the Name*n* keys.

NOTE *Always quit NetMeeting before restarting your computer. If you don't quit NetMeeting, you may still be listed on the ILS after you restart your computer. This is because NetMeeting does not automatically log you off the ILS unless you quit NetMeeting manually (as opposed to having Windows shut down NetMeeting automatically, as happens when you restart your computer with NetMeeting still running).*

Can't Connect Through a Firewall

If your computer connects to the Internet through a firewall, you may be able to run NetMeeting without problems—or you may run into various kinds of problems, depending on how the firewall is configured and what its capabilities are.

In order for NetMeeting to work fully, the firewall needs to be configured to pass through primary TCP connections (on ports 389, 522, 1403, 1720, and 1731) and secondary UDP connections (on dynamically assigned ports in the range 1024 to 65535). Here's the brief version of what happens: NetMeeting uses port 1720 for the H.323 call setup protocol, which dynamically negotiates a TCP port for the call. Then the audio call control protocol, using port 1731, and the H.323 call setup protocol (still using port 1720) negotiate UDP ports from the range of available, dynamically assignable ports for the Real-Time Protocol (RTP), which runs on top of UDP. NetMeeting uses two ports on either side of the firewall for streaming audio and video.

Here's a breakdown of the IP ports NetMeeting uses and what it uses them for:

Port	Use	Protocol
389	Internet Locator Server	TCP
522	User Locator Server	TCP
1503	T.120	TCP
1720	H.323 call setup	TCP
1731	Audio call control	TCP
Dynamic	H.323 call control	TCP
Dynamic	H.323 streaming	RTP over UDP

If your firewall can handle the TCP connections but not the UDP connections, NetMeeting will provide basic functionality but no audio or video.

If your firewall can't virtualize internal IP addresses or can't virtualize them on-the-fly, you'll be able to establish outgoing NetMeeting connections through the firewall, but you won't be able to receive incoming connections from computers located outside the firewall.

Let People Connect to You from a Web Page

If you want to enable people to connect to you via NetMeeting from a Web page, create a call on the page to hyperlink to your IP address (if you have a fixed IP address), DNS name, or ILS logon name. Use the following formats:

Format	Example
callto:IP_Address	callto:192.168.0.44
callto:DNS_Name	callto:asterion.headquarters.local
callto:ILS/logon_name	callto:ils.microsoft.com/andy_rondolophberger@hotmail.com

For example, the hyperlink to an IP address might look like this:

```
<a href="callto:192.168.0.44">Chat with Me</a>
```

When someone clicks a hyperlink such as this, Internet Explorer activates or launches NetMeeting, which then attempts to place a call to the specified address. (This assumes that the URL: CallTo Protocol file type is registered to NetMeeting. If it's not, use the File Types page of the Folder Options dialog box to register it.)

The preceding method works with NetMeeting 2 or later and Internet Explorer 3 or later. If you want to ensure compatibility with earlier versions of NetMeeting or Internet Explorer, you need to go an extra mile. Create a SpeedDial entry to the address you want the hyperlink to call; then copy the SpeedDial to the appropriate Web folder and create a link to it on the page.

You can also create a SpeedDial file that causes NetMeeting to dial a phone number. To do so, open Notepad or another text editor and create a text file that contains these lines:

```
[ConferenceShortcut]
ConfName=Conference_Name
Address=Phone_Number
CallFlags=2
Transport=8
```

Save the file with the .CNF extension. (If you're using Notepad, enter the filename and extension in double quotation marks so that it doesn't get a .TXT extension after the .CNF extension.) Then place the file in a folder used for the Web page and put a link to the file on the Web page.

Chat with NetMeeting

Unlike Messenger, NetMeeting doesn't automatically dump you in a chat window the moment you establish a call. Instead, it lets you decide what you want to do: chat with text, voice, or video (or all three); share programs to collaborate on projects; transfer files to each other; or use the Whiteboard to brainstorm. This section discusses how to use the chat feature. The other features we'll visit in subsequent chapters.

To chat with the people in your call, click the Chat button. NetMeeting displays a Chat window on each participant's computer. Figure 5-22 shows an example of the Chat window.

Most of the chat features are easily grasped: You type the message in the text box and click the Send Message button to send it. By default, NetMeeting sends the message to every participant in the call, but you can choose to send a private message to a particular participant by using the

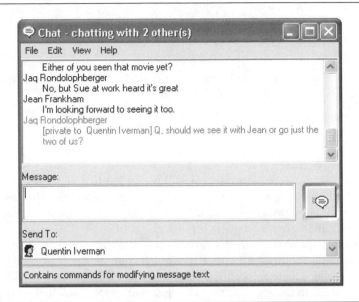

FIGURE 5-22   NetMeeting's Chat window provides modest but effective chat features,
including the ability to send private messages to individual participants.

Send To drop-down list. These messages appear in gray font and with "[private]" on the recipient's
computer and "[private to *participant's name*]" on the sender's (and, of course, don't appear in
the other participants' Chat windows).

You can paste text into the Chat text box; but if it's too long, it'll be truncated. On most versions
of NetMeeting, you can paste in 900 to 1,000 characters. NetMeeting doesn't warn you if you
paste in more characters than the buffer can hold—it just goes ahead and truncates the extra
characters without warning.

You can save a chat session at any time by choosing File | Save As. NetMeeting displays the
Save As dialog box. Specify the filename and location, choose the file type (either HTM or HTML
chat files or TXT or DOC text files), and click the Save button. Once you've saved a chat session,
you can save later versions of it (for example, when further chat has occurred) by choosing
File | Save.

When you close the Chat window, NetMeeting prompts you to save unsaved changes to Chat.

NOTE   *NetMeeting 2.11 prompted you to save Chat when a new participant joined in.*
Subsequent versions of NetMeeting don't do this.

Troubleshoot Chat in NetMeeting

When using NetMeeting to chat, audio conference, video conference, or collaborate with other Windows users, you may run into the problems detailed in the following subsections.

As before, this section ends with more of a tip than a problem: how to remove the evidence of your NetMeeting calls from NetMeeting.

Chat Initially Says "Not in a Call"

The Chat window displays "Not in a Call" in its title bar until NetMeeting has successfully communicated with the copies of NetMeeting running on the other participants' computers and made sure that the Chat window has been opened on their computers. The Chat window then displays in its title bar the number of people in the call—for example, "chatting with 2 other(s)."

Microsoft would probably claim this is a design feature of some kind, but I can't imagine what. Most people would consider it more of a clumsy implementation at best, but it's easy enough to work around.

"Unknown" Chat Participant

If a participant in Chat is listed as "Unknown," it usually means that they're using NetMeeting 2.*x* on Windows 95 or NT 4 and that they've quit the Chat session and then rejoined it. The workaround is for everyone to quit Chat and then restart it. Alternatively, you might want to ask "Unknown" who they are and continue anyway.

For another cause of an "Unknown" chat participant, see the next item.

NetMeeting 2.*x* Clients Can't See All Chat Participants

NetMeeting 2.*x* clients in a chat with NetMeeting 3.*x* clients may not be able to see all participants in Chat. This typically occurs when a NetMeeting 3.*x* user joins an existing chat—the T.120 protocol used by Chat fails to update correctly because NetMeeting 3.*x* uses H.323 to start a call, and as a result, the NetMeeting 2.*x* user sees the new user listed as "Unknown." The only solution is to upgrade from NetMeeting 2.*x* to NetMeeting 3.*x*.

Windows NT 4 Problems

Running NetMeeting when using the default VGA video driver may make NT crash with a blue screen of death and the message "STOP: 0x0000001E: KMODE_EXCEPTION_NOT_HANDLED." To avoid this, use a different video driver for your video card.

NetMeeting 2.*x* Problems

NetMeeting 2.*x* on Windows 95, 98, or NT 4 may automatically reopen a Chat window you've tried to close when you're chatting with someone who's using NetMeeting 3.0 or later. There's no workaround but to upgrade from NetMeeting 2.*x*.

NetMeeting 2.*x* on Windows 95 or NT 4 may cause the participant to be listed as "Unknown" if they quit Chat and then join back in.

"Your Program Is Making an Invalid Dynamic Link Call to a .DLL" Error Message

This error message, which you may see on NetMeeting running on Windows 95 and 98, usually means that the Rfmk2v.dll file (a 16-bit multimedia file described as "S3 Ready for Multimedia Video Processor/ScalarS3") is in the Windows\System folder. You may be able to work around this problem by renaming the Rfmk2v.dll file and remarking out the following lines in your system.ini file (to remark out a line, put a semicolon at its beginning):

```
[386Enh]
dci=RFMDCI
...
[Display]
DCI-Support=On
```

Be aware that doing this may prevent NetMeeting from working with the video stream from your camera.

Remove the Evidence of Your NetMeeting Calls

Just as you can erase (though not rewrite) your History in Internet Explorer and wipe out the record of your recent documents in Explorer, you can remove the evidence of the NetMeeting calls you've placed by removing the entries from the Address box in the New Call dialog box.

To do so, run the Registry Editor (choose Start | Run, enter **regedit** in the Open text box in the Run dialog box, and click the OK button), navigate to the HKEY_CURRENT_USER\ Software\Microsoft\Conferencing\UI\CallMRU key, and remove any Name*n* or Addr*n* entries that you wouldn't want other people to see—or change the entries to those of people or computers you want the nosy to think you've called.

Host a Meeting

NetMeeting calls are fine for on-the-fly conversations and ad hoc gatherings, but if you want to get a large group of people together online and keep the result manageable (as opposed to the melee of the average unregulated chat room), you'll probably want to host a meeting instead. By hosting a meeting, you can limit participants to people who know the password (which you set for each meeting), prevent participants from letting other people join the meeting by connecting to them, and prevent participants from using tools other than those you've specified.

Set Up a Meeting

To set up a meeting, choose Call | Host Meeting and specify the details in the Host a Meeting dialog box (see Figure 5-23).

FIGURE 5-23   The Host a Meeting dialog box lets you set a password, security restrictions, and tool restrictions for the meeting.

Change the default name of Personal Conference to something that describes the meeting (so that people joining it will know they've reached the right meeting) and set a unique password in the Meeting Password text box. Communicate this password as securely as possible to each meeting participant.

Select the Require Security for This Meeting (Data Only) check box to use encryption (and, depending on the digital certificates involved, authentication) for the meeting. You won't be able to effectively use audio or video for a meeting involving multiple people, so there's no downside to requiring security.

If you want to restrict participation in the meeting to people whose entry you approve, select the Only You Can Accept Incoming Calls check box and the Only You Can Place Outgoing Calls check box. Otherwise, anyone you let into the meeting will be able to admit other people by accepting calls from them or by calling them.

If you want to maintain control over the tools used during the meeting, select the appropriate check boxes in the Meeting Tools group box. Once you've selected the check box for a tool, nobody else but you can start the tool, but everyone can use it once you've started it. For example, you might want to prevent meeting participants from using sharing and file transfer so that they don't get distracted (or squander their bandwidth on frivolities) during the meeting.

Once you've finished choosing restrictions for the meeting, click the OK button to close the Host a Meeting dialog box and start the meeting. NetMeeting acts a bit confused in that its window announces you're "not in a meeting," but it puts your name in the Participant List box, indicating that you are in fact in the meeting but on your own.

Admit or Repel Boarders

When someone tries to join the meeting, NetMeeting displays the NetMeeting – Incoming Call dialog box as usual, so you can accept or ignore the call.

Add Other Participants

You can add other participants to the meeting by placing calls to them as usual. When you do so, NetMeeting doesn't prompt them for a password, but it displays the Meeting Properties dialog box so that they know the name of the meeting and the restrictions you've imposed on it.

Remove a Participant from a Meeting

To remove a participant from a conference, right-click their entry in the Name list box in the main NetMeeting window and choose Remove from Meeting from the context menu.

Join a Meeting

To join a meeting, place a call (secure, if necessary) to the meeting host, just as you would place a regular NetMeeting call. If the meeting host has set a password for the meeting, NetMeeting displays the Enter Password dialog box (see Figure 5-24). Enter the meeting password and click the OK button. If you get it right, NetMeeting displays the NetMeeting – Incoming Call dialog box to the host, who gets to decide whether they want you in the meeting.

FIGURE 5-24   When joining a meeting that the host has protected with a password, you'll see the Enter Password dialog box.

If the host accepts your call, the Meeting Properties dialog box, shown in Figure 5-25, is displayed to notify you of any restrictions the host has set on the meeting. When you click the OK button (there's no alternative) to dismiss the Meeting Properties dialog box, you're in the meeting.

If the host rejects your call, NetMeeting displays a message box telling you that they didn't let you into the meeting.

End the Meeting

To end a meeting (and thus remove all participants from it), hang up.

Summary

In this chapter, you've learned the advantages and disadvantages that Messenger and NetMeeting bring to the chat party. You've seen how to configure Messenger to eliminate some of its worst excesses, and how to set up NetMeeting and configure it to work as well as possible with your hardware. You've learned to make insecure calls for chat with Messenger and secure calls for chat with NetMeeting. You've also seen how to use NetMeeting to set up secure meetings in which you can control the tools available to participants.

FIGURE 5-25   The Meeting Properties dialog box details any restrictions the host has placed on the meeting participants.

Yet (I hardly need tell you) in this brave, new multimedia world, mankind does not chat by text alone—most people prefer to chat with sound and video, if possible—and both Messenger and NetMeeting make audio and video chat easy, as discussed in the next chapter. Because you've got the tedious details of configuring Messenger and NetMeeting out of the way, we'll be able to move along quickly. Let's go!

Chapter 6

Make Free Worldwide Voice and Video Conference Calls

This chapter discusses how to make voice and video calls using your PC and your Internet connection. By using Messenger, NetMeeting, and Phone Dialer, you can make PC-to-PC calls that cost you nothing more than the cost of your Internet connection. These calls can be to any computer in the world that has an Internet connection. And by using Messenger with a suitably configured voice service provider, you can also make calls from your PC to a phone anywhere in the world.

Most of the chapter concentrates on Messenger and NetMeeting, because these are the programs you're likely to want to use for most of your computer-based voice and video calls. However, both Messenger and NetMeeting are limited as of this writing to two-party voice and video calling, whereas the humble Phone Dialer program can make voice and video calls to up to six people. So at the end of the chapter I show you how to use Phone Dialer to make voice and video calls involving more than two parties.

This chapter concentrates on making computer-to-computer calls because once you have your Internet connection, the calls are essentially free. But toward the end of the Messenger section, I also discuss the features that Messenger provides for making calls from your computer to a telephone at the other end. The advantage of this is that you can use your computer to call anybody in the world who has a telephone—they don't have to have a computer, or if they do have one, they don't have to be at it in order to receive the call. The disadvantage is that many of the services for PC-to-phone calling charge per minute—in some cases, about the same amount as the low-cost long-distance and international carriers. This removes the advantage of using your PC to place calls—so unless you're really attached to your PC, you might as well not bother.

> **NOTE** *This chapter assumes that you've configured Messenger and NetMeeting as discussed in the previous chapter. If you haven't, please go back and do so—or at least have the grace to thrash about on your own without complaining that I haven't told you how to do the configuration.*

Should You Use Messenger or NetMeeting?

Before we start, cast your mind back briefly to the differences between Messenger and NetMeeting that I mentioned at the beginning of Chapter 5: With Messenger, every move you make is tracked by the .NET Messenger Service, which means you're providing a lot of information on your habits, preferences, and contacts when you're using Messenger. By contrast, with NetMeeting, you can make calls without anybody but your ISP knowing.

This chapter discusses Messenger first because it's marginally easier to use than NetMeeting. But if you want security, choose NetMeeting over Messenger every time.

> **NOTE** *One quick thing that should be obvious but that a surprising number of people miss— because Messenger and NetMeeting establish a direct connection between your computer and that of the person you're conversing with, your communication speeds are limited by the slower of the two Internet connections. For example, if you have a fiber-optic connection but your interlocutor has a modem connection, things will take place at modem speeds.*

Choose and Set Up Audio and Video Hardware

At the risk of stating the obvious, your computer needs to have sound hardware installed and working in order for you to make voice calls.

Audio Hardware

In most cases, you'll want a sound card, a microphone, and either speakers or headphones. (If you have an immovable sound card that's wretched beyond belief, you may want to use USB to bypass it. USB speakers, headphones, and microphones are all available.)

Most sound cards that are compatible with XP (and that have drivers for XP) will work fine for voice conferencing with Messenger, NetMeeting, and Phone Dialer. The key requirement is that the sound card be able to handle full-duplex sound—sending and receiving sound at the same time. If the card is capable only of half duplex (either sending or receiving at any given point, but not both at once), your conversations will be unsatisfactory at best.

TIP   *If you don't know whether your sound card supports full duplex, you can check quickly by opening two instances of Sound Recorder (Start | All Programs | Accessories | Entertainment | Sound Recorder). In the first instance of Sound Recorder, open a WAV file of a decent length (for example, one of the standard XP sounds in the \Windows\ Media\ folder), and set it playing. In the second instance of Sound Recorder, click the Record button to start recording a file. If the WAV file continues to play and the recording is successful, your sound card supports full duplex and is correctly configured for it. Another way of finding out whether your sound card supports full duplex is to check its spec sheet, but doing so won't tell you whether the sound card is correctly configured for full duplex.*

If you're using speakers, connect them to the correct output on your sound card and position them so that they produce the type of stereo or surround image they're supposed to—stereo, 5.1, 7.1, or whatever. Check the setting on the Speakers page of the Advanced Audio Properties dialog box to make sure that XP knows what type of speaker setup you're using. (To display the Advanced Audio Properties dialog box, click the Advanced button on the Volume page of the Sounds and Audio Devices Properties dialog box.)

Connect your microphone to your sound card's microphone input and position it where it will pick up your voice without catching too much input from the speakers. Unless you like to transmit rasping and spluttering, keep the microphone out of your breath stream and spit-field. Usually, positioning the microphone to the side of your mouth or by your throat works well. Most headset microphones are designed with this in mind.

Video Hardware

Most Webcams that are compatible with XP (and that have drivers for XP) will work okay for videoconferencing with Messenger, NetMeeting, and Phone Dialer. None of these programs can handle a resolution higher than 352×288 pixels, which is the resolution that even the cheesiest Webcams provide, so you don't need to go for a super-high-end Webcam with 800×600 or

1024×768 resolution for conferencing. (By contrast, if you're planning to use the Webcam to record video, a higher resolution will benefit you.) But cheaper Webcams do tend to provide lower image quality at a given resolution than their better-constructed counterparts.

CAUTION *Many Webcams sold for (or with) Windows 98 and Windows Me PCs won't work with XP because no drivers for them are available. At this writing—four months after XP was released—some major vendors have yet to provide XP drivers for their Webcams. (Creative and Kensington, I'm looking at you here.) Others, such as Dexxa, have decided not to provide XP drivers for some products currently being pumped through the retail channels.*

You may also be able to use a digital video camcorder or a camera that attaches to your PC using an analog TV tuner adapter.

Position the camera where it catches you from the best angle, while making it look as though you're looking soulfully into the camera—and make sure you're adequately lit. If the camera has zoom or focus controls, use them.

Voice and Video with Messenger

This section discusses how to make voice and video calls with Messenger. Messenger makes it as easy as possible to add voice and video to your existing conversations, so this section is relatively short. There's not even much troubleshooting information on this topic to share.

NOTE *If you're interested in making PC-to-phone calls with Messenger, see the section "Make PC-to-Phone Calls with Messenger" in the middle of the chapter for details on how to get started doing this.*

Run the Audio and Video Tuning Wizard

If you haven't configured Messenger to use your audio and video hardware, it's a good idea to run the Audio and Video Tuning Wizard to set up the hardware. If you don't run the wizard, it springs into action when you try to add audio or video (or both) to a call—which can be awkward if you're midway through a conversation at the time.

To run the Audio and Video Tuning Wizard, choose Tools | Audio Tuning Wizard. The wizard walks you through the following steps, with one step to a page:

1. Close other programs that "show video, or play or record sound" (read: just about any program, but especially Windows Media Player, Sound Recorder, Windows Movie Maker, and similar programs), and make sure your hardware devices are plugged in and turned on.

2. Select the camera you want to use (if you have only one, obviously you'll use that one).

3. Preview the image the camera is getting so that you can reposition it or yourself, as necessary, or maybe focus or zoom the camera.

4. Position your speakers and microphone relative to yourself and each other.

5. Choose the microphone and speakers to use (again, unless you're serious about your multimedia, you probably won't have a choice here) and specify whether you're using headphones. (Selecting the I Am Using Headphones check box turns off acoustic echo cancellation. More on this in the "Troubleshoot Messenger Audio and Video" section.)

6. Test your speaker volume.

7. Set your microphone sensitivity. (Read the provided text—or declaim free verse—at your normal conversational volume. Otherwise, you'll get a sensitivity setting that won't match your normal delivery.)

If the wizard detects any obvious problems, such as a total lack of input when your free verse should be making its virtual toes curl, it notifies you of them so that you can fix them and try again.

If your environment for using Messenger changes (for example, it gets noisier or quieter), or you change your hardware or move the hardware around, run the Audio and Video Tuning Wizard again to retune your settings.

Hold a Voice Conversation

You can start a voice conversation from scratch or add voice to an existing conversation. Here's how:

■ To start a voice conversation from scratch, click the Start a Voice Conversation link in the action pane and use the Start a Voice Conversation dialog box to select the victim on the My Contacts page or the Other page. (Note that the Start a Voice Conversation dialog box is the Send an Instant Message dialog box shown in Figure 5-10 in the previous chapter, but now in another disguise.) Messenger gives your victim a pop-up telling them that you're sending them an invitation.

■ To add voice to an existing conversation, click the Start Talking button in the Conversation window or choose Actions | Start Talking.

In the Conversation window, your victim sees an announcement that you want to have a voice conversation with them. The announcement contains an Accept link and a Decline link that they can click to respond to the invitation.

If they click the Accept link, Messenger sets up the audio channel between you, and you should be able to talk to each other. Use the Speakers control to control the speaker volume and the Microphone control to adjust the microphone sensitivity. The Speakers control is linked to the master volume control for XP. For example, if you use the Volume icon in the notification area to adjust the volume, you'll see the Speakers control reflect this change. Similarly, the Microphone control is linked to the microphone control for recording. (More on this in the "Troubleshoot Messenger Audio and Video" section, coming right up.)

To end a voice conversation, click the Close button in the Conversation window or choose File | Close. To end the voice part of the conversation but continue chat (and other tools such as program sharing), click the Stop Talking button or choose Actions | Stop Talking.

> **NOTE** *Even though Messenger leaves the Invite Someone to This Conversation link available when you're in a voice or voice-and-video call, you can't add another person to the call. If you choose this link, Messenger adds to the Conversation window a message telling you so.*

Hold a Voice and Video Conversation

As with voice, you can start a voice and video conversation from scratch or add voice and video to an existing conversation. Here's how:

- To start a voice and video conversation from scratch, click the Start a Video Conversation link in the action pane (if necessary, click the More item at the bottom of the initial I Want To list and select the link from the continuation of the list). Then use the Start a Video Conversation dialog box (which is another disguised version of the Send an Instant Message dialog box) to select your victim. Again, Messenger gives the victim a pop-up telling them that you want to see and be seen.

- To add voice and video to an existing conversation, click the Start Camera button in the Conversation window or choose Actions | Start Camera.

In the Conversation window, your victim sees an announcement that you want to have a video and voice conversation with them. The announcement contains an Accept link and a Decline link that they can click to respond to the invitation.

> **NOTE** *Before you ask—you can't have a video conversation in Messenger without using voice as well. Microsoft probably justifies this on the basis that anyone wanting to have a video call will necessarily want to use voice as well—and that if you have the bandwidth to send video, you can afford to send voice, too. This is all true enough, but it doesn't let people with low-bandwidth connections use text chat enhanced by the occasional video picture (perhaps at a minimal frame rate) but unburdened by voice. Which is a pity, because it'd be nice to be able to do this. I guess you can save a quick digital snap of yourself as a file and use file transfer to get it to whomever you're chatting with, but it's not the same as a live feed—even a very slow one.*

If the other person clicks the Accept link, Messenger sets up the audio and video channels between you two. Figure 6-1 shows an ongoing voice and video conversation.

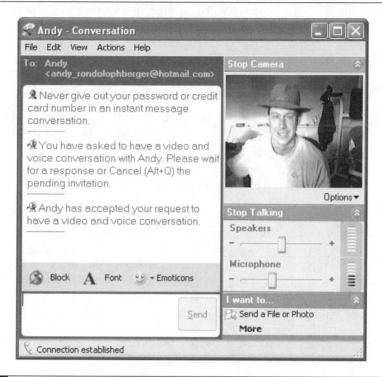

FIGURE 6-1 A voice and video conversation in Messenger

Messenger offers a couple of options when you're sending video. You can access each option either from the View menu or from the menu Messenger displays when you click the Options button below the video window. These are the options:

- The Stop Sending Video command stops transmitting video without tearing down the video connection between you and the other party. This is a toggle setting, so you issue the same command again to restart video. Stopping the video momentarily like this is useful for recovering from a bandwidth crunch or taking a timeout to scratch yourself in an embarrassing place without the camera betraying you.

- The Show My Video As Picture-in-Picture command toggles your video preview on and off. This command is available only when you're sending video.

To end a voice and video conversation, click the Close button on the Conversation window or choose File | Close. To end the voice and video part of the conversation but continue using other tools (for example, chat and Whiteboard), click the Stop Camera button or choose Actions | Stop Camera. (Stopping the camera also stops the audio.)

Troubleshoot Messenger Audio and Video

This section discusses some of the most common problems with audio and video on Messenger.

Microphone Slider in the Conversation Window Seems Not to Work

If the Microphone slider in the Conversation window seems not to adjust the recording volume, Messenger's microphone setting may be associated with XP's microphone control for playback rather than for recording.

To change the association, open the volume control by clicking the Advanced Volume Controls link in the See Also task list on the Sounds, Speech, and Audio Devices page in Control Panel (select Start | Control Panel, and then click the Sounds, Speech, and Audio Devices link). Be aware that the volume control goes by various names, depending on your audio hardware—it may be called Master Volume, Play Control, or something else.

Choose Options | Properties to display the Properties dialog box, select the Recording option button in the Adjust Volume For group box, and click the OK button. XP switches the volume control display to that of the recording control and (in most cases) changes the name of the window to something like Recording Control or Record Control. (Again, the name depends on your hardware and software.)

At this point, you might feel you need to adjust the microphone settings in the window. Do so if you feel like it; but if not, just close the Recording Control window (or whatever it's called on your computer). This little rigmarole should have associated the Messenger Microphone slider with the microphone control for recording.

Microphone Slider Moves When You Move the Speaker Slider

If you find that moving the Speaker slider to adjust the volume of a call causes the Microphone slider to move as well, rest assured that this is normal behavior because of the automatic gain control, which attempts to equalize sound volume. (Unlike NetMeeting, Messenger doesn't let you turn off automatic gain control, deeming it good for you, so you can't do much about this quirk.)

Messenger Delivers Feedback or Echo

If you get echoing or feedback on your Messenger audio calls, download the Messenger fix that contains the Acoustic Echo Cancellation (AEC) update from the Microsoft Support Web site (support.microsoft.com). At this writing, AEC works only with USB cameras that use Microsoft USB audio, but Microsoft may have improved the fix by the time you read this—so it's worth checking the Microsoft Support Web site even if your camera doesn't match that description. (Search for "Windows Messenger" and "Acoustic Echo Cancellation.")

XP doesn't include AEC, so Messenger needs to implement AEC itself. Messenger's Options dialog box doesn't give you an option for turning AEC on and off, but the I Am Using Headphones check box on the Select the Microphone and Speakers You Want to Use page of the Audio Tuning Wizard turns off AEC.

If AEC doesn't work with your hardware, try repositioning your microphone and speakers, or use headphones instead of speakers.

Messenger Doesn't Support Your DV Camcorder or Analog TV Tuner Adapter

If Messenger doesn't support your digital video camcorder or analog TV tuner adapter, download the Messenger fix that contains the Acoustic Echo Cancellation (AEC) update, as described in the preceding section. This fix includes support for digital video camcorders and analog TV tuners (although AEC itself doesn't work with them).

Make PC-to-Phone Calls with Messenger

As mentioned at the beginning of this chapter, you can also use Messenger to make calls from your PC to a regular phone. For PC-to-phone calls, Messenger uses .NET Voice Services— another component in the plethora of .NET services.

In order to use .NET Voice Services, you need to sign up with a voice service provider (VSP)—a company that provides telephony services compatible with .NET Voice Services.

At this writing, .NET Voice Services doesn't work through Network Address Translation (NAT), including Internet Connection Sharing (ICS) and many wireless network systems, so you can use it only on a PC that has a direct connection to the Internet. Microsoft is working to upgrade .NET Voice Services to work with NAT—so check to see if they've finished.

Choose Your Voice Service Provider

The first step in making PC-to-phone calls with Messenger is to choose your VSP. The way Messenger is set up, you can use only one voice service provider at a time, so do your homework before signing up with one.

The easiest way to sign up for a VSP is to click the Make a Phone Call link in the Action pane or choose Actions | Make a Phone Call. Messenger displays the Phone window, checks that your computer has a suitable connection to the Internet (in other words, no NAT at this writing), and offers you a Get Started Here button. Click it, and Messenger displays the Select a Voice Service Provider window with links to providers. Investigate the providers, choose the one that best meets your needs, sign up for it, and buy some minutes to use. (If you get a message that tells you your voice service account information is temporarily unavailable and invites you to click a link to check .NET Service status, wait for a while and then try again.)

Once you've signed up for a VSP, its name appears in the Phone window. Figure 6-2 shows an example.

FIGURE 6-2 The Phone window lists your VSP and provides basic controls for making PC-to-phone calls via your Internet connection.

Make a Call

To make a call, display the Phone window by clicking the Make a Phone Call link in the Action pane or by choosing Actions | Make a Phone Call. Specify the country and the phone number and click the Dial button.

To call a contact, you can click the Contacts icon and use the resulting Make a Phone Call dialog box (the Send an Instant Message dialog box in yet another disguise) to select the contact. The Phone window phone-number drop-down list displays the contact's numbers so that you can choose the right one.

For the recipient, the call appears to be a regular incoming call on their telephone, except that because of the analog-to-digital and digital-to-analog conversions, the quality is much lower than that of a regular voice call.

Change Your Voice Service Provider

In order to change to a different VSP, you need to cancel your existing VSP account, so it's not a change to make on the spur of the moment.

To change your VSP, choose Tools | Change Voice Service from the Phone window. Messenger connects to your VSP, which walks you through the process of canceling your account. You can then sign up for a new account with another VSP by clicking the Get Started Here button in the Phone window.

Voice and Video with NetMeeting

This section discusses how to make two-person voice and video calls with NetMeeting. As you'll remember from the previous chapter, NetMeeting can make secure data-only calls, but all calls involving voice and video are insecure and can be monitored easily by any security agency that can tap into the ISP at either end.

Run the Audio Tuning Wizard

If you've added your audio and video hardware to your computer since you set up NetMeeting, run the Audio Tuning Wizard to make sure NetMeeting knows which hardware you want to use and has the speaker and microphone levels set sensibly.

Hold an Audio Conversation

If you have functioning audio hardware on your computer, all you need to do to start an audio conversation with another user is place an insecure call to them. (By default, NetMeeting sets up audio on insecure calls.)

To change the audio levels, click the Adjust Audio Volume button to make NetMeeting display the audio controls, shown in Figure 6-3, in place of the participant list. You can then select or clear the Mute/Unmute Microphone check box to mute or unmute the microphone, drag the Adjust Microphone Volume slider to adjust the microphone sensitivity, select or clear the Mute/Unmute Speakers check box to mute or unmute the speakers, and drag the Adjust Speaker Volume slider to adjust the speaker volume.

Hold a Video Conversation

If you've selected the Automatically Send Video at the Start of Each Call check box and the Automatically Receive Video at the Start of Each Call check box in the Sending and Receiving Video group box on the Video page of the Options dialog box, NetMeeting automatically starts sending and receiving video when you establish a connection to another NetMeeting user.

TIP   *Although you can set NetMeeting to start video automatically at the beginning of each call, it's usually better to start video manually once you've established the call and ascertained that audio works correctly. This is because, if you get a low-bandwidth connection at either end, trying to use video will prevent you from using audio to figure out the problem and deciding how to deal with it, so you'll have to fall back on text chat.*

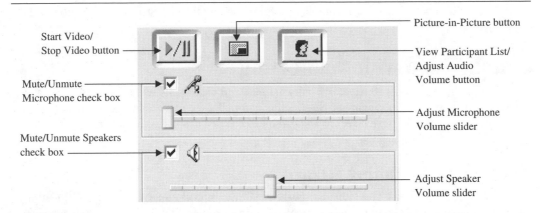

Start Video/
Stop Video button

Mute/Unmute
Microphone check box

Mute/Unmute Speakers
check box

Picture-in-Picture button

View Participant List/
Adjust Audio
Volume button

Adjust Microphone
Volume slider

Adjust Speaker
Volume slider

FIGURE 6-3   Display the audio controls to adjust the speaker volume or microphone volume.

If you haven't chosen to send video automatically, you can start sending it by clicking the Start Video/Stop Video button (the leftmost of the three buttons under the video window) or by choosing Tools | Video | Send once you've set up an insecure call. Figure 6-4 shows a video call underway.

To display the video image you're sending as a picture-in-picture miniature on the lower-right corner of the video window, click the Picture-in-Picture button or choose View | Picture-in-Picture.

To view the video image you're sending at its full size (instead of at the picture-in-picture size), choose View | My Video.

To stop and start receiving video, right-click the video picture and select Pause from the context menu or choose Tools | Video | Receive.

You can't change the size of the video image being sent to you, but you can change the size at which NetMeeting displays it on your computer. To do so, right-click the video window, select the Window Size item from the context menu, and choose 100%, 200%, 300%, or 400% from the submenu. (Alternatively, choose Tools | Video | Window Size and choose the size from the submenu.) The bigger you pump the image up, the grainier it'll be, but increasing the size by a modest amount can make it easier to see.

Record a NetMeeting Call

NetMeeting doesn't include any functionality for recording audio calls, but you can do so easily by using conventional analog hardware or by piping the output signal from the conference back

FIGURE 6-4   A video call in NetMeeting

into a soundcard other than the one NetMeeting is using and then using a sound-recording program to capture it.

Remember that the legalities of recording a phone call vary from state to state. In many states, you have to obtain the other party's express or implied consent. (For example, when your credit card company's voicemail message announces that they may record your call "for training purposes" or "for quality assurance," your consent is implied by your not dropping the line.)

> **TIP** *To capture a still image of the video being sent to you, right-click the video picture and choose Copy from the context menu. Then paste the image into a graphics program such as Paint.*

Troubleshoot Audio Problems in NetMeeting

This section discusses how to troubleshoot the most common audio problems in NetMeeting. The section breaks these problems down into two basic categories: First, you can't get any audio. Second, you can get audio, but it sounds bad.

Troubleshooting audio problems in NetMeeting is doubly exciting because it can be hard to tell whether the problems are being caused at your end of the connection or at your would-be interlocutor's end. As before, in this section, I mention problems and solutions for problems involving older versions of NetMeeting and Windows, as well as those versions for XP, because the person you're trying to speak to may be running an older version of NetMeeting or Windows.

No Audio

This subsection discusses how to troubleshoot the lack of sound or loss of sound in NetMeeting. The next subsection discusses how to troubleshoot assorted problems with the sound you're getting.

Check the Sound Card, Speakers or Headphones, and Your Ears   Start with the basics:

- Do you have a sound card, and is it working?
- Can you play sounds from other programs through your sound card and speakers or headphones?
- Is the volume control set to a reasonable volume, or has muting somehow been applied to all sound? When you start NetMeeting, it picks up the current master volume setting from the PC—so if you've turned that all the way down, you won't be getting any sound in NetMeeting.
- Do the speakers require power?
- If you have two or more sound cards, has NetMeeting selected the right one? If not, use the Audio Tuning Wizard to select the right one.

Okay. Good. We can proceed.

Turn Off Other Audio Sources   If you're not able to get audio in NetMeeting, turn off any other audio source that you're using. For example, if you're listening to an Internet radio station, playing back MP3 files, or ripping a CD and listening to it, you may be unable to get audio in NetMeeting at the same time.

Use TCP/IP to Establish the Conference   NetMeeting transfers audio and video using the H.323 videoconferencing protocol over TCP/IP. If you're using a connection established using any protocol other than TCP/IP (for example, if you're using the TCP/IP emulator SLiRP), you won't be able to use NetMeeting's audio and video features. To use these features, use TCP/IP to establish the NetMeeting connection.

TCP/IP is so firmly engrained in all versions of Windows since Windows 98 that it's easy to forget it wasn't installed by default on Windows 95. So, if you're using Windows 95, you may need to install TCP/IP manually, configure IP addresses (or set the computer to use DHCP), and perhaps even configure a HOSTS file for resolving domain names and an LMHOSTS file for resolving other names.

> **NOTE**   *NetMeeting versions before 2.1 supported IPX and PSTN (public-switched telephone network—in other words, modem-to-modem connections) protocols. NetMeeting 2.1 and later versions support only TCP/IP over a LAN or a dial-up connection.*

Disable TCP/IP Header Compression on the Dial-up Networking Connection   (This applies only to Windows 95, Windows 98, Windows 98 Second Edition, and Windows NT 4.)

If one of the ISPs involved doesn't support IP header compression, you may be unable to start audio or video. To work around this, disable IP header compression on the dial-up networking connection by clearing the Use IP Header Compression check box on the TCP/IP Settings page of the Server Type dialog box for the dial-up connection.

NetMeeting 2.*x* Can't Resume Audio or Video after Stopping Audio or Video   Sometimes when a NetMeeting 2.*x* client stops audio or video in a call with a NetMeeting 3.*x* client, the NetMeeting 2.*x* client can't resume audio or video in the call. The only solution is to end the call and make another. (Better, upgrade to the latest version of NetMeeting unless you have a compelling reason to stay with NetMeeting 2.*x*.)

Set the Sample Rate Conversion Quality to "Best"   With some versions of NetMeeting, you may need to set Sample Rate Conversion Quality to the Best setting in order to enable audio with NetMeeting.

For example, in Windows XP, display the Advanced Audio Properties dialog box by clicking the Advanced button in the Sound Playback group box on the Audio page of the Sounds and Audio Devices Properties dialog box. (You can display the Sound and Audio Devices Properties dialog box by right-clicking the Volume icon on the Taskbar and choosing Adjust Audio Properties from the context menu, or by going through Control Panel.) On the Performance page, move the Sample Rate Conversion Quality slider to the Best setting and then click the OK button.

Start NetMeeting Fully Before Accepting an Incoming Call   If you accept an incoming call while you're starting up NetMeeting and before it has fully started up, you may be unable to use audio or video during the call. This happens when NetMeeting on your computer hasn't started up enough to respond to an incoming request for a connection using the H.323 protocol. The calling computer takes this lack of response to mean that your version of NetMeeting can't handle H.323. It then attempts to establish a connection using T.120, which your computer (which has probably fully started NetMeeting by now) accepts.

If you run into this problem, disconnect the call and establish it anew.

Proxy Server Ports 1720 and 1731 Must Be Open   If you're connecting through a proxy server, and everything else seems okay but you're unable to get audio, check whether ports 1720 and 1731 are open. (Ask your server administrator if need be.) NetMeeting needs these ports to be open on the proxy server in order to send audio.

Audio Sounds Bad

This subsection discusses problems that may make the audio in NetMeeting sound bad and what, if anything, you can do about them.

Too Much Background Noise   If you're using NetMeeting in a noisy environment, your microphone may be picking up too much background noise for it to convey your voice clearly. Reduce the background noise, if possible, or reposition the microphone so that it picks up less of the noise. Run the Audio Tuning Wizard to retune the microphone.

Audio Quality Is Low   Several problems can cause low audio quality, including lack of processing power, lack of bandwidth, and poor microphone placement or tuning. If you have an older computer, minimize the demands on it by quitting any programs that you don't need to have running while you're using NetMeeting. Similarly, if you have limited bandwidth, prevent other programs from using it for the duration. Check for obvious deficiencies in the positioning of your microphone and run the Audio Tuning Wizard to see if it can tune the microphone better.

Audio Is Inaudible   The usual problem here is one of the two obvious contenders—the microphone may be too far from the sound source (for example, your voice), or its record volume may be set too low. Try moving the microphone nearer to the sound source or using the Audio Tuning Wizard to increase the record volume. If necessary, do both.

Audio Is Distorted   Again, two predictable offenders here—the microphone may be too close to the sound source (for example, your voice), or its record volume may be turned up too high. Try moving the microphone farther away or using the Audio Tuning Wizard to reduce the record volume (or do both).

If the volume is satisfactory but you're getting annoying static on plosives and fricatives, try moving the microphone out of your breath stream. Position the microphone to the side of your mouth or nearer your throat.

Audio Has Interference   Interference can be a brute to troubleshoot, because it can have so many causes and can occur at either end of the connection or on the connection itself. But there's one cause that's worth mentioning here because you might not think of it—the interference may come from inside your computer—fans and video cards (which these days increasingly have their own fans, either from design or from necessity) can cause interference on nearby sound cards. To reduce interference, you may need to move your sound card to a slot as far as possible from your video card (or cards) and from noisy fans.

Audio Is Choppy   Choppy audio may indicate several different problems. Of these, the most likely is that your sound card can't handle full-duplex audio satisfactorily. If this is the case, drop back to half-duplex audio by clearing the Enable Full-Duplex Audio So I Can Speak while Receiving Audio check box in the General group box on the Audio page of the Options dialog box (Tools | Options).

You may also need to turn off DirectSound. To do so, clear the Enable DirectSound for Improved Audio Performance check box in the General group box on the Audio page of the Options dialog box.

Next most likely is that NetMeeting isn't getting the bandwidth to transfer audio. Unless you can increase the bandwidth on your connection (for example, by adding a second ISDN channel or another modem to a multilink connection), the only way to improve matters is to stop any other applications using that bandwidth—turn off the Internet radio station and any stock tickers, stop any automatic checking of e-mail, and so on.

Audio Has Echoes   Echoes in NetMeeting audio usually means that the person you're talking to has gotten their speakers too close to their microphone for the current sensitivity of the microphone. You might also have done this yourself, since you won't usually notice the problem.

The cures are simple enough: put more distance between the microphone and the speakers; turn down the speaker volume; decrease the gain on the microphone (either manually or by running the Audio Tuning Wizard); or use headphones instead of speakers. If none of these works and the echo is driving you nuts, you can probably kill it by switching from full duplex to half duplex—but in normal circumstances, this is more curse than cure.

Computer Temporarily or Permanently Incapable of Producing Quality Audio   If your computer usually produces quality audio but can't seem to do so at the moment, you may be running too many programs, you may be running a program that's cornered the local market in memory, or you may be running another sound program that's interfering with the sound.

If you have the Taskbar displayed, you shouldn't have any difficulty telling whether you're running a large number of programs. If you're not, display Task Manager (right-click the notification area and choose Task Manager from the context menu) and check the Mem Usage column on the Processes page to see whether any program is being unusually greedy. (You may also want to display the VM Size column to see the amount of virtual memory the programs are using. To display this, choose View | Select Columns and select the Virtual Memory Size check box in the Select Columns dialog box.) Close the offender.

If you're running another sound program, try closing it and see whether the audio quality in NetMeeting improves.

If your computer is permanently incapable of producing quality audio, you may need to invest in a new sound card. If your computer is a laptop, consider using USB speakers or USB headphones to bypass an underperforming sound card that you can't replace, or try an external sound card such as the Sound Blaster Extigy.

Audio and Other NetMeeting Features Suffer from Lack of Bandwidth   If you have a low-bandwidth Internet connection (for example, a modem connection), you're probably already painfully aware of its limitations. But because of the demands that audio and video place on your bandwidth, you may need to be even more careful than usual when using NetMeeting. For example, you may not be able to get decent audio quality while receiving files or video. In this case, you'll need to decide where your priorities lie.

If both you and the person you're talking to have fast connections that normally deliver speedy uploads and downloads, the problem may be with one of your ISPs. Some ISPs throttle back greedy applications at times of heavy demand. You're more likely to have this happen to you if you're trying to transmit a large video picture as well as audio.

Program sharing demands a surprising amount of bandwidth. In particular, moving a shared program window on the Desktop requires NetMeeting to transmit a large amount of information. If you're collaborating over a low-bandwidth connection, expect audio to suffer at times like this.

Network Bandwidth Is Set Too High   As mentioned in the discussion of configuring NetMeeting, the Network Bandwidth dialog box lets you specify the approximate speed of the connection you're using for your NetMeeting calls. Your choices are 14400 bps Modem; 28800 bps or Faster Modem; Cable, xDSL or ISDN; and Local Area Network. NetMeeting uses this setting to determine the rate at which to send audio and video. If you specify a faster connection than you're actually using, NetMeeting will try to send too much information, which can result in a choppy or broken signal.

The solution, as you'd guess, is to display the Network Bandwidth dialog box (choose Tools | Options to display the Options dialog box; then click the Bandwidth Settings button on the General page) and choose a lower bandwidth setting.

Even Half-Duplex Audio Doesn't Work Properly   If you find that even half-duplex audio doesn't work properly, chances are that ambient noise on the full-duplex end is holding open the receive channel on the half-duplex end of the call, thus preventing it from sending. Reduce ambient noise and run the Audio Tuning Wizard at the full-duplex end to eliminate this problem.

Hardware Known to Cause Audio Problems with NetMeeting   The ATI All-in-Wonder video adapter is known to cause problems with NetMeeting 3.01 in Windows 95, 98, and 98SE. When you use All-in-Wonder to capture video, you may not be able to use the microphone or audio features. If you run into this problem, try specifying the microphone as the recording source manually in the Recording Properties dialog box. You may also need to edit the Registry by adding a DWORD value called NoRecLevelMute with the value 1 to HKEY_LOCAL_MACHINE\SOFTWARE\ATI Technologies\Capture Driver\Settings\Sounds.

The Yamaha OPL3-SAx sound card may not be able to play sound in NetMeeting when it's sharing an IRQ (an interrupt request) with another device. The solution is to change the sound card's IRQ assignment so that it's not sharing an IRQ.

Troubleshoot Video Problems in NetMeeting

This section discusses how to troubleshoot video problems in NetMeeting. These problems range from not getting any video to not getting satisfactory video.

Video Image Is Jerky

Jerky video is pretty much a fact of life when you're videoconferencing over limited-bandwidth connections, so the first order of business is to get your expectations in line with reality.

Here are the basics. None of them should cause you much surprise:

■ NetMeeting adjusts its frame rate depending on the bandwidth available at both ends of the connection. If you have a T1 line but the person at the other end has a V.90 dial-up connection (which gives 33.6 Kbps upstream), you'll get a slow frame rate because that's all the other person's connection can send. Likewise, they'll get a slowish frame rate because, even though your connection can pump through a high frame rate, their connection can't receive any faster than 56 Kbps.

■ In general, the smaller the video image, the higher the frame rate you get. With most video hardware, NetMeeting offers three formats in the Send Image Size group box on the Video page of the Options dialog box: Small, Medium, and Large. Large is Common Interchange Format (CIF), which has a resolution of 352×288 pixels; Medium is Quarter Common Interchange Format (QCIF), which has a resolution of 176×144 pixels; and Small is Sub-Quarter Common Interchange Format (SQCIF), which has a resolution of 128×96 pixels. (Many postage stamps are actually larger than SQCIF on a normal-sized screen.)

> **NOTE** *What's that about "most video hardware"? Well, when NetMeeting encounters a video-capture device that isn't registered with it, NetMeeting queries the device for its default capture frame size. If the default capture frame size is 320×240 or a similar size, NetMeeting offers the Large, Medium, and Small options. It then creates the QCIF image by downsampling the 320×240 image and the SQCIF image by cropping the QCIF image to 128×96. But if the default capture frame size is 160×120 or a similar size, NetMeeting offers only the Medium and Small options in the Send Image Size group box. It then black-bands the 160×120 image to produce the 176×144 image for QCIF (and again crops the 160×120 image for SQCIF).*

■ If bandwidth isn't a problem, and the video camera supports a high frame rate, *and* your computer's video hardware is up to scratch (less a problem these days than it used to be), you should be able to get SQCIF or QCIF up to 30 frames per second (fps), which gives smooth movement but a small picture. You'll be lucky to get CIF above 15 fps because each frame contains four times as much information as QCIF.

> **NOTE** *Because NetMeeting doesn't support video overlay mode, your CPU is involved in all video that you send and receive via NetMeeting. So to get a high frame rate in NetMeeting, your computer needs to be running at a decent speed. Generally speaking, this, too, is less of a problem these days than it used to be in the late twentieth century. If your computer is powerful enough to run Windows XP at a decent speed, it should be able to handle NetMeeting's video demands.*

Enable Video

If you want to automatically establish a video connection at the beginning of each call you make, select the Automatically Send Video at the Start of Each Call check box on the Video page of the Options dialog box (Tools | Options).

Change Your Video Device

When you change the video device selected in the The Video Capture Device I Want to Use Is drop-down list in the Video Camera Properties group box on the Video page of the Options dialog box, you may need to close the Options dialog box and reopen it in order to force the Send Image Size group box to list the image sizes that the video device provides.

Poor-Quality Video or Wrong Colors in the Video Window

If the video quality is wretched, or if the wrong colors appear in parts of the video window, either you've chosen a larger video image size than your bandwidth and computer can handle or you've set the image quality too low. (A third possibility is that there's not enough light on the video camera's subject, but this tends to be easier to diagnose.)

If you've chosen too large an image size, decrease it and close any superfluous programs. If you've set too low an image quality, increase the I Prefer to Receive slider setting in the Video Quality group box on the Video page of the Options dialog box. (By default, NetMeeting chooses the Faster Video setting when you specify 28.8 Kbps bandwidth.)

Black Screen in the Video Window

If the video window in NetMeeting is showing a black screen, try the following:

- If you have two or more video-capture devices, make sure NetMeeting is set up to use the correct one. (Use the The Video Capture Device I Want to Use Is drop-down list in the Video Camera Properties group box on the Video page of the Options dialog box.)

- Once you're sure the video-capture device is right, check the video format you're using to make sure it's a format that NetMeeting supports.

- Make sure that the video-capture device isn't set to use video overlay mode. NetMeeting doesn't support video overlay mode. (Video overlay mode lets the video-capture device bypass the processor and send video directly to memory on the video-capture card. Generally, video overlay mode is a good idea—but only if the program involved supports it.)

NOTE   *In NetMeeting 2.1 and NetMeeting 3.01 for Windows 95, 98, and NT 4, you may need to remove any video-capture device beyond the first (or at least disable it in Device Manager).*

NetMeeting Through Microsoft Proxy Server, Darkly

If you're using Windows 95 or Windows 98 with NetMeeting 2.1 or 3.01, and you're connecting to the Internet through a proxy server that's running Microsoft Proxy Server 2.0, *and* you're using Microsoft Winsock 2.0, you may find yourself unable to use audio and video in NetMeeting. To get around this problem, you'll need to edit the Registry. The standard cautions apply: you should understand what the Registry is and does, you should have a full backup of the Registry available in case Windows doesn't agree with the changes you make, and you should know how to restore the Registry from the backup.

If you're okay on those fronts, run Registry Editor (Start | Run, enter **regedit**, and click the OK button) and add a DWORD value entry named DisableWinsock2 with the value 1 to the HKEY_ LOCAL_MACHINE\SOFTWARE\Microsoft\Internet Audio\NacObject\ key for NetMeeting 2.1 or to the HKEY_LOCAL_MACHINE\software\microsoft\conferencing\rrcm key for NetMeeting 3.01.

Can't Disconnect and Reconnect Video Camera During a Call

NetMeeting doesn't support disconnecting and reconnecting video sources during a call; so if you disconnect your camera and then reconnect it (or connect another camera), NetMeeting will probably not display the new image. If you need to change your camera or reconnect it for other reasons (for example, to untangle its cable), end the call, adjust the camera, and then establish a new call.

Can't Send Video in NetMeeting If CUCORE Is Running

The CUCORE program, a component of CUseeME Pro, can prevent NetMeeting 2.*x* from accessing a video camera on Windows 95 or 98. You can work around this issue by terminating CUCORE before starting a NetMeeting session.

Uninstall pcAnywhere 8 Removes a Vital Video File for NetMeeting 2.1

Uninstalling pcAnywhere 8 removes a file named Msvcrt.dll, which NetMeeting 2.1 needs to send video. See Q176052 in the Microsoft Knowledge Base (support.microsoft.com/default.aspx?) for instructions on downloading, extracting, and installing a replacement copy of this file.

Hardware Known to Cause Video Problems with NetMeeting

The Hauppauge Wincast video card may cause Windows 95 to hang when you're running NetMeeting 2.0 or 2.1. See Q168026 in the Microsoft Knowledge Base for a solution that involves editing the Registry.

The Kodak USB DVC323 video camera doesn't work well with NetMeeting 3.0 or 3.01 on Windows 95, 98, or 98SE—the advanced camera settings aren't available. There's no workaround.

Unable to Change the Image Size You're Sending During a Call

Some 2.*x* versions of NetMeeting aren't able to change the size of the video image you're sending during a call when connected through ICS—attempting to change the video size disconnects you from the meeting you're in. There's no solution beyond the "don't *do* that, then" solution of setting the video image size before connecting through ICS.

Phone Dialer

Compared to the multifaceted NetMeeting and to the even more talented Messenger, which represents various of the hydra heads of Microsoft's .NET services, Phone Dialer is a small, boring, and modest program. But, it boasts a capability that neither Messenger nor NetMeeting has that may be of interest to you—whereas Messenger and NetMeeting can manage audio and video between only two participants, Phone Dialer lets you get up to six people in an audio and video conversation.

This capability can be useful when you absolutely must have a conversation with two or more other people, but it's important to understand Phone Dialer's limitations:

- First, Phone Dialer doesn't do data at all—it's a telephony application that runs over POTS or a network or Internet connection. Phone Dialer can do a voice conversation, or a voice and video conversation, between two to six participants. But it can't do chat, file transfer, application sharing, or any of the other tricks Messenger and NetMeeting perform so impressively.

- Second, if you're making calls over POTS, you're limited by the number of phone lines you have available.

- Third, if you're making calls over a network connection or Internet connection, you're limited by your bandwidth. Even if the connection is very fast, there's usually a lag between one person speaking and the other person receiving the audio—like old-time satellite calls, if you remember them.

- Fourth, each video image is tiny, as you'll see in a moment. Even so, if you have several video streams squeezing through your Internet connection, each will have a pretty miserable frame rate. To be cruel, the video quality that Phone Dialer delivers makes CCTV look quite passable.

Enough negativity—I mean, *realism*. Phone Dialer *does* work. Let's see how.

Run Phone Dialer

To run Phone Dialer, enter **dialer** in the Run dialog box (Start | Run) and click the OK button. Alternatively, create a shortcut to the dialer command in a convenient location and then double-click it when you need to run Phone Dialer. (You shouldn't need to specify the path to the executable; but if you do, it should be in your \Program Files\Windows NT\ folder.)

Figure 6-5 shows the Phone Dialer interface. Phone Dialer has a regrettable tendency to run in a much larger window than necessary, which highlights its paucity of menus and toolbars. But you can easily drag the Phone Dialer window down to a more reasonable size, as in the figure.

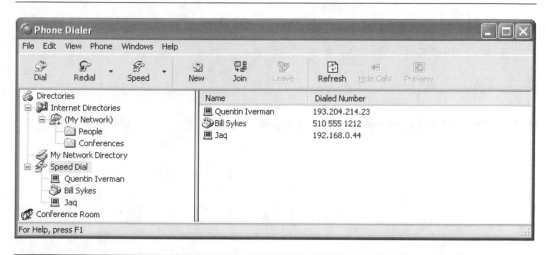

FIGURE 6-5 The Phone Dialer window

> **NOTE** *Like NetMeeting, Phone Dialer comes configured to use the Microsoft Internet Directory server network. Because this server network has been "upgraded" to Messenger Service, its previous functionality has been removed, and you can no longer use it for Phone Dialer features such as creating and joining conferences. However, if you can access a third-party ILS server, you can use these Phone Dialer features. On the basis that you're probably not accessing a third-party ILS server, I don't discuss these features in this chapter.*

Configure Phone Dialer

By default, Phone Dialer comes sensibly configured for general use, but it's a good idea to at least check its settings to make sure they suit you. To do so, choose Edit | Options to display the Options dialog box.

Choose the Lines to Use for Calling

The Lines page of the Options dialog box, shown in Figure 6-6, contains options for specifying your preferred line for calling (choose the Phone option button or the Internet option button) and for specifying which line to use for phone calls, Internet calls, and Internet conferences. The default setting for the options in the Line Used For group box is Auto-Select, which tells Phone Dialer to select the best line available for the purpose. If necessary, specify the phone line or the H323 line. (H323 is an Internet conferencing protocol.)

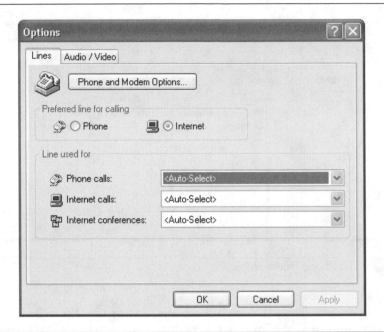

FIGURE 6-6 The Lines page of Phone Dialer's Options dialog box lets you specify your preferred line for different types of calls.

Use a Telephone Handset

If you have a telephone handset connected to your PC and want to use it for all calls, select the Use The Telephone Handset Connected To This PC For All Calls check box on the Audio/Video page of the Options dialog box (see Figure 6-7). If you don't have a telephone handset, this check box is unavailable, as in the figure.

Enable or Disable Acoustic Echo Cancellation

If you're hearing your own voice echoing through your speakers, select the Enable Acoustic Echo Cancellation check box on the Audio/Video page of the Options dialog box. (Alternatively, reposition your speakers or microphone, or try using headphones.)

Choose the Devices to Use for Each Type of Call

In the Devices Used For Calling group box, specify the audio and video devices to use for each type of call you plan to make: in the Line drop-down list, select the Phone Calls item, the Internet Calls item, or the Internet Conferences item; then use the Audio Record drop-down list, the Audio Playback drop-down list, and the Video Recording drop-down list to specify the audio

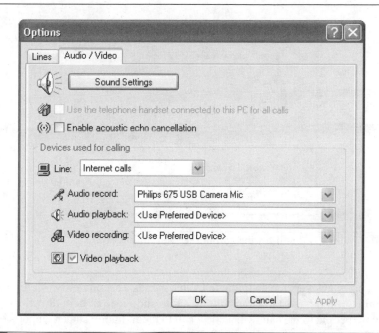

FIGURE 6-7   The Audio/Video page of Phone Dialer's Options dialog box lets you specify which devices to use for audio pickup and playback.

and video devices you want to use for the call. Repeat the procedure for the other line types, as necessary.

For Internet conferences, the Devices Used For Calling group box displays a Maximum Video Windows text box in which you specify the maximum number of video windows you want to have open. (The default setting is 6.)

Make a Call

Provided that your audio hardware (and, if necessary, video hardware) is connected and functional, and that you have an Internet connection or a phone line available, making a call with Phone Dialer is a kissing cousin of simplicity itself.

Click the Dial button to display the Dial dialog box (see Figure 6-8). Then enter the IP address or phone number in the Connect To text box. (If it's an IP address or a phone number you've connected to before with Phone Dialer, select it from the Connect To drop-down list.) Check that Phone Dialer has selected the appropriate option button—the Phone Call option button or the Internet Call option button—in the Dial As group box. (Phone Dialer chooses the option button based on what you've entered in the Connect To text box.) If you want to create a Speed Dial entry for this IP address or phone number, select the Add Number To Speed Dial List check box. Then click the Place Call button.

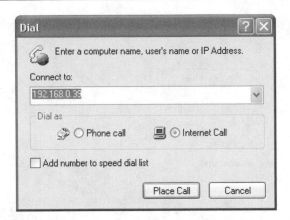

FIGURE 6-8   Enter the detail for the call in the Dial dialog box.

If the other party answers the call, Phone Dialer spends a second or two setting up its audio and video terminals, and then starts transmitting audio and video in both directions. At this point, you can add more people to the call by placing a call to them: Phone Dialer supports only one call at a time, so it adds them into the existing call. Figure 6-9 shows a video call with two other people. The top pane is your preview pane and displays your outgoing video stream if you have a Webcam up and running. (In the figure, the recipient of the call doesn't have a Webcam.)

To end a call, click the Disconnect button.

Take a Call

When someone calls you, Phone Dialer slides a couple of hefty panels across the upper-left corner of your screen on top of all other programs, so you can hardly fail to notice the incoming call. Figure 6-10 shows an example.

Click the Take Call button to accept the call or the Reject Call button to reject it.

NOTE   *You need to have Phone Dialer running in order for it to pick up incoming calls. Phone Dialer warns you about this when you issue an Exit command.*

Hide the Phone Dialer Window and Call Panes

You can hide the Phone Dialer window by choosing File | Hide Phone Dialer Window. To display it again, click the Phone Dialer icon in the notification area and choose Open from the menu.

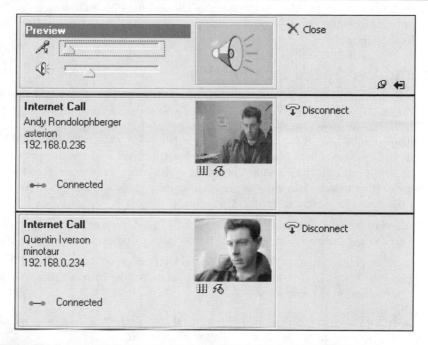

FIGURE 6-9   Phone Dialer making a video call with two other people

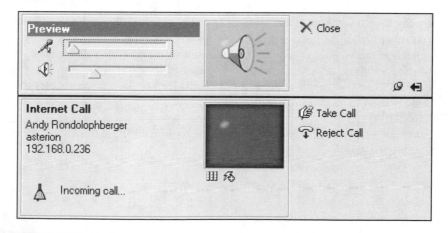

FIGURE 6-10   Phone Dialer displays two hefty panels in the upper-left corner of your screen when you receive an incoming call.

Similarly, you can hide the current call panes by clicking the Phone Dialer icon and choosing Hide Current Calls from the menu. As you'd imagine, you choose Show Current Calls from the menu to redisplay the calls.

Create and Use Speed Dial Entries

If you call certain numbers or addresses frequently using Phone Dialer, you'll probably want to create Speed Dial entries for them. You can do so in any of several easy ways:

- When using the Dial dialog box to specify the details for a call, select the Add Number To Speed Dial List check box. This isn't the most satisfactory way, since Phone Dialer gives the Speed Dial entry a name consisting of the phone number or IP address you entered rather than the name of the person or computer associated with it. But you can edit the Speed Dial entry later to add the relevant name.

- Choose Edit | Add To Speed Dial List (or click the Add button in the Edit Speed Dial List dialog box) and use the Speed Dial dialog box to specify the details of the Speed Dial entry.

- From an ongoing call, click the Add To Speed Dial button on the call pane. Phone Dialer displays the Speed Dial dialog box with information for the current caller so that you can edit or just accept the new entry.

To edit a Speed Dial entry, choose Edit | Speed Dial List. In the resulting Edit Speed Dial List dialog box, select the entry you want to edit and click the Edit button.

To use a Speed Dial entry, select the Speed Dial entry in Phone Dialer's left pane and then double-click the entry in the right pane.

Summary

This chapter has shown you how to use Messenger and NetMeeting for audio and video chat with one other participant. Because audio and video tend to be ticklish, especially across Internet connections and with the possibility of different versions of the software at each end of the connection, much of this chapter has concentrated on troubleshooting.

For the times when two-person audio and video calls aren't enough, this chapter has also discussed how to use Phone Dialer for audio and video calls with anywhere from one to five other participants.

The next chapter discusses how to use Messenger, NetMeeting, and other tools for effective file sharing. Turn the page.

Chapter 7

Enjoy Unrestricted, Untraceable File Sharing

This chapter discusses how to share files using the programs and tools that come with XP. There's good news and bad news on this front. The good news is that XP provides strong features for shunting files from A to B without C or D being able to tell that you're doing so. The bad news is that Microsoft points you toward tools that can be monitored. The good news is that you've got this book. The bad news is that you have to read at least some of it....

This chapter takes as a given that many people want to share files securely, without the files being intercepted in transit and without the details of what they've sent and received being easily accessible to outside parties—much as they don't want other people reading their e-mail without permission or opening their snail mail without a warrant. *Pace* the NSA and its proposals for the Clipper chip, wanting privacy or security or using encryption doesn't necessarily mean you're doing anything illegal—there are plenty of reasons for needing privacy or secrecy on business-related files or personal files.

However, many people do share files illegally, so this chapter also briefly discusses the legalities of file sharing. Computers make it so easy to share almost any digital file that it's the work of a second to commit a copyright violation that could deprive you of a serious chunk of your income or send you to jail for the short-term future. If you're going to share with other people files that you don't have a specific right to distribute, you owe it to yourself (and to any that love you) to understand the legalities of sharing files and the ease with which many of the more popular ways of sharing files can be traced back to you.

> NOTE *Apart from XP's built-in features, there are many other ways to share files, including the ever-changing plethora of peer-to-peer (P2P) technologies, which include the late lamented Napster, audioGnome, Freenet, LimeWire, BearShare, and others. This chapter doesn't discuss these technologies, but you may want to investigate them on your own.*

Understand the Basics of File Sharing

Before I show you how to share files using the technologies built into XP, you need to understand the basics of file sharing, starting with the law.

The Law

This section discusses briefly what the law allows you to do with digital files of copyrighted content and what it doesn't allow you to do. This section also illustrates the penalties for some of the actions that fall on the illegal side of the fence.

First, though, a quick quiz.

A Quick Quiz

To give us an idea of where you're coming from, try the following quiz. Each item is either legal or illegal under most prevailing circumstances in U.S. law.

	Action	Legal	Illegal
1.	Lend a friend a CD so that they can rip and encode it.	❏	❏
2.	Scan a picture of Gisele or Leonardo and post it on your Web site.	❏	❏
3.	Scan and perform optical character recognition (OCR) on a short newspaper article and include it in a paper you're writing.	❏	❏
4.	Burn a copy of a music CD for a friend.	❏	❏
5.	Give a digital music file that you've bought and downloaded (to your computer) to a friend so that they have the original file and you no longer have a copy of it.	❏	❏
6.	Borrow a CD from a friend and create WMA files from it.	❏	❏
7.	Rip a DVD to files on your hard disk.	❏	❏
8.	Download a Metallica track that someone's sharing via Freenet.	❏	❏
9.	Install a software package that your friend brought over so that they can use it on your computer as well as on theirs.	❏	❏
10.	Move your copy of certain software from your old computer to your new computer.	❏	❏

Okay, there were some easy ones there—or were there?

All these actions are illegal in most circumstances. There are specific cases when each is okay, but most of these actions infringe copyright.

Items 1 through 9 involve making an illegal digital copy of a digital original (1 and 4 through 9) or of a hard-copy original (2 and 3). Item 10 involves breaking the licensing agreement for tightly restricted software. (These products are licensed for use only on one computer—ever.) For example, lending a CD to a friend is fine. But if they create a copy of it (which is what ripping and encoding the CD's contents is), they've broken the law.

Of course, there are exceptions to the prevailing circumstances. Most of these exceptions involve the copyright holder permitting you to make a copy of the copyrighted work, either by granting you permission for an individual act or by putting the work in the public domain (a notional area that contains all works not protected by copyright). Apart from works deliberately placed by the copyright holder in the public domain, these works include works whose copyright has been lost or has expired, works that aren't copyrightable, and many U.S. government publications.

For example, Metallica might choose to make some of their tracks freely distributable via the Internet. (Given that Metallica played a significant part in the legal assault on Napster in 2000, this seems exceedingly unlikely.) And many software authors choose to release their programs under a copyright alternative called *copyleft*, which allows people to freely copy the works provided that they meet various conditions, such as including the full source code with the copies, and to freely modify the works, provided that they make their modifications available to other people.

What Copyright Says

Copyright provides protection for intellectual property. If you'll allow me to simplify horribly (thank you—I thought you would), copyright law essentially says that when someone has created an original work in a tangible format, they have copyright on that work from the time it was created until 70 years after their death. The creator of the work doesn't have to put a copyright notice on it in order for the work to be copyrighted, nor do they have to register the copyright with the Copyright Office—although if a dispute arises about copyright, it helps if the copyright holder can use the copyright registration as proof that the work had been created by a certain date.

Copyright gives the holder the reproduction right (making copies of the work), the distribution right (distributing copies of the work), the derivative works right (creating other works from the work), the public performance right (performing, say, a theater piece or showing a movie in its usual order), and the public display right (transmitting the work to the public, displaying a sculpture, or showing a movie out of its usual order). People other than the copyright holder can't do any of those things to the work without getting permission from the copyright holder, other than in some circumstances we'll visit shortly.

With a few minor wrinkles that we needn't get into here, copyright applies internationally; so, in most cases, you can't circumvent copyright law by committing the copyright violation in another country.

By preventing other people from ripping off a copyrighted work, copyright encourages artists to create works in the hope of being able to profit from them, either materially or in reputation, and encourages publishers to distribute the works.

> **NOTE** *Here's an important point—copyright covers the expression of ideas, not ideas themselves. Here's an example of an idea: a two-wheeled, self-balancing scooter for personal transport, work, and so on. Here's an example of the execution of the idea: the Segway scooter. Dean Kamen has copyright (and several bucketfuls of patents) on the Segway, so nobody can legally make a two-wheeled, self-balancing scooter that looks just like the Segway or that uses its patented technologies. But they can make any number of different two-wheeled, self-balancing scooters because the idea can't be copyrighted. Similarly, Damien Hirst can't use copyright to prevent other people from chainsawing animals in two and exhibiting half of the results, and Martin Creed can't prevent anyone else from creating a room in which the lights go on and off at regular intervals and claiming that's it's a work of art, unless their room with lights going on and off is so similar to Creed's that it's deemed to be a direct copy.*

So What *Can* You Legally Do?

After reading the last couple of sections, you may well be wondering what you can legally do with digital files of copyrighted content. The answer may well be "Less than you'd like to"— but there *are* various things you can legally do. You should probably know what they are before you proceed.

If you hold the copyright to a work, and you haven't granted those rights to anyone else, you can do pretty much what you want with digital files of your copyrighted content: publish them on media such as CD, DVD, or floppy; sell them; distribute them via the Internet; derive further works from them; broadcast or perform them; and so on. So if you want to distribute MP3 files of your original hip-hop opera, post photos you've taken on your Web site, or transmit streams of videos you've shot, you have every right to do so.

If you license the appropriate rights from the copyright holder, you have the freedom conferred by those rights. For example, I've granted to Osborne the right to publish and distribute this book, so they're allowed to do just that.

Likewise, a copyright holder may explicitly grant people permission to freely distribute copies of their works, usually in the hope of either gaining publicity (and thus perhaps benefiting from other works they create) or benefiting the community. For example, in late 2000, the Smashing Pumpkins had an impressive rift with their record company and ended up releasing their work *Machina II* as digital files, which they encouraged their fans to copy and pass along to others ("take, share; this is our music that is given unto you…," as it were), together with a token 25 copies on vinyl for nostalgia's sake. You could argue that the Pumpkins were hoping to both benefit the community and to perhaps gain from increased sales of their other works (or concert tickets, or paraphernalia) as well as taking an interesting quixotic (and perhaps Pyrrhic) revenge on their record company.

Similarly, someone who wrote a report on industrial pollution in, say, Houston might decide to encourage people to distribute it freely on the Internet so that more people could learn about it. This would most likely benefit the community. (It might also have other effects.)

If the work is copyrighted, but you don't hold the copyright, you haven't licensed any rights for the work from the copyright holder, and the copyright holder hasn't granted any rights, you're unlikely to be able to share files of the copyrighted work legally. This is likely to be the case for many of the works of which you own copies.

Here are some examples:

- If you buy a DVD of a movie, you can watch it until you wear it out if you want to. It's arguable whether you can legally rip the DVD to your computer so that you can watch it from another device (for example, a computer without a DVD drive). But even if you can legally rip it, you can't legally share the resulting files with other people.

- If you buy a CD, you can rip and encode its tracks to MP3 or WMA files (or a different format) so that you can store them on your PC or download them to a portable device and play them there. But, again, you can't legally share these files with other people, even though you can lend them the physical CD.

- If you buy a book, you probably can't legally scan and perform optical character recognition (OCR) on the whole thing to make an electronic version of it that you could read on a computer or a handheld device, and you certainly can't legally distribute an electronic version of the book. (You can't legally photocopy the whole book either, but photocopying a whole book is usually so much more expensive than buying another hard copy that this is seldom an issue.)

- If you buy software, the license tightly restricts what you can do with it. For example, most shrinkwrap agreements allow you to install the software on only one computer at a time, but they allow you to move the software from one computer to another. Other agreements force you to agree to install the software on only one computer ever—so if you get a new computer, you'll need to get a new copy of the software.

- If you buy a picture, you can't legally scan it to a file and distribute it.

If you've read this list, and the list of the Ten Forbidden Things in the quiz, you'll have noticed that some copying actions are (or may be) legally permitted, whereas others definitely aren't. For example, you can legally create digital-audio files (such as MP3 files) from a CD, even though doing so involves copying. But you can't legally make a copy of software, except for backup.

This apparent discrepancy results from various legal rulings on concepts such as personal use, time-shifting, and place-shifting:

- **Personal use**   This was established by the Audio Home Recording Act (1992), which makes it legal for you to make a copy of an audio recording using a "digital audio recording device" provided that the copy is for your personal use. Now, technically, a computer isn't a digital audio recording device, although a stand-alone CD-ripper-and-encoder box is one. But most people feel that ripping a CD using a computer is close enough to the Audio Home Recording Act's intent to qualify as personal use.

- **Time-shifting**   This is the term for copying a broadcast work so that you can watch or listen to it later. For example, if you videotape a ballgame so that you can watch it the next day, you've time-shifted it. Likewise, if you record a radio show so that you can listen to it later.

- **Place-shifting**   This is the term for copying a work so that you can watch it, listen to it, or otherwise experience it in a different location than you would have been able to with the medium on which you have the work. For example, if you create MP3 files from an LP so that you can listen to them while jogging, you've place-shifted them. Likewise, if you transfer video files to a handheld computer so that you can watch them while skydiving.

There's a fourth term you should understand as well: fair use. *Fair use* lets you use part or (very occasionally) the whole of a copyrighted work "for purposes such as criticism, comment, news reporting, teaching . . ., scholarship, or research." For example, fair use might cover a teacher making copies of an article for a class, or a reviewer quoting a short passage from a book or movie to illustrate a point in a review, or a rap artist sampling short sections of other people's tracks in order to parody them. Fair use is assessed on four very fluid criteria (the purpose and character of the use, the type of copyrighted work involved, the percentage of the copyrighted work used, and the effect the use will have on the value of the copyrighted work) that together form a high hurdle for the user to clear. Fair use very seldom applies to copying entire works, with the exception of really short works (for example, a haiku or a five-second song). The reason you need to know about fair use is that people often claim that copying a copyrighted work is "fair use." They're almost always wrong.

> **NOTE** *Many of the things that you can legally do with copyrighted content have been established by individual court decisions chipping away at copyright law. For example, when videocassette recorders were first released, it was illegal to use them to record a television program, and it took the Supreme Court (in the 1984 Betamax Decision) to establish that recording for personal use was legal. Similarly, the legality of recording an audio track onto a cassette was the matter of much legal back-and-forth between the record companies and the consumers. This culminated in a small royalty on all blank cassettes to compensate the artists and record companies for the putative losses they might sustain through illegal taping. The Audio Home Recording Act offered some concessions to the music industry and at the same time provided consumers with personal use.*

Penalties for Copyright Violations

If you commit a copyright violation, you can face heavy penalties. For example, the No Electronic Theft Act (NET Act) of 1997 threatens you with up to a year's imprisonment and a fine for copying or distributing a copyrighted work or works with a retail value of more than $1,000. If the value of the works is $2,500 or more, and you've reproduced or distributed ten or more copies, you can get up to three-years' imprisonment and a fine for a first offense; for a second offense, you can get up to six-years' imprisonment and a fine.

At this point, you're probably wondering what work is worth $1,000 or $2,500—a nice painting, perhaps, or a post-modern statue? But no: The court gets to decide what the value of the work is, and it can factor in the number of copies you have or might have distributed. For example, even sharing one track of the ten on a CD that cost you $15 to buy might count as a work worth $1,000 (or $2,500) because you might have shared the track with many people.

The Digital Millennium Copyright Act, passed in 1998, adds savage penalties for cracking the copy-protection mechanism on copyrighted works: fines of up to $500,000 and up to five years in prison for a first offense, and double both for a second offense.

Compression and Zip Archives

Unless both you and the person to whom you're transferring files (or from whom you're receiving files) have unlimited bandwidth, it's a good idea to consider compressing any uncompressed file larger than, say, 500KB or 1MB. Windows XP has basic compression functionality built in (and installed by default), so there's no excuse not to use it. If you find Windows XP's compression clumsy (and you wouldn't be alone in that opinion), you can easily add a third-party compression solution. Big names include WinZip (www.winzip.com), TurboZip (www.turbozip.com), and PKZip (www.pkware.com). All these companies offer trial versions of their products to get you hooked.

Any file in a format that's already compressed is likely to be a poor candidate for compression. For example, MP3 files are compressed about as far as they'll go. If you create a Zip file containing an MP3 file, chances are that it won't be any smaller than the MP3 file—it may well be bigger, because there's a little overhead in the Zip file format. So there's not much point in zipping an MP3 file unless you're trying to disguise its identity or protect it with a password.

But you may want to create a Zip file containing several MP3 files so that you can transfer them in a single operation with a program that can transfer only a single file at a time. For example, Messenger can transfer only one file at a time, so sometimes you may want to make that file a Zip file so that you and the recipient don't have to stay glued to your computers for the whole transfer session—you to start each new transfer, and they to accept each so that it runs.

Monitoring and Traffic Analysis

As discussed in Chapter 3, various people and organizations can monitor the actions you perform online: your ISP, your local friendly security agency, a less friendly global security agency, or a determined individual. Depending on the tool you're using, others may be able to monitor your actions too. For example, .NET Messenger Service can see and log every action you take while you're signed into Messenger, all on the pretext that knowing what you're doing is vital to delivering you the interactive, real-time services you need (or crave).

If you've encrypted the files you're transferring (for example, using PGP), anybody monitoring your communication sessions will be able to see the data you're sending and receiving, but they won't be able to make sense of it as such. However, they may be able to perform *traffic analysis* on the data—studying your communications patterns in order to work out what types of information you're transferring or what relationship you and the people you're communicating with have with each other.

This is less far-fetched than it might sound. Consider this example, which Bruce Schneier mentions in *Secrets and Lies*: Pizza deliveries to the Pentagon increased one hundredfold in the hours before the U.S. started bombing Iraq in 1991, whereas pizza deliveries to the CIA stayed the same. Anyone tracking pizza movements could have figured something was up, though they wouldn't have known exactly what. Heck, even someone delivering 500 quad-pepperonis to the Pentagon in place of the usual five would have noticed a surge of enthusiasm for the sausage.

Similarly, if a communications session between Andy and Billie shows Andy sending small multiple amounts of data and Billie responding with a corresponding number of large amounts of data, traffic analysis might conclude that Andy is requesting files and Billie is supplying them. The size of the data transmissions may make particular file types more likely—for example, if a file is between 100KB and 400KB, it might well be a graphics file; if it's between 2MB and 10MB, it might well be a music file; if it's bigger than 10MB, it might be a video file. These categories are crude, but I'm sure you see the point.

Up to this point, traffic analysis has been largely a tool of the military and intelligence services, but as encryption moves into the mainstream, more companies will probably start using it to try to work out what their customers are doing.

XP's Tools for Sharing

The main tools XP provides for sharing files are NetMeeting, Messenger, and HyperTerminal. XP also makes it easy to access and manage online storage locations, which can be great for sharing files asynchronously, and to send files via e-mail, which can also provide effective asynchronous sharing. I'll start with NetMeeting, because it provides secure sharing, and then discuss Messenger (which doesn't) and HyperTerminal (which can). Toward the end of the chapter, I'll briefly discuss considerations for sharing files via online storage locations and e-mail. And at the end of the chapter, I'll spend a fair amount of time on virtual private networks (VPNs) because, although they're not exactly designed for sharing files, they offer a very appealing combination of security, privacy, and flexibility.

> **NOTE** *There are all kinds of other tools and technologies for sharing, many of which you can install on XP (or on earlier versions of Windows). In the last couple of years, peer-to-peer (P2P) technologies such as Napster, audioGnome, gnutella, Freenet, and others have made the P2P sharing model very popular. You may well want to investigate the latest crop of P2P technologies on your own.*

Transfer Files with NetMeeting

As I mentioned in Chapter 5, NetMeeting lets you make secure data-only calls and conferences with anywhere from one other person to dozens of people. These secure calls can include file transfers, making NetMeeting a powerful tool for sharing files securely.

> **NOTE** *If you haven't already configured NetMeeting, turn back to "Set Up and Configure NetMeeting" in Chapter 5 for a discussion of its options.*

Before Receiving Files

Before you receive any files with NetMeeting, it's a good idea to change your received files folder—the folder in which NetMeeting places files you receive via file transfer. By default, this folder is the \Program Files\NetMeeting\Received Files folder. This isn't a great place for it because not only is the folder normally hidden by XP's don't-touch-the-program-files security screen, but the same folder is used by each NetMeeting user, which gives the users access to each other's files. (That said, there's some good news on this front—NetMeeting is smart enough not to overwrite an existing file in the received files folder that has the same name as a new incoming file. Instead, it renames the incoming file with *Copy(n) of* at the beginning of the filename, where *n* is the lowest unused number.)

To change your received files folder, click the Transfer Files button (or choose Tools | File Transfer or press CTRL+F) to display the File Transfer window. Then choose File | Change Folder, use the resulting Browse for Folder dialog box to select the folder to use, and click the OK button to close the dialog box and set the folder.

Send Files via File Transfer

To send files with NetMeeting, display the File Transfer window by clicking the Transfer Files button (or choosing Tools | File Transfer or pressing CTRL+F). Figure 7-1 shows the File Transfer window with some files being transferred.

To send files to another user, you add the files to the File Transfer window, specify who the files are going to, and send them. Here's what to do:

- To add the files, you can drag them from your Desktop or from an Explorer window to the File Transfer window, but usually it's easier to click the Add Files button (or choose File | Add Files) and use the resulting Select Files to Send dialog box (a common Open dialog box in disguise) to select the files to send.

- To specify the recipient, select their entry in the Select the Person You Want to Send Files drop-down list. The default selection is Everyone.

- To send all the files in the File Transfer window, click the Send All button (or right-click a file and choose Send All from the context menu, or choose File | Send All). To send just one file, right-click it and choose Send a File from the context menu. Alternatively, select the file and choose File | Send.

To stop sending a file, click the Stop Sending button on the toolbar in the File Transfer window or choose File | Stop Sending. NetMeeting displays a message box confirming the cancellation.

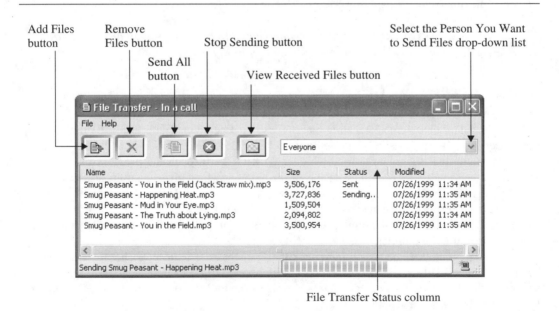

FIGURE 7-1   Use NetMeeting's File Transfer window to send files to other NetMeeting users.

NOTE

If you try to send a shortcut, NetMeeting sends the file itself. This happens by design rather than by accident, on the assumption that the location that the shortcut points to will probably not be available to the recipient—which is largely true if you're sending the shortcut to someone remote, but may well not be true if you're both on the same company network (LAN or WAN). The exception to this rule is when the shortcut is a URL: NetMeeting transfers URLs as they are.

Receive Files via File Transfer

When NetMeeting detects an incoming file, it displays a file transfer window giving the file's name, who it's coming from, and the progress of the file transfer. Here's an example:

As you can see here, you can choose to accept or delete the incoming file while it's being transferred. Clicking the Accept button closes the file transfer window, preventing you from seeing the details of the rest of the transfer operation, so you may want to leave the file transfer window open so that you can see what's happening. When NetMeeting has received the whole file, the file transfer window makes the Open button available and displays a Close button in place of the Accept button. You can click the Open button to open the file, but usually it's best to virus-check it first. This is because clicking the Open button issues an Open command for the file's real file type, which may not be the same as the file type that its extension claims—so if the file is a script file or an executable masquerading as, say, a JPG, issuing the Open command executes the script or runs the executable.

NOTE

If you receive multiple files, NetMeeting displays a window for each, cascading them across your screen. You don't need to acknowledge a file transfer in order to receive the next.

To examine the files you've received (and perhaps to virus-check them), choose File | Open Received Folder from the File Transfer window to look at these files (for example, to virus-check them). NetMeeting opens an Explorer window and displays the contents of your received files folder in it.

If you don't want to accept the incoming file, click the Delete button. NetMeeting terminates the inbound transfer and cancels any other inbound transfers from the same source.

Troubleshoot File-Transfer Problems in NetMeeting

This section discusses a couple of problems you may encounter when using NetMeeting to transfer files.

Meeting Participant Doesn't Appear in File Transfer Window

If anyone in a conference is using NetMeeting 2 on Windows 95, you may find you can't send that person a file because NetMeeting's file-transfer element seems not to see their presence, even if they're showing up in other NetMeeting windows, such as the Chat window.

To get around this problem, have the person using NetMeeting 2 transfer a small file to you first. This forces NetMeeting to register the presence of the node using NetMeeting 2 and usually solves the problem.

File Transfer Doesn't Stop Immediately

If you're communicating via a modem with someone who's using an older version of NetMeeting, that older version of NetMeeting may sometimes take a minute or two to stop sending a file when the sender or the recipient cancels the transfer. This is because NetMeeting transfers the file to a memory buffer before sending it over the wire, and the transfer may not end until the buffer is empty. Usually the best thing to do when this happens is wait for the buffer to clear. The alternative is to get the person sending the file to quit NetMeeting and restart it, but that means they'll leave the conference, including all chat and shared program windows.

Transfer Files with Messenger

Messenger offers simple file-sharing capabilities that can be effective provided you're aware of its limitations. The first limitation is that Messenger can transfer only one file at a time to a person in a conversation. This means that if you want to transfer a number of files to the same person, you'll need to be at your computer so that you can send them one by one, instead of being able to stack them as you can with NetMeeting.

The second limitation is that, if you're in a Messenger conversation with multiple people, you can send a file to only one of them in a file-transfer operation. You can then start another transfer to send the same file to another person in the conversation, but you're effectively transferring the file twice, so if all other things are equal, the transfer will take twice as long. (In case you're wondering—a form of multicast distribution would be better, in which you upload the file once to a server that distributes copies of it to each of the people you've designated as recipients.)

You can get around this by using a compression utility, such as the limited Zip-file functionality built into XP (or, better, a more powerful compression utility such as WinZip), to create an archive file and send that as the single file. At the same time, it's not a good idea to send colossal files over any but the fastest of connections, because you can waste a huge amount of time if the file transfer gets broken off for any reason and you have to restart it from the beginning.

Send a File with Messenger

Messenger makes it trivially easy to send a file to somebody you're in a conversation with. Start by clicking the Send a File link in the Conversation window or choosing File | Send a File or Photo.

If there's only one other person in the conversation with you, Messenger knows to whom you want to send the file or photo. If there's more than one other person, Messenger displays the Send a File dialog box, which lists the contacts in the conversation so that you can select which of them should receive the file. Once you've selected the contact, Messenger opens a new Conversation window with just that contact, thus keeping the details of the file transfer out of the original Conversation window.

Messenger then displays the Send a File to *Contact's Name* dialog box, which is yet another renamed Open dialog box. Select the file and click the Open button, and the contact receives a notice in the Conversation window that you want to send them a file. The notice contains an Accept link and a Decline link. If the contact chooses the Accept link, Messenger starts the file transfer and keeps both you and the recipient informed of its progress. If the contact chooses the Decline link, you get a notice telling you that they declined the transfer.

If you're not already in a conversation with the person to whom you want to send the file, you can start the file-transfer process by clicking the Send a File or Photo link in the Action pane of the main Messenger window or choosing Action | Send a File or Photo. Messenger displays the Send a File dialog box, in which you specify the contact or other person. Messenger then opens a Conversation window and displays the Send a File to *Contact's Name* dialog box, and the process continues as described earlier.

> TIP   *Another way of starting a file transfer is to drag a file from your Desktop or an Explorer window and drop it on a contact in the main Messenger window.*

Receive a File with Messenger

If you read the previous section, you'll have had no difficulty working out what happens when someone sends you a file with Messenger—if you're in a conversation with them, you get a notice in the Conversation window inviting you to accept or decline the file transfer; if you're not in a conversation with them, you get a screen pop-up to bring your attention to the new Conversation window that's flashing on your Taskbar. Click the Accept link or the Decline link, as appropriate.

As you saw in the section titled "Change the Folder into Which Transferred Files Are Placed" in Chapter 5, Messenger places files by default in your \My Documents\My Received Files\ folder. You can change this by using the Browse button on the Preferences page of the Options dialog box (Tools | Options).

Troubleshoot File Transfers with Messenger

Thanks to the determined efforts of Microsoft's software engineers, file transfers with Messenger are usually easy. Still, you may run into the problems described in this section.

> **NOTE** *Before we start, remember Messenger's limitations: You can transfer only one file at a time to each contact—you can't stack up multiple file transfers to the same person the way you can with NetMeeting. And you can perform a maximum of ten file transfers at a time.*

Can Transfer Only One File at a Time

If Messenger doesn't let you start further file transfers after you've got one going, the problem is likely to be that your firewall is configured with only one port open for file transfers.

For file transfer, Messenger uses ports 6891–6900. If only port 6891 is open, you'll be able to perform only one file transfer—either inbound or outbound—at a time. If you have access to your firewall, check its configuration and open more ports in the range 6891–6900 if possible. (If you don't have access to the firewall, ask the administrator responsible for it, but be warned that they may have deliberately restricted the number of files you can transfer.)

> **NOTE** *If the problem isn't with your firewall, it may be with your ISP. In this case, contact the ISP, ask them about it, and yell at them to open more ports if necessary.*

Can't Send Files from Behind ICF

If you can't send files from an ICS client that connects through a connection protected with ICF, ports 6891–6900 (discussed in the previous section) probably aren't open. If you can configure ICF, add entries to the Services page of the Advanced Settings dialog box to open these ports for Messenger file transfers. (See the section "Open Ports Manually on ICF" in Chapter 2 for details on opening ports.)

Can't Send Files from Behind a Corporate Firewall

If you're using Messenger from behind a corporate firewall, you may not be able to send files because ports 6891–6900 are closed. If your network administrators have deliberately closed these ports, you'll probably have a hard time persuading them to reopen the ports for file transfer. However, if the ports are open but transfers still aren't working, suggest mildly that the administrators configure the TCP ports so the sockets on them remain open for an extended period of time. (If the sockets time out quickly, Messenger file transfers may get interrupted.)

If you get no joy on the administrator front, you may want to use another means of transferring the file, such as using online storage or e-mail. See the next sections for a discussion of these two means of file transfer.

Can't Send Files from Behind a NAT Device

If the NAT device through which Messenger is connecting to the network doesn't support Universal Plug and Play (UPnP), Messenger won't be able to perform file transfers through it. Either upgrade the NAT device (for example, by flashing it with an update) or use an alternative means of file transfer (again, see the next sections for suggestions).

Online Storage

Another effective way of sharing files is to use an online storage locker, also sometimes called an *online drive*. I'll discuss the basic parameters of choosing and using online storage in Chapter 9; so for now, I'll mention just the basic advantages of online storage for transferring files:

- First, online storage is *asynchronous*, meaning one person can upload the files at their convenience and at the maximum upload speed of their Internet connection, and the other person can download the files whenever it suits them and at the maximum download speed of their Internet connection. Because most Internet connections are asymmetrical, offering marginally (in the case of modems) or hugely (in the case of DSLs and cable connections) faster connections downstream than upstream, uploading files to online storage and then downloading them at a different time can be both fast and convenient.

- Second (and hinted at in the first point), each person can use the full speed of their Internet connection rather than getting stuck at the lowest speed going. For example, Andie can spend ten hours uploading a colossal video file via her poky 14.4 Kbps modem. Billy can then suck the file down in ten seconds with his Camaro cable connection.

- Third, because multiple people can download the file from the online storage location once you've uploaded it, it's a great way to distribute the file to several people without needing to transfer it more than once.

Transfer Files via E-mail

Another method of transferring files is by attaching them to e-mail messages. This method has a couple of advantages:

- First, you and the person (or people) you're sending the file or files to don't have to be online at the same time. You can send the files at your leisure, and they can pick up the files at theirs. This works particularly well if one of you has a much faster Internet connection than the other because the faster party doesn't get restrained to the speed of the slower connection.

- Second, you can send the files to multiple recipients at the same time while needing to transmit each file only once—your computer uploads the message and the attached files once to your ISP's mail server, and the mail server distributes the various copies of the message and the attached files from there.

Life can't be that good—and of course it isn't—transferring files via e-mail has disadvantages as well as advantages. First, your ISP or a recipient's ISP may keep records of the e-mail messages you send and the attachments these messages have. So, if you're transferring sensitive files, you'll need to encrypt them before sending them in order to preserve your privacy.

Second, to protect their mail servers, most ISPs block attachments larger than a certain size. Some ISPs set a maximum message size (with attachments) of a megabyte or less, whereas other ISPs allow you to send up to several megabytes per message. Check what your ISP permits, either empirically or by asking them, and if necessary use Outlook Express's Break Apart Messages Larger than *NN* KB option (in the Sending area of the Advanced page of the Properties dialog box for the account) to break down large messages into smaller parts. (See Chapter 4 for more information on configuring Outlook Express.) Many other e-mail clients offer similar features, because obese e-mail messages have long been a problem on the Internet.

HyperTerminal

As I mentioned in Chapter 1, HyperTerminal is a basic telephony program that you can use for point-to-point connections. These connections can be established either via phone lines (POTS or ISDN) or via IP across your Internet connection.

Because of the capabilities of NetMeeting and Messenger, you're likely to find HyperTerminal useful for file transfer in only a few circumstances. For example, if you want to communicate with someone running another operating system, such as Linux, you won't be able to communicate with them via Messenger (at least, not at this writing); and if they don't have a conferencing client that can communicate with NetMeeting, that'll be out, too. Online storage or e-mail will work fine from any OS, of course, but if you want synchronous communication, a modest utility such as HyperTerminal fits the bill very nicely.

To run HyperTerminal, choose Start | All Programs | Accessories | Communications and choose the HyperTerminal item from the Communications submenu. (If there are two HyperTerminal items on the Communications submenu, choose the one that doesn't have the folder icon and submenu arrow. Once you've created and saved dial-up configurations in HyperTerminal, XP displays the HyperTerminal submenu off the Communications submenu so that you can access them directly from the Start menu, without having HyperTerminal encourage you to create a new connection.)

The first time you run HyperTerminal, it displays the Default Telnet Program? dialog box, which recommends that you make HyperTerminal your default client for Telnet (remote networking). Choose the Yes button or the No button, as appropriate. Whichever way you choose, you'll probably want to select the Don't Ask Me This Question Again check box to prevent HyperTerminal from displaying this dialog box each time you run it.

HyperTerminal then displays the Connection Description dialog box, prompting you to create a new connection. Create the incoming connection or the outgoing connection as described in the next two subsections.

Create the Incoming Connection

HyperTerminal considers each discrete set of communications information a "connection," which works well for outgoing calls—you can create a connection for each number or host you need to call with anything approaching regularity and then open the connection when you need to call that host.

For incoming calls, the logic seems a bit tortured, especially as the New Connection dialog box contains fields that apply only to outgoing calls. Essentially, what you want to do is tell HyperTerminal to wait for a call and (if applicable) to listen for TCP/IP rather than a modem. But you need to define a connection in order to convey this information.

Fair enough: Let's create the incoming connection. Take the following steps:

1. Display the Connection Description dialog box by clicking the New button on the toolbar or by choosing File | New Connection. The illustration here shows the Connection Description dialog box:

2. Enter the name for the connection in the Name text box and select an icon in the Icon list box. Then click the OK button. HyperTerminal displays the Connect To dialog box, shown here:

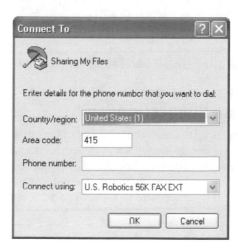

3. By default, HyperTerminal assumes that you want to connect via a modem. If you want to connect via TCP/IP instead, select the TCP/IP (Winsock) item in the Connect Using drop-down list. Doing so makes the Connect To dialog box display a different set of controls, as shown here:

4. Now, for an outgoing connection, you'd specify the details for the connection here. For a phone connection, you specify the country or region, the area code, and the phone number. For a TCP/IP connection, you specify the address of the host (for example, an IP address) and the port number. But, in this case, this computer is the computer that's being called, so you don't need to tell HyperTerminal the phone number information or the host address. You do need to specify the device (in the Connect Using drop-down list) and the port number (if the connection will use TCP/IP).

5. Click the OK button to close the Connect To dialog box and create the connection.

Now that you've created the connection, you can set HyperTerminal to answer the phone automatically by choosing Call | Wait For A Call. (To end waiting for a call, choose Call | Stop Waiting.)

NOTE   *HyperTerminal can take only one incoming connection at a time.*

Create the Outgoing Connection

Next, you (or the other party) need to create the outgoing connection. Follow the steps in the previous section, but this time, specify the full set of information, including the phone number information (if you're using a modem) or the host name or IP address (if you're using TCP/IP). If you're using TCP/IP, make sure the port number on the outgoing connection and the incoming connection match each other. (HyperTerminal defaults to port 23, but you can change this if necessary.)

Establish a Connection

To establish a connection, open the connection (if it's not already open, which it will be if you've just created it), and click the Call button on the toolbar or choose Call | Call. HyperTerminal places the call and connects if the host answers.

Send and Receive Files with HyperTerminal

Once you've established a connection with HyperTerminal, you can transfer files easily enough. HyperTerminal differentiates between sending text files (files that contain only text—for example, Notepad documents) and sending binary files (files that contain binary data—in short, just about anything other than a text file). Most of the time, you'll be sending binary files, such as documents, spreadsheets, music, or movies.

To start sending a binary file, choose Transfer | Send File. Specify the file in the resulting Send File dialog box, and, if necessary, select a different protocol in the Protocol drop-down list. (The default setting, Zmodem with Crash Recovery, is the best bet for general-purpose use.) Then click the Send button.

Under most circumstances, HyperTerminal receives files automatically when they're sent. But, occasionally you may need to receive a file manually by issuing the Transfer | Receive File command, specifying the destination and protocol in the resulting Receive File dialog box, and clicking the Receive button.

When you've finished sending and receiving files, close the connection by clicking the Disconnect button on the toolbar or choosing Call | Disconnect.

Share Files via Virtual Private Network (VPN) Connections

If you want to make files available to other people so that they can choose what to download instead of having you specify the files for transfer (as with the solutions discussed so far in this chapter), you may want to use a virtual private network (VPN) connection. XP includes a stripped-down version of Microsoft's remote access server, which provides the features you need for implementing virtual private networking on your computer or your network.

A VPN connection is a secure private network connection established over an insecure public network—typically, but not always, the Internet. VPNs use either the Point-to-Point Tunneling Protocol (PPTP) or the Layer Two Tunneling Protocol (L2TP) to establish a secure and encrypted connection across the insecure network.

To create a VPN connection, you need to set up one computer to accept incoming connections and the other computer (or computers) to call those connections. The computer that hosts the connections has to have an IP address or name that you can access via the Internet. Usually, it's easiest to have a static IP address that you can hard-code in the computers that call the connection. But you can also create a VPN using a dynamic IP address—one that changes from session to session. In this case, the VPN host will need to inform the callers of the host's current IP address after establishing their Internet connection, and each caller will need to enter the current IP address in the Host Name or IP Address of Destination text box on the General page of the Properties dialog box for the connection.

Another method for providing files for download and letting other users browse them is to run an FTP server. Because XP Home Edition doesn't include an FTP server, running one on XP Home Edition means using add-on software, so I don't cover it in this book. But if one of your computers is running an OS that includes an FTP server—for example, Linux—this may be a good solution for some of your file-sharing needs.

Set XP to Accept Incoming Connections

To set up XP to accept incoming connections, take the following steps:

1. Start the New Connection Wizard by choosing Start | All Programs | Accessories | Communications | New Connection Wizard or by clicking the Create a New Connection link in the Network Tasks list on the Network Connections page of Control Panel.

2. Click the Next button on the introductory page. The wizard displays the Network Connection Type page, shown here:

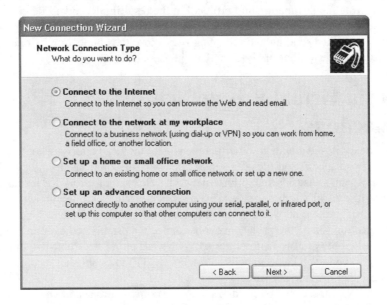

3. Select the Set Up an Advanced Connection option button and click the Next button. The wizard displays the Advanced Connection Options page, shown next:

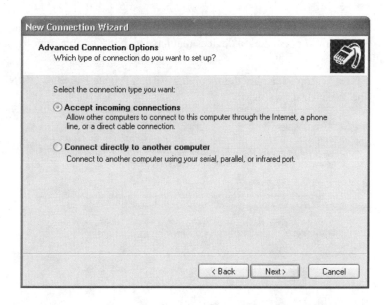

4. Leave the Accept Incoming Connections option button selected (as it is by default) and click the Next button. The wizard displays the Devices for Incoming Connections page, shown here:

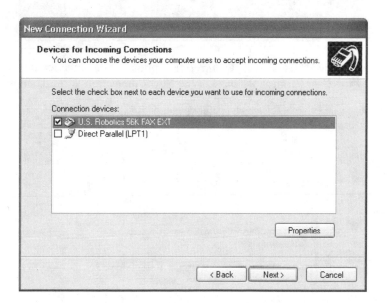

5. Select the check boxes for the devices on which you want to accept incoming connections. In the preceding illustration, the choices are a modem and the parallel port, so you'd want to choose the modem. Depending on your computer's configuration, you may have other choices. If applicable, you can set properties for the selected connection by clicking the

Properties button and working in the resulting Properties dialog box. Note that XP doesn't disable this button for connection devices that have no configurable options, such as a parallel port.

6. Click the Next button to display the Incoming Virtual Private Network (VPN) Connection page of the Wizard, shown next:

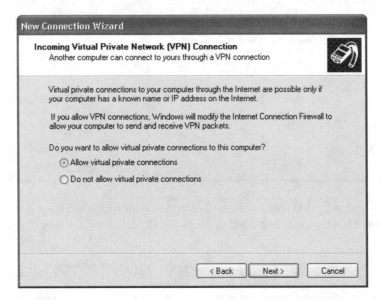

7. Select the Allow Virtual Private Connections option button and click the Next button to display the User Permissions page of the New Connection Wizard, shown here:

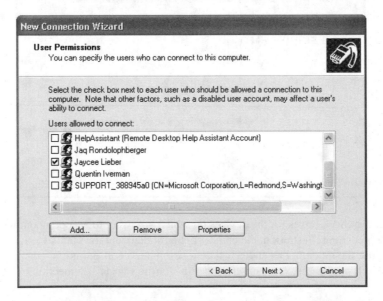

8. Use the controls on the User Permissions page to specify which users can connect to the computer via the VPN connection:

- To enable a user listed in the Users Allowed to Connect list box to connect via the VPN connection, select their check box. As you can see in the illustration, the list includes a couple of users you haven't created manually: HelpAssistant and SUPPORT_*nnnnn*. The HelpAssistant user is used by Remote Assistance, and the SUPPORT_ user is used by Microsoft Assisted Support.

- To add a new user to the list, click the Add button and specify the user's username, full name, and password in the resulting New User dialog box.

- To change the password or to specify callback options for a selected user, click the Properties button and work in the resulting Properties dialog box. You're unlikely to need to use callback for a VPN connection, but XP lets you set the options anyway.

- To remove a selected user from being able to use the VPN connection *and* from the local list of user accounts, click the Remove button. XP displays the Incoming Connections Warning dialog box to warn you that this action removes the user from your system, as well as from the VPN connection. Click the Yes button to remove the user permanently or the No button to step back. (If you don't want an existing user to be able to use the VPN connection, simply clear their check box in the Users Allowed to Connect list box.)

9. When you've finished specifying users, click the Next button to display the Networking Software page of the New Connection Wizard, shown here:

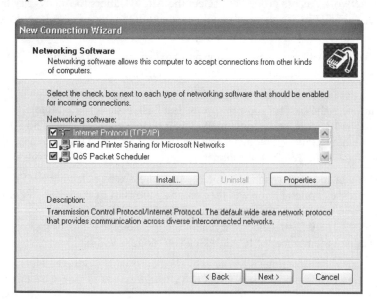

10. If you set up XP on your computer yourself, you'll probably recognize the dialog box from the Setup routine. Under most circumstances, it lists entries for Internet Protocol (TCP/IP), File and Printer Sharing for Microsoft Networks, QoS [Quality of Service]

Packet Scheduler, and Client for Microsoft Networks. This is the set of networking software that a standard XP setup will be running anyway. But there's a crucial difference. Select the Internet Protocol (TCP/IP) entry in the Networking Software list box and click the Properties button to display the Incoming TCP/IP Properties dialog box, shown next:

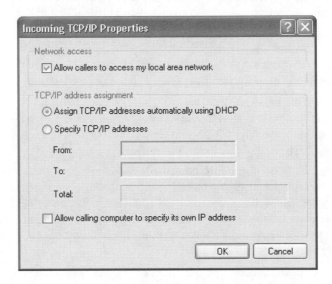

11. In the Network Access group box, select the Allow Callers to Access My Local Area Network check box if you want people connecting via the VPN to be able to access the other computers connected to this computer. If not, make sure this check box is cleared.

12. In the TCP/IP Address Assignment group box, specify how you want XP to handle IP addresses for computers that connect via the VPN:

   ■ The default setting, the Assign TCP/IP Addresses Automatically via DHCP option button, is the best for most purposes. If a DHCP server is available, such as ICS, it assigns IP addresses automatically when people connect; and if no DHCP server is available, XP uses Automatic Private IP Addressing (APIPA) to assign a random IP address in the 169.254.$n.n$ subnet.

   ■ You can specify a range of available IP addresses by selecting the Specify TCP/IP Addresses option button and then entering the start of the range in the From text box and the end of the range in the To text box (for example, From 192.168.0.220 To 192.168.0.230). Check the readout in the Total text box to make sure you've assigned the number of IP addresses you thought you had.

   ■ If you want incoming callers to provide their own IP address, select the Allow Calling Computer to Specify Its Own IP Address check box. Use this option if you want to use an IP address to identify a particular caller, but understand that the address the calling computer specifies might conflict with the IP address of a computer already on the network.

13. Click the OK button to close the Incoming TCP/IP Properties dialog box.

14. On the Networking Software page, click the Next button to display the Completing the New Connection Wizard page, which tells you that the connection you've specified will be saved under the name Incoming Connections in the Network Connections folder.

15. Click the Finish button to close the New Connection Wizard.

At this point, XP has created the VPN connection and activated it, so your computer is listening for incoming calls. If you check the Services page of the Advanced Settings dialog box for the Internet connection being used for the VPN, you'll see that XP has added services for Incoming Connection VPN (L2TP), Incoming Connection VPN (PPTP), and IP Security (IKE).

> TIP
>
> *The Incoming Connection VPN (PPTP) connection uses TCP port 1723. If you're using ICS and you need to map the incoming VPN connection to an ICS client, enter the client's details in the Name or IP Address of the Computer Hosting This Service on Your Network text box in the Service Settings dialog box for the Incoming Connection VPN (PPTP) connection.*

Create the Incoming VPN Connection

To create the VPN connection on the computer that will call in, take the following steps:

1. Start the New Connection Wizard by choosing Start | All Programs | Accessories | Communications | New Connection Wizard or by clicking the Create a New Connection link in the Network Tasks list on the Network Connections page of Control Panel.

2. Click the Next button on the introductory page. The wizard displays the Network Connection Type page, shown in step 2 in the previous section.

3. Select the Connect to the Network at My Workplace option button and click the Next button to display the Network Connection page of the wizard, shown here:

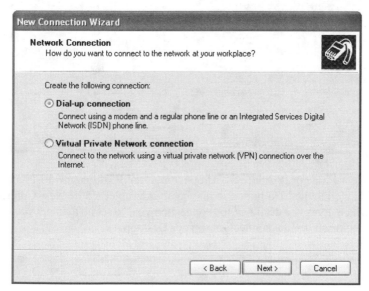

4. Select the Virtual Private Network Connection option button and click the Next button to display the Connection Name page of the wizard.

5. In the Company Name text box, enter the name you want to assign to the VPN connection. You're probably not connecting to a company (and even if you were, the name for the connection wouldn't need to have anything to do with the company), so enter whatever name you want to use for the connection. Then click the Next button to move on to the Public Network page or the VPN Server Selection page.

6. If the computer on which you're creating the connection has a dial-up connection to the Internet, the wizard displays the Public Network page, which lets you specify whether XP should automatically dial the initial connection to the Internet before establishing the VPN connection and, if so, which connection it should dial. If you have a dial-up connection that you keep open automatically or manually, select the Do Not Dial the Initial Connection option button on this page because, if you select the Automatically Dial This Initial Connection option button, XP will try to redial the connection if it's already open.

7. If the wizard displayed the Public Network page, click the Next button to display the VPN Server Selection page, shown here:

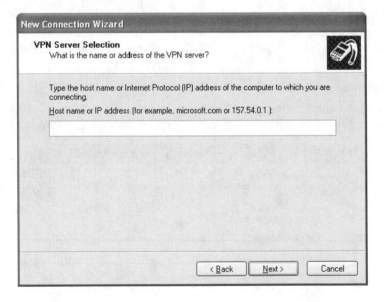

8. In the Host Name or IP Address text box, enter the IP address or host name of the VPN host. Then click the Next button to display the Completing the New Connection Wizard page, which gives you details of the connection you've set up and lets you choose whether to add a shortcut for the connection to your Desktop.

9. Click the Finish button to close the Wizard.

Connect via a VPN Connection

To connect via the VPN connection you've created, choose Start | Connect To and choose the item for the VPN connection from the Connect To submenu. XP displays the Connect dialog box for the connection.

> **TIP** *If you're connecting to a VPN host that uses a dial-up connection that gets its IP address dynamically assigned (rather than having a static IP address), you'll need to get the current IP address from the host for each session (for example, by e-mail or chat). Then right-click the VPN connection and choose Properties from the context menu to display the Properties dialog box, enter the IP address in the Host Name or IP Address of Destination text box on the General page, and click the OK button.*

Enter your username and password, specify as usual whether to save the username and password (and, if so, whether for yourself only or for other users as well), and then click the Connect button. XP connects to the VPN server using the same sequence of steps and dialog boxes as for connecting to an ISP.

Once you've connected, you'll be able to access your network drives and other resources (for example, printers) as if you were working locally, except that the connection speed will be that of your Internet connection rather than a LAN speed.

You can disconnect a VPN connection in the same ways as an Internet connection. For example, right-click the VPN's icon in the notification area and choose Disconnect from the context menu.

Share Files via a VPN Connection

To share files via a VPN connection, place the files (or copies of them) in a folder or folder structure that people connecting via the VPN connection will be able to access. They will then be able to download the files as necessary. If they have the Create right in the folders available to them, they'll also be able to upload files.

Summary

This chapter has discussed how to share files effectively and securely using some of the Internet tools included in XP. It has also shown you how to share files effectively but insecurely using Messenger and has reminded you of the extent to which .NET Messenger Service monitors your actions while you're using Messenger. It has also lectured you briefly on what you may and may not legally do with other people's copyrighted digital content.

Enough of that kind of sharing; it's time for a different kind. The next chapter discusses how to work with your friends, family, or coworkers (or, indeed, just about anybody you choose to work with) on collaborative projects online.

Chapter 8

Work with Friends, Family, or Coworkers on Online Projects

NetMeeting and Messenger offer powerful capabilities for working on projects with your friends, your family, or your coworkers—or with members of all three groups at once.

These capabilities fall into two parts: using the whiteboarding features built into NetMeeting and Messenger to brainstorm or sketch out ideas, and using NetMeeting's and Messenger's program-sharing and Desktop-sharing features to work with other people on other documents. For example, you might share WordPerfect to work together on drafting a document, or you might share Excel to work together on improving a spreadsheet.

This chapter also discusses NetMeeting's Remote Desktop Sharing feature, which lets you access your own Desktop remotely and securely. Because of XP's multiuser technology, Remote Desktop Sharing isn't as useful or as easy to use as the Remote Desktop feature built into XP Professional, but it's a good tool to have available for accessing a computer running XP Home. (XP Home doesn't have Remote Desktop, though it does have Remote Desktop Connection for connecting to Remote Desktop.) Messenger doesn't offer Remote Desktop Sharing (presumably because Microsoft would prefer you to use XP Professional and Remote Desktop instead).

Because NetMeeting and Messenger offer many of the same collaboration features, I discuss them together for much of the chapter. There'd be no point in having a section on using Whiteboard with NetMeeting and a parallel section on using Whiteboard with Messenger with 90 percent of the contents similar, would there? And as you'll see, most of the commands are very similar between the two applications. Where they're different, I point out the differences.

Use Whiteboard with NetMeeting and Messenger

Whiteboard provides a virtual whiteboard for brainstorming and planning during your conferences. It combines ease of use with enough power to be useful for a variety of purposes.

Whiteboard has advantages and disadvantages compared to sharing a program. The main advantages are that Whiteboard is designed for brainstorming, so it provides suitable tools, and it's optimized for use over networks, so it will run at an acceptable speed even over dial-up connections. By contrast, sharing a fatter application can make modem connections seem frustratingly arthritic.

Another advantage is that you can use Whiteboard as a kind of sandbox: Though you're working with other people on your computer (and on theirs at the same time), none of you can take any action on anyone else's computer. By contrast, if you're sharing a program, the other people can take actions in it that you might not want. For example, if you're sharing a VBA-enabled program, another user might execute some VBA code. Or if you're sharing an Explorer window, another user could delete some of your files. Sure, you'd see them do it, but you might not be quick enough to prevent it.

The main disadvantage to Whiteboard is, as you'd imagine, that its capabilities are limited compared to most programs you might want to share—Whiteboard is essentially a version of Microsoft Paint with a couple of twists and with collaboration features tacked on. These features are pretty solid: you can create multiple pages on Whiteboard, you can unsynchronize a page so that you can work on it without other people interfering, and you can lock Whiteboard to stop anybody fouling up the masterwork that's been painstakingly assembled by legion hands. But if you want to collaborate on editing text, say, or manipulating a graphic, Whiteboard won't get you far. For operations such as those, you'll need to share a program.

Differences Between Whiteboard in NetMeeting and Messenger

As mentioned a moment ago, Whiteboard is largely the same in Messenger as it is in NetMeeting. And that's little wonder because Messenger borrows Whiteboard directly from NetMeeting.

But there are a couple of crucial differences. First, NetMeeting lets multiple people participate in a Whiteboard session, whereas Messenger lets only two people participate. Having only two people in a collaboration speeds things up a great deal over your average connection, but it greatly limits the amount of collaboration you can achieve at once.

Second, Whiteboard in Messenger works only with XP, not with earlier versions of Windows. Whiteboard in NetMeeting, on the other hand, works with all known versions of 32-bit Windows for desktop computers, with a few quirks that we'll examine a bit later in this chapter—in particular, NetMeeting isn't 100-percent compatible with ICS, which can cause problems.

So Messenger gives you greater ease of use, but NetMeeting gives you more flexibility. If that sounds a bit like what you read in the last couple of chapters, I couldn't exactly contradict you. And, as usual, you can establish secure connections with NetMeeting, whereas Messenger monitors your every action.

> **NOTE** *You can run Messenger and NetMeeting at the same time, but you can't run their sharing features at the same time. If you do, XP displays a message box telling you that another application is using the sharing features when you try to add the second program to the party. XP then cancels the launch of the second program.*

Whiteboard Basics

To start a Whiteboard session in a NetMeeting conference, click the Whiteboard button in the main NetMeeting window. Alternatively, choose Tools | Whiteboard or press CTRL-W. NetMeeting opens Whiteboard on all the computers in the conference without prompting any of the other users in the conference.

> **NOTE** *NetMeeting 3.x includes two versions of Whiteboard: the regular version, which you invoke by using the commands just described, and a Whiteboard 2.x version that's compatible with NetMeeting 2.x and NetMeeting 1.x and that you can invoke by choosing Tools | Whiteboard (1.0–2.x). Whiteboard 2.x offers almost all the same features as Whiteboard 3, but its menu configuration and interface are a little different. This section discusses Whiteboard 3.*

To start a Whiteboard session in Messenger, click the Start Whiteboard link in the I Want To list or choose Actions | Start Whiteboard. (You can take either of these actions from an existing conversation or from the main Messenger window to establish a new conversation.) If you issue one of these commands from the main Messenger window or in a Conversation window that contains two or more other participants, Messenger displays the Start Whiteboard dialog box to let you pick the contact or other person with whom to start the Whiteboard session. If you issue one of these commands in a Conversation window in which there's only one other protagonist, Messenger starts the Whiteboard session with that person.

If you've used Paint, Whiteboard's drawing tools should seem familiar and straightforward. Figure 8-1 shows the Whiteboard window with a brainstorming session in progress. Figure 8-2 shows the Whiteboard toolbar buttons and navigation buttons.

Most of these tools are self-explanatory. For example, to select an item, you click the Selector button so that the mouse pointer changes to the Selector arrow and then click the item you want to select. To erase an item, you click the Eraser button so that the mouse pointer changes to the Eraser arrow and then click the item you want to erase.

Some of the tools, such as Lock Contents and Unsynchronize, aren't so obvious. The next sections discuss these tools.

If you start Whiteboard from Messenger, Messenger also displays the Sharing Session toolbar, shown in Figure 8-3, from which you can easily start Whiteboard or program sharing, and from which you can quickly close your sharing session.

Work with Text

In some ways, Whiteboard carries the analogy of working on a whiteboard a bit further than you might like—most notably in that once you've placed an object on the page and finished creating

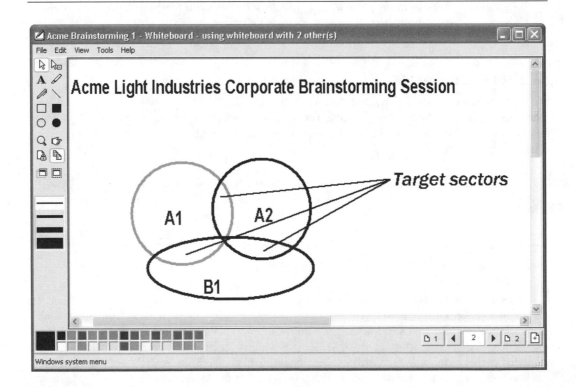

FIGURE 8-1   NetMeeting's Whiteboard is Microsoft Paint bulked up with collaboration tools.

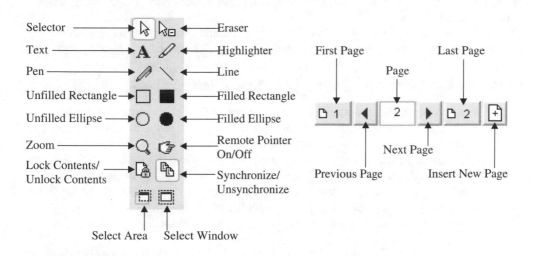

Selector — Eraser

Text — Highlighter

Pen — Line

Unfilled Rectangle — Filled Rectangle

Unfilled Ellipse — Filled Ellipse

Zoom — Remote Pointer On/Off

Lock Contents/ Unlock Contents — Synchronize/ Unsynchronize

Select Area   Select Window

First Page   Last Page

Page

Next Page

Previous Page   Insert New Page

FIGURE 8-2   Whiteboard's toolbar buttons and navigation buttons.

it, you can move it or apply basic formatting to it, but you can't otherwise edit it. This is a particular problem with text, which tends to need editing much more than visual elements do.

TIP   *Whiteboard 2.x (in NetMeeting) lets you edit the text in a text box. For whiteboarding involving serious amounts of text, you may want to use Whiteboard 2.x rather than Whiteboard 3 because of this capability. If you choose, you can run Whiteboard 2.x and Whiteboard 3 at the same time, but doing so risks causing confusion. To perform group editing on text, share a text editor (such as Notepad) or a word processor (such as WordPad).*

To add text to the current page, click the Text button. The mouse pointer changes to an insertion point. Click the page at the point where you want the upper-left corner of the text

FIGURE 8-3   The Sharing Session toolbar gives you easy access to Whiteboard and program sharing.

to appear. Whiteboard displays a text box with a flashing cursor. Type the text for the text box, pressing ENTER to break lines as necessary or create paragraph breaks. When you've finished working in the text box, click the Selector button to deselect the text box. (Alternatively, click to start another text box.)

To format the text in a text box, right-click the text box and choose Font from the context menu, and use the Font dialog box to specify the formatting. (Alternatively, select the text box by clicking in it. Then choose Tools | Font to display the Font dialog box.)

All the text in any given text box has to have the same formatting, so you don't need to select any text before applying formatting—selecting the text box is enough. That means you need to use a different text box for each text element that requires different formatting. But given that you can't edit text once you've finished creating its text box, you'll probably want to create each paragraph—perhaps even each line—as a separate text box.

The Whiteboard is primarily a means of assembling information. It's not a great means of exchanging text or graphical information. However, you *can* copy a text box or a graphical object from the Whiteboard and paste it into another application. For a text box, you get just the text without the formatting. For a graphical object, you get the whole object, including color.

To exchange larger amounts of text, send it via chat or via file transfer.

> **NOTE**   *The Edit | Select All command lets you quickly select all the objects on a Whiteboard page. This command is primarily useful for copying all the contents of a page to another page. (You can also use it to delete all the objects from a page, but the Edit | Clear Page command is quicker and more convenient.) Copying all the contents of a page works only for Whiteboard—if you paste what you've copied into another program, you get only the contents of the first text box on the page.*

Add, Delete, and Synchronize Pages

Whiteboard lets you create multiple pages in the same file, so you can create several drafts of the work in progress or let each member of the conference work on a separate page to brainstorm different approaches.

Here's how to work with pages:

- To insert a page after the current page, click the Insert New Page button, press CTRL++ (that's CTRL and the "plus" key), or choose Edit | Insert Page After. To insert a page before the current page, choose Edit | Insert Page Before.

- To navigate from one page to another, use the navigation buttons and the Page text box. (In NetMeeting versions before NetMeeting 3, choose Edit | Page Sorter and use the Page Sorter dialog box.)

- To delete a page, choose Edit | Delete Page or press CTRL+– (CTRL and the "minus" key).

- To clear the current page, choose Edit | Clear page or press CTRL+DEL.

By default, Whiteboard synchronizes the pages, so all participants in the conference see the changes being made—when one participant makes a change to a page that's being synchronized, Whiteboard displays that page on the other participants' Whiteboard windows as well. By unsynchronizing a page, you can work on it without the changes you make being automatically displayed to the other participants, but they can still access the page manually and see the changes you're making.

To unsynchronize a page, click the Unsynchronize button. When you're ready to synchronize the pages again, click the Synchronize button.

Move and Copy Information

To move an item, use the Selector to select it and then drag the item to where you want it to appear. To move two or more items at the same time, select the first item, hold down CTRL, select each of the other items, and then drag them to the new location.

To move one or more items from one page to another, select the item or items, cut them from the page they're on, and paste them onto the other page. Alternatively, copy the items and paste copies onto the other page.

If one object overlaps another, you can use the Bring to Front command or the Send to Back command to specify which object appears on top of the other. These commands are on the context menu for objects, as well as on the Edit menu.

Copy a Program Window into Whiteboard

Whiteboard doesn't let you paste in a screenshot captured by using a technique such as ALT-PRTSCN, but it does include commands for pasting either a program window or a selected area of the screen into Whiteboard:

- ■ To paste a program window into Whiteboard, click the Select Window button or choose Tools | Select Window and then click the window you want to paste.

- ■ To paste an area of the screen into Whiteboard, click the Select Area button or choose Tools | Select Area, and then use the resulting crosshair to select the area of the screen.

For either command, Whiteboard displays an information message box explaining the command until you tell it to desist. Whiteboard then hides itself so that you can make your selection; then it pastes in the window or selected area at the upper-left corner of Whiteboard.

 *Bear in mind that graphics such as screenshots contain much more information than text, lines, and simple graphical shapes, so they take much longer to transfer over a slow or moderate-speed connection.*

Lock Whiteboard

Any user can lock Whiteboard to prevent other people from making further changes to its contents. Once you've locked it, you yourself can make changes to your heart's content; others can only save or print Whiteboard.

To lock Whiteboard, click the Lock Contents button on the toolbar or choose View | Lock Contents. To unlock Whiteboard, click the Unlock Contents button that replaces the Lock Contents button.

You can't lock Whiteboard when another user has open an object that requires locking. For example, a text box is locked until the user currently working in it removes the focus from it. So when someone's working in a text box, you can't lock Whiteboard. If you try, Whiteboard displays a Lock message box warning you that "Another Whiteboard has one or more objects locked on this page" or "Cannot lock the Whiteboard, the object has focus on another computer." To release the lock, you need to get the user with the locked object to remove the focus from that object.

You also can't lock Whiteboard when it's not synchronized. When Whiteboard isn't synchronized, the Lock Contents button is dimmed and unavailable. When you synchronize Whiteboard, it makes the Lock Contents button available.

Save Whiteboard

You can save the contents of Whiteboard by using the File | Save command and the resulting Save As dialog box. Once you've saved a file, you can save later versions to the same file by reissuing the File | Save command, or you can save later versions in separate files by using the File | Save As command and specifying a new filename, as usual.

NetMeeting 3.*x* Whiteboard files use the NMW file format. Earlier versions use the WHT file format. The NMW file format is compatible with T126—one of the T.120 standards that cover the data-sharing element of a multimedia teleconference. This means you can open NMW files in other teleconferencing (or, more specifically, *whiteboarding*) programs.

If you haven't saved the contents of Whiteboard when you close the Whiteboard window or exit NetMeeting or Messenger, Whiteboard prompts you to save the contents. NetMeeting also prompts you to save the contents if you have Whiteboard open with unsaved contents when you join a new conference.

Open a Saved Whiteboard File

You can open a saved Whiteboard file by issuing an Open command (File | Open or CTRL-O) from Whiteboard, or by double-clicking the file in an Explorer window or on the Desktop.

Troubleshoot Whiteboard

This section discusses some common problems involving Whiteboard.

Whiteboard from NetMeeting May Not Work on Windows 98 ICS Host

Windows 98's version of ICS and NetMeeting aren't fully compatible with each other because (in Microsoft's words) "the ICS address table has a problem using the H.323 protocol." This can have a couple of different results: first, Whiteboard, file transfer, program sharing, or chat may not work on the ICS host; second, ICS clients may not be able to receive incoming NetMeeting calls even though they can place outgoing NetMeeting calls with no problem.

The only solution to Whiteboard (or other NetMeeting components) not working on the ICS host is to disable ICS for your NetMeeting sessions. I need hardly point out that disabling ICS prevents your ICS clients from connecting to the Internet. You might also consider upgrading the Windows 98 computer to XP.

Whiteboard from NetMeeting Doesn't Work on Windows Me ICS Host or ICS Client

Windows Me's version of ICS typically has a Registry value set incorrectly that prevents Whiteboard, chat, program sharing, and file transfer from working on either the ICS host or its ICS clients.

If you run into this problem, you can fix it by editing the Registry. As before, the standard cautions apply: you should understand what the Registry is and does, you should have a full backup of the Registry available in case Windows doesn't agree with the changes you make, and you should know how to restore the Registry from the backup.

To edit the Registry, run Registry Editor (Start | Run, enter **regedit**, and click the OK button). Navigate to the HKEY_LOCAL_MACHINE\System\CurrentControlSet\Services\ICSharing\ Mappings\Installed\H323\0001 key and modify the Translation value entry to **H323**. Then exit Registry Editor and restart the computer.

"Error 0x80ee000c. SIP Transaction Timed Out" Error

If you get this error when you start a Whiteboard session from Messenger, it means your NAT device isn't Universal Plug and Play (UPnP) compliant. Because Messenger works only across UPnP-compliant NAT devices or direct connections, the NAT device prevents Messenger from establishing the Whiteboard session. See if the device's manufacturer has an update to make the NAT device UPnP compliant. If not, you'll need to use Messenger on a direct connection rather than through NAT for Whiteboard to work.

NOTE   *Because you ask—SIP is the abbreviation for Session Initiation Protocol, an application-layer signaling protocol used for setting up and handling multimedia calls.*

You Respond to a Messenger Invitation, but the Inviter Is Gone

If you respond to a Messenger invitation for Whiteboard or program sharing but find that the person who invited you doesn't seem to be there, they may have used XP's Fast User Switching feature to switch to a different account (or someone else may have logged onto the computer) without either ending their XP session or signing out of Messenger Service. XP lets Messenger sessions run in disconnected XP sessions—it doesn't terminate them the way it terminates NetMeeting sessions in disconnected XP sessions.

Windows 95/98/NT 4 User Can't See Whiteboard in a NetMeeting Call

If you add a user who's running NetMeeting 2.x (for example, on Windows 95, Windows 98, or NT 4) to a call in which NetMeeting 3.x users have already established a Whiteboard session, the NetMeeting 2.x user won't be able to see Whiteboard because NetMeeting is using the NetMeeting 3.x–only version of Whiteboard rather than the backward-compatible version (Whiteboard 1.0–2.x) that NetMeeting 3.x also includes. NetMeeting automatically starts the appropriate version of Whiteboard for the clients in the call, so the problem arises only if you add a NetMeeting 2.x user to an existing NetMeeting 3.x session.

If this problem occurs, run Whiteboard 1.0–2.*x* by choosing Tools | Whiteboard (1.0–2.*x*). You can copy information across from Whiteboard 3 by using the Copy and Paste commands as usual, but be aware that issuing an Edit | Select All command and copying and pasting the result pastes the information into Whiteboard 1.0–2.*x* as a single uneditable item rather than as the individual components.

Can't Use Whiteboard, Chat, or File Transfer
When Sending Video in NetMeeting on Windows Me

NetMeeting 3.01 for Windows Me has a bug that prevents you from using Whiteboard, chat, or file transfer once you've started using video in a call. This problem occurs with any use of video but is worst if you've selected the Automatically Send Video at the Start of Each Call check box on the Video page of the Options dialog box, because that cripples Whiteboard, chat, and file transfer from the beginning of the call.

To work around this problem, clear the Automatically Send Video at the Start of Each Call check box and avoid starting video manually for calls on which you want to use Whiteboard, chat, or file transfers.

Highlight Pen in NetMeeting on Windows 95 Blacks Out Details

The highlight pen in Whiteboard in NetMeeting version 2 on Windows 95 sometimes gives trouble. Either you can't see the line it's drawing or it blacks out the pixels of the bitmap. The workaround is to change the color combination you're using. You may get better results with a bitmap that has a white background.

Share a Program—or Your Desktop—Using NetMeeting or Messenger

NetMeeting and Messenger both let you share either one or more programs or your whole Desktop with other people in a meeting or call so that you can work together on documents, demonstrate how to use software, or show off.

NetMeeting's and Messenger's program-sharing features are almost identical, so I discuss them together in this section. Where there's a difference between NetMeeting's and Messenger's implementation of a feature, or when one program has a feature that the other does not, I point it out—starting with the key difference, which is that Messenger lets you share programs with only one other person whereas NetMeeting lets you share programs with multiple people.

Program sharing has good points and bad points, in roughly equal amounts. On the plus side, you can work together with one (with NetMeeting or Messenger) or more (with NetMeeting) other people, and only one of you needs to have the shared program (or programs) installed on your computer. You can chat with the people in the meeting or call about the sharing. (If there's just one other person in the call, you can use audio and video, as well as chat to discuss what you're sharing, but your bandwidth needs will be prodigious.) And you can either share only the display of the program (or Desktop) or share the display and allow others to control it. If you choose to share control, you can allow requests for control automatically for convenience or screen each one manually for security.

The minus side of program sharing involves security and performance. Sharing a program without allowing control is relatively safe, provided that you don't let the participants in the meeting or call see anything you don't want them to see. But allowing control of a shared program, let alone your Desktop, raises major security issues because another participant may take actions you don't want before you can prevent them.

So, before you allow control of a shared program, sit back and assess the risks involved. The more limited the capabilities of the program you let other users control, the less damage they can do—intentionally or otherwise. Balance against that the actions you need to be able to take in the program. For example, if you're creating a text document, consider whether you need to use Word, or whether WordPad—or even Notepad—would do. Will you just be hacking text in tandem (or in chorus), or will you need to use features such as revision marks? Does Word's VBA functionality pose a threat? Remember that most applications use common dialog boxes (such as the Open dialog box and the Save As dialog box) that include commands for creating, renaming, and deleting folders, and for deleting and renaming files, as well as commands for copying or cutting both files and folders.

Before you allow control of your Desktop, ask yourself why you're sure it's safe to do so. Unless you're certain of the good will and the skills of the other person or people, don't do it.

To share a program, take one of the following steps:

- In NetMeeting, display the Sharing window by choosing Tools | Sharing, clicking the Share Programs button in the main NetMeeting window, or pressing CTRL-S.

- In Messenger, issue a Start Application Sharing command from the I Want To list or the Actions menu in a Conversation window or in the main Messenger window. Messenger establishes the connection, displays the Sharing Session toolbar (shown in Figure 8-3, earlier in this chapter), and displays the Sharing window.

Figure 8-4 shows the Sharing window with some sharing underway (so that you can see all the controls more clearly). Because I've allowed control of the programs (again, the better for you to see the controls), NetMeeting has replaced the Allow Control button with the Prevent Control button, its evil twin.

To share a program, select it in the Share Programs list box and click the Share button. To stop sharing a program, select it and click the Unshare button. To stop sharing all the programs you're sharing, click the Unshare All button.

To share your Desktop, select the Desktop item in the Share Programs list box and click the Share button. (You'll need to stop sharing any previously shared programs first.) To stop sharing your Desktop, click the Unshare button or the Unshare All button.

Share in True Color

If you want to share the program in true color, select the Share in True Color check box. Sharing a program in true color is a bad idea unless everyone with whom you're sharing the program has a very fast connection (for example, an Ethernet connection) to the meeting *and* you actually need to use true color. For example, if you're collaborating on tweaking a photograph in Photoshop or another graphics editor, you might need true color in order to be able to see what you're doing. For other programs, such as working together on documents, spreadsheets, presentations, or

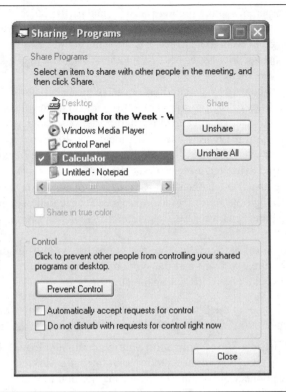

FIGURE 8-4 The Sharing window lets you designate the programs you want to share and whether you want other participants to be able to control them.

programming, you'll do better to let NetMeeting or Messenger reduce the color to a depth more practical for the speed of the connection. In some cases, you may see noticeable dithering as NetMeeting or Messenger reduces the color. In other cases, you may see false colors—pinks instead of whites, that kind of thing. In most cases, the dithering or color substitution is mild and not bothersome. But if the pink is verging on red and you get a touch of the McCarthys, you may need to try true color instead.

Allow Control of the Shared Program or Desktop

If you choose, you can allow the other participants in the call or meeting to take control of the shared program or Desktop. As discussed earlier in this chapter, allowing control presents a real security risk to the integrity of data on your computer. But if you trust the other participant or participants in the meeting to do nothing bad (or incompetent) with the shared program, you may decide to go ahead and allow control.

To allow control of all the programs you're sharing, click the Allow Control button. Once you've clicked it, you can choose whether to automatically accept requests for control. The default setting is *not* to automatically accept requests for control. If you leave this setting, when someone requests control of a shared program, NetMeeting or Messenger notifies you and lets you accept or deny the request. This manual evaluation of requests for control gives you better security than automatic acceptance of requests, but it makes the process of working together in the shared program slower.

When you're sharing control of a program, things can get hectic if several people are trying to input changes at the same time. If you need to calm things down and give yourself a break, you can select the Do Not Disturb with Requests for Control check box in the Sharing window. Anyone who then requests control gets a message box saying that you're "busy right now."

In NetMeeting, any program you choose to share is shared with all the other computers you're conferencing with. You can't limit sharing to one or more specific computers. (In Messenger, you can share only with one other computer at a time.)

The shared window displays the name of the participant sharing a program or their Desktop, so it's usually easy enough to keep straight which computer any given program is running on. Any unshared programs positioned in front of the shared programs' windows appear as blanked-out areas. Because you won't see this problem on programs you're sharing, make sure the windows you're sharing are clear of obstruction. The classic candidates for being in the way are the NetMeeting program window, the Sharing window, and (in Messenger) the Sharing Session window. Figure 8-5 shows a shared Programs window with the Sharing Session window at the upper-left corner to illustrate the problem.

When you allow control of a program, you have control of it by default. Other participants in the meeting or call see a window titled *Yourname's* Programs – Controllable. They can request control by double-clicking in the shared window or choosing Control | Request Control. If you haven't selected the Automatically Accept Requests for Control check box in the Sharing window, you then get a Request Control dialog box with an Accept button and a Reject button so that you can decide whether to grant the request or refuse it.

If they get control of the programs one way or another, they can release it by choosing Control | Release Control.

If you're sharing from NetMeeting with two or more other people, they can use the Control | Forward Control submenu to forward control of the programs to a specified participant.

Troubleshoot Sharing Programs

This section discusses how to troubleshoot program sharing. Most of these items are for NetMeeting because Messenger's sharing is limited to XP, whereas NetMeeting's sharing works (more or less) for all 32-bit desktop versions of Windows.

Program Sharing Doesn't Work on Windows Me ICS Host or ICS Client

As mentioned earlier in this chapter, Windows Me ICS has a Registry problem that prevents program sharing from working properly. See "Can't Use Whiteboard, Chat, or File Transfer When Sending Video in NetMeeting on Windows Me," earlier in this chapter, for the solution.

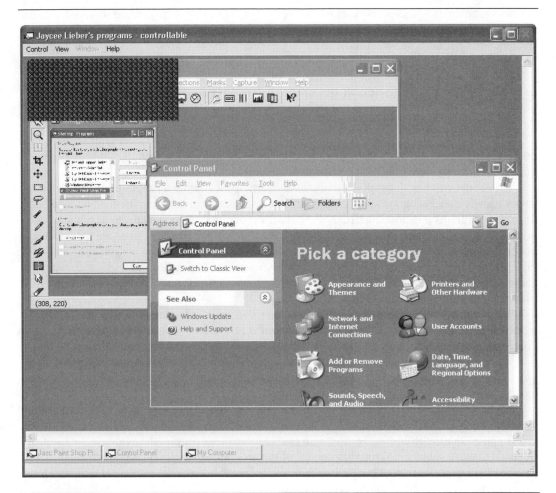

FIGURE 8-5   The shared programs appear in a Programs window like this on the other computer's screen. The Desktop appears blanked out if it's not being shared, and unshared programs can obscure the shared programs.

Program Sharing Doesn't Work on Windows 98 ICS Host

As mentioned earlier in this chapter, NetMeeting and the Windows 98 implementation of ICS don't entirely agree with each other. One result is that program sharing may not start on the ICS host. The solution is to disable ICS for the NetMeeting session.

Two Participants Can't Share Programs at the Same Time

Some versions of NetMeeting can't successfully implement program sharing if the first request for program sharing in a conference comes from two directions at once—in other words, if two participants try to share a program at the same time before any other program has been shared.

To get around this problem, share only one program at first. Once that program has been shared successfully, you should be able to share multiple programs at once without problems.

NetMeeting 2.*x* Can't Control Programs Shared by NetMeeting 3

Because NetMeeting 3 uses a different specification for sharing programs (a specification that, incidentally, lets NetMeeting 3 implement Remote Desktop Sharing), NetMeeting 2.*x* clients can't control programs shared by NetMeeting 3 clients.

NetMeeting 2.*x* Can't Share a Program at the Start of a Conference

NetMeeting 2.*x* occasionally manifests problems with sharing programs the moment that the NetMeeting conference is established. This is because NetMeeting needs a moment or two to get synchronized before it can share programs. If you run into this problem, wait a few seconds (more if you're using a slow connection) after establishing the conference and before trying to share a program.

NetMeeting 2.*x* Displays the Wrong Initials on the Shared Program Window

NetMeeting 2.*x* sometimes displays on the shared program window the initials of the previous person who controlled the program instead of the initials of the person currently controlling the program.

To refresh the display of the pointer, move it outside the NetMeeting window. Alternatively, minimize NetMeeting and then restore it.

NetMeeting 2.*x* Doesn't Work Properly with Office 2000 Meet Now Feature

The Office 2000 Meet Now feature sometimes doesn't work properly if some computers are running NetMeeting 2.*x* and you start collaborating by using the Meet Now feature when NetMeeting isn't running.

To work around this problem, start NetMeeting on each computer before invoking the Meet Now Feature.

NetMeeting Doesn't Share Internet Explorer When You Start It from a Shared Program

Some versions of NetMeeting sometimes fail to share Internet Explorer when you start it from a shared program, such as a Microsoft Office program. When this happens, there's no workaround except to share Internet Explorer manually by using the Sharing dialog box.

System Policy Prevents Collaboration During a Conference with NetMeeting 2.x

If an administrator has applied to your computer a system policy that restricts program sharing, you won't be able to collaborate during a conference with NetMeeting 2.x, even if the collaboration features appear to be available.

NetMeeting Shares Programs Without Consulting You

Internet Explorer 4 and NetMeeting 2.1 on Windows 95 produced an interesting bug—if another user in a call with you closed a shared copy of Explorer or Internet Explorer that had been running on your computer, NetMeeting would automatically share each program you started after that. The only workaround was to hang up the call and quit NetMeeting.

Unless you're running the programs just listed, you're unlikely to see this problem on your computer. But if you run into someone who apparently shares all sorts of interesting programs against their interests, this might be the explanation.

General Protection Fault (GPF) When You Quit NetMeeting While Transferring a File

NetMeeting 2.1 on Windows 95 and NT 4 may give a general protection fault (GPF) or a Dr. Watson error message if you quit NetMeeting while you're transferring a file *and* using a shared program. The solution is to upgrade from NetMeeting 2.1 or not quit NetMeeting while transferring a file.

NT 4 Requires Service Pack 3 to Share Programs

If you're using NT 4, you won't be able to share programs unless you install Service Pack 3 or a subsequent service pack.

Colors Are Weird in Shared Programs

If the colors in shared programs are strange, but everything else seems to be working fine, the problem is probably that the computers sharing the programs are using different color palette settings.

Briefly, if one of the computers in the conference is using a color setting with fewer colors than 24-bit True Color, NetMeeting downgrades the color setting of the shared program to 256 colors. This can make it look strange. Likewise, when a computer using a 256-color palette is sharing a program with computers using more colors, those computers will display dithered colors in the program window shared by the computer using fewer colors.

Shared Program Is Called "Untitled Application"

With NetMeeting 2 and Internet Explorer 4 running on Windows 95, a shared program may appear as "Untitled Application," the Windows Taskbar may also be shared, and sharing Internet Explorer also shares Explorer without your say-so.

Microsoft recommends upgrading NetMeeting to fix the problem, and it's hard to see any reason not to. Of course, upgrading Windows 95 to Windows XP automatically upgrades NetMeeting and Internet Explorer as well....

Known Issues with Other Programs

Here are a couple of known issues with other programs that you might just run into.

pcAnywhere 7.5   pcAnywhere 7.5's aw_host.sys driver prevents NetMeeting 2.0 on NT 4 from sharing programs. The solution is to upgrade to pcAnywhere 8 or later. However, if you upgrade to pcAnywhere 8, don't remove it because (as discussed in the previous chapter) doing so removes the file MSVCRT.DLL, which NetMeeting 2.1 needs to send video.

Word 6 for Windows   In Word 6 for Windows, if a remote user in a collaboration session attempts to customize a Word toolbar, the computer running the shared instance of Word may freeze for a while. (It usually recovers after a few moments.) There's no workaround beyond having the host customize the toolbar instead of the remote user doing it.

Known Issues with Hardware

Diamond Viper display drivers may cause GPFs (general protection faults—in other words, *crashes*) with NetMeeting 2.*x* on Windows 95, 98, or NT 4 when you're sharing programs. The solution is to upgrade to NetMeeting 3.*x*.

NetMeeting 2.*x* or NetMeeting 3.*x* running on NT 4 on a computer using an Accel Permedia II video adapter may hang the computer when you share a program or the Desktop. The solution is to change the value of the DisablePCIDisconnect value entry in the Registry from 0 to 1 and then restart the computer.

Use Remote Desktop Sharing in NetMeeting

NetMeeting's Remote Desktop Sharing feature lets you control your computer remotely. Remote Desktop Sharing is like a cut-down NetMeeting conference—it exists only for one person at a time, and you have to log on using your user account.

NOTE   *In order to access a computer via Remote Desktop Sharing, you need to have a Computer Administrator account on XP. Limited users and the Guest user needn't apply.*

To set up Remote Desktop Sharing, choose Tools | Remote Desktop Sharing from the main NetMeeting window. NetMeeting starts the Remote Desktop Sharing Wizard, which guides you through a short and unexciting setup process. If you're not already using a password-protected screensaver, the setup process more or less forces you to use one.

If you're using Windows XP Professional on the computer you want to access, you have the option of using Remote Desktop Connection rather than Remote Desktop Sharing. In this case, it's almost always a good idea to use Remote Desktop Connection rather than Remote Desktop Sharing because Remote Desktop Connection is fully integrated into the Windows XP multiuser mindset, whereas with Remote Desktop Sharing, you'll need to leave your user logged on and Remote Desktop Sharing running in order to be able to connect. If anyone logs you off, you won't be able to connect.

To start Remote Desktop Sharing, choose Call | Exit NetMeeting and Activate Remote Desktop Sharing. NetMeeting closes its main window and puts an icon called NetMeeting Remote Desktop Sharing in the notification area.

Troubleshoot Remote Desktop Sharing

All other things being equal, it's probably no surprise that Remote Desktop Sharing gives its fair share of trouble, but it's unfortunate all the same. The worst part of this is that trouble usually occurs when you're attempting to access Remote Desktop Sharing remotely and aren't there in presence to fix any problems. So, if you can practicably do so, test Remote Desktop Sharing locally before you need to use it in earnest.

Correct Password Is Deemed Incorrect on Windows 95 or 98

If NetMeeting denies your attempts to connect via Remote Desktop Sharing and claims that your password is invalid, make sure you're connecting via a TCP connection. If you have Client for Microsoft Networks or Microsoft Family Logon installed on your computer, select the I Want to Enable NetBIOS over TCP/IP check box on the NetBIOS page of the TCP/IP Properties dialog box and then restart your computer.

Remote Desktop Sharing Is Not Activated

In NT 4, you need to set the permissions for the NMCOM.DLL file in the Program Files\ NetMeetingNT folder so that the Everyone group or the System account has Read permission. If neither the Everyone group nor the System account has Read permission on this file, Remote Desktop Sharing typically is not activated by choosing Call | Exit NetMeeting and Activate Remote Desktop Sharing, even though the NetMeeting Remote Desktop Sharing icon appears in the notification area.

Can't Resume Remote Desktop Sharing After ISP Drops the Call

Remote Desktop Sharing in NetMeeting is a little flaky in that it can't always detect when a connection is dropped by accident instead of being terminated formally. For example, if you're enjoying a Remote Desktop Sharing session from somewhere not just remote but far away, and your ISP or the phone system drops your connection, the Remote Desktop Sharing session may not be terminated on the host. And because the host thinks that the Remote Desktop Sharing session is still going on, it doesn't bother to listen for other incoming connections—in fact, it deliberately shuts them out (because Remote Desktop Sharing is designed to accept only one connection at a time for security).

So, when you try to reconnect, you'll see error messages such as "The call was not accepted" or "The person you are calling cannot accept NetMeeting calls." There are two workarounds, but neither is exactly workable because both involve direct access to the host computer—the computer you're trying to access remotely. Still, in case you're asking, here they are:

- The easier workaround is to exit Remote Desktop Sharing on the host machine and restart it.

- The longer workaround is to exit Remote Desktop Sharing, run winipcfg or ipconfig (as appropriate for the version of Windows you're using), and use it to first release all connections and then renew all connections. Then restart Remote Desktop Sharing.

Summary

This chapter has discussed how to use NetMeeting and Messenger to collaborate with other people on projects online. You've seen how to use the Whiteboard to brainstorm or kick around ideas, how to share programs or your Desktop with others, and how to use Remote Desktop Sharing to access your computer remotely.

The next chapter discusses how to build online communities that you can use for sharing information with others.

Chapter 9

Build Your Own Free
Online Communities

The previous two chapters have discussed the tools and techniques that XP provides for sharing files with other people. Apart from e-mail, most of these tools and techniques involved synchronous communication: both you and the other person need to be online at the same time in order to share the files.

Of course, one of the great things about the Internet is that you can make material available online by creating a place for it, uploading it, and just leaving it there. Anyone who happens to come across the material—by chance or by design—can view it and download any files you've provided for download.

This short chapter discusses the following topics:

- How to create MSN communities so that you can share files and hold discussions
- Other possibilities for storing and exchanging information online
- The tools that XP provides for uploading files to and downloading files from online sites

Create and Use MSN Communities

An MSN community is a Web site and discussion area hosted by MSN, the Microsoft Network. You can create either a personal community, which is essentially an online folder in which you can store documents but which (at least in theory) nobody else can access, or a community that's open to other people—either to everyone or to people whom you allow to join in.

Each community with members provides the following:

- A What's New area, which acts as the home page
- A Pictures area in which you can create photo albums and share pictures
- A Chat area in which members can chat
- A Calendar of Events area for the community
- A Documents folder for any document that's not a picture
- A Links page to which you can easily add links to other sites

As with Hotmail e-mail accounts and MSN e-mail accounts, a basic MSN community is free to anyone who cares to sign up for it. As you'd imagine, you need to have a .NET Passport to create an MSN community, but that's about as difficult as it gets. Also as you might imagine if you've read the chapters about .NET Passport and Hotmail, a basic MSN community provides just enough space to get a small community up and running; but if your community attracts more than a few active members, or if you want to post a number of photos or other files, you'll soon run out of space. At that point, you'll need to either delete content or purchase more space—and the latter, of course, involves giving Microsoft information on your true identity, address, and means of payment.

Compared to a standard Web site, an MSN community is much easier to use, provided that the features it offers meet your needs. It's much less expandable than a Web site and (depending on the ISP that you use or would use for your Web site) much more tightly managed. Because they're free, MSN communities are certainly worth trying if you're considering getting a Web site, but they're not to all tastes.

Create an MSN Community with Members

You can create an MSN community with members by using either your Web browser or the Add Network Place Wizard:

- With your Web browser, open communities.msn.com/home, sign in using your .NET Passport, and then click the Create a Community link.

- Choose Start | My Network Places to display your My Network Places folder. Then, in the Network Tasks list, click the Add a Network Place link to start the Add Network Place Wizard.

The site or the wizard then walks you through its Create Your Own Community process. The site and the wizard break up the steps differently, but the main points (covered in the next subsections) are the same.

Name and Describe Your Community

Make the name as catchy, concise, and descriptive as possible. Use the description to explain clearly what the community is for so that you get only people who are interested in the appropriate things (if this is to be a public community) or so that the people who access the community can be sure they're in the right place and not in a different community with a similar name.

Specify Parameters for Your Community

You then get to specify the parameters for your community. These are discussed next.

Rate the Community   Choose the appropriate rating for your community:

- **General**   Safe for all ages
- **Mature**   May not be suitable for all audiences
- **Adult**   Explicit or graphic content

Choose a Membership Policy   Choose the type of membership policy for your community:

- **Public**   Anyone can view the community or become a member.
- **Public Restricted**   Anyone can view the community and apply to join, but you, as the manager of the community, get to approve applications.
- **Private**   Nobody can even view the community without your approving their membership.

Specify Whether the Community Will Be Moderated   Specify whether the community is unmoderated (all messages posted to the community automatically go to the message board) or moderated (you get to check the messages and decide which go to the message board and which go into the bit bucket).

Specify Whether the Community Is Listed or Unlisted   Choose whether the community is listed in the community directory and search engine or is unlisted. Private communities don't appear in the search engine.

Choose the Category and Subcategory for the Community   MSN categorizes its communities to help people find communities that interest them, so you need to specify the category and subcategory for the community. For example, you might choose the Entertainment category and the Music: Urban/R&B subcategory.

Choose the Preferred Language for the Community   Next, choose the preferred language for the community. (This is the language in which the community is displayed. Members can use other languages as necessary.)

Choose Options for Participating in the Community

The setup process or the wizard asks you to confirm your e-mail address (which it has extracted from your .NET Passport), choose the nickname you want to use in the community, and decide whether other people in the community are allowed to see your e-mail address.

You also get to specify how you want to read community messages. You can have community messages routed to your Inbox individually, have them sent as a daily digest (in other words, all lumped together in the order in which they arrived), or simply read them on the message board. You can also choose between plain text and HTML for e-mail messages you receive.

Accept the Code of Conduct

Next, you have to accept the Code of Conduct for MSN Communities. You'll need to read the Code of Conduct in detail, of course; but as you'd imagine, it lists a wide variety of things that aren't allowed on MSN communities (everything from spam to child pornography, bigotry, and copyrighted content to which you don't have the appropriate rights) and tells you that Microsoft can delete any of your content or pull the plug on your community if they see something they don't like.

Create the Community—or Choose a Different Name

Once you've clicked the Create My Community button, the setup process creates a community e-mail address based on the name you gave the community and displays the home page for the community with the Manager's Tools list and manager's links shown.

If you've chosen for your community a name that's already been used or that Microsoft blocks for whatever reason, the setup process displays the Invalid Community Name page for you to choose a different name. Enter it and click the Create My Community button.

Edit the Welcome Message for the Community

If you have any sense of the appropriate, you'll want to edit the Welcome message for the community because the default text is bland beyond belief. To edit the message, click the Edit Welcome Message link on the community's home page for the manager and work on the resulting page, which provides formatting controls that'll seem very familiar if you've used Hotmail's rich-text formatting. If you want to manipulate the HTML codes directly, select the Use HTML to Create Your Page check box. Click the Save Welcome Message button when you've finished, and MSN adds your message to the Welcome page for the community.

Create a Personal MSN Community

As well as creating an MSN community that has (or can have) members or instead of creating one, you may want to create your own personal MSN community for storing your documents online.
    To do so, take these steps:

1. Run the Add Network Place Wizard by clicking the Add a Network Place link in the Network Tasks list on the My Network Places page (Start | My Network Places).

2. On the first Select Where You Want Your Files Stored page of the wizard, select the Create a New MSN Community to Share Your Files item.

3. On the second Select Where You Want Your Files Stored page, choose the Personal option button.

4. On the Set Up My Web Documents page, check that the wizard has entered the right e-mail address (from your .NET Passport) and then accept the Code of Conduct.

5. On the How Do I Find My Community? page, note the address at which your personal community is located and choose whether to have the wizard create a favorite for it.

NOTE   *Your personal community is located at www.msnusers.com/mywebdocuments. Your .NET Passport differentiates your personal community from other people's personal communities.*

6. On the Your Files Will Be Published to This Community page, change the folder for your image files and the folder for your non-image files, if necessary.

7. On the Completing the Add Network Place Wizard page, click the Finish button.

Manage Your Community

To manage your community, sign in as manager and use the Manager Tools links on the home page. These links take you to pages for actions such as the following:

-   Adding, managing, and deleting pages.

-   Inviting other people to join your community. If you chose not to list your community, sending invitations and generating good word of mouth will be your main tools for building the community.

-   Sending a message or an announcement to all the members of the community.

-   Sending a message to the managers of the community.

-   Editing your member profile (the information that other people can see about you).

- Changing your e-mail settings (for example, deciding to receive the digest rather than each message individually).

- Examining the member list, changing their roles (for example, making a member a manager or an assistant manager), and banning members who don't make the grade.

- Changing the community settings (for example, changing the community from Public to Public Restricted, or from Moderated to Unmoderated).

> **TIP** *To delete a community, use the Delete Community link on the Community Settings page (click the Community Settings link on the home page).*

Alternatives to MSN Communities

MSN communities aren't for everyone. If you want freedom of action, you may well prefer to use a regular Web site on which you can build the pages you need, rather than using a canned site like the communities do. Or, if you just want to store some files online, you might prefer to use an online drive rather than an MSN community. The following subsections discuss these possibilities.

Web Sites

Most ISPs offer their customers storage space for a Web site, together with some mechanism for posting pages on the site. Depending on the ISP's focus (consumer, small business, big business, and so on), the ISP may also provide tools for creating Web pages and Web sites. Such tools vary widely in their features, friendliness, and usefulness.

If you're still shopping for an ISP, add to the criteria discussed in the section "Choose an ISP" in Chapter 2 the amount of storage space you'll need for your Web site and the approximate amount of traffic it's likely to generate. Any ISP worth using will gladly sell you more storage space and a larger bandwidth allowance, but you'd do well to start off at roughly the right level of service to make sure your Web site is available when you expect it to be.

Online Drives

If you find MSN communities too restrictive for the amount of files you want to store online (or share with others by storing online), you may want to investigate online drives. Online drives are sites that (with varying degrees of sophistication and friendliness of interface) let you store files online so that you can retrieve them from anywhere you can access the Internet.

> **TIP** *Online drives are also great for keeping a backup of a relatively small amount of crucial files. But, because the security of any online drive is likely to be far less than that of your local computer, it's vital to encrypt the files you place there using strong encryption, in case anybody unauthorized is able to access them.*

While e-commerce was booming, there were more online drives offering free storage than you could shake a stick at: 10MB here, 50MB there, even a massive 3GB on MyPlay (yes, you read that correctly—three marketing gigabytes, 2.86 real gigabytes—but with some tortuous legal restrictions on them). But with the dotcom crunch, most of the free storage has fallen by the wayside, and legal challenges to the multitude of illegal files stored on other online drives has driven the companies to mutate the services they offer toward a more copyright-friendly model.

But there are still a variety of online drives left, such as these:

- **Yahoo! Briefcase (briefcase.yahoo.com)**   Offers 30MB of space for free and an extra 50MB for $29.95 per year.

- **FreeDrive (www.freedrive.com)**   Currently offers 65MB of space for $4.95 per month, or 150MB of space for $9.95 per month. (FreeDrive's eponymous free offering has fallen by the wayside, but, at this writing, the site still bills itself as a "free Internet hard drive." Go figure.)

- **Xdrive (www.xdrive.com)**   Currently offers 75MB of space for $4.95 per month. You can purchase further blocks of space (in sizes of 75, 150, 500, or 1,000MB) as you need them. Xdrive is integrated with the Web Publishing Wizard, making it easy to publish your files to Xdrive.

- **My Docs Online (www.mydocsonline.com)**   Offers 50MB of space for $9.95 per quarter, 100MB for $14.95 per quarter, 200MB for $21.95 per quarter, 300MB for $29.95 per quarter, and 1GB for $109.95 per quarter.

- **IBackup (www.ibackup.com)**   Offers plans ranging from 50MB (for $30 per year) and 100MB (for $54 per year) up to 100GB ($8,640 per year). You're probably not going to go for the ton o' gigs, but IBackup has one nice feature worth mentioning: you can drop files into your IBackup account by e-mailing them to your user account at IBackup.

- **FloppyCenter (www.floppycenter.com)**   Offers 100MB for $4.99 per month.

Access Online Sites

XP provides four main tools for accessing online sites to upload and download information: network places, the Web Publishing Wizard, Internet Explorer, and the command-line FTP client. The following subsections discuss these three tools in turn.

If none of these tools is to your liking, you may want to get a graphical FTP client such as CuteFTP (www.cuteftp.com or www.globalscape.com) or WS_FTP (www.ipswitch.com). Both of these offer strong features and an evaluation version that lets you find out how you like them before breaking out the plastic to buy them.

Use Network Places to Access Online Sites

Network places provide perhaps the easiest way of accessing online sites:

- To add a network place, run the Add Network Place Wizard from a My Network Places window, as described earlier in the chapter.

- To open a network place, double-click the appropriate entry in a My Network window. You can then copy files to or from the network place as you would for local folders.

Use the Web Publishing Wizard to Publish Files or Folders to the Web

For copying files and folders to an MSN community or an online storage location run by a provider affiliated with Microsoft (such as Xdrive), you can use the Web Publishing Wizard. To do so, open an Explorer window to the appropriate folder, select the file or folder you want to publish, and then click the Publish This File to the Web link or the Publish This Folder to the Web link. The Web Publishing Wizard walks you through the process of choosing the files you want to publish, adjusting the sizes of pictures (to fit in a 640×480 window, an 800×600 window, or a 1024×768 window), if necessary, and then copying the files.

Access FTP Sites with Internet Explorer

Internet Explorer provides basic but unexciting features for accessing FTP sites. In the Address bar or the Open dialog box, enter the address of the FTP site together with your username and your password in this format:

```
ftp://username[:password]@ftpservername/url
```

Obviously, you substitute your username for *username*, your password for *password*, the name of the FTP server for *ftpservername*, and the URL for *url*. Your password is optional: if you don't enter it at this point, the FTP site prompts you for it with the Login As dialog box. Not entering the password is better for security, especially if you create an Internet Explorer favorite for the FTP site. (Otherwise, your password is saved in the favorite, enabling you to access the FTP site with minimal effort.)

Use XP's Command-Line FTP Client

Given that most file-transfer operations over the Internet use FTP, it'll come as no surprise that XP has an FTP client built into it that provides the underpinnings for features such as Network Places. This FTP client is command-line only, so it's not the prettiest thing in the Western Hemisphere. But, if you don't like doing things through XP's GUI and you don't want to use a third-party graphical FTP client, XP's FTP client may appeal to you. (If it doesn't, stop reading right here.)

To run the FTP client, enter **ftp** in the Run dialog box (Start | Run) and click the OK button. XP opens a command-prompt window and starts the FTP client.

These are the commands that the FTP client supports:

Command	Meaning
!	Run the command on the local computer.
?	Displays a list of the commands the FTP client supports. Same as **help**.
append	Appends the specified local file to the specified file on the remote computer.

Command	Meaning
ascii	Sets the file transfer type back to ASCII, for downloading a plain-text file. Because ASCII is the default, you shouldn't need to use this command until you've issued the **binary** command.
bell	Toggles the setting for a bell to ring after the client completes a file transfer command. The bell is off by default to help keep the peace, but you may find it useful, especially when downloading large files.
binary	Sets the file transfer type to binary. Issue this command before transferring any binary files, such as programs, pictures, or audio.
bye	Closes the FTP session with the remote computer and exits the FTP client. Same as **quit**.
cd	Changes the current directory on the remote computer. (Use **lcd** to change the directory on the local computer.)
close	Closes the FTP session with the remote computer (but doesn't exit the FTP client).
debug	Toggles the debugging setting. Debugging is off by default.
delete	Deletes the specified file on the remote computer.
dir	Displays a list of the files and subdirectories in the specified remote directory.
disconnect	Disconnects your computer from the remote computer.
get	Copies a file from the remote computer to the local computer. Same as **recv**.
glob	Toggles the setting for *globbing*, the use of wildcard characters (such as *) in filenames or paths. Globbing is on by default, but you may need to turn it off occasionally if you find yourself getting globs you don't want.
hash	Toggles the setting for the printing of hash marks (#) during file transfer. By default, hash mark printing is off; but if you turn it on, the FTP client displays a hash mark for each 2,048-byte block of data transferred. Hash mark printing can be useful for giving a visual representation of a transfer's progress.
help	Displays a list of the commands the FTP client supports. Same as the **?** command.
lcd	Changes the directory on the local computer (as opposed to on the remote computer).
literal	Sends a RAW command to the remote FTP server. This command is most commonly used to enable passive-mode transfers, such as you might need when accessing an FTP site via a NAT or a company firewall. Same as **quote**.
ls	Displays a list of the files and subdirectories in the specified remote directory. Similar to **dir** but displays abbreviated information.
mdelete	Deletes the specified multiple files on the remote computer. Useful with wildcards.
mdir	Displays a list of the files and subdirectories in the specified remote directory or directories. You can use wildcards with **mdir** to list the contents of multiple directories meeting the criteria you specify.
mget	Copies multiple files from the remote computer to the local computer.
mkdir	Creates a directory on the remote computer.

Command	Meaning
mls	Displays a list of the files and subdirectories in the specified remote directory or directories. As with **mdir**, you can use wildcards with **mls** to list the contents of multiple directories meeting the criteria you specify. This command displays more abbreviated information than **mdir**.
mput	Copies the specified multiple files from the local computer to the remote computer.
open	Opens a connection to the specified FTP server.
prompt	Toggles prompting on and off. Prompting is on by default, but you may want to turn it off when using **mget** and **mput** so that the FTP client starts the next operation in the series without waiting and prompting you.
put	Copies the specified file from the local computer to the remote computer. Same as **send**.
pwd	Prints the working directory (the current directory) on the remote FTP server.
quit	Closes the FTP session with the remote computer and exits the FTP client. Same as **bye**.
quote	Sends a RAW command to the remote FTP server. This command is most commonly used to enable passive-mode transfers, such as you might need when accessing an FTP site via a NAT or a company firewall. Same as **literal**.
recv	Copies a file from the remote computer to the local computer. Same as **get**.
remotehelp	Displays help available on the remote FTP server.
rename	Renames the specified remote file.
rmdir	Deletes the specified remote directory.
send	Copies the specified file from the local computer to the remote computer. Same as **put**.
status	Displays the status of your FTP connections and toggle settings.
trace	Toggles packet tracing on and off. Tracing is off by default. When on, tracing displays the route of each packet when you run a command.
type	Displays or sets the file transfer type (ASCII or binary).
user	Specifies the user to the remote FTP server.
verbose	Toggles verbose output on and off. Verbose output is on by default and displays the key command responses.

TIP *You can abbreviate most of the FTP commands down to enough letters to distinguish them from any other command. For example, you can use o for open because no other command starts with o, bi or bin for binary, and del for delete.*

Summary

This chapter has discussed how to build your own online communities so that you can share information with people and have them share information with you. The chapter has concentrated on MSN communities because they're the online communities that XP makes easy to create and administer; but it has also discussed other online storage options, such as online drives, and different methods of accessing them.

This is the last chapter in the book, but in a page or two you'll find a glossary of the interesting terms included in the book.

Glossary

I n most cases, where a term has an acronym or abbreviation, I've defined the term and referred to the term from the acronym or abbreviation. But where the acronym or abbreviation is more widely used than the term itself, I've put the definition with the acronym or abbreviation and referred to that entry from the term itself. For example, almost everyone uses the abbreviation "TCP/IP" rather than "Transmission Control Protocol/Internet Protocol," so I've put the definition with the abbreviation.

> NOTE
>
> *Words shown in **boldface** are terms that appear in the Glossary.*

access token A means of establishing identity or authorization to access a place or a system. Access tokens can be physical or virtual—anything from a physical key to a digital certificate.

ADSL The abbreviation for **Asymmetric DSL**.

Asymmetric DSL A form of **DSL** that delivers faster downstream speeds than upstream speeds.

Bambleweeny 57 Sub-Meson Brain The mythical computer in *The Hitch Hiker's Guide to the Galaxy* used to power Infinite Improbability Drive.

basic rate interface The standard consumer version of **ISDN**: two 64 Kbps bearer (B) channels and one 16 Kbps data (D) channel. Abbreviated to *BRI*.

biometrics The use of measurements of parts of the body (such as fingerprints, handprints, retinal scans, DNA, and photographs), or their movements (such as signatures) to establish or verify identity.

BRI The abbreviation for **basic rate interface**.

brute-force attack A cryptographic attack that attempts to guess a cryptographic key by trying all possible keys until finding the one that succeeds.

CA The abbreviation for **certification authority**.

callto A network protocol for placing an **H.323** call.

CDSL abbreviation for **Consumer DSL**.

certification authority A body that issues **digital certificates**. Also called *certificate authority*. The abbreviation for either term is *CA*.

CIF See **Common Interchange Format**.

click-stream The data you generate while browsing the Web.

Common Interchange Format A video format with a resolution of 352×288 pixels. The acronym is *CIF*.

Consumer DSL A splitterless version of **DSL** designed for fast and easy implementation in consumer premises. Abbreviated to *CDSL*.

cookie   A text file written by a Web browser to the user's hard drive in which an Internet server can store information about the user for customization or tracking. *Session cookies* are deleted at the end of a browsing session, whereas *permanent cookies* remain on the user's drive unless deleted manually.

copyleft   A rights structure that allows people to freely copy or modify a work, provided they meet various conditions for doing so—for example, making their modifications freely available to other people.

copyright   A form of legal protection to the creators of original works, such as music, painting, sculpture, and so on.

cracker   A malicious **hacker**.

dial-return satellite service   Satellite service in which the satellite handles downstream data only, and you use your phone line for upstream data. Better described as *one-way satellite service*.

digital certificate   A collection of identity information that's encrypted and signed with the digital signature of the **certification authority** that issued it. Digital certificates are used for purposes such as adding a digital signature to e-mail messages, making sure messages haven't been tampered with, and encrypting messages and attachments so that only the specified recipient can read them.

digital ID   Another term for **digital certificate**. In particular, Microsoft programs such as Address Book and Outlook Express use *digital ID* instead of *digital certificate*.

digital subscriber line   Abbreviated to *DSL*. A digital phone line that's faster than **ISDN**.

digital subscriber line access multiplexer   A telephony device used to connect the central-office end of the **DSL** to the telco's equipment. The acronym is *DSLAM*.

DSL   The abbreviation for **digital subscriber line**.

DSL Lite   A form of **digital subscriber line** that's implemented without a splitter device. Also known as *G.Lite*, *Universal ADSL*, and *Splitterless DSL*.

DSLAM   The acronym for **digital subscriber line access multiplexer**.

dual-line modem   A modem that can handle two phone lines. Also called a *shotgun modem*.

dynamic IP address   An **IP address** that's allocated from a pool of addresses when you connect to the server. Contrast **static IP address**.

ECHELON   The code name for an automated global interception and relay system run by the NSA, the U.K.'s General Communications Headquarters (GCHQ), Canada's Canadian Security Intelligence Service (CSIS), Australia's Defence Signals Directorate (DSD), and New Zealand's Government Communications Security Bureau (GCSB).

entropy   In encryption, a measure of how "uncertain" something is. A password or pass-phrase with high entropy is much harder to crack than one with low entropy.

Extensible Markup Language   A markup language that can be used for page layout (like HTML) and also for describing the structural elements of a document, thus enabling the transfer of structured information from one application to another. The abbreviation is *XML*. XML is extensible in that you can create new markup elements, rules, and markup languages for different types of content.

fair access policy   A part of a service provider's agreement that allows the provider to restrict your bandwidth to prevent you from hogging the service. The abbreviation or acronym is *FAP*.

FAP   The abbreviation or acronym for **fair access policy**.

firewall   A hardware device or software program for protecting a computer or a network. A firewall examines all incoming **TCP/IP** packets (and, in some cases, outgoing traffic) and allows to pass only those packets that either match predefined rules or that are replies to outgoing packets. A firewall can be **stateful** or **stateless**.

General Protection Fault   One of the various Microsoft terms for a serious computer error. A General Protection Fault (the abbreviation is *GPF*) occurs when one Windows 9*x* program accesses memory assigned to another program, thus corrupting the data in those memory registers. Windows NT, 2000, and XP protect memory against such incursions.

GPF   The abbreviation for **General Protection Fault**.

H.323   An Internet telephony protocol used by **NetMeeting** and **Phone Dialer** (among many other programs).

hacker   An expert and enthusiast who delights in pushing software or hardware to (or beyond) its design limits. *Hacking* is used for both well-intentioned and ill-intentioned manipulation of the software or hardware, and to cover both legal and illegal actions. For clarity, a hacker is sometimes described as a *white-hat hacker* (good) or a *black-hat hacker* (bad). The term *cracker* is also used for a malicious hacker.

Hotmail   Microsoft's Web-based e-mail service, which offers both free accounts and paid accounts.

HTTP   The abbreviation for **Hypertext Transport Protocol**.

HyperTerminal   A basic telephony program included with XP and other recent versions of Windows.

Hypertext Transport Protocol   The protocol on which much of the Web is based. Also used in Microsoft's .NET initiative. The abbreviation is *HTTP*.

ICF   The abbreviation for **Internet Connection Firewall**.

ICS   The abbreviation for **Internet Connection Sharing**.

ICS client   A computer that connects to the Internet via **Internet Connection Sharing** running on an **ICS host**.

ICS host   The computer that runs the **Internet Connection Sharing** service and provides Internet connectivity to the **ICS clients**.

ILS   The abbreviation for **Internet Locator Server**.

IMAP   The acronym for **Internet Mail Access Protocol**.

Integrated Services Digital Network   A digital telephone line that offers moderate data rates but greater distance from the telco's central office than **DSL**. The abbreviation is *ISDN*. The usual home or SOHO ISDN offering is **basic rate interface** (BRI), which uses two 64-Kbps bearer (B) channels for data transfer and one 16-Kbps data (D) channel for signaling.

Internet Connection Firewall   A software **firewall** built into XP. The abbreviation is *ICF*.

Internet Connection Sharing   A feature built into XP (and several earlier versions of Windows) for sharing an Internet connection with clients on a small network. The abbreviation is *ICS*. ICS combines a Domain Name System (DNS) proxy or DNS forwarder and a Dynamic Host Configuration Protocol (DHCP) allocator (a simplified DHCP server) with **Network Address Translation** (NAT). ICS is integrated with **Internet Connection Firewall**.

Internet Locator Server   A server on a server network that Microsoft used to run for conferencing and communications programs such as **NetMeeting** and **Phone Dialer**. The abbreviation is *ILS*. Microsoft has dismantled the ILS network and transformed it into Microsoft Internet Directory, which is designed for use with **Windows Messenger**.

Internet Mail Access Protocol   A protocol for Internet e-mail that lets you store copies of your messages on the mail server and manipulate them there.

Internet service provider   A company that provides Internet connectivity to consumers or businesses. The abbreviation is *ISP*.

IP address   An Internet Protocol address.

ISDN   The abbreviation for **Integrated Services Digital Network**.

ISP   The abbreviation for **Internet service provider**.

key pair   The **public key** and **private key** used in **public key cryptography**.

Liberty Alliance   A project backed by Sun Microsystems for creating a digital identity. The Web site is at http://www.projectliberty.org.

Messenger   See **Windows Messenger**.

MSN   The abbreviation for *Microsoft Network*, Microsoft's online service.

MSN Messenger   See **Windows Messenger**.

NAT   The acronym for **Network Address Translation**.

.NET   Microsoft's platform for delivering **XML** services over the Internet. Pronounced "dot-net."

.NET clients   The devices that can access **.NET services** across the Web—for example, handheld devices or PCs that support XML.

.NET experiences   The user end of Microsoft's .NET initiative, such as **.NET Passport** and MSN.

.NET Passport   A form of digital identity tied to an e-mail address. .NET Passport is an essential component of Microsoft's **.NET** strategy and for most users forms the entry point to **.NET services**.

.NET servers   Server software used to create the infrastructure for deploying, managing, and using **XML** Web services: Windows 2000 Server, Windows .NET Server, Exchange Server, SQL Server, and other Microsoft servers.

.NET services   The building blocks of functionality for creating **.NET** programs.

.NET tools   Tools for building, deploying, and running **XML** Web services.

NetMeeting   A conferencing and collaboration program included with most 32-bit desktop versions of Windows, including XP.

Network Address Translation   Converting internal **IP addresses** to external IP addresses so that computers on an internal network (for example, a home or office network) can access an external network (for example, the Internet).

one-way satellite service   A term describing satellite service in which the satellite handles downstream data only, and you use your phone line for upstream data. Also known as *dial-return satellite service*.

online drive   An Internet site on which consumers or businesses can store files for backup or for universal availability. Also called (more accurately) *online storage* or an *online storage locker*.

Passport Express Purchase   A **.NET** feature for online merchants that allows users with a **Passport Wallet** to transfer payment information easily and quickly to the merchant.

Passport Wallet   An add-on feature to **.NET Passport** that lets you store payment information (such as your credit card details and your billing address) online so that you can easily share it with **Passport Express Purchase**–enabled Web sites for monetary transactions. Unlike the basic .NET Passport, Passport Wallet requires proof of identity, such as a valid credit card.

permanent cookie   A **cookie** that remains permanently on the user's computer. Compare **session cookie**.

Phone Dialer   A basic telephony program included with most 32-bit desktop versions of Windows.

phreak   To manipulate the telephone system illegally.

PKI   The abbreviation for **public key infrastructure**.

place-shifting   Recording a (usually, copyrighted) work to a different format or medium so that you can listen to, watch, or otherwise experience it in a different place than with its current medium. For example, making MP3 files from a CD so that you can listen to them somewhere you don't have a CD player. Compare **time-shifting**.

plain old telephone service   Analog telephone service over copper wires. The jocular (but widely used in all seriousness) acronym is *POTS*.

point of presence   An access point to a network—for example, a dial-up number for connecting to an **Internet service provider**.

POP   The acronym for **point of presence** and for **Post Office Protocol**.

Post Office Protocol   A protocol for handling e-mail messages. Abbreviated to *POP* or *POP3*.

POTS   The acronym for **plain old telephone service**.

PRI   The abbreviation for **Primary Rate Interface**.

Primary Rate Interface   A form of **ISDN** targeted at businesses. The abbreviation is *PRI*. In the U.S.A. and Canada, PRI uses twenty-three 64 Kbps bearer (B) channels and one 16 Kbps data (D) channel, delivering 1.536 Mbps. In Europe, PRI uses thirty 64 Kbps bearer channels and one 16 Kbps data channel, delivering 1.920 Mbps

private key   The key in a **key pair** for **public key cryptography** that you keep to yourself. You use your private key to sign and/or encrypt outgoing documents and messages, and to decrypt incoming documents and messages that others have encrypted with your **public key**.

public domain   A legal area that contains all works that are not in **copyright** or that are not copyrightable.

public key   The key in a **key pair** for **public key cryptography** that you distribute freely to those who want to contact you or whom you want to contact. Other people use your public key to decrypt messages that you've signed with your **private key** and to encrypt messages that they're sending to you.

public key cryptography   Cryptography that uses a **key pair** (a **private key** and a **public key**) to secure and encrypt data.

public key infrastructure   An arrangement among **certification authorities** and other bodies for making **public keys** accessible to those that need them. The abbreviation is *PKI*.

QCIF   The abbreviation for **Quarter Common Interchange Format**.

Quarter Common Interchange Format   A video format with a resolution of 176×144 pixels. The abbreviation is *QCIF*.

RTP   The abbreviation for **Realtime Transport Protocol**.

sandbox   A logical area in which you (or a program, or the operating system) can safely execute unknown or suspect code without its being able to access protected parts of the operating system.

Secure Password Authentication   A protocol used to secure passwords being transmitted across a network. The abbreviation (or, for some, the acronym) is *SPA*.

session cookie   A temporary **cookie** that is deleted at the end of a user session. Compare **permanent cookie**.

shotgun modem   Another term for **dual-line modem**.

signature   A short file that's added automatically to the end of outgoing e-mail messages. Traditionally, a signature contains information about the sender, an aphorism or quote, or both.

Simple Object Access Protocol   One of the protocols used by Microsoft's **.NET** initiative. The acronym is *SOAP*.

SOAP   The acronym for **Simple Object Access Protocol**.

social engineering   The practice of obtaining passwords or other confidential information by asking users for it while pretending to be someone authorized to ask—for example, impersonating a systems administrator and asking a user for their password in order to update their account.

SPA   The abbreviation (or, some would have it, acronym) for **Secure Password Authentication**.

spam   Unsolicited e-mail messages. Some people draw a distinction between *unsolicited commercial e-mail* (from a company that they've dealt with—or a company affiliated with one they've dealt with) and wholly unredeemable messages (mail-order Filipinas, Viagra, pyramid and multi-level marketing schemes, spamming software, and so on), but most people use the term more loosely to refer to all junk-mail messages.

splitter   A device used to logically divide a **digital subscriber line** into data and voice segments.

SQCIF   The abbreviation for **Sub-Quarter Common Interchange Format**.

stateful   (Of a **firewall** or protocol) Retaining a memory of connections that have passed through it. A stateful firewall stores the details of connections in dynamic connection tables and uses them to decide which incoming packets should be allowed and which should be blocked. Contrast **stateless**.

stateless   (Of a **firewall** or protocol) Retaining no memory of the connections that have taken place, and so treating each connection through it as a new connection. Contrast **stateful**.

static IP address   An **IP address** that remains the same from one connection to another. Most **ISDN**, **DSL**, and cable connections use static IP addresses, whereas dial-up modem connections almost always use a **dynamic IP address**.

Sub-Quarter Common Interchange Format   A video format with a resolution of 128×96 pixels. Abbreviated to *SQCIF*.

T.120   A group of communications protocols and applications protocols for real-time communications. Used by **NetMeeting**, among other programs.

TA   The abbreviation for **terminal adapter**.

TCP   The abbreviation for Transmission Control Protocol, one of the protocols in the **TCP/IP** protocol suite. TCP is a **stateful** protocol.

TCP/IP   The abbreviation for **Transmission Control Protocol/Internet Protocol**, the suite of network protocols on which most of the Internet runs. Because the full term is such a mouthful, most people use the abbreviation instead most of the time.

terminal adapter   A digital device used to connect an **ISDN** line to a computer. Abbreviated to *TA*.

time-shifting Recording a (usually copyrighted) work that's being published via broadcasting so that you can listen to, watch, or otherwise experience it at a later time. For example, using a TiVo or a VCR to record a TV show so that you can watch it later. Compare **place-shifting**.

traffic analysis Studying communication patterns. Used for analyzing encrypted data with the aim of working out its contents.

Transmission Control Protocol/Internet Protocol See **TCP/IP**.

UDDI The abbreviation for **Universal Description, Discovery, and Integration**.

UDP The abbreviation for User Datagram Protocol, one of the protocols in the **TCP/IP** protocol suite. UDP is a **stateless** protocol.

ULS See **User Locator Server**.

Universal Description, Discovery, and Integration One of the protocols used by Microsoft's **.NET** initiative. The abbreviation is *UDDI*.

Universal Plug and Play An architecture that lets devices advertise their services on a network to other networked devices and to control points via the Simple Service Discovery Protocol (SSDP). The abbreviation is *UPnP*.

UPnP The abbreviation for **Universal Plug and Play**.

User Locator Server A server used by early versions of **NetMeeting** to maintain lists of users and connect to them. Now obsolete. The abbreviation is *ULS*. See also **Internet Locator Server**.

V.90 A communications standard for modems that provides 56 Kbps downstream (limited by the FCC to 53.3 Kbps) and 33.6 Kbps upstream.

V.92 A communications standard for modems that offers features including Quick Connect and Modem-on-Hold, together with V.44 data compression. V.92 modems can manage upstream speeds of up to 48 Kbps, compared to **V.90**'s 33.6 Kbps upstream.

virtual private network A secure private network connection established over an insecure public network, such as the Internet. The abbreviation is *VPN*.

VPN The abbreviation for **virtual private network**.

Windows Messenger Microsoft's messaging client for XP. Earlier versions were called *MSN Messenger*. Usually referred to as *Messenger*.

XML The abbreviation for **Extensible Markup Language**.

Index

A

Accel Permedia II video adapters, 297
access tokens, 57, 59, 312
access tokens, digital. *See* digital certificates
Acoustic Echo Cancellation (AEC) updates, 232-233
Add a Contact Wizard, Messenger, 190-192
Add Alternate Phone Numbers dialog box, 26-27
Add Network Place Wizard, 7, 305, 307-308
Add Someone to This Conversation dialog box, Messenger, 194-195
Address Book, Outlook Express
    adding correspondents, 129
    creating new messages, 149
    digital IDs in, 84, 136
ADSL (Asymmetric DSL), 15, 312
Advanced Calling dialog box, NetMeeting, 214
Advanced Security Settings dialog box, 30
Advanced Settings dialog box
    ICF security logging, 45-46
    ICMP requests, 44
    incoming services via ICS, 42-44
    modem options, 23
    opening ports manually on ICF, 46-47
    Outlook Express, 133-134, 136
AEC (Acoustic Echo Cancellation) updates, 232-233
alerts, 109-111
    Hotmail, 112

Messenger options, 183, 185, 191-192, 194
.NET, 71, 73-74
Allow List list box, Messenger, 184-185
Alternate Phone Numbers dialog box, 26-27
anonymity. *See* privacy/anonymity
Anonymizer.com, 69
Apply Rules Now dialog box, Outlook Express, 167
Asymmetric DSL (ADSL), 15, 312
attachments, Outlook Express, 133, 157
Audio and Video Tuning Wizard, 228-229, 235
Audio Tuning Wizard, NetMeeting, 199-200
authentication
    digital certificates and, 84
    establishing identity and, 56-58, 58-60
    NetMeeting, 202-203, 210-211
Automatic Dialing and Hanging up dialog box, Internet connections, 34-35

B

B2B (business-to-business), 81
Bambleweeny 57 Sub-Meson Brain, 83, 312
bandwidth
    cable modems and, 17
    demand for, 11
    NetMeeting, conference calls, 242
    NetMeeting, configuring setting for, 202
    NetMeeting, increasing clients in call, 212
    optical-fiber connections and, 17

Base64 Encoded X.509 format, digital certificates, 97
basic rate interface (BRI), 12-13, 312
Bigfoot e-mail account, 174
biometrics, 56-59, 312
Block command, Messenger, 192
Block Sender link, Hotmail, 109
Blocked Senders list, Outlook Express, 168-169
blocks, ICF, 41-42
BRI (basic rate interface), 12-13, 312
browsing, privacy/anonymity and, 69
brute-force attacks, 312
business cards, Outlook Express, 127-128, 154

C

C2C (consumer-to-consumer), 81
CA (certification authority), 84, 312
cable modems
        adding router, 24
        overview of, 16-17
        troubleshooting, 47, 49
callto, defined, 312
CCTV (closed-circuit television) systems, 67-68
CDs, copyrights, 255-256, 257-258
CDSL (Consumer DSL), 15, 312
Certificate Export Wizard, 96-97
Certificate Import Wizard, 89-91
Certificates dialog box
        editing, 95
        exporting, 96-98
        installing, 89
        removing, 94
        scrutinizing, 91-93
certification authority (CA), 84, 312
Change My Message Font dialog box, 180-181
Chat window, NetMeeting, 217-219
chats. See Messenger; NetMeeting
CIF (Common Interchange Format), 312
click-stream, 64, 312

closed-circuit television (CCTV) systems, 67-68
Code of Conduct, MSN community, 304
color, sharing programs in, 291-292, 296
command line
        starting NetMeeting from, 200
        using FTP client, 308-309
Common Interchange Format (CIF), 312
communities. See online communities
compression, file transfers, 259-260, 264-265
conference calls. See Messenger, conference calls; NetMeeting, conference calls; Phone Dialer
connections, backup, 19
connections, Internet. See Internet connections
connections, Messenger, 193-195
connections, NetMeeting. See NetMeeting
Consumer DSL (CDSL), 15, 312
consumer-to-consumer (C2C), 81
contact lists, Messenger, 184-185, 190-192
cookies
        defined, 313
        .NET Passport security, 79
        permanent, 316
        session, 317
copyleft, defined, 313
copyright, 254-259
        defined, 313
        overview of, 255-256
        penalties for violations of, 259
        quiz, 254-255
        what you can legally do, 256-259
crackers, defined, 313
Create SpeedDial dialog box, NetMeeting, 209
credit card security, 78, 79
cryptographic keys, 134
CUCORE program, 245

D

Deleted Items folder, Outlook Express, 138
DER Encoded Binary X.509 format, 97-98
DES Deep Crack, 135

desktop/program sharing, 290-297
    allowing control, 292-293
    overview, 290-291
    troubleshooting, 293-297
    in true color, 291-292
DHCP (Dynamic Host Configuration
    Protocol), 37
Dial dialog box, Phone Dialer calls, 249-250
dial-return satellite service, 313
dial-up connections
    configuring, 27-29
    creating, 25
    ISPs, 18
    Outlook Express, 137-138
    storage location of, 35
    troubleshooting, 47
    via POTS, 11-12
Diamond Viper display drivers, 297
digital certificates, 82-98. *See also* digital IDs,
    Outlook Express
    changing information on, 95
    creating new RSA Exchange Key, 87-88
    defined, 313
    exporting, 96-98
    getting, 84-87
    installing, 88-91
    NetMeeting, 202-204
    overview of, 82-84
    removing, 93-94
    scrutinizing, 91-93
    security of, 59-60
digital identity
    establishing online, 58-60
    identity in physical world, 56-58
digital IDs, Outlook Express
    choosing for e-mail account, 144
    defined, 313
    getting, 84
    overview of, 136
digital signatures
    applying or removing, 152
    overview of, 133
    specifying digital ID for, 144

digital subscriber line. *See* DSL (digital
    subscriber line)
digital subscriber line access multiplexer
    (DSLAM), 313
Directory dialog box, NetMeeting, 214
directory information, NetMeeting, 201-202
directory server, NetMeeting errors, 213-214
display names, Messenger
    adding contacts, 189-191
    changing, 179-180
    troubleshooting, 187-188
document transfer. *See* file sharing
DoubleClick, Inc., 64
Driver's Privacy Protection Act, 63
DSL (digital subscriber line)
    adding router, 24
    defined, 313
    overview of, 15-16
    splitters, 318
    troubleshooting, 47
DSL Lite, 15, 313
DSLAM (digital subscriber line access
    multiplexer), 313
dual-line, defined, 313
DVDs, copyright law, 255-256, 257
Dynamic Host Configuration Protocol
    (DHCP), 37
dynamic IP address, 313
dynamic link calls, NetMeeting, 220
dynamic port mapping, ICF, 53

E

e-mail
    Blocked Senders lists, 168-169
    body text, entering, 151-152
    business cards, adding, 154
    digital signatures, 152
    encryption, 152-154, 158-159
    ISP selection, 18-19
    local file clean up, 169-171
    privacy issues, 67-69
    Read Receipts, granting, 157-158

Read Receipts, requesting, 154
replies, creating, 150-151
satellite connections and, 15
spam protection, 159-161
subject, entering, 151
transferring files via, 267-268
working offline, 159
e-mail attachments
receiving, 157
sending, 152
e-mail mail rules
applying, 166-167
arranging, 166
creating, 161-165
modifying, 168
e-mail messages
addressing, 150
creating, 147-149
forwarding, 150
reading, 155-157
sending, 154-155
e-mail services. *See also* Hotmail;
    Outlook Express
Bigfoot, 174
HushMail, 172
MSN, 304
Netscape Mail, 173
Yahoo! Mail, 171
EAP (Extensible Authentication Protocol), 30
ECHELON, 66-67, 313
emoticons, Messenger
entering in messages, 195
showing or suppressing, 181
troubleshooting, 196
encryption
connection security and, 30
digital certificates and, 94
.NET Passport and, 80
public key cryptography and, 83
transferring files and, 260
Web-based services for e-mail, 69

encryption, NetMeeting
accepting calls, 210-211
certificates for, 202-203
hosting calls, 221
encryption, Outlook Express
adding e-mail accounts, 144
opening message, 158-159
options for, 133
overview of, 134-136
sending/receiving e-mail, 152-154
Enter Password dialog box, NetMeeting, 222
entropy, 135, 313
Europol (European Police Office), 66
Extensible Authentication Protocol (EAP), 30
Extensible Markup Language (XML),
    69-70, 314

F

fair use, 258
FAP (fair access policy), 14-15, 314
file sharing
compression and zip archives, 259-260
e-mail and, 267-268
HyperTerminal and, 268-271
legalities of, 254-259
monitoring and traffic analysis of, 260
online storage and, 267
secure, 69
troubleshooting ICF, 53
XP tools for, 261
file sharing, Messenger
configuring folder for, 183
overview of, 264-265
receiving files, 265
sending files, 265
troubleshooting, 266-267
file sharing, NetMeeting
GPF and, 296
before receiving files, 261
receiving files, 263-264

sending files, 262-263
troubleshooting, 264
file sharing, VPN
connecting via, 278
incoming connections, accepting, 272-277
incoming connections, creating, 277-278
overview of, 271-272
file transfer. *See* file sharing
File Transfer Protocol (FTP), 308-309
File Transfer window, NetMeeting
receiving files, 261, 263-264
sending files, 262-263
troubleshooting, 264
Files and Settings Transfer Wizard, 25
filters
Hotmail, applying to incoming mail, 109-112
Hotmail, Junk Mail Filter setting, 107-109
protecting POP3 mailbox from spam, 159-161
Find Someone dialog box, NetMeeting, 209, 210
fingerprints, 58
firewalls
defined, 314
overview of, 40
poking holes in, 42
troubleshooting Messenger, 188, 266
troubleshooting NetMeeting, 216
flags, in Outlook Express, 155
fonts
Messenger, 180-181
NetMeeting, 284-286
Outlook Express, 127
Found New Hardware Wizard, 19
frame rate, NetMeeting video, 243
FTP (File Transfer Protocol), 308-309

G

gateways/gatekeepers, NetMeeting, 202
General Protection Fault (GPF), 296, 314
government agencies, online monitoring by, 65-67
GPF (General Protection Fault), 296, 314

H

H.323, 314
hackers, 79, 314
Hailstorm, 71
hardware
Messenger conference calls and, 226-227
NetMeeting audio and, 242
NetMeeting video and, 245
program sharing and, 297
highlight pen, NetMeeting Whiteboard, 290
Hotmail, 102-117
accessing via Web, 106
defined, 5, 314
history of, 102-104
setting up account, 104-106
tasks performed with, 7
Hotmail, configuring, 106-117
accessing via Outlook Express, 117
alerts, 112
applying signatures, 113-114
expiring sessions, 116
filtering mail, 109-112
free newsletters/special offers, 107
getting POP mail, 112-113
Hotmail Member Directory, 107
junk mail, 107-109
Mail Display Settings, 114-116
Personal Profile/Password/Secret Question, 106
Sent Message Confirmation, 116
Hotmail Member Directory listing, 107

HTML (HyperText Markup Language),
  128-129
HTTP (Hypertext Transport Protocol),
  142-143, 314
HushMail, 69, 172
HyperTerminal
    defined, 314
    file transferring with, 268-271
    multilink modem setup, 33-34
    overview of, 6
HyperText Markup Language (HTML),
  128-129, 142-143, 314

I

ICF (Internet Connection Firewall), 39-47
    Advanced options for, 32
    allowing ICMP requests, 44-45
    blocks, 41-42
    configuring incoming services, 42-44
    defined, 315
    enabling, 41
    opening ports manually, 46-47
    overview of, 39-40
    poking holes in firewalls, 42
    security logging feature, 45-46
    troubleshooting in Messenger,
        188-189, 266
    turning on for Internet connection, 26
ICMP (Internet Control Message Protocol)
    requests, 44-45
icon display, NetMeeting, 202
ICS (Internet Connection Sharing)
    Advanced options for, 32
    alternatives to, 39
    configuring incoming services, 42-44
    connecting Messenger to Internet via, 186
    defined, 315
    ICF blocks and, 41-42
    ICS clients, 314
    ICS hosts, 314

NetMeeting and, 36
overview of, 36-39
satellite connections and, 15
troubleshooting program sharing,
    293-294
troubleshooting Whiteboard, 288-289
identity. *See* digital identity
ILS (Internet Locator Server), 215-216, 315
IMAP (Internet Mail Access Protocol)
    authentication with, 142-143
    changing mail server information,
        142-143
    choosing options, 146-147
    defined, 315
    removing deleted messages, 139
    specifying server port
        numbers/timeouts, 144-145
Incoming call dialog box, NetMeeting, 211
Incoming Connection VPN (PPTP), 277-278
Integrated Services Digital Network.
    See ISDN (Integrated Services
    Digital Network) connections
Internet communication tools, 1-8
    advantages of, 2-3
    Hotmail and Outlook Express, 5
    HyperTerminal, 6
    .NET Passport, 5
    NetMeeting, 4
    Phone Dialer, 6
    tasks and programs that perform
        them, 6-7
    Windows Messenger, 3-4
Internet Connection Firewall. *See* ICF
    (Internet Connection Firewall)
Internet Connection Wizard, 117-119
Internet connections
    choosing ISPs, 17-19
    making Outlook Express hang up, 138
    Messenger, preventing sign-in during,
        182-183
    troubleshooting, 47-49

Internet connections, configuring
    advanced options, 32
    automatic dialing/hanging up, 34-35
    dialing options, 27-29
    general options, 26-27
    multilink modem or ISDN, 33-34
    networking options, 31
    security options, 29-31
Internet connections, ICF and
    allowing ICMP requests, 44-45
    blocks, 41-42
    enabling, 41
    incoming services, 42-44
    opening ports manually, 46-47
    overview of, 39-40
    poking holes in firewall, 42
    security logging feature, 45-46
    troubleshooting, 52-53
Internet connections, ICS and
    connection sharing, 36-39
    troubleshooting, 49-52
Internet connections, setting up
    adding cable or DSL router, 24
    adding modem, 19-23
    adding terminal adapter, 24
    connecting communications device, 19
    creating, 24-26
Internet connections, types
    cable modem, 16-17
    dial-up via POTS, 11-12
    DSL, 15-16
    ISDN, 12-13
    optical-fiber, 17
    overview of, 10-11
    satellite, 14-15
    wireless, 13-14
Internet Control Message Protocol (ICMP)
    requests, 44-45
Internet Explorer
    accessing FTP sites with, 308
    connecting to NetMeeting from
        Web page and, 217

    digital certificates in, 84
    formats for exporting digital certificates,
        96-97
    installing digital certificates and, 88-91
    program sharing in NetMeeting and,
        295-296
Internet Locator Server (ILS)
    defined, 315
    troubleshooting NetMeeting, 215-216
Internet Options dialog box, digital
    certificates, 88-89
Internet service providers. *See* ISPs
    (Internet service providers)
IP addresses
    NetMeeting and, 208, 210
    sharing files via VPN, 271-272
    static, 318
    troubleshooting, 214
ipconfig command, troubleshooting, 49, 50-52
ISDN (Integrated Services Digital Network)
    connections
        choosing ISPs for, 18
        defined, 315
        overview of, 12-13
        setting up multilink, 34
        troubleshooting, 47
ISPs (Internet service providers)
    building pages on Web sites, 306
    choosing, 17-19
    finding, 10
    Internet connections and, 24-26
    multiple phone numbers and, 26-27
    satellite connections and, 14
    security and, 29-30
    troubleshooting Internet connections
        and, 48
    troubleshooting Remote Desktop
        Sharing and, 297-298
    using ICS and, 37
    V.92 modem support of, 12

J

junk mail, 107-109, 164-165

K

key pair, defined, 315

L

laws, copyright, 254-259
Liberty Alliance project, Sun Microsystems, 60, 315
Linux boxes, 52
Local File Clean Up dialog box, Outlook Express, 169-171
Location Information dialog box, Internet connection, 20
locks, Whiteboard, 287-288
logging, ICF security, 45-46

M

Macintosh computers, ICS and, 52
Magic Carpet, AOL Time Warner, 60
Mail Display Settings, Hotmail, 114-116
mail rules, Outlook Express, 159-168
    applying, 166-167
    arranging into order, 166
    deriving new rule from existing rule, 168
    examples, creating, 161-165
    modifying, 168
    protecting POP3 mailbox from spam, 159-161
mail servers, Outlook Express, 142-143
Meeting Properties dialog box, NetMeeting, 221, 223
membership policy, MSN community, 303-304
message header display, Hotmail, 114
Message Rules dialog box, Outlook Express, 166
message store location, Outlook Express, 140

Messenger, 176-197. *See also* desktop/program sharing; Whiteboard
    changing status, 196
    comparing NetMeeting with, 176
    connecting with, 193-195
    contract groups, 196
    defined, 319
    ending sessions, 195
    entering emoticons, 195
    how it works, 177
    inviting contact to NetMeeting, 210
    .NET Passport and, 81-82
    overview of, 2-3
    preventing Outlook from signing you into, 119-120
    privacy implications of, 178-179
    tasks performed with, 6-7
    transferring files with, 264-267
    troubleshooting, 187-188, 196-197
Messenger, conference calls, 226-235
    Audio and Video Tuning Wizard, 228-229
    hardware, 226-227
    NetMeeting and, 226
    PC-to-phone calls, 233-235
    troubleshooting, 232
    voice and video conversations, 230-232
    voice only conversations, 229-230
Messenger, configuring, 179-192
    alerts, 183-184
    choosing "Away" intervals, 183
    connecting via proxy servers, 186-187
    contact lists, 184-185, 189-192
    display in Windows, 187
    display name, 179-180
    emoticon display, 181
    font and font size, 180-181
    My Allow/My Block Lists, 184-185
    .NET Passport, 185-186
    preventing automatic Internet sign-in, 182-183
    preventing automatic operation of, 182

publishing phone numbers, 180
tab display, 186
transferred file folders, 183
troubleshooting, 187-188
Messenger Service
configuring Messenger with, 179
overview of, 177
privacy implications of, 178
microphones
Audio and Video Tuning Wizard and, 228-229
Messenger, 226, 232, 240
NetMeeting, 199-200, 204-206
Microsoft .NET Passport. *See* .NET Passport
Microsoft Network (MSN), 302-306, 315
Microsoft Proxy Server, 244-245
Microsoft Windows. *See* Windows
mIRC, 36-37
Modem-on-Hold feature, V.92 modems, 11
Modem Troubleshooter, 47
modems. *See also* cable modems;
multilink modems
adding for Internet connection, 19-23
dial-up connection via POTS and, 11-12
troubleshooting dial-up connections, 47
Moore's Law, 11
MP3 files, compressing, 260
MSN (Microsoft Network), 302-306, 315
multilink modems
dial-up connection via POTS and, 12
Internet connections and, 33-34
ISPs and, 19
My Block List list box, Messenger, 184-185

N

NAT (Network Address Translation)
defined, 316
hardware solution, 39
ICS using, 37-38
troubleshooting Messenger file transfers, 267
troubleshooting Whiteboard, 289

.NET, 69-75
advantages of, 70-72
detriments of, 73-74
overview of, 69-70
protecting yourself from, 74-75
.NET alerts, 71, 73-74
.NET clients, 315
.NET documents, 71-72
.NET experiences, 70, 315
.NET Messenger Service, 226
.NET My Services, 71, 72, 73-74
.NET Passport, 75-82
appeal of, 71-72
defined, 316
detriments of, 73-74
editing profile, 77
getting and adding to XP, 75-76
Messenger configuration and, 179, 185-186
overview of, 5
Passport Wallet and, 77-81
privacy implications of, 178
protecting yourself from, 74
what happens when using, 81-82
.NET servers, 70, 316
.NET services, 70, 316
.NET tools, 70, 316
NetMeeting, 207-223
accepting call, 210-211
adding person to calls, 211-212
chats and, 217-220
comparing Messenger with, 3, 74-75, 176
connecting from Web page, 216-217
defined, 316
hanging up call, 213
hosting meetings, 220-223
ICS and, 36
increasing clients in call, 212
increasing number of clients in call, 212
inviting contacts to join sessions, 209-210
overview of, 4
placing call, 208
Remote Desktop Sharing, 297-299

removing evidence of calls, 208
removing person from call, 212
secure document transfers, 69
SpeedDial entries, 209
tasks performed with, 6-7
troubleshooting configuration, 213-216, 219-220
troubleshooting program sharing, 295-296
NetMeeting, conference calls, 235-245
    Audio and Video Tuning Wizard, 235
    audio conversations, 235
    compared with Messenger, 226
    recording calls, 237
    troubleshooting audio, 238-242
    troubleshooting video, 242-245
    video conversations, 235-237
NetMeeting, configuring, 199-207
    Audio Tuning Wizard and, 199-200
    automatic start, 202
    bandwidth settings, 202
    directory information, 201-202
    encryption/authentication, 202-203
    gateway/gatekeeper, 202
    icon display, 202
    microphone, 204-206
    security, 203-204
    starting, 197-200
    version numbers, 200
    video, sending/receiving, 206-207
NetMeeting, file transfer, 261-267
    overview, 264-265
    before receiving files, 261
    receiving files, 265
    receiving files via FTP, 263-264
    sending files, 265
    sending files via FTP, 262-263
    troubleshooting, 264, 266-267
NetMeeting, online projects.
    See also Whiteboard
    Remote Desktop Sharing, 297-299
    sharing programs/desktop, 290-297

Netscape Mail, 173
network adapters, 48, 52
Network Address Translation. *See* NAT (Network Address Translation)
Network Setup Wizard
    ICF and, 39-41
    Internet connection options, 31
    troubleshooting ICS, 50
    troubleshooting Internet connections, 48
New Call dialog box, NetMeeting, 220
New Connection Wizard, VPN
    creating incoming connection, 277-278
    creating Internet connection, 25-26
    setup for incoming connections, 272-277
newsgroups, 18
newsletters, Hotmail, 107
notification, e-mail messages, 129-130

O

OCR (optical character recognition), 255-256, 257
offline, working, 159
one-way satellite service, defined, 316
online communities, 301-310
    accessing, 307-309
    alternatives to MSN, 306-307
    MSN, 302-306
online drives
    defined, 316
    overview of, 306-307
    sharing files, 267
online projects, 281-300
    sharing programs/desktops, allowing control, 292-293
    sharing programs/desktops, in true color, 291-292
    sharing programs/desktops, overview of, 290-291
    sharing programs/desktops, troubleshooting, 293-297

Whiteboard, adding/deleting/
synchronizing pages, 286-287
Whiteboard, advantages/
disadvantages, 282
Whiteboard, basics of, 283-284
Whiteboard, locking, 287-288
Whiteboard, moving/copying
information, 287
Whiteboard, NetMeeting vs.
Messenger, 283
Whiteboard, Remote Desktop Sharing
and, 297-299
Whiteboard, saving, 288
Whiteboard, troubleshooting, 288-290
Whiteboard, working with text, 284-286
online storage, 267, 305
optical character recognition (OCR),
255-256, 257
optical-fiber connections, 17
Outlook Express, 117-146
accessing Hotmail via, 117
certification authorities and, 84
digital certificates in, 84
overview of, 5
setting up accounts, 117-119
tasks performed with, 7
Outlook Express, configuring, 119-146
Address Book, adding to
automatically, 129
authentication with POP3 or
IMAP server, 143-146
AutoComplete, 129
automatic Messenger sign-in,
preventing, 119
checking for mail, 141
compacting old messages, 139-140
default mail handling, 119
Deleted Items folder, emptying, 138-139
deleted messages, removing, 139
dial-up connections, changing, 137
e-mail accounts, adding, 140-146
easy reading, 120-125
fonts/stationery/business cards, 127-128

HTML/plain text formatting, 128-129
Internet connection, hanging up, 138
mail server information, 142-143
message store location, 140
messages, sending/checking for, 125-127
notification of new messages, 129-130
original message, including in reply, 129
secure mail, sending, 133-136
signatures, applying, 130-132
spelling options, 137
tooltips, displaying, 123
user information changes, 141
virus-protection options, 132-133

P

PAP (Password Authentication Protocol), 31
Passport Express Purchase, 316
Passport Wallet, 77-81
benefits of, 81
defined, 316
detriments of, 73-74
overview of, 77-78
security and, 78-80
Password Authentication Protocol (PAP), 31
Password link, Hotmail, 106
passwords
connection security and, 29-30
encrypting, 135
establishing identity and, 57, 59
.NET Passport security and, 79-80
NetMeeting calls and, 222
PayPal, 81
pbreak, defined, 316
PC-to-phone calls, Messenger, 233-235
pcAnywhere 7.5, 297
permanent cookie, defined, 316
Personal Profile link, Hotmail, 106
PGP (Pretty Good Privacy), 69
Phone Dialer, 246-252
comparing Messenger with, 3
configuring, 247-249
defined, 316

hiding Phone Dialer window/call panes, 250-252

limitations of, 246

making calls, 249-250

running, 246-247

setting up multilink modem connection, 33-34

SpeedDial entries, 252

taking calls, 250

tasks performed with, 6-7

phone numbers, publishing, 180

photographs, biometrics, 58

PKCS #12 format, 97

PKCS #7 format, 97

PKI (public key infrastructure), 317

Place a Call dialog box, NetMeeting, 208

place-shifting, 258, 316

plain old telephone service (POTS), 11-12, 316

plain text e-mail, 128-129

POP (point of presence), 316-317

POP3 accounts

authentication with, 142-143

defined, 317

Hotmail, 112-113

mail server information, changing, 142-143

messages, leaving on server, 145-146

protecting from spam, 159-161

server port numbers/timeouts, 144-145

ports

opening manually, 46-47

Outlook Express server port numbers, 144

troubleshooting, 53, 216

POTS (plain old telephone service), 11-12, 316

PPTP (Incoming Connection VPN), 277-278

Pretty Good Privacy (PGP), 69

Preview pane, Outlook Express, 120-123

PRI (Primary Rate Interface), 317

privacy/anonymity, online, 60-69

comparison of, 61-63

erosion of privacy, 61

government agencies and, 65-67

illusion of, 63

implications of Messenger for, 178

inquisitive individuals and, 67

ISPs and, 63-64

monitoring and, 64-65

protecting, 69

surveillance and, 67-68

visited Web sites and, 64

private keys, defined, 317

program sharing. *See* Desktop/program sharing

proxy servers, Messenger, 186

public domain, 317

public key cryptography, 83-84, 317

public key infrastructure (PKI), 317

public keys, 317

Q

QCIF (Quarter Common Interchange Format), 317

queues, Outlook Express, 126-127

Quick Connect feature, V.92 modems, 11

R

RADSL (Rate-Adaptive DSL), 15

read receipts, Outlook Express

granting, 157-158

requesting and returning, 124-125

requesting manually, 154

recording, NetMeeting conference calls, 237

Regulation of Investigatory Powers (RIP), 67

Remote Desktop Sharing, NetMeeting, 297-299

Request Read Receipt, Outlook Express, 154

Revocation Checking area, Outlook Express, 136

RIP (Regulation of Investigatory Powers), 67

RSA Exchange key, 86-88

Run dialog box, 197-199, 246-247

S

Safe List, Hotmail, 108
Sample Rate Conversion quality,
    NetMeeting, 239
sandbox, 317
satellite connections
    dial-return, 313
    disadvantages of using ICS, 37
    ISPs for, 18
    overview of, 14-15
    troubleshooting, 47-48
SDSL (Symmetric DSL), 15
Secret Question link, Hotmail, 106
Secure Password Authentication (SPA), 318
Secure Receipt Options dialog box, Outlook
    Express, 124-125
security. *See also* ICF (Internet
    Connection Firewall)
    cable modems, 16
    connection options, 29-31
    digital certificates and, 82-84
    file transfer and, 260-261
    NetMeeting, 203-204
    Outlook Express, 133-136
    Passport Wallet, 77-81
    program/desktop sharing, 291, 292
    RSA Exchange key and, 87-88
    Web-based access to e-mail and, 18
Select Certificate Store dialog box, 90-91
SELFCERT.EXE, 85
Send an Instant Message dialog box,
    Messenger, 193
Send Messages Immediately check box,
    Outlook Express, 126-127
Sent Message Confirmation, Hotmail, 116
servers, troubleshooting, 53
Service Settings dialog box, ICF, 46-47
session cookies, 317
Session Expiration link, Hotmail, 116
shotgun modem, 317

signatures, e-mail
    defined, 317
    Outlook Express, 130-132, 133
    overview of, 113-114
SOAP (Simple Object Access Protocol),
    defined, 318
social engineering, 318
software
    copyright laws for, 255-256, 257
    processor cycles and, 11
sound cards, 226, 238
SPA (Secure Password Authentication), 318
spam, 159-161, 164
speakers
    Messenger conference calls, 226,
        229-230
    NetMeeting conference calls, 238
speed
    ISPs and, 18
    Messenger compared with
        NetMeeting, 226
    NetMeeting configuration and, 198
Speed Dial, Phone Dialer, 252
SpeedDial, NetMeeting, 209, 217
spelling options, Outlook Express, 137
splitters, 318
SQCIF (Sub-Quarter Common Interchange
    Format), 318
Start a Voice Conversation dialog box,
    Messenger, 229-232
Start Whiteboard dialog box, NetMeeting, 283
stateful firewalls, 40, 318
stateless firewalls, 40, 318
static IP addresses, 318
stationery, Outlook Express, 127
status, Messenger, 183, 196
Sub-Quarter Common Interchange Format
    (SQCIF), 318
surveillance, 67-68
Symmetric DSL (SDSL), 15

T

T.120, 318
tab display, Messenger, 186
TAs (terminal adapters)
    adding, 24
    connecting ISDNs with, 12-13
    defined, 318
TCP/IP (Transmission Control
  Protocol/Internet Protocol), 239, 297, 318
TCP (Transmission Control Protocol), 318
terminal adapters. *See* TAs (terminal adapters)
Thawte Certification, 86
time-shifting, 258, 319
timeouts, Outlook Express, 144
tooltips, Outlook Express, 123
traffic analysis, 260, 319
Transmission Control Protocol/Internet
  Protocol (TCP/IP), 239, 297, 318
The Transparent Society (Brin), 63
troubleshooting, 47-53
    desktop/program sharing, 293-297
    ICF, 52-53
    ICS, 49-52
    Internet connections, 47-49
    Messenger chats, 196-197
    Messenger conference calls, 232
    Messenger configuration/connections,
      187-188
    NetMeeting audio, 238-242
    NetMeeting connections, 213-216
    NetMeeting file transfers, 264-265
    NetMeeting video, 242-245
    Remote Desktop Sharing, 297-299

U

UDDI (Universal Description, Discovery,
  and Integration), 319
UDP (User Datagram Protocol), 319
Uninstall pcAnywhere 8, 245

Universal Description, Discovery, and
  Integration (UDDI), 319
Universal Plug and Play (UPnP), 38, 319
The Unwanted Gaze (Rosen), 61, 62
upload caps, 17
UPnP (Universal Plug and Play), 38, 319
User Datagram Protocol (UDP), 319
USL (User Locator Service), 319

V

V.90 modems, 319
V.92 modems, 11-12, 319
VBA (Visual Basic for Applications), 72
video conference calls, Messenger.
  See Messenger, conference calls
video conference calls, NetMeeting.
  See NetMeeting, conference calls
video conference calls, Phone Dialer.
  See Phone Dialer
Video Privacy Protection Act, 63
virus-protection options, Outlook Express,
  132-133
Visual Basic for Applications (VBA), 72
voice conference calls, Messenger.
  See Messenger, conference calls
voice conference calls, NetMeeting.
  See NetMeeting, conference calls
voice conference calls, Phone Dialer.
  See Phone Dialer
voice service provider (VSP), Messenger,
  233-235
VPN (virtual private network), 271-278
    accepting incoming connections,
      272-277
    connecting via, 278
    creating incoming connections, 277-278
    defined, 319
    overview, 271-272
VSP (voice service provider), Messenger,
  233-235

W

Web
 accessing Hotmail via, 106
 building Web pages, 306
 connecting to NetMeeting from,
  216-217
 digital certificates, getting, 84
 MSN community in, 303
 online anonymity, 64
 publishing files or folders to, 308
Web of Trust, 86
Web Publishing Wizard, 308
Web site information, 69, 259
Webcams, Messenger, 226-227
Welcome message, MSN community,
 304-305
Whiteboard, 282-289
 adding/deleting/synchronizing pages,
  286-287
 basics, 283-284
 locking, 287-288
 moving and copying information, 287
 NetMeeting vs. Messenger, 282-283
 saving, 288

 troubleshooting, 288-290
 working with text, 284-286
Windows 95/98/ME, 288-290, 288-290, 293
Windows Media Player, audio problems, 53
Windows Messenger. *See* Messenger
Windows NT 4, 219, 289-290, 297
Windows, using ICS with early versions of, 52
WinFax Pro, 215
wireless connections, 13-14, 47-48
Word 6 for Windows, 297
working offline, Outlook Express, 159

X

XML (Extensible Markup Language),
 69-70, 314

Y

Yahoo! Mail, 171

Z

Zero Knowledge Systems, Inc., 69
Zip files, 259-260, 264-265

INTERNATIONAL CONTACT INFORMATION

AUSTRALIA
McGraw-Hill Book Company Australia Pty. Ltd.
TEL +61-2-9417-9899
FAX +61-2-9417-5687
http://www.mcgraw-hill.com.au
books-it_sydney@mcgraw-hill.com

CANADA
McGraw-Hill Ryerson Ltd.
TEL +905-430-5000
FAX +905-430-5020
http://www.mcgrawhill.ca

GREECE, MIDDLE EAST,
NORTHERN AFRICA
McGraw-Hill Hellas
TEL +30-1-656-0990-3-4
FAX +30-1-654-5525

MEXICO (Also serving Latin America)
McGraw-Hill Interamericana Editores S.A. de C.V.
TEL +525-117-1583
FAX +525-117-1589
http://www.mcgraw-hill.com.mx
fernando_castellanos@mcgraw-hill.com

SINGAPORE (Serving Asia)
McGraw-Hill Book Company
TEL +65-863-1580
FAX +65-862-3354
http://www.mcgraw-hill.com.sg
mghasia@mcgraw-hill.com

SOUTH AFRICA
McGraw-Hill South Africa
TEL +27-11-622-7512
FAX +27-11-622-9045
robyn_swanepoel@mcgraw-hill.com

UNITED KINGDOM & EUROPE
(Excluding Southern Europe)
McGraw-Hill Education Europe
TEL +44-1-628-502500
FAX +44-1-628-770224
http://www.mcgraw-hill.co.uk
computing_neurope@mcgraw-hill.com

ALL OTHER INQUIRIES Contact:
Osborne/McGraw-Hill
TEL +1-510-549-6600
FAX +1-510-883-7600
http://www.osborne.com
omg_international@mcgraw-hill.com